A**Global** **Agenda**

Issues before the 60th General Assembly of the United Nations

Edited by Angela Drakulich

Published by the United Nations Association
of the United States of America

New York, New York

UNITED NATIONS ASSOCIATION, USA, Inc.

Published in the United States of America
by the United Nations Association of the United States of America.
801 Second Avenue, New York, NY 10017

ISBN 1-880632-71-3
LCCN 2005901859

Editor: Angela Drakulich
Designer: Charlotte Staub
Copyeditor: Ruth O'Brien
Indexer: Claudi Peterfreund

Contributing Editors: Suzanne DiMaggio, Steven A. Dimoff, William H. Luers, John Washburn and Lawrence Woocher

Researchers: Dana Butunoi, Andrew Fargnoli, Andreea Florescu, Micky Hingorani, Lindsey Iorg, Joyce Man, Kristine McNeil and Liz Shryock

Cover photos: Secretary-General Kofi Annan addresses the General Assembly on the report of the High-level Panel on Threats, Challenges and Change, December 2004. The UN60 logo is the official United Nations logo for its 60th anniversary, 2005.

Printed in the United States of America

Contents

Maps and Tables

Contributors

Ishtiaq Ahmad (Peacekeeping in Asia) is an associate professor in the Department of International Relations, Quaid-i-Azam University, in Islamabad, Pakistan. Formerly, he served as assistant professor/vice chair of international relations at Eastern Mediterranean University, North Cyprus; senior research fellow at the Area Study Centre, QAU; and as a diplomatic correspondent for *The Nation* in Islamabad. Dr. Ahmad has authored a number of books on security issues in south and west Asia, including Gulbuddin Hekmatyar: An Afghan Trail from Jihad to Terrorism (2004), and India and Pakistan: Charting a Path to Peace (2004).

Assefaw Bariagaber (Peacekeeping in Africa) is an associate professor at the John C. Whitehead School of Diplomacy and International Relations of Seton Hall University, New Jersey. He serves as a member of the executive committee of the Third World Studies Association, and secretary of the Eritrean Studies Association. Dr. Bariagaber has written several articles on conflicts and refugee formations in Africa for journals such as the *Journal of Modern African Studies*, *International Migration* and *Ethnic and Racial Studies*. He also serves as an associate editor of the *Eritrean Studies Review*.

Dana Butunoi (Special Sections) is a UNA-USA intern. She is currently pursuing a joint M.B.A.-M.A. in Diplomacy and International Relations at Seton Hall University, New Jersey. Ms. Butunoi also holds a bachelor of laws from Al. I. Cuza State University, Romania.

Simon Chesterman (UN Reform) is executive director of the Institute for International Law and Justice at New York University School of Law. Previously, he was a senior associate at the International Peace Academy and director of UN relations at the International Crisis Group. Mr. Chesterman has worked for the Office for the Coordination of Humanitarian Affairs in Belgrade; taught at the Universities of Melbourne, Oxford, Southampton and Columbia; and interned at the International Criminal Tribunal for Rwanda in Arusha. He is the author of You, The People: The United Nations, Transitional Administration, and State-Building (2004) and Just War or Just Peace? Humanitarian Intervention and International Law (2001).

Roger Coate (Millennium Development Goals) is a professor of international relations at the University of South Carolina. He is author or co-author of numerous books, including The United Nations and Changing World Politics (2004) and the forthcoming United Nations Politics: Responding to a Challenging World. Dr. Coate directs the Creating Effective Partnerships for Human Security Project, a transnational, collaborative research and professional development program undertaken in cooperation with the United Nations University, the executive office of the UN secretary-general, the Central European University and other partners.

Lorna Davidson (Human Rights) is the deputy director of British Irish Rights Watch, a human rights nongovernmental organization based in London. Previously, she was a senior associate at Human Rights First (formerly the Lawyers Committee for Human Rights). Ms. Davidson has worked at Columbia Law School, the International Crisis Group and in the chambers of the International Criminal Tribunal for the former Yugoslavia. She has a master's degree in law from the University of Cambridge and Columbia Law School, and a law degree from the University of Glasgow, Scotland.

Espen Barth Eide (Peacekeeping in Europe) is director of the Department of International Politics at the Norwegian Institute of International Affairs (NUPI). From 2000-2001, he served as deputy foreign minister in the Norwegian government, primarily responsible for US and European affairs, security policy and relations with Russia. Prior to this appointment, he was a researcher and director of the UN Program at NUPI, and campaign director and acting secretary-general of the Norwegian European movement leading up to Norway's European Union referendum. Mr. Eide is co-editor of the London-based journal *International Peacekeeping*, and a member of the Resource Group of the UN High-level Panel on Threats, Challenges and Change. He received a degree in political science from the University of Oslo, Norway.

Andreea Florescu (Peacekeeping in the Americas, Special Sections) is a UNA-USA intern and a graduate student at the John C. Whitehead School of Diplomacy and International Relations at Seton Hall University, New Jersey where she is specializing in human rights, international economics and development. Ms. Florescu holds a bachelor's degree in political science and philosophy from Gettysburg College, Pennsylvania.

Jacques Fomerand (Humanitarian Assistance) was director of the United Nations University's North America office from 1992 to 2003. Previously, he served in the UN secretariat's office of the under-secretary-general of the Department of Economic and Social Affairs. He has published numerous works on the UN and is currently completing a dictionary of the UN. Dr. Fomerand studied political science and law at the University of Aix-en-Provence, France and earned a Ph.D. in political science at the City University of New York. He now teaches at John Jay College of the City University of New York and at Occidental College.

Micky Hingorani (Looming Conflicts) is a UNA-USA intern. He is currently a doctoral candidate in global affairs at the Rutgers University Center for Global Change and Governance, where his work focuses on the Internet and its effects on political participation. Mr. Hingorani holds a bachelor's degree in psychology from New York University.

Yanzhong Huang (Global Health) is an assistant professor at the John C. Whitehead School of Diplomacy and International Relations of Seton Hall University, New Jersey. He serves as director of the school's Center for Global Health Studies, and was a participant in the L20 Summit project initiated by Canadian Prime Minster Paul Martin. Dr. Huang has recently written articles for *Asia Perspective, Journal of Contemporary China* and *Harvard Asia Quarterly*, as well as chapters for books published by Cambridge University Press and the National Academies Press. Dr. Huang received a Ph.D. in political science from the University of Chicago.

Rebecca Johnson (Disarmament and Terrorism) is the founding executive director of The Acronym Institute for Disarmament Diplomacy in London and editor of *Disarmament Diplomacy*, an international journal on multilateral arms control and global security. She is currently vice chair of the board of the Bulletin of the Atomic Scientists and senior adviser to the Weapons of Mass Destruction Commission, launched by Sweden. Dr. Johnson has authored numerous articles and reports on disarmament and arms control negotiations, civil society, British defense policy, space weaponization and international security. She holds a Ph.D. from the London School of Economics.

Gail Karlsson (Sustainable Development) is an attorney specializing in international environmental law. She is currently working as a consultant to the UN Development Programme where she has recently designed and facilitated a training course on environmental policy and sustainable development. She is also the New York coordinator for the Citizens Network for Sustainable Development.

Jean Krasno (Peacekeeping in the Middle East) is the Yolanda Moses Scholar at the Colin Powell Center for Policy Studies at the City College of New York and an International Security Studies fellow at Yale University. She is also an adjunct professor of international relations at the City College of New York. Dr. Krasno was executive director of the Academic Council on the United Nations System from 1998 to 2003. She previously served as deputy director of the Yale-UN Oral History Project and taught as a visiting scholar at Wesleyan University. Dr. Krasno has co-authored The United Nations and Iraq: Defanging the Viper (2003), and edited both The United

Nations: Confronting the Challenges of a Global Society (2004) and Leveraging for Success in UN Peace Operations (2003). She holds a Ph.D. from the City University of New York Graduate Center.

David Lynch (Trade) is an associate professor of political science at Saint Mary's University, Minnesota. With a doctorate from the University of California, Santa Barbara, Dr. Lynch's published works have focused on American trade policy, the World Trade Organization and regional trade agreements such as the North American Free Trade Agreement.

Anthony Mango (UN Finance and Administration) worked for the UN Secretariat from 1960 to 1987 and the UN Pension Board from 1983 to 1987. Between 1970 and 1983, he headed the Secretariat of the Advisory Committee on Administrative and Budgetary Questions. Since retirement, he has continued to consult for the UN and recently edited the third edition of the Encyclopedia of the United Nations and International Agreements (Routledge, 2003).

Lawrence C. Moss (International Law) is a lawyer in private practice specializing in litigation, arbitration and international law. He has served as chair of the Special Committee on the UN of the Association of the Bar of the City of New York, as the Association's representative to the UN, as one of the founders of the Lawyers Committee for the UN and as an adviser to various nongovernmental organizations. Mr. Moss has been elected to eight terms as member of the New York State Democratic Committee representing the 66th Assembly District and served as chair of both the Reform Caucus of the Democratic State Committee and the New York State New Democratic Coalition. He holds a bachelor's degree in history from Brown University and a J.D. from Stanford Law School.

Pernille Rieker (Peacekeeping in Europe) is a senior researcher and coordinator for the research program on European and Transatlantic Security at the Norwegian Institute of International Affairs. She holds a Ph.D. from the University of Oslo in political science and has published various articles.

Essayists

Diego Arria, former Permanent Representative of Venezuela to the United Nations and visiting scholar at Columbia University

Baki Ilkin, Permanent Representative of Turkey to the United Nations

Gaia Larsen, World Federation of the United Nations Associations

Anders Lidén, Permanent Representative of Sweden to the United Nations

Kishore Mahbubani, former Permanent Representative of Republic of Singapore to the United Nations and current dean of the Lee Kuan Yew School of Public Policy, National University of Singapore

Gunter Pleuger, Permanent Representative of Germany to the United Nations

Stephanie Rossi, World Federation of the United Nations Associations

M. Javad Zarif, Permanent Representative of the Islamic Republic of Iran to the UN

Prologue

In 1945, delegates of many nations gathered in San Francisco to build a new forum for international cooperation out of the ruins of the Second World War—the United Nations. Sixty years later, in September 2005, world leaders will meet at a summit of the UN at its headquarters in New York. I believe they should use this opportunity to update the institutions created by their forebears, and to agree on key priorities and policies to guide multilateral cooperation in a world very different from that which even the visionary founders of the UN could have foreseen.

To help them rise to this challenge, I have placed before the member states of the UN a series of proposals on how the organization might adapt to its new challenges. These are contained in my March 2005 report, *In Larger Freedom: Towards Development, Security and Human Rights for All*. The phrase "in larger freedom" is taken from the preamble to the *Charter of the UN*; it encapsulates my conviction that our world will not enjoy development without security or security without development, and it will not enjoy either without respect for human rights. To advance this agenda, the September 2005 summit should address four challenges.

The first is to translate consensus on development into concrete global action. Three years ago, a bargain was struck in Monterrey between developed and developing countries. The time has come to implement it fully. I therefore call on each developing country to adopt and begin to implement, by next year, a comprehensive national strategy bold enough to achieve the UN Millennium Development Goals by 2015. And I call on developed countries to support these efforts with action on aid, trade and debt relief. For example, I urge them to lay down timetables to meet, by 2015, the agreed target of spending 0.7 percent of their gross national income on official development assistance.

The second challenge is to agree on a new vision of collective security, and to update our shared instruments in order to give effect to it. States expect a collective security system to address the threats they most fear—whether the threat is international war, weapons of mass destruction, terrorism and organized crimes, state collapse and civil conflict, deadly infectious disease, extreme poverty or environmental destruction. If the UN is to live up to those expectations, member states must work through it to develop stronger anti-terrorism, nonproliferation, disarmament and crime prevention regimes. They must also provide more support for UN mediation and peacekeeping missions. To ensure a more strategic approach in helping countries make the transition from war to lasting peace, a new UN body—a peace-building commission—should be established. And member states should agree on basic principles to help guide decisions on the use of force by the UN Security Council.

The third challenge is to reduce the gap between the impressive normative regime of human rights and fundamental freedoms that has been developed under UN auspices over the past six decades and its implementation in each country. I therefore ask the UN's member states to embrace the principle of the "responsibility to protect," as a basis for collective action against genocide, ethnic cleansing and crimes against humanity. I urge them to support a democracy fund at the UN to assist countries seeking to strengthen democracy. And I hope they will agree to replace the Commission on Human Rights, which suffers from declining professionalism and credibility, with a smaller human rights council to help advance the protection of *all* human rights, in *all* countries, *all*-year-round.

This leads me to the fourth and final challenge—the challenge of revitalizing the UN itself. In addition to creating the new bodies I have mentioned, the time has come to update existing ones. The General Assembly should rationalize its agenda, focus on major substantive issues of the day and fully engage with civil society. The Security Council should be more broadly representative of the international community as a whole, as well as of the geopolitical realities of today. The Economic and Social Council should be more strategic in helping to make and implement coherent UN policies for development. And we should build on the extensive reforms of the Secretariat undertaken over the past eight years to ensure that it is more flexible, transparent and accountable in serving the priorities of member states.

My report makes other important recommendations on issues as diverse as humanitarian response capacity, climate change and migration. Taken as a whole, the proposals seek to strike a careful balance across a broad range of issues, and between the needs and interest of the various countries and regions. Of course, the decisions on reform quite properly rest with the member states of the UN. They must negotiate and agree on how to proceed. But I hope that my proposals will assist them in reaching a global deal to advance development, security and human rights for all.

We all share an interest in an effective, efficient and equitable multilateral system that addresses *all* the serious threats and challenges facing humanity. In 2005, 60 years after the United Nations was founded, our world must move decisively in this direction.

Kofi Annan
Secretary-General of the United Nations

Introduction

The Secretary-General has called 2005 "a time for renewal" for the United Nations. With reform proposals on the table, he has asked the world's leaders to act to make the UN better once and for all. Questions about the world body's effectiveness and relevance have plagued the UN since early 2003, when the United States and its coalition entered into war in Iraq without the authority of the Security Council; this cloud of criticism grew over the course of 2004 when serious questions and investigations arose in regard to corruption within the UN-led Oil-for-Food Programme. For these reasons and others, Secretary-General Kofi Annan initiated a thorough review of the UN system with an eye toward making much-needed improvements.

SG Annan established the High-level Panel on Threats, Challenges and Change in fall 2003 to recommend clear and practical measures for ensuring effective collective action to today's threats, be it bioterrorism or infectious disease. The year before, in 2002, he had set up the Millennium Project to develop a global plan to achieve the Millennium Development Goals (MDGs), which have been lagging in progress since agreed upon by member states in 2000. While many nations, including the US, were at first skeptical of such massive reform efforts, a number of governments and institutions have come to pay serious attention to the results and recommendations presented in the High-level Panel and Millennium Project reports, which were issued in December 2004 and January 2005, respectively. The US Congress even called for its own Task Force on the UN to examine ways in which the organization is meeting its *Charter* goals and how the US can take a greater lead in helping the UN meet those goals in today's political climate.

As described in SG Annan's Prologue, a special summit of heads of state and governments is to take place in September 2005 to review the proposals set forth in his March 2005 report, *In Larger Freedom: Towards Development, Security and Human Rights for All*, which draws from both the High-level Panel and Millennium Project recommendations. Delegates of the General Assembly will discuss reform and review progress made thus far on the MDGs.

The various reform proposals laid out and the progress made on the MDGs are discussed in Chapters 1 and 3 of this book, respectively. Simon Chesterman takes a deep look into the collective responses required for the world to prevent and manage today's threats, from weapons of mass destruction and terrorism to infectious disease and human rights violations. His paper presents the path the UN might take to improve the global institutions tasked with managing these threats, from amending the *UN Charter* in order to increase the size of the Security Council to replacing the Commission on Human Rights with a smaller Human Rights Council. Roger Coate and Gail Karlsson, in turn, tackle the challenges presented to the world community by the MDGs. Their research highlights those regions that are making progress as well as those that are falling behind and what can be done to get the world on course.

While much attention is being paid to keeping the MDGs on track, the UN's peace and humanitarian efforts are also a high priority for the General Assembly. Missions and operations to manage peace and security are expanding like never before. In 2004 and early 2005 alone, the UN's Department of Peacekeeping developed five new missions while remaining active in 13 others, delivered much-needed food aid and other supplies to people in around 20 regions or countries, and assisted approximately 19 million refugees and internally displaced persons worldwide. Chapters 2 and 4 cover the UN actions taken to address these issues in some of the most war-torn, devastated regions, from serving a transitional government in Haiti to negotiating independence in Kosovo to ending violence in Sudan.

In addition to peace and security, the High-level Panel reminds us that one of the major threats to today's global community is that of infectious disease. There are now approximately 40 million people living with HIV/AIDS. Emerging diseases such as the Marburg virus, and re-emerging diseases, such as polio, continue to plague society, many of them reaching epidemic, if not pandemic levels. Yanzhong Huang explains the risks at stake and what the UN is doing to control them in Chapter 5.

Just as health security has a global reach, so does trade, and the year 2005 is especially pertinent for countries to put their differences aside and work toward agreement on the Doha round of World Trade Organization (WTO) negotiations. From trade barriers to WTO membership, David Lynch discusses in Chapter 6 why developed and developing nations alike need to make both sacrifices and compromises to get the most out of today's world economy.

The growth in scope of international criminal law is also of utmost importance to the UN's member states. Not only has Prosecutor Luis Moreno Ocampo set the International Criminal Court into action, but he has five cases before him—all of them in Africa. Meanwhile, as the international criminal tribunals in the former Yugoslavia and Rwanda are nearing the halfway mark of finishing their work by the 2010 target deadline, the special courts in Sierra Leone and Cambodia are just beginning. As explained by Lawrence C. Moss in Chapter 7, of specific consequence to this year's General Assembly are questions regarding the use of force and the Security Council's law-making authority.

While the world turns toward renewing the UN in 2005, it is also celebrating in 2005, looking back on its 60 years in action to June 25, 1945 when the *United Nations Charter* was signed. Appendix A of this book highlights 60 key events in the UN's history that led to it becoming the world's greatest and only forum for all nations. In this regard, we have asked several prominent individuals from a range of regions to discuss their thoughts and hopes for the UN as it moves into its next 60 years. In the Essay section of this book, you will find writings from the current or former ambassadors to the UN of Sweden, Germany, Iran, Venezuela, Singapore and more.

In the words of SG Annan, there is no doubt that the last year or so has been an *annus horribilis* for the UN, but it is important to note that it also has been a bad year for the world. With responsibility for the Oil-for-Food Programme resting on all member states' shoulders, the demand for billions of dollars in aid to assist civilians and governments rebuild the tsunami-impacted region as well as those "forgotten emergencies," the call for cheaper and better access to medicines to help those suffering from HIV/AIDS and other diseases, the need for greater communication and negotiations between developing and developed nations to improve global trade, the initiative to unleash greater rule of law and justice worldwide, and the mandate to promote peace and security in nations doused in conflict, the member states of the UN have more than a full plate on their hands. For all these reasons, now is the time for the General Assembly to move toward strengthening the capacity, efficiency and reputation of its home—the United Nations.

In this context and in this anniversary year, the 2005-2006 edition of *A Global Agenda* not only looks back at the UN's 60 years of learning and progress, but also looks forward to a time when the UN will be better equipped and better supported by its member states to meet the needs of the world. Thanks to the reform initiatives proposed over the past year, we now know what needs to be accomplished to meet the tasks ahead and we have the solutions in hand.

Angela Drakulich
Managing Editor, UNA-USA

William H. Luers
President, UNA-USA

Chapter 1

Reform: Managing Peace and Security in the 21st Century

Simon Chesterman

As globalization shrinks distances around the globe and these issues become increasingly interconnected, the comparative advantages of the United Nations become ever more evident. So too, however, do some of its real weaknesses. From overhauling basic management practices and building a more transparent, efficient and effective United Nations system to revamping our major intergovernmental institutions so that they reflect today's world and advance the priorities set forth in the present report, we must reshape the organization in ways not previously imagined and with a boldness and speed not previously shown.

—United Nations Secretary-General Kofi Annan
In Larger Freedom: Towards Development, Security and Human Rights for All, March 2005

The United Nations has always faced crises of expectations. At the beginning of the 1990s, the United States, while proclaiming itself the victor of the Cold War, magnanimously asserted that this provided an opportunity for the UN to fulfill its long-promised role as the guardian of international peace and security. The Security Council saw new possibilities for action without the paralyzing veto. Secretary-General Boutros Boutros-Ghali laid out grand plans with *An Agenda for Peace.* And in the words of US President George H.W. Bush, the rule of law could finally supplant "the rule of the jungle."[1]

The rhetoric was euphoric, utopian and short-lived. International security issues continued to be resolved by reference to "great power" interests and development remained an area where words were more plentiful than resources. Rhetoric did have some impact, however. The language of human rights and the rule of law became more accepted through this period, as did the principle of greater international engagement in areas previously considered to lie solely within the domestic jurisdiction of member states. Whether such principles should be supported by action remained a bone of some contention.

In this context, the question of reform has always begged the question of whether it must take place primarily in the structures, procedures and personnel that make up the UN, or in the willingness of member states to use them. As the UN prepares for its 60th General Assembly, taking place in fall 2005, similar questions of expectations, principles and practice confront the member states and the Secretariat.

Past efforts at creating and changing the international institutions of peace and security have tended to follow a time of crisis. World War I was the backdrop for establishment of the League of Nations; the League's failure to prevent World War II led to its replacement by the UN. US President Franklin Roosevelt pushed for the negotiation of the *UN Charter* to be held in San Francisco while the bombs of World War II were falling elsewhere. Unlike the covenant of the League of Nations, which was negotiated as one agreement among many at Versailles in 1919, the *Charter's* references to "the scourge of war" were reinforced by daily reports from final battles in the worldwide conflict.

For some, the US-led invasion of Iraq in March 2003 was a similar challenge not merely to the institutions of the UN but to the very idea of international order. The war split the Security Council, divided the North-Atlantic Treaty Organization (NATO) and prompted the creation of a high-level panel to rethink the very idea of collective security in a world dominated by US military power. In the wake of the Iraq war, anxiety concerning the role and relevance of the UN was widespread. But leadership on the reform agenda came, unusually, from the Secretary-General. It was Kofi Annan who appointed the High-level Panel on Threats, Challenges and Change in September 2003 to grapple with US concerns while broadening discussion of international threats beyond its counter-terrorism and non-proliferation agenda.[2] SG Annan had already commissioned Jeffrey Sachs' UN Millennium Project to propose strategies for achieving the Millennium Development Goals.[3] And in March 2005, these security and development agendas were joined by a third, human rights, in his report—one that has been noted for its ambition and rhetoric.

That report, *In Larger Freedom: Towards Development, Security and Human Rights for All*, is intended to set both the tone and substantive agenda for the 60th General Assembly, which includes a special summit of the world's heads of state in September 2005. The report is broad in scope, seeking to define a new security consensus based on the interdependence of threats and responses, and narrow in detail, setting specific targets for official development assistance, calling for the creation of a peace-building commission and a new, small human rights council, and outlining a long-awaited definition of terrorism. On the most contested political question of Security Council expansion, however, the report endorses the fence-sitting position of the High-level Panel, laying out options but not choosing between them, while urging member states to make a decision on expansion even if consensus is not possible.[4]

As the member states gather in New York, there will be much talk of consensus, though this may be a veil for the underlying issues of politics and expectations. In political terms, arguments over consensus imply divergent views as to whether the UN should be a forum for intergovernmental cooperation or an independent actor that can lead on issues of global import. The former view tends to lean toward a lowest-common denominator approach to standards and implementation; the latter could lead to greater effectiveness but at the risk of the UN's legitimacy as a club of states. (Whether, in a world of interdependent threats, it makes sense for states to retain their privileged position in such a forum is well beyond the scope of the UN itself to determine.)

In terms of expectations, SG Annan has consciously put pressure on member states not to leave New York empty-handed. He has tied his own legacy to the outcome of the push for reform. This is certainly a more desirable legacy than any other news story that has come out of the UN in the past two years, but it points to the ambiguous position occupied by the Secretary-General. Serving as the world's top ranking civil servant and, in a sense, secular pope, he depends on states for both the legitimacy and resources that make the UN possible. At the same time, the disparate national interests of those states depend on the UN and its Secretary-General to work together effectively and to respond adequately to threats unanswerable by any one state alone.

Whether or not the Security Council is expanded, the year ahead will at the very least see a change in rhetoric. Political compromises will, as they must, compromise the vision of reform laid out in the Secretary-General's blueprint. But the link between the security, development and human rights priorities of the UN is likely to endure. The role of the UN's chief administrative officer in articulating a vision of global order will persist. And expectations for what can be achieved by the organization will continue to be disappointed—even as they continue to rise.

With this background in mind, this chapter focuses on the peace and security reforms recommended by the SG's High-level Panel on Threats, Challenges and Change and by the Secretary-General himself in his *In Larger Freedom* report. (The work of the UN Millennium Project is considered together with an evaluation of the Millennium Development Goals in Chapter 3; further analysis of the UN's human rights institutions can be found in Chapter 4.) These issues will come before the General Assembly in its 60th session. Before discussing in detail the reforms proposed by the High-level Panel, as well as other reforms, it is important to examine the UN's history in dealing with change.

Looking Back

Many discussions of reform tend to suggest that major changes in the UN are both too hard and too easy. Those who say reform is too hard forget that, in the right circumstances, likeminded countries were able to negotiate the *UN Charter* and amend it three times—including an expansion of the Security Council in the face of superpower reluctance. Those who suggest reform is easy forget that the most significant reform (the near doubling of the membership) took two years to complete and depended on a perfect set of circumstances driving reform corresponding directly to the reform agenda. The *UN Charter* is much like a constitution. And, like most constitutions, it is designed to be difficult to amend. Article 108 of the *Charter* points out that an amendment has to be ratified by two-thirds of the UN member states, including all five permanent members of the Security Council (P-5). The three *Charter* amendments that did occur all took place between 1963 and 1973. The first expanded Security Council membership from 11 to 15 and increased the number of votes necessary to pass a resolution from seven to nine; it also expanded the membership of the Economic and Social Council (ECOSOC) from 18 to 27. The second corrected the amendment procedures themselves, in line with the increased size of the Security Council, requiring that nine (rather than seven) members be required to support a call for a General Conference of member states for the purposes of reviewing the *Charter*. The third further increased the membership of ECOSOC from 27 to 54.

Since the Security Council is widely viewed as the most influential part of the UN system, much discussion of reform focuses on its membership. In 1993, the General Assembly established an open-ended working group (that is, open to all members of the UN) to consider, among other things, the question of increasing Council membership.[5] Now more than a decade into its deliberations, there is still no agreement on an appropriate formula for Security Council representation, and the body is jokingly referred to as the "never-ending working group." Issues of general consensus are that the Council should be expanded and probably include new permanent members—but perhaps without granting newcomers the coveted veto, currently held by only the P-5.

In March 1997, Razali Ismail, chairman of the working group, presented a paper synthesizing the majority view on expansion of the Security Council. Now known as the "Razali Plan," it proposed increasing Council membership from 15 to 24 by adding five permanent members (one each from the developing states of Africa, Asia, Latin America and the Caribbean, and two from the industrialized states—generally recognized as Germany and Japan) and four non-permanent members (one each from Africa, Asia, Eastern Europe, and Latin America and the Caribbean). Though unable to generate much enthusiasm, the Razali Plan became the benchmark for other reform proposals.[6]

Efforts to abolish the veto itself are not presently taken seriously. Even proposals to limit it—such as that discussed in the report of the International Commission on Intervention and State Sovereignty titled *The Responsibility to Protect*, which outlined a possible "code of conduct" whereby permanent members without vital national interest at stake would agree not to use their veto to block a resolution responding to a humanitarian crisis— appear to be off the table following the severe disagreements in the Council over the handling of Iraq.[7]

The barriers to change are significant. There is, however, much that can be done to improve the effectiveness of the UN without amending its *Charter*. Indeed, in the case of the Security Council, there is a tendency to conflate the question of the Council's "representativeness" with that of its effectiveness. Would expanding the Council's membership make it more capable of responding to threats to international peace and security? It is arguable that other areas of reform, such as transparency of the Council's decision-making practices, the analytical role of the UN Secretariat, the availability of forces under UN command, and financial and human resources devoted to peacekeeping would better address the problems the Security Council currently faces. For this reason, the position of some governments is to support Council expansion in theory while opposing any specific reforms to membership in practice.

The High-level Panel

The High-level Panel on Threats, Challenges and Change was set up in response to the political crisis that followed the US-led invasion of Iraq in March 2003. Speaking to the General Assembly that September, SG Annan was blunt about the challenges confronting the UN:

"Excellencies, we have come to a fork in the road. This may be a moment no less decisive than 1945 itself, when the United Nations was founded. At that time, a group of far-sighted leaders, led and inspired by President Franklin D. Roosevelt, were determined to make the second half of the 20th century different from the first half. They saw that the human race had only one world to live in, and that unless it managed its affairs prudently, all human beings may perish. So they drew up rules to govern international behaviour, and founded a network of institutions, with the United Nations at its centre, in which the peoples of the world could work together for the common good.

"Now we must decide whether it is possible to continue on the basis agreed then, or whether radical changes are needed. And we must not shy away from questions about the adequacy, and effectiveness, of the rules and instruments at our disposal."[8]

The aim of the panel was to "recommend clear and practical measures for ensuring effective collective action, based upon a rigorous analysis of future threats to peace and security, an appraisal of the contribution collective action can make, and a thorough assessment of existing approaches, instruments and mechanisms, including the principal organs of the United Nations." Specifically, the panel's terms of reference asked it to:

1) Examine today's global threats and provide an analysis of future challenges to international peace and security. While a diversity of perception on the relative importance of the various threats facing particular member states on an individual basis continues to exist, it is important to find an appropriate balance at a global level. It is also important to understand the connections between different threats.

2) Identify clearly the contribution that collective action can make in addressing these challenges.

3) Recommend the changes necessary to ensure effective collective action, including but not limited to a review of the principal organs of the United Nations.[9]

On November 3, 2003, the SG announced the 16 members of the panel in a letter to the president of the General Assembly. Chaired by Anand Panyarachun, a former prime minister of Thailand, the panelists included Robert Badinter of France, João Clemente Baena Soares of Brazil, Gro Harlem Brundtland of Norway, Mary Chinery-Hesse of Ghana, Gareth Evans of Australia, David Hannay of the United Kingdom, Enrique Iglesias of Uruguay, Amre Moussa of Egypt, Satish Nambiar of India, Sadako Ogata of Japan, Yevgeny Primakov of Russia, Qian Qichen of China, Nafis Sadik of Pakistan, Salim Ahmed Salim of Tanzania and Brent Scowcroft of the United States.[10]

The panel met for the first time in Princeton, NJ, on December 5-7, 2003. It was originally asked to report back to the SG by August 15, 2004—a deadline that was later pushed back to December 2004. Subsequent formal meetings were held in Switzerland in February 2004, Ethiopia in April 2004, Austria in July 2004, and the US in September and November 2004. Panel members also took part in a variety of side meetings and consultations around the world.

Speaking to the General Assembly in September 2003, the Secretary-General had referred to "hard" and "soft" threats—with the latter denoting "the persistence of extreme poverty, the disparity of income between and within societies, and the spread of infectious diseases, or climate change and environmental degradation."[11] The final sentences of the terms of reference stated that "the Panel's work is confined to the field of peace and security, broadly interpreted. That is, it should extend its analysis and recommendations to other issues and institutions, including economic and social, to the extent that they have a direct bearing on future threats to peace and security."

In place of "hard" and "soft" threats, in early meetings the panel turned its attention to six "baskets" of threats: 1) intrastate violence; 2) interstate rivalry and war, including genocide; 3) economic and social issues, including poverty and infectious diseases; 4) weapons of mass destruction; 5) terrorism; and 6) organized crime. A point of ongoing discussion for the panel was whether these threats should be prioritized, and how the "soft" threats figured into discussions of peace and security.

Since the Security Council passed a resolution in 2000 stressing that HIV/AIDS "if unchecked, may pose a risk to stability and security," it has been accepted that "soft" threats such as infectious disease may have an impact on traditional security questions—most obviously through the impact of the HIV/AIDS pandemic on the armed forces of various African countries. But some argue that defining poverty, for example, as a threat on par with terrorism or interstate violence does little more than render the word "threat" vague. Poverty may be a partial cause–or, in some cases, an effect–of conflict, but there are other policy frameworks in place to deal with this and related issues, most prominently the Millennium Development Goals (MDGs).

One way of resolving this question was to explicitly recognize the disparate ways in which different stakeholders perceive threats. While the combination of terrorism and weapons of mass destruction is the primary fear of many countries in the industrialized North, economic concerns dominate in the South. Some thought it might be possible, therefore, to link these issues and secure greater support and cooperation by countries in the South for counter-terrorism and counter-proliferation activities in exchange for greater development assistance and reform of agricultural subsidies by countries in the North. This "grand bargain" approach was not fully embraced, though the report and the Secretary-General's synthesis document, *In Larger Freedom*, bear distinct traces of its philosophy.

By far the greatest speculation on the panel's deliberations focused on the question of reform of the Security Council. In his September 2003 speech, SG Annan drew attention "to the urgent need for the Council to regain the confidence of States, and of world public opinion—both by demonstrating its ability to deal effectively with the most difficult issues, and by becoming more broadly representative of the international community as a whole, as well as the geopolitical realities of today." Noting that the composition of the Security Council had been on the agenda of the General Assembly for over a decade, he stressed the need to address the issue with greater urgency. The terms of reference for the panel, however, emphasized the need for effectiveness, calling on the panel to "recommend the changes necessary to ensure effective collective action, including but not limited to a review of the principal organs of the United Nations."[12]

Indeed, in the report of the High-level Panel, one of the interesting contradictions is that the Security Council is said to have become more effective and more willing to act, remaining the UN body "most capable of organizing action and responding rapidly to new threats." It is nonetheless said to be urgently in need of reform.

The Report

Shared Threats, Collective Responses

The report is organized into four parts. The first part outlines the argument for a new security consensus. The world, it is said, poses new and evolving threats that could not have been anticipated when the UN was founded in 1945. These threats are not answerable through a unilateral response; every state—even the most powerful—requires international cooperation to make it secure. In addition to the prospect of catastrophic attacks using weapons of mass destruction (WMD), this new security consensus is also built upon the foundation of globalization. Global economic integration means that a major terrorist attack anywhere in the industrial world would have devastating consequences for the well-being of millions in the developing world. The report points out that, while the 700 million international airline passengers every year bring many benefits, they could also carry deadly infectious diseases. And, as Afghanistan showed, the erosion of state capacity may weaken the protection of every state against transnational threats such as terrorism and organized crime.

The second, third and fourth parts of the report address efforts at collective response through prevention, the regulation of the use of force and institutional changes proposed for the UN. These will be considered in turn.

Prevention and Collective Responses

Poverty, Infectious Disease and Environmental Degradation

The panel called on all states to commit themselves to the goals of eradicating poverty, achieving sustained economic growth and promoting sustainable development. The MDGs should be at the center of this poverty-reduction strategy, it argues, with the many donor countries that currently fall short of the United Nations 0.7 percent gross national product (GNP) target for official development assistance (ODA) establishing a timetable for reaching it.[13]

In addition to greater assistance and debt relief, the panel also called, indirectly, for a reduction in agricultural subsidies:

"In Monterrey and Johannesburg, leaders agreed that poverty alleviation is undermined by continuing inequities in the global trading system. Seventy percent of the world's poor live in rural areas and earn their income from agriculture. They pay a devastating cost when developed countries impose trade barriers on agricultural imports and subsidize agricultural exports. In 2001, the World Trade Organization (WTO) *Doha Declaration* explicitly committed signatories to put the needs and interests of developing countries at the heart of negotiations over a new trade round. WTO members should strive to conclude the Doha development round at the latest in 2006."[14]

On HIV/AIDS, the panel acknowledged that resources devoted to combating the disease had risen from about $250 million in 1996 to about $2.8 billion in 2002, but more than $10 billion annually is needed to stem the pandemic. To raise the profile of the problem and formulate an appropriate strategy, the panel urged that the Security Council convene a second special session on HIV/AIDS as a threat to international peace and security. In addition to greater support to local and national public health systems through the developing world, the report urged for better disease monitoring capabilities, in particular through increasing resources to the World Health Organization's (WHO) Global Outbreak Alert and Response Network.[15]

On the question of climate change, the panel stopped short of endorsing the *Kyoto Protocol* and calling on states (most obviously the US) to sign it. Instead, the report asked member states "to reflect on the gap between the promise of the *Kyoto Protocol* and its performance, re-engage on the problem of global warming and begin new negotiations to produce a new long-term strategy for reducing global warming beyond the period covered by the Protocol," which expires in 2012.[16]

Conflict between and within States

The threat of interstate war has declined but far from disappeared, said the panel. Intrastate conflict, meanwhile, has appeared to be undergoing a period of growth, although in fact the actual number of civil wars has declined since 1992; in the last 15 years, more civil wars were ended through negotiation than in the previous two centuries.[17]

How much responsibility the UN may claim for these changes is open to debate. The prohibition on the use of force enshrined in Article 2(4) of the *UN Charter* is routinely called into question—as it was, prominently, by the US-led invasion of Iraq in 2003—and yet remains the normative benchmark against which states are judged. This may have been more of an issue domestically for United Kingdom Prime Minister Tony Blair than for US President George W. Bush, but the US also articulated clear legal arguments in support of its position on the continuing operation of past Security Council resolutions on Iraq allowing for an exception to *Charter* Article 2(4).[18]

The panel suggested that the resolution of civil wars was possible "in large part because the United Nations provided leadership, opportunities for negotiation, strategic coordination, and the resources needed for implementation. Hundreds of thousands of lives were saved, and regional and international stability were enhanced." Such successes, however, were sometimes overshadowed by failures. Mediation efforts succeeded in only one-quarter of civil wars, and of those, not all received the international attention and resources necessary for effective implementation. Those which did not, such as the 1991 Bicesse Agreement in Angola, the 1993 Arusha Accords for Rwanda and periodic efforts to consolidate peace in Afghanistan in the early 1990s, greatly increased the number of deaths attributable to war.[19]

But the biggest failures of the UN in civil violence have been in failing to halt ethnic cleansing and genocide. Take, for instance, Rwanda, where, as the HLP report says:

"Secretariat officials failed to provide the Security Council with early warning of extremist plans to kill thousands of Tutsis and moderate Hutus. When the genocide started, troop contributors withdrew peace-keepers, and the Security Council, bowing to US pressure, failed to respond. In Bosnia and Herzegovina, UN peacekeeping and the protection of humanitarian aid became a substitute for political and military action to stop ethnic cleansing and genocide. In Kosovo, paralysis in the Security Council led NATO to bypass the UN. Only in one instance in the 1990s—in East Timor—did the Security Council, urged on by the Secretary-General, work together with national governments and regional actors to apply concerted pressure swiftly to halt large-scale killing."[20]

Improving this record of prevention requires political will. But the panel also outlined some of the tools that may be used. First, "the Security Council should stand ready to use the authority it has under the *Rome Statute* to refer cases to the International Criminal Court." Such an indication that the Council is carefully monitoring a conflict may deter parties from committing crimes against humanity and violating the laws of war. Second, better mechanisms are required to govern the management of natural resources for countries emerging from or at risk of conflict. Evidence from Sierra Leone and Angola suggests that efforts to cut down on illicit trade in "conflict diamonds" and other goods contributed to the end of their civil wars (*see Chapter 2 for further details*). Third, the UN should draw upon the experience of regional organizations in developing frameworks for minority rights and protection of democratically elected governments from unconstitutional overthrow. These networks are important both as early-warning systems and as normative standards that can guide preventive efforts. Fourth, better controls on small arms—the weapon of choice in most civil wars—would be an important constraint on civil wars, but progress in this direction has barely moved beyond rhetoric to action.[21]

Nuclear, Chemical and Biological Weapons

Disarmament and weapons of mass destruction are covered in Chapter 2 of this book. Consideration here is limited to reform proposals, which were intended to reduce both demand and supply.

On the demand side, the panel stressed the "lackluster" efforts by nuclear-weapon states in their obligations under the nonproliferation regime, undermining its ability to constrain proliferation. These states were called upon to honor their obligations under the Nonproliferation Treaty (NPT) to move toward disarmament and to reaffirm previous commitments not to use nuclear weapons against non-nuclear-weapon states. The Security Council argued the High-level Panel should support this by explicitly pledging to take collective action in response to a nuclear attack or the threat of such an attack on a non-nuclear-weapon state.[22]

In order to reduce supply, the UN's International Atomic Energy Agency (IAEA) requires greater powers. Only one-third of states parties to the NPT have ratified the *Model Additional Protocol to the Treaty*, which provides for more stringent inspection rules. The panel therefore recommended that the IAEA Board of Governors recognize the *Additional Protocol* as the standard for IAEA safeguards, with the Security Council prepared to act in response to non-compliance with these standards. The IAEA should be empowered to act as a guarantor of the supply of fissile material to civilian nuclear users. To combat illicit trade, states are encouraged to join the (voluntary) Proliferation Security Initiative (PSI), which the US initiated in 2003 and now claims more than 60 supporting states.[23]

Terrorism

The terrorist threat has grown in recent years due to the emergence of terrorist actors with global reach and the possibility that such actors will obtain access to weapons of mass destruction. Recommendations are made to help dissuade disaffected populations from turning to terrorism, improving instruments for global counter-terrorism cooperation, building state capacity and controlling dangerous materials. Endorsing the approach of the Counter-Terrorism Committee (CTC) established by Security Council Resolution 1373 in 2001, member states are asked by the panel to ratify all 12 international conventions against terrorism, with the CTC facilitating inter-state cooperation and capacity-building.[24]

Probably the most important contribution to the discussion of terrorism within the UN, however, is the definition of terrorism given by the High-level Panel. Agreement on a definition is typically undermined by two issues. The first is the question of whether it should include acts undertaken by states. As the panel argued, the use of force by states is comparatively well-regulated and prohibits most acts that might otherwise be classified as terrorism. The second issue is the objection that peoples under foreign occupation have a right to resistance that should not be overridden by a broad definition of terrorism. This conflates ends and means, however: there is nothing in the fact of occupation that justifies the targeting and killing of civilians and non-combatants. The definition proposed for adoption by the General Assembly, as part of a comprehensive convention on terrorism, includes four elements:

1) Recognition, in the preamble of the *Charter*, that state use of force against civilians is regulated by the *Geneva Conventions* and other instruments, and, if of sufficient scale, constitutes a war crime by the persons concerned or a crime against humanity;
2) Restatement that acts under the 12 preceding anti-terrorism conventions are terrorism, and a declaration that they are a crime under international law; and restatement that terrorism in time of armed conflict is prohibited by the *Geneva Conventions* and *Protocols*;
3) Reference to the definitions contained in the 1999 *International Convention for the Suppression of the Financing of Terrorism* and Security Council Resolution 1566 (2004); and
4) Description of terrorism as "any action, in addition to actions already specified by the existing conventions on aspects of terrorism, the *Geneva Conventions* and Security Council Resolution 1566 (2004), that is intended to cause death or serious bodily harm to civilians or non-combatants, when the purpose of such act, by its nature or context, is to intimidate a population, or to compel a government or an international organization to do or to abstain from doing any act."[25]

This was summarized by SG Annan in his report as providing that an action constitutes terrorism if "it is intended to cause death or serious bodily harm to civilians or non-combatants with the purpose of intimidating a population or compelling a Government or an international organization to do or abstain from doing any act."

Transnational Organized Crime

Combating transnational organized crime would both improve human and state security. Drug trafficking in particular has major security implications. The $300 to $500 billion illegal trade in narcotics is the largest single source of income for organized criminal groups. The consequences of this trade range from the spread of HIV/AIDS through intravenous drug use to the destabilization of governments confronting criminal enterprises wealthier than the state. Afghanistan in particular also demonstrates a clear link between opium and terrorist financing (*see Chapter 2 for further details*).

Addressing this problem requires better international regulatory frameworks and better capacity-building in weak states. States are asked by the panel to ratify the 2000 UN *Convention Against Transnational Organized Crime*, its three protocols, the 2003 UN *Convention against Corruption*, as well as the *Protocol to Prevent, Suppress and Punish Trafficking in Persons, Especially Women and Children*. The panel also concludes that a new convention on money-laundering is necessary.[26]

Collective Security and the Use of Force

As the High-level Panel emphasized, "the maintenance of world peace and security depends importantly on there being a common global understanding, and acceptance of when the application of force is both legal and legitimate. One of these elements being satisfied without the other will always weaken the international legal order—and thereby put both state and human security at greater risk."[27] The following section takes a look at these common goals.

Legality

The *UN Charter* prohibits the use of force with two exceptions: self-defense under Article 51 and enforcement action authorized by UN Security Council under Chapter VII. During the Cold War, these rules were frequently violated; the Council was paralyzed and Article 51 only rarely provided credible cover for military adventures. In the post-Cold War era, the Council became more active, but problems of defining the limits of Article 51 remain, as do questions of what should happen when the Security Council is divided (as it was over Kosovo and Iraq), and what general principles are emerging, if any, as to how the UN should treat threats that are primarily internal.

The first question, self-defense, was clearly aimed at recent assertions that a right of preemptive action might be allowed in response to a gathering threat. Intimations that this was the justification for the US-led invasion of Iraq led to accusations that the US had conflated anticipatory self-defense and preventive war. (This was despite the formal legal argument that the action was undertaken by the US in support of past Security Council resolutions dating back to Iraq's invasion of Kuwait.)[28] The panel stressed in this section of its report that "a threatened State, according to long established international law, can take military action as long as the threatened attack is imminent, no other means would deflect it and the action is proportionate."

This is debatable as a matter of law, but usefully separated out the most controversial aspect of the argument of expanded self-defense: where the threat in question is not imminent but still claimed to be real—such as the acquisition, with allegedly hostile intent, of the capability to make nuclear weapons. Might a state act unilaterally in such circumstances? The answer given by the panel is worth quoting at length:

"Those who say 'yes' argue that the potential harm from some threats (e.g., terrorists armed with a nuclear weapon) is so great that one simply cannot risk waiting until they become imminent, and that less harm may be done (e.g., avoiding a nuclear exchange or radioactive fallout from a reactor destruction) by acting earlier.

"The short answer is that if there are good arguments for preventive military action, with good evidence to support them, they should be put to the Security Council, which can authorize such action if it chooses to. If it does not so choose, there will be, by definition, time to pursue other strategies, including persuasion, negotiation, deterrence and containment—and to visit again the military option.

"For those impatient with such a response, the answer must be that, in a world full of perceived potential threats, the risk to the global order and the norm of non-intervention on which it continues to be based is simply too great for the legality of unilateral preventive action, as distinct from collectively endorsed action, to be accepted. Allowing one to act is to allow all."[29]

On the question of what to do when the Security Council is divided, the panel adopted a similar position to that of the International Commission on Intervention and State Sovereignty. The commission's 2001 report, The Responsibility to Protect, argued that "the task is not to find alternatives to the Security Council as a source of authority but to make the Council work better than it has." Nonetheless, the High-level Panel was realistic about the ability of the Council alone to constrain states that feel that they have both the obligation to their own citizens, and the capacity, to do "whatever they feel they need to do, unburdened by the constraints of collective Security Council process." Although such an approach might have been tolerated during the Cold War, the panel said, "the world has now changed and expectations about legal compliance are very much higher."[30]

The panel incorporated the substance of Responsibility to Protect in its recommendations on Security Council response to internal threats. In particular, it embraced the rhetorical and political move from considering the inviolability of governments to their responsibility. This reflects the growing awareness that the pertinent question is not whether there is a "right to intervene" but what obligations there are on a state to protect the population within its territory. And, as the panel noted, there is a growing acceptance that when a government is unwilling or unable to fulfill such obligations, they may devolve to the international community. Whether the options available to international actors include the use of force remains controversial.

The least controversial response to questions of the use of force remains recourse to the Security Council, but it has been inconsistent and sometimes ineffective. Action has come too late, hesitantly, or not at all. Nevertheless, there has been a gradual recognition that Chapter VII of the UN Charter can appropriately authorize military action to redress catastrophic internal wrongs that reach the level of a "threat to international peace and security."[31]

The UN's Responsibility to Protect

Three months after the North-Atlantic Treaty Organization concluded its controversial 78-day campaign over Kosovo in 1999, Secretary-General Kofi Annan presented his annual report to the UN General Assembly. In it, he outlined in stark terms the dilemma confronting those who privileged international law over the need to respond to gross and systematic violations of human rights:

"To those for whom the greatest threat to the future of international order is the use of force in the absence of a Security Council mandate, one might ask—not in the context of Kosovo—but in the context of Rwanda: If, in those dark days and hours leading up to the genocide, a coalition of States had been prepared to act in defence of the Tutsi population, but did not receive prompt Council authorization, should such a coalition have stood aside and allowed the horror to unfold?"[32]

The hypothetical neatly captured the ethical dilemma as many of the acting states sought to present it. Could international law truly prevent such "humanitarian" intervention? The problem, however, is that this was not the dilemma faced in the context of Rwanda. Rather than international law restraining a state from acting in defense of the Tutsi population, the problem in 1994 was that no state wanted to intervene at all.

The capriciousness of state interest is a theme that runs throughout the troubled history of humanitarian intervention. While much ink has been spilt on the question of the legality of using military force to defend human rights, it is difficult to point to actual cases that demonstrate the significance of international law on this issue. States do not appear to have refrained from acting in situations like Rwanda (or Kosovo) simply from fear of legal sanction. Nor, however, do any of the incidents frequently touted as examples of "genuine" humanitarian intervention correspond with the principled articulation of such a doctrine by legal scholars.

Returning to the Secretary-General's analogy, the type of problem confronting human rights today is not Kosovo but Rwanda. Put differently, the problem is not the legitimacy of humanitarian intervention, but the overwhelming prevalence of non-intervention. Empowering the UN, in this context, requires mobilizing the political will of member states as much as it does the creation of new legal rules. In this context, the rhetorical shift adopted by the International Commission on Intervention and State Sovereignty—from a right of intervention to the responsibility to protect—may mark the strongest advance in this contested area of international relations.

As recent years have demonstrated, enthusiasm about intervention can be a mixed blessing. For this reason, the panel limited the responsibility to protect—understood as authorizing military intervention as a last resort, in the event of genocide and other large-scale killing, ethnic cleansing or serious violations of international humanitarian law which sovereign governments have proved powerless or unwilling to prevent—to being exercisable by the Security Council alone.

Guidelines for the Use of Force

The panel proposed guidelines that could form the basis for Security Council deliberations. The aim is not to produce agreed conclusions or guarantee that the best outcome will prevail. Instead, the aim is to maximize the possibility of achieving Council consensus as to when it is appropriate to use force, to maximize international support for Council decisions and to minimize the possibility of individual member states bypassing the Council:

1) *Seriousness of threat.* Is the threatened harm to state or human security of a kind, and sufficiently clear and serious, to justify prima facie the use of military force? In the case of internal threats, does it involve genocide and other large-scale killing, ethnic cleansing or serious violations of international humanitarian law, actual or imminently apprehended?

2) *Proper purpose.* Is it clear that the primary purpose of the proposed military action is to halt or avert the threat in question, whatever other purposes or motives may be involved?

3) *Last resort.* Has every non-military option for meeting the threat in question been explored, with reasonable grounds for believing that other measures will not succeed?

4) *Proportional means.* Are the scale, duration and intensity of the proposed military action the minimum necessary to meet the threat in question?

5) *Balance of consequences.* Is there a reasonable chance of the military action being successful in meeting the threat in question, with the consequences of action not likely to be worse than the consequences of inaction?[33]

The panel suggested that the Council might adopt these principles in a declaratory resolution, but also stressed that member states generally subscribe to them as the appropriate guidelines for Council decision-making.[34] Whether the Security Council is best served by acting in a principled manner remains something of an open question. When first established, it is clear that there was no intention for the Council to be bound by anything other than the political will of those states that were victorious in World War II. As the UN and the Security Council have become more active, however, taking on far greater responsibilities not merely in responding to threats to peace but also acting to keep the peace in a far broader sense, the panel argued that legitimacy requires more than reliance on discretion granted by the *Charter*:

"The effectiveness of the global collective security system, as with any other legal order, depends ultimately not only on the legality of decisions but also on the common perception of their legitimacy—their being made on solid evidentiary grounds, and for the right reasons, morally as well as legally."

In order for the Security Council to maintain the respect it needs to fulfill its role effectively, the panel argued that its most important decisions have to be "better made, better substantiated and better communicated." On questions of the use of force, the Council should develop agreed guidelines "going directly not to whether force can legally be used but whether, as a matter of good conscience and good sense, it should be."[35]

Peace Enforcement and Peacekeeping Capability

The accepted wisdom within the UN community, articulated most recently in the 2000 Brahimi Report, is that a successful UN peace operation should ideally consist of three sequential stages. First, the political basis for peace must be determined. Then a suitable mandate for a UN mission should be formulated. Finally, that mission should be given all the resources necessary to complete the mandate.[36] The accepted reality is that this usually happens in the reverse order: member states determine what resources they are prepared to commit to a problem and a mandate is cobbled together around those resources—often in the hope that a political solution will be forthcoming at some later date.

This suggests that many of the problems confronting the UN in its peace and security responsibilities are political, but even if there is agreement on the Security Council about the appropriate response to a crisis, resources to implement that response are not always available. Necessary resources include not only numbers of troops, but also their abilities and, importantly, their willingness to implement their mandate.

As Brigadier-General Anthony Zinni, deputy for operations of the Unified Task Force in Somalia, once dryly observed in the second UN operation, there, the various contingents came to the battlefield with many different rules of engagement, "which makes life interesting when the shooting begins." Mogadishu airport in Somalia was defended by the forces of no less than eight nations: "Was that because the airfield was so big or so threatened? No. It was because the forces of those eight nations could go no farther than the airfield when they got off the airplane."[37] The obvious solution would be for the UN to develop standard rules of engagement, which might follow the production of standard operating procedures and standard form mandates from the Security Council. Member states of the UN have, however, been reluctant to allow it to develop doctrine in the area of peace operations. Members of the Non-aligned Movement are said to have rejected the very idea of creating a unit in the Department of Peacekeeping Operations with the word "doctrine" in the unit's title.[38]

Resistance on the part of certain member states is bolstered by those who adhere to the strict divide between peacekeeping and enforcement actions. UN Under-Secretary-General Shashi Tharoor, for example, has argued that "it is extremely difficult to make war and peace with the same people on the same territory at the same time."[39] This position was reflected in the General Guidelines for Peacekeeping, which stated: "Peacekeeping and the use of force (other than in self-defence) should be seen as alternative techniques and not adjacent points on a continuum. There is no easy transition from one to the other."[40] Sir Brian Urquhart, who joined the UN at its founding, put it best when he stressed that a true peacekeeper has no enemies, just a series of difficult and sometimes homicidal clients.[41]

As the panel emphasized, however, discussion of the necessary capacities has led to a misunderstanding about the differences between peacekeeping and peace enforcement, understood in shorthand as "Chapter VI operations" and "Chapter VII operations." In particular, this has led to a troubling assumption that the former do not involve the use of force for purposes other than self-defense, while the latter do:

"There is a distinction between operations in which the robust use of force is integral to the mission from the outset (e.g., responses to cross-border invasions or an explosion of violence, in which the recent practice has been to mandate multinational forces) and operations in which there is a reasonable expectation that force may not be needed at all (e.g., traditional peacekeeping missions monitoring and verifying a ceasefire or those assisting in implementing peace agreements, where blue helmets are still the norm).

"But both kinds of operation need the authorization of the Security Council (Article 51 self-defense cases apart), and in peacekeeping cases as much as in peace-enforcement cases it is now the usual practice for a Chapter VII mandate to be given (even if that is not always welcomed by troop contributors). This is on the basis that even the most benign environment can turn sour—when spoilers emerge to undermine a peace agreement and put civilians at risk—and that it is desirable for there to be complete certainty about the mission's capacity to respond with force, if necessary. On the other hand, the difference between Chapter VI and VII mandates can be exaggerated: there is little doubt that peacekeeping missions operating under Chapter VI (and thus operating without enforcement powers) have the right to use force in self-defense—and this right is widely understood to extend to 'defense of the mission.'

"The real challenge, in any deployment of forces of any configuration with any role, is to ensure that they have 1) an appropriate, clear and well understood mandate, applicable to all the changing circumstances that might reasonably be envisaged, and 2) all the necessary resources to implement that mandate fully."[42]

The most troubling aspect of the resource problems confronting peace-keeping is the lack of adequately trained personnel. The supply of peace-keepers is constrained by the configuration of many armed forces for Cold War duties, with the result that less than 10 percent of those in uniform are available for active deployment. In addition, few states have sufficient transport and logistic capacities to move and supply those who are available. The panel is discreet about suggesting that developed states have "particular responsibilities here, and should do more to transform their existing force capacities into suitable contingents for peace operations." Others have been more blunt, referring to the current situation, where more than three-quarters of peacekeepers operating under UN command come from developing countries, as "peacekeeping apartheid."[43]

Other Recommendations

The panel made further recommendations related to collective security to increase the UN's capacity to implement peace agreements by calling on the Secretary-General "to recommend and the Security Council to authorize troop strengths sufficient to deter and repel hostile factions."[44] In addition, the increased law and order responsibilities of the UN have been repeatedly undercut by the slow deployment of police contingents. The UN, the panel said, should therefore establish "a small corps of senior police officers and managers (50-100 personnel)" to undertake mission assessments and start-up police components of peace operations. The General Assembly is called upon to authorize this capacity.[45] Coordination is addressed primarily through the proposed establishment of a peace-building commission and a peace-building support office (*discussed below*), but also through giving greater power to special representatives of the Secretary-General and through funding disarmament and demobilization programs from assessed budgets rather than voluntary contributions.

Institutional Change

Given the inclusion of models for Security Council expansion, many readers of the High-level Panel's report have focused on the recommendations regarding institutional change, as outlined here.

General Assembly

The General Assembly embodies unique legitimacy through its near universal membership of states. Nevertheless, an "unwieldy and static agenda" has led to repetitive debates. The GA has frequently squandered its normative role on debates about minutiae or thematic topics overtaken by real-world events and its inability to achieve concrete conclusions on issues has undermined its relevance. Achieving the potential of this body, the panel wrote, requires more than procedural fixes. Instead, a new attitude toward the Assembly is required in order to enable it to perform its function as the main deliberative organ of the UN as stated by the panel: "This requires a better conceptualization and shortening of the agenda, which should reflect the contemporary challenges facing the international community. Smaller, more tightly focused committees could help sharpen and improve resolutions that are brought to the whole Assembly."

The High-level Panel also endorsed the role of civil society and non-governmental organizations in providing knowledge and perspective on global issues. It endorsed the recommendation of the Panel of Eminent Persons on United Nations-Civil Society Relations, in particular through establishing a better mechanism to enable systematic engagement with civil society organizations.[46]

Security Council

The one issue on which the panel was unable to reach agreement concerned the expansion of the Security Council—both the method for determining criteria for Council membership and the models ultimately proposed in the report. Presaging the debates by member states, Panel Chair Anand Panyarachun noted: "Some members of the Panel believe strongly that only the model involving expansion of permanent membership, albeit without a veto, will equip the Security Council to deal with the new century's threats. Others believe equally strongly that the alternative model involving elected, long-term but non-permanent members is the better way to proceed."[47]

The panel settled on four principles for reform of the Security Council:

1) Any reform should increase the involvement of those who contribute most to the UN financially, militarily and diplomatically. This should be understood as meaning contributions to assessed budgets, participation in mandated peace operations, contributions to voluntary activities of the UN in the areas of security and development, and diplomatic activities in support of the world body's objectives and mandates. Among developed countries, achieving or making substantial progress toward the internationally agreed level of 0.7 percent of GNP for official development assistance should be considered an important criterion of contribution.

2) Reform should bring into the decision-making process countries more representative of the broader membership, especially of the developing world.

3) Any such reform should not impair the effectiveness of the Security Council.

4) Reform should increase the democratic and accountable nature of the body.[48]

The panel further proposed two models which distributed seats on the

Security Council between four major regional areas. The four regions were not defined but simply identified as "Africa," "Asia and Pacific," "Europe" and "Americas." This in itself is a departure from the status quo agreed to in 1963 at the time of the expansion of the Council, that the elected 10 members would be allocated along the following lines: five "African and Asian states"; one "Eastern European state"; two "Latin American and Caribbean states"; and two "Western European and Other" (WEOG) states.[49] The change would merge Eastern Europe into "Europe," while moving Australia and New Zealand, and Canada and the United States from the "Other" into "Asia and Pacific" and "Americas," respectively. Israel, which only joined WEOG in 2000, might remain part of "Europe" or join the Asia group.

Model A provides for six new permanent seats, with no veto being created, and three new two-year term non-permanent seats, divided among the major regional areas as follows:

Table 1: High-level Panel Security Council Expansion Model A[50]

REGIONAL AREA	NO. OF STATES	PERMANENT SEATS (CONTINUING)	PROPOSED NEW PERMANENT SEATS	PROPOSED TWO-YEAR SEATS (NON-RENEWABLE)	TOTAL
Africa	53	0	2	4	6
Asia and Pacific	56	1	2	3	6
Europe	47	3	1	2	6
Americas	35	1	1	4	6
Total	191	5	6	13	24

Model B provides for no new permanent seats but creates a new category of eight four-year renewable-term seats and one new two-year non-permanent (and non-renewable) seat, divided among the major regional areas as follows:

Table 2: High-level Panel Security Council Expansion Model B[51]

REGIONAL AREA	NO. OF STATES	PERMANENT SEATS (CONTINUING)	PROPOSED FOUR-YEAR RENEWABLE SEATS	PROPOSED TWO-YEAR SEATS (NON-RENEWABLE)	TOTAL
Africa	53	0	2	4	6
Asia and Pacific	56	1	2	3	6
Europe	47	3	2	1	6
Americas	35	1	2	3	6
Total	191	5	8	11	24

The panel concluded that there was no practical way of changing existing permanent members' veto powers, but neither model included provisions to expand the veto to new permanent members. An interesting proposal frequently overlooked in the wake of the report was the suggestion of a system of "indicative voting" whereby members of the Security Council could call for a public indication of positions on a proposed action. A "no" under such circumstances would not have a veto effect; indeed, the vote itself would have no legal force. But it might provide a modest improvement in accountability for the use of the veto function.[52]

Economic and Social Council

The UN Charter recognizes the connections between peace and security on the one hand, and development on the other. Two of the three councils established in the Charter deal with these issues: the Security Council and the Economic and Social Council respectively. The third council, the Trusteeship Council, now exists in name only, the last trust territory having become independent in 1994. The role of the UN in international economic matters is not quite so anachronistic, but decision-making on such matters, especially in the areas of finance and trade, has long left the United Nations for organizations such as the International Monetary Fund, World Bank, World Trade Organization and others.

Nonetheless, the panel found three areas in which the UN might play a significant role in economic and social development: providing normative and analytical leadership on topics such as the social and economic aspects of security threats; providing an arena in which states measure their commitments to achieving key development objectives; and engaging the development community at the highest level in a kind of "development cooperation forum." Doing this effectively requires abandoning much of ECOSOC's current agenda, which tends to focus on administrative issues and program coordination, in favor of a more focused agenda built around major themes in the Millennium Declaration.[53]

Commission on Human Rights

An important and provocative argument in the report concerned the Commission on Human Rights, which was said to have been undermined by "eroding credibility and professionalism":

> "Standard-setting to reinforce human rights cannot be performed by States that lack a demonstrated commitment to their promotion and protection. We are concerned that in recent years States have sought membership of the Commission not to strengthen human rights but to protect themselves against criticism or to criticize others. The Commission cannot be credible if it is seen to be maintaining double standards in addressing human rights concerns."[54]

Identifying membership as the most difficult and sensitive issue, the panel recommended avoiding the problem through universal membership. Though it was generally accepted that the panel's diagnosis of the problem with the Commission on Human Rights was correct, the Secretary-General's response (discussed below) took a different tack by proposing more limited membership on a human rights council, whose members would be elected directly by the GA by a two-thirds majority.[55]

Peace-building Commission

The other major institutional change proposed by the panel was the creation of a peace-building commission. The report rightly criticized the UN's post-conflict operations as characterized by "countless ill-coordinated and overlapping bilateral and United Nations programmes, with inter-agency competition preventing the best use of scarce resources."[56]

Its key recommendation to remedy this situation was the call for a peace-building commission to be established as a subsidiary organ of the UN Security Council under Article 29 of the *UN Charter*:

"The core functions of the Peace-building Commission should be to identify countries which are under stress and risk sliding towards State collapse; to organize, in partnership with the national Government, proactive assistance in preventing that process from developing further; to assist in the planning for transitions between conflict and post-conflict peace-building; and in particular to marshal and sustain the efforts of the international community in post-conflict peace-building over whatever period may be necessary."

While the precise composition, procedures and reporting lines of the peace-building commission will need to be established, the panel states the commission should take account of the following guidelines:

1) It should be reasonably small.
2) It should meet in different configurations, to consider both general policy issues and country-by-country strategies.
3) It should be chaired for at least one year and perhaps longer by a member approved by the Security Council.
4) In addition to representation from the Security Council, it should include representation from the Economic and Social Council.
5) National representatives of the country under consideration should be invited to attend.
6) The Managing Director of the International Monetary Fund, the President of the World Bank and, when appropriate, heads of regional development banks should be represented at its meetings by appropriate senior officials.
7) Representatives of the principal donor countries and, when appropriate, the principal troop contributors should be invited to participate in its deliberations.
8) Representatives of regional and sub-regional organizations should be invited to participate in its deliberations when such organizations are actively involved in the country in question.[57]

These recommendations rightly addressed the need for coordination, though it is debatable whether they would resolve these problems that manifest in practice. Such problems tend to arise at three levels: the strategic level (e.g., for example, the final status of Kosovo); the operational level (e.g., competing donor agencies in Bosnia and Herzegovina); and the national level (e.g., getting international actors to sign onto a national development framework in Afghanistan).

If it is to be successful, two additional coordination dynamics need to be addressed. The first is the problem of coordination across time. This embraces both the conflicting time-tables of internationals (diminishing interest) and locals (increasing absorptive capacity), as well as the tension between demands for quick impact and gap-filling projects versus the development of sustainable institutions. The second coordination dynamic is the emergence of local actors as an independent political force. Consultation through an instrument such as a peace-building commission would be helpful, but not if it complicates the more important consultative mechanisms on the ground that manage day-to-day political life in the post-conflict territory. The most important aspect of this second dynamic is clarity: clarity about who is in charge at any given time, but also clarity about who is going to be in charge.

UN Charter

Any expansion of the Security Council would require amendment of Article 23 of the *Charter*. The panel recommended three further changes to the *Charter* reflecting the changed circumstances in which the UN finds itself today. First, references to enemy states in Articles 53 and 107 should be deleted. As the report notes, the *UN Charter* should reflect the hopes and aspirations of the present rather than the fears of 1945. Second, Chapter 13 on the Trusteeship Council should be deleted. After the independence of Palau in 1994, the Trusteeship Council amended its rules of procedure to remove the obligation to meet annually, agreeing instead to meet as required.[58] The Council now meets by its decision or the decision of its president, or at the request of a majority of its members or the General Assembly or the Security Council, but some states have periodically urged that the Trusteeship Council be recast as a forum through which member states could exercise their collective trusteeship over areas of common concern. For instance, it might focus on the environment or high seas.[59] There has been no evidence of enthusiasm for such a move, but since the Council no longer meets, has almost no staff, and uses no UN resources, there has been little impetus to shut it down.

Third, Article 47 on the Military Staff Committee (and reference to it in Articles 26, 45 and 46) should be deleted. The Military Staff Committee was intended to advise and assist the Security Council on the "employment and command of forces placed at its disposal," but remains little more than a curiosity. Its published records indicate that the committee has met once every two weeks since February 1946; in almost 60 years, it has done nothing of substance since it reported to the Council in July 1948 that it was unable to complete the mandate given to it two years previously. Meetings presently last a couple of minutes.[60]

Report Response

Responses to the High-level Panel report were generally positive, particularly given the low expectations that had dominated early discussion of its ability to produce an important policy document. Predictably, those states seeking permanent membership of the Security Council commenced a lobbying campaign to secure their seats under "Model A" for Council expansion. Hesitation about the choice of two African states to push for bids meant that Japan, Germany, India and Brazil—widely regarded as the most likely contenders for permanent seats—launched themselves independently as the "Group of 4" or "G-4." Other aspirants to a greater role on the Council, perhaps best secured through the occasional rotation of "Model B," formed a "coffee club" of opposition, later recasting itself as the happily titled "Uniting for Consensus" group. Of the permanent members themselves, the US explicitly endorsed Japan's bid but was openly skeptical of Germany's claim to a seat. China cultivated an extraordinary level of domestic opposition to Japan's possible role on the Council. As discussed earlier, however, the permanent members must ratify any *Charter* amendment to change the Council's representation, but this is not the same as having a veto. In 1963, France and the Soviet Union voted against Council expansion, only to ratify the amendment, which came into force almost two years later when the US (which had abstained in the General Assembly vote) became the last permanent member to ratify it.

Criticism of the Commission on Human Rights was generally well-received, though, as indicated above, the transformation of the commission into a body that might resemble the General Assembly was greeted with some horror. The idea of a peace-building commission was seen as a positive contribution, though in significant part because different constituencies understood it very differently—as variously as a standing pledging conference, a coordination mechanism or a new Trusteeship Council.

The most important response, as detailed below, came from the Secretary-General, whose *In Larger Freedom* report cherry-picked from the work of the High-level Panel and Jeffrey Sachs' UN Millennium Project report.

The Secretary-General's Proposals: *In Larger Freedom*

The report of the Secretary-General that attempts to lay out the reform agenda for the 2005 Summit is ambitious in both its scope and its rhetoric. *In Larger Freedom: Towards Development, Security and Human Rights for All* takes its title from the preamble to the *UN Charter*, which outlines the determination of "we the peoples" in the areas of peace ("to save succeeding generations from the scourge of war, which twice in our lifetime has brought untold sorrow to mankind"), human rights ("to reaffirm faith in fundamental human rights, in the dignity and worth of the human person, in the equal rights of men and women and of nations large and small"), justice ("to establish conditions under which justice and respect for the obligations arising from treaties and other sources of international law can be maintained"), and development ("to promote social progress and better standards of life in larger freedom").

Some of the report's language consciously echoed US President Franklin

Roosevelt, notably his 1941 "Four Freedoms" State of the Union Address. The High-level Panel had quoted President Harry Truman's injunction to the final plenary session of the founding conference of the UN that "we all have to recognize—no matter how great our strength — that we must deny ourselves the license to do always as we please."[61] The Secretary-General, in turn, quoted FDR's call for leaders to demonstrate "the courage to fulfill [their] responsibilities in an admittedly imperfect world."[62] Both references, of course, had the additional intent of demonstrating the importance to the UN of the strong and active participation of the US. (Two months earlier, US President George W. Bush had delivered a second inaugural address that used the word "freedom" no less than 27 times.)

The "in larger freedom" conceit runs through the document and attempts to bind three hitherto separate fields of activity within the UN system:

"Even if he can vote to choose his rulers, a young man with AIDS who cannot read or write and lives on the brink of starvation is not truly free. Equally, even if she earns enough to live, a woman who lives in the shadow of daily violence and has no say in how her country is run is not truly free. Larger freedom implies that men and women everywhere have the right to be governed by their own consent, under law, in a society where all individuals can, without discrimination or retribution, speak, worship and associate freely. They must also be free from want—so that the death sentences of extreme poverty and infectious disease are lifted from their lives—and free from fear—so that their lives and livelihoods are not ripped apart by violence and war. Indeed, all people have the right to security and to development."[63]

In Larger Freedom adopted President Roosevelt's calls for freedom from want and freedom from fear in its sections on development and security respectively. FDR's two other freedoms (of speech and thought, and of worship) were replaced with a broader concept of freedom to live in dignity. This was said to embrace respect for the rule of law, human rights and democracy. It also suggested a certain symmetry in the Secretary-General's call for the Commission on Human Rights to be replaced with a human rights council, alongside ECOSOC, and the Security Council.

The first leg, freedom from want, endorsed the Millennium Development Goals and called for priority action in 2005 on the adoption and implementation of "national development strategies bold enough to meet the Millennium Development Goals targets for 2015." At the same time, developed countries "should establish timetables to reach the 0.7 percent of gross national income for official development assistance by no later than 2015, starting with significant increases no later than 2006 and reaching 0.5 percent by 2009." On trade, SG Annan called for the Doha round of multilateral trade negotiations to fulfill its development promise and be completed no later than 2006 (*see Chapter 6 for further details*). And, "as a first step, states should provide duty-free and quota-free market access to exports from least developed countries."[64]

The second leg, freedom from fear, began by noting that while the UN's development agenda suffers from a lack of implementation, its security agenda begins without even a basic consensus on the most pressing issues for the UN. The Secretary-General embraced the "broad vision...of collective security" articulated in the High-level Panel's report and sought to make the case that collective security today means "accepting that the threats which each region of the world perceives as most urgent are in fact equally so for all." At times this blended arguments that were analytical, normative and ethical:

> "On this interconnectedness of threats we must found a new security consensus, the first article of which must be that all are entitled to freedom from fear, and that whatever threatens one threatens all. Once we understand this, we have no choice but to tackle the whole range of threats. We must respond to HIV/AIDS as robustly as we do to terrorism and to poverty as effectively as we do to proliferation. We must strive just as hard to eliminate the threat of small arms and light weapons as we do to eliminate the threat of weapons of mass destruction. Moreover, we must address all these threats preventively, acting at a sufficiently early stage with the full range of available instruments."[65]

Largely endorsing the High-level Panel's recommendations, the Secretary-General highlighted four areas key to successful reforms:

1) To prevent catastrophic terrorism, he endorsed with minor modifications the panel's definition of terrorism (*quoted earlier*) and outlined a strategy based on five pillars: dissuading people from resorting to terrorism or supporting it; denying terrorists access to funds and materials; deterring states from sponsoring terrorism; developing state capacity to defeat terrorism; and defending human rights.

2) To limit the dangers of nuclear, biological and chemical weapons, he emphasized the responsibilities of nuclear weapons states to reduce stockpiles and provide negative security assurances (assurances of non-use of nuclear weapons) to non-nuclear powers. He also endorsed the expanded role of the IAEA (*discussed earlier*).

3) In the area of conflict, the proposal for a Deputy Secretary-General for Peace and Security was dropped, but the peace-building commission was, in large part, endorsed. Notable changes included the renunciation of an early warning or monitoring capacity, and an increased role for ECOSOC, to which the Commission would report "in sequence" after the Security Council depending on the phase of a conflict.

4) On the question of the use of force, the Secretary-General adopted a similar position to the High-level Panel on self-defense: that Article 51 of the *UN Charter* covers self-defense against an "imminent attack." This dropped even those limited qualifications in the High-level Panel's description—that no other means would deflect the threatened attack and that the response is proportionate—but this was presumably for

economy of language rather than to mark a normative shift. He also called on the Security Council to adopt a resolution (leaving out the additional call for the General Assembly to do so also) setting out the principles according to which it would use force.[66]

The third leg, freedom to live in dignity, was the most novel and, perhaps, the most controversial. By embracing the language of "responsibility to protect," SG Annan challenged member states to put deeds behind words in their commitment to international humanitarian law in particular:

"While I am well aware of the sensitivities involved in this issue, I strongly agree with this approach. I believe that we must embrace the responsibility to protect, and, when necessary, we must act on it. This responsibility lies, first and foremost, with each individual State, whose primary raison d'être and duty is to protect its population. But if national authorities are unable or unwilling to protect their citizens, then the responsibility shifts to the international community to use diplomatic, humanitarian and other methods to help protect the human rights and well-being of civilian populations. When such methods appear insufficient, the Security Council may out of necessity decide to take action under the *Charter of the United Nations*, including enforcement action, if so required."[67]

In this context, he encouraged member states to "cooperate fully with the International Criminal Court and other international or mixed war crimes tribunals, and to surrender accused persons to them upon request," but stopped short of recommending that the Security Council use its power to refer matters to the ICC.[68]

The institutional changes necessary at the UN broadly reflect those articulated in the report of the High-level Panel, with the notable exception of the proposed human rights council. In recommending a smaller, standing council, the Secretary-General sought to address the politics of membership by reducing rather than expanding it, while at the same time proposing that member states consider creating a body that puts human rights on par with the development and security agendas of the UN. On strengthening the Secretariat, the Secretary-General noted that, instead of appointing a Deputy Secretary-General, he had decided to create a cabinet-style decision-making mechanism. In the wake of the scandals surrounding the Oil-for-Food Programme and alleged sexual abuse by peacekeepers in the Democratic Republic of Congo and elsewhere, the Secretary-General also emphasized the importance of accountability and oversight, proposing a comprehensive review of the Office of Internal Oversight Services.

Each of SG Annan's concrete recommendations is listed in Table 3, together with corresponding references to the reports of the High-level Panel and the Millennium Project.

Table 3: Reform Recommendation Comparison

RECOMMENDATIONS	SECRETARY-GENERAL	HIGH-LEVEL PANEL	MILLENNIUM PROJECT
FREEDOM FROM WANT			
Reaffirm and commit to Monterrey Consensus and goals outlines at the World Summit on Sustainable Development (Johannesburg)	5(a)	1, 2, 5-10, 86(c)	Various references
Developing countries recommit themselves to taking primary responsibility for their own development by strengthening governance, combating corruption and putting in place the policies and investments to drive private-sector-led growth and maximize domestic resources to fund national development strategies	5(a)(i)	45 (corruption through transnational organized crime)	2
Developed countries undertake to support these efforts through increased development assistance, a more development-oriented trade system, and wider and deeper debt relief	5(a)(ii)	3, 4	7, 8
Recognize the special needs of Africa	5(b)	86(c) (donor countries to work with the AU)	Various references
Each developing country with extreme poverty to adopt by 2006 and begin to implement a comprehensive national strategy to meet the MDGs	5(c)	1	1
Developed countries to donate 0.7 percent of their GNP for official development assistance	5(d)	2	7
Redefine debt sustainability	5(e)	4	7
Complete the WTO Doha round	5(f)	3	8
Launch an International Financial Facility	5(g)		(Chapter 17)
Launch "quick win" initiatives to realize immediate progress of the MDGs (*See Chapter 3*)	5(h)		5
Ensure that the international community responds urgently to HIV/AIDS and fully fund the Global Fund to Fight AIDS, Tuberculosis and Malaria (*See Chapter 5*)	5(i)	5-8	5
Reaffirm gender equality	5(j)		2
Significantly increase international support for scientific research and development to address the special needs of the poor	5(k)		9
Ensure global action to mitigate climate change	5(l)	11	9
Establish a worldwide early warning system for natural disasters	5(m)		(Chapter 11)
Developing countries that put forth sound, transparent and accountable strategies to receive increases in aid	5(n)		4

RECOMMENDATIONS	SECRETARY-GENERAL	HIGH-LEVEL PANEL	MILLENNIUM PROJECT
FREEDOM FROM FEAR			
Affirm and commit to the implementation of a new security consensus based on the fact that threats are interlinked and that no state can protect itself acting alone	6(a)	Various references	Various references
Pledge full compliance with all articles of the *Treaty on the Non-Proliferation of Nuclear Weapons*, the *Biological and Toxin Weapons Convention* and the *Chemical Weapons Convention*	6(b)	21-37	
Develop legally binding international instruments to regulate small arms and light weapons; ensure effective monitoring and enforcement of arms embargoes	6(c)	15, 50(a)	
Define and renounce terrorism	6(d)	38, 39, 44	
Implement the comprehensive UN counter-terrorism strategy presented by the Secretary-General; deny terrorists access to funds and materials; deter states from sponsoring terrorism; develop state capacity to defeat terrorism; and defend human rights	6(e)	38, 41-43	
Resolve to accede to all 12 international conventions against nuclear terrorism and a comprehensive convention on nuclear terrorism before the end of the 60th General Assembly	6(f)	39, 44	
Accede to all relevant international conventions on organized crime and corruption	6(g)	45	
Security Council to adopt a resolution that sets out principles for the use of force	6(h)	56-57	
Establish a peace-building commission and a voluntary standing fund for peace-building	6(i)	82-85	
Create strategic reserves for UN peacekeeping; support efforts by the EU, the AU and others to establish standby capacities; establish a UN civilian police standby capacity	6(j)	59, 60, 86(d)	
Enforce Security Council sanctions effectively, including by strengthening capacity, establishing monitoring mechanisms and mitigating humanitarian consequences	6(k)	50-52	
FREEDOM TO LIVE IN DIGNITY			
Strengthen the rule of law; respect human rights and fundamental freedoms; promote democracy	7(a)	14, 38(a), 38(c), 49	2
Embrace the "responsibility to protect" as a basis for collective action against genocide, ethnic cleansing and crimes against humanity	7(b)	55	

RECOMMENDATIONS	SECRETARY-GENERAL	HIGH-LEVEL PANEL	MILLENNIUM PROJECT
FREEDOM TO LIVE IN DIGNITY			
Ratify all treaties relating to protection of civilians	7(c)	66	
Support democracy, including through a democracy fund	7(d)	14, 38(a)	(Chapter 7)
Support the International Court of Justice	7(e)		
STRENGTHENING THE UN			
Rationalize and speed up the work of the General Assembly; focus its agenda on major substantive issues; engage with civil society	8(b)	71-72	
Make the Security Council more representative by agreeing to expand its membership before September 2005, if necessary by a vote	8(c)	73(d), 74-77	
Make ECOSOC a high-level development cooperation forum	8(d)	87-89	
Replace the Commission on Human Rights with smaller standing human rights council	8(e)	90-92 (with universal membership)	
General Assembly to review all mandates older than five years	8(f)(i)		
Provide the Secretary-General with authority and resources to pursue a one-time staff buyout	8(f)(ii)	96(d)	
Undertake a comprehensive review of the UN budget and human resources rules	8(f)(iii)	96(b)	
Endorse the Secretary-General's past management reform proposals	8(f)(iv)	96(c)	
Strengthen the Office of Internal Oversight services	8(f)(v)		
Coordinate representatives on the governing boards of the various development and humanitarian agencies	8(g)		
Commit to protecting humanitarian spaces; developing new funding arrangements for emergency funding; supporting the Secretary-General's effort to strengthen responses to the needs of internally displaced persons	8(h)		
Integrate structures for environmental standard-setting and monitoring	8(i)		
Strengthen the relationship between the UN and regional organizations; develop and implement a 10-year plan for capacity-building with the African Union	8(j)	86(b)-(d)	
Eliminate *UN Charter* references to "enemy States" in Articles 53 and 107; delete Article 47 on the Military Staff Committee and references to it in Articles 26, 45, and 46; delete Chapter XIII on the Trusteeship Council	8(k)	98-100	

Process

Apart from his substantive contributions, the Secretary-General made three important contributions in terms of process. First, he endorsed an accelerated process for resolving the question of expanding the Security Council, stating that member states should agree to take a decision on this important issue before the summit in September 2005. It would be very preferable for member states to take this vital decision by consensus, but if they are unable to reach consensus this must not become an excuse for postponing action.[69]

This was seen by some as an implicit endorsement of Germany and Japan's bid to have a vote on expansion at the beginning of the summer. It was also intended, presumably, to get the politicking of Security Council membership out of the way before what might be more construionctive dialogue on reforms on other matters. A danger, however, was that by encouraging a vote, the very process intended to unite the member states might itself cause disharmony.

Second, by proposing a "comprehensive agenda," he expressed the hope that member states would approach the reform package as a whole and negotiate "in a spirit of give and take";[70]

"In any such list of proposals, there are items which seem more important to some than to others, and items about which some have reservations, while others consider them essential. The temptation is to treat the list as an à la carte menu, and select only those that you especially fancy.

"In this case, that approach will not work. What I am proposing amounts to a comprehensive strategy. It gives equal weight and attention to the three great purposes of this Organization: development, security and human rights, all of which must be underpinned by the rule of law.

"But I do not need to remind you that this is an Organization of 191 member states. We all know that global problems can best be solved if all states work together. We must also accept that that will only happen if, within the common strategy, all states see their specific concerns addressed.

"I argue in the report, and I am profoundly convinced, that the threats which face us are of equal concern to all. I have called the report *In Larger Freedom*, because I believe those words from our *Charter* convey the idea that development, security and human rights go hand in hand. The cause of larger freedom can only be advanced if nations work together; and the United Nations can only help if it is remoulded as an effective instrument of their common purpose.

"You may or may not find my argument convincing. But please remember, in any event, that if you need the help of other states to achieve your objectives, you must also be willing to help them achieve their objectives. That is why I urge you to treat my proposals as a single package."[71]

This argument was essentially rejected. Member states immediately began negotiating on selected issues in which they had specific interests. This horse-trading seemed likely to continue until the High-level plenary in September.

Third, SG Annan appointed five envoys to use their good offices to promote *In Larger Freedom*: Dermot Ahern, minister for foreign affairs of Ireland; Ali Alatas, former foreign minister of Indonesia; Joaquin Chissano, former president of Mozambique; Vaira Vike-Freiberga, president of Latvia; and Ernesto Zedillo, former president of Mexico. Within the UN, this was complemented by the appointment by 59th General Assembly President Jean Ping of 10 facilitators organized around four "clusters" of reform: 1) freedom from want, or socioeconomic development; 2) freedom from fear, or peace and security; 3) freedom to live in dignity, or law and human rights; and 4) strengthening the UN, or institutional reform.

Other Reforms

Various other initiatives have been underway in parallel with the official UN reform agenda discussed in this chapter, building on the various initiatives of the Secretary-General since his 1997 "Program for Reform." Within the world body itself, several initiatives have been established. The General Assembly held its second High-level Dialogue on Financing for Development in June 2005 at UN headquarters in New York. The dialogue is the major intergovernmental focal point for the follow-up to the Monterrey Conference on Financing for Development. Other mechanisms include the Panel of Eminent Persons on United Nations-Civil Society Relations (the Cardoso Panel) and General Assembly working groups. In April 2004, the President of Mexico established a "Group of Friends for the Reform of the United Nations," which issued 14 non-papers on various reform issues. The US Institute of Peace was directed by Congress in December 2004 to create a Task Force on the UN to assess the extent to which the UN is fulfilling the purposes stated in its *Charter* and to recommend an actionable agenda for the US on the UN. The task force, while not an official US government effort, was obligated to provide its report to Congress over the summer of 2005. Other governments have undertaken similar reform projects.

A further reform initiative worthy of note was established by a network of young professionals working within or alongside the UN system (including the author of this chapter). Working on a voluntary basis, this group sought to identify reforms that would greatly improve the day-to-day operations of the UN but not require a *Charter* amendment, significant resources or high-level political negotiations. In contrast to the High-level Panel, this group termed itself the "Low-level Panel" and released its first report in June 2005.[72]

Where Does the Capital Master Plan Fit In?

As part of its capital master plan, the United Nations is seeking to refurbish its 52-year-old headquarters building on Manhattan's East River, commencing in 2007. Original plans had called for the UN to build a 35-story tower as swing space on an adjacent property that currently serves as a playground and a dog run. During the renovation, 3,600 staff would have been moved from the headquarters building into the swing building. When work had been completed, around 2010, these employees would return to the refurbished headquarters and the dozens of agencies and offices scattered around Turtle Bay would be consolidated in the new building, UNDC-5.

New York State Republican legislators, however, reportedly irritated by recent scandals at the UN as well as perceived anti-Americanism and alleged anti-Semitism, denied approval for the use of the land. The UN had proposed a riverside esplanade to compensate for the lost public space, and the Department of Homeland Security had studied the security issues. Nonetheless, it is probably too late now to use the swing space even if approval were granted quickly, so other possibilities have been canvassed, ranging from sites in Brooklyn's Navy Yard, across the East River in Queens, and even the largely unused Governor's Island near the Statue of Liberty. Difficulties in renting out proposed properties in the new World Trade Center site led some to suggest moving the UN there. In a report released on May 10, 2005, the most likely venue was said to be part of a larger development in downtown Brooklyn.[73]

On February 25, 2005, the US Congress approved a loan offer of $1.2 billion to finance the costs of the project. This was conditional on a loan agreement being in place by September 30, 2005. The Secretary-General has recommended that the General Assembly accept this loan during its 60th session.[74]

Looking Forward

Secretary-General Kofi Annan's report was formally welcomed by the General Assembly on April 25, 2005, in a resolution that set the stage for a summit-level commemoration of the United Nations' 60th anniversary in September 2005. On September 14-16, leaders will gather in New York City for the "High-level Plenary Meeting of the General Assembly to Review Progress in Fulfillment of Commitments Contained in the UN *Millennium Declaration.*" This will be the focal point for the current reform push, but much of the real work will happen before and after that meeting.

At the time of publication, it was expected that member states would work to lay the foundation for a consensus document—possibly in the wake of a divisive vote over Security Council expansion. Many key issues were likely to be left unresolved before the September summit, such as the precise nature and composition of the proposed peace-building commission and human rights council. Work on the details of such institutional changes is likely to continue well beyond the summit.

Commentary:
The Shared Link among Today's Threats
Simon Chesterman

A t the heart of the substantive reform agenda—in particular the Secre-tary-General's efforts to link security, development and human rights—is a paradox of globalization. Globalization has long been seen as a tool of integration, binding states into a network of financial, political and cultural relationships that should make conflict less likely because the severance of those relationships was in no state's interests. But globalization is now seen as a threat, not merely an economic opportunity; integration into global net-works may expose a state to attack by non-state actors or biological hazards.

A dilemma for the High-level Panel on Threats, Challenges and Change had been how far to push the linkage between security and development. Some suggested that participation by developing states in the "global war on terror" might plausibly be linked to greater action on, for example, reduction of agricultural subsidies by the developed world. This approach was not, in the end, adopted, largely because it was seen as politically unrealistic.

The linkage remains, however, in varying degrees through the High-level Panel report and the Secretary-General's *In Larger Freedom* report. Unfortunate-ly, even this level of connection was sometimes misunderstood as suggesting that the only reason development assistance should be a priority is because fail-ing to invest in development might give rise to a threat along the lines of the collapse of Afghanistan prior to the 2001 attacks on the United States. Action on the development front should indeed help provide security for all, in the broad sense intended here, but development should also be a priority simply because it protects and improves the quality of life of fellow human beings.

The changed approach to the problem of "failed states" is suggestive of the opportunities and dangers of this approach. Recognition that weak states—archetypically Afghanistan—can create threats that reach beyond their bor-ders may increase the level of international interest in supporting those states, indirectly providing benefits to the populations. This argument has been made, for example, to encourage intervention for human protection purposes in Liberia by the US and in the South Pacific by Australia, although in both cases the link with terrorism was tenuous. The connection was also made in the new US National Security Strategy, which stressed that when violence erupts and states falter, the US will "work with friends and partners to alleviate suf-fering and restore stability." When interventions are justified by the national interest, however, this may lower the standards to which state-building and development activities are held. The level of physical and economic security required in Afghanistan to prevent it from becoming a terrorist haven, for example, is not the same as that required for the basic peace and prosperity of the general population.

None of this, of course, is new. Coercive diplomacy, the use of force and military occupation, has long been used by powerful states to further their interests. From an assistance perspective, the longer-term concern arising from the "war on terror" is that an obsessive focus on reacting to terrorism misunderstands the nature of threats as experienced around the world. Inequality and poverty remain the dominant concern of the most vulnerable and a key question confronting the human development agenda is how to ensure that international attention does not focus solely on countries of "strategic" importance. None of these strategic considerations have changed the experiences of populations at risk. A key challenge for the humanitarian and development communities is to establish the relevance of non-strategic assistance to populations at risk.

The report of the High-level Panel admirably set out the different types of threats that confront vulnerable populations, though it did not join the dots as clearly as it might have on the linkage between those threats. The concept of a "grand bargain" may yet be helpful—if only as a rhetorical device—in calling upon the industrialized nations to accept that their concerns about terrorism and weapons of mass destruction occupy a similar place that concerns about poverty and disease do in the global south.

Endnotes

1. George H.W. Bush, "Address before a Joint Session of the Congress on the Persian Gulf Crisis and the Federal Budget Deficit," September 11,1990.
2. *A More Secure World: Our Shared Responsibility* (Report of the High-level Panel on Threats, Challenges and Change), December 1, 2004. Hereafter, referred to as "HLP."
3. *Investing in Development: A Practical Plan to Achieve the Millennium Development Goals* (Report of the UN Millennium Project to the Secretary-General), January 17, 2005.
4. *In Larger Freedom: Towards Development, Security and Human Rights for All,* (Report of the Secretary-General to the General Assembly), March 21, 2005. Hereafter referred to as "ILF."
5. UN Document A/RES/48/26 (1993).
6. Paper by the Chairman of the Open-Ended Working Group on the Question of Equitable Representation on and Increase in the Membership of the Security Council and Other Matters Related to the Security Council, March 20, 1997.
7. *The Responsibility to Protect* (Report of the International Commission on Intervention and State Sovereignty, International Development Research Centre, Ottawa), December 2001.
8. Secretary-General's address to the UN General Assembly, September 23, 2003.
9. UN Document SG/A/857 (2003).
10. Ibid.
11. Secretary-General's address to the UN General Assembly, September 23, 2003.
12. Ibid.
13. HLP, paras 59-60.
14. HLP, para 62.
15. HLP, paras 64, 67, 69.
16. HLP, para 72.
17. HLP, para 82.
18. *See* for example: William H. Taft IV and Todd F. Buchwald, "Preemption, Iraq, and International Law," *American Journal of International Law,* Issue 97 (2003).
19. HLP, paras 85-86.
20. HLP, para 87.

21. HLP, paras 90-97.
22. HLP, paras 118-122.
23. HLP, paras 129-132. / US Department of State website.
24. HLP, paras 147-150.
25. HLP, paras 163-164.
26. HLP, paras 165-166, 171-172, 174-175.
27. HLP, para 184.
28. See for example: William H. Taft IV and Todd F. Buchwald, "Preemption, Iraq, and International Law," American Journal of International Law, Issue 97 (2003).
29. HLP, paras 189-191.
30. HLP, para 196.
31. HLP paras 201-203.
32. UN Document SG/SM/7136-GA/9596, (1999).
33. HLP, paras 206-207.
34. HLP, paras 206-209.
35. HLP, paras 204-205.
36. Brahimi Report (Report of the Panel on UN Peace Operations), August 21, 2000.
37. Anthony Zinni, "It's Not Nice and Neat," Proceedings, US Naval Institute 121, No. 8 (1995).
38. Trevor Findlay. The Use of Force in UN Peace Operations. (SIPRI & Oxford University Press, 2002).
39. Ibid.
40. UN Document UN/210/TC/GG95 (1995).
41. Brian Urquhart. A Life in Peace and War. (W.W. Norton, 1987).
42. HLP, paras 212-214.
43. David M. Malone and Ramesh Thakur, "Racism in Peacekeeping," Globe and Mail (Toronto), October 30, 2000.
44. HLP, para 222.
45. HLP, para 223.
46. HLP, paras 242-243.
47. HLP report.
48. HLP, para 249.
49. HLP, para 251. / General Assembly Resolution 1991A (XVIII) (1963).
50. HLP report.
51. Ibid.
52. HLP, paras 256-257.
53. HLP, paras 275-279.
54. HLP, para 283.
55. HLP, paras 283, 285.
56. HLP, para 38.
57. HLP, paras 264-265.
58. Trusteeship Council Resolution 2200 (LXI) (1994).
59. See for example: UN document A/RES/50/55 (1995).
60. Sydney D. Bailey and Sam Daws. The Procedure of the Security Council. 3rd ed. (Clarendon Press, 1998).
61. HLP, Synopsis.
62. ILF, para 222.
63. ILF, para 15.
64. ILF, paras 34, 49, 55.
65. ILF, para 81.
66. ILF, paras 87-94, 115-116, 124, 126, 188. / HLP, para 267.
67. ILF, para 135.
68. ILF, paras 135, 188. / HLP, para 90.
69. ILF, para 170.
70. UN Document SG/SM/9828 (2005).
71. UN Document SG/SM/9770 (2005).
72. More information is available at www.lowlevelpanel.org.
73. Maggie Farley, "UN Seeks Temporary Site," Los Angeles Times, April 4 2005. / UN Document A/59/441/Add.1 (2005).
74. UN Document GA/AB/3663 (2005). / UN Document A/59/441/Add.1 (2005).

Chapter 2

Peacekeeping & Disarmament: Protecting the World's Peoples

Assefaw Bariagaber, Ishtiaq Ahmad, Andreea Florescu,
Espen Barth Eide, Pernille Rieker, Jean Krasno,
Micky Hingorani and Rebecca Johnson

In an era of globalization and interdependence, security strategies founded merely on the priorities of individual countries or groups of countries can only be a short-term solution. As Secretary-General Kofi Annan recently stated, 'collective security today depends on accepting that the threats which each region of the world perceives as the most urgent are in fact equally so for all.'
—International Atomic Energy Agency Director-General Mohamed ElBaradei
Address to the opening of the Treaty on the Nonproliferation of Nuclear Weapons Review Conference, May 2005

Recent developments contain contradictory messages about the trends in international peace and security. The year 2003 was dominated by the Iraq war, which epitomized ill-thought-through military adventurism. By 2004, as official investigations in the United Kingdom and United States raised serious questions about the decision-making processes, accountability and selective uses of intelligence, multilateral approaches appeared to be making a comeback. The Iraq Survey Group, established by the US to hunt for weapons of mass destruction (WMD)[1] in Iraq reported in September 2004 that Saddam Hussein had not been capable of posing any kind of WMD threat in 2002-2003. The credibility of its intelligence in tatters, with Iraq suffering further disintegration and a catastrophic resurgence of terrorist acts, Washington appeared to acknowledge that international assistance and legitimacy were necessary for making significant progress in combating terrorism or developing the institutions to promote peace and stability, whether in Afghanistan or the Middle East. Meanwhile, conventional wars, characterized by racial and religious intolerance, violence against women and the indiscriminate use of cheaply-acquired small arms and light weapons, have continued to claim thousands of lives.

As reflected in the following maps, the United Nations is currently running 18 peacekeeping missions to assist such conflicts through its Department of Peacekeeping Operations (DPKO), five of which have begun since January 2004. There are 11 political and peace-building missions[2] being managed by the UN's Department of Political Affairs (DPA). Two political and peace-building missions, one in Afghanistan and one in Timor-Leste, have fallen under the umbrella of DPKO.

ONGOING PEACEKEEPING MISSIONS

* Political mission directed and supported by the Department of Peacekeeping Operations

Map No. 4000(E) R29   UNITED NATIONS
June 2005

Department of Peacekeeping Operations
Cartographic Section

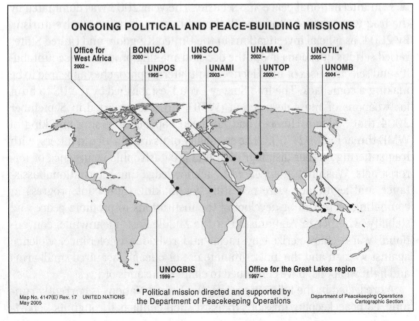

ONGOING POLITICAL AND PEACE-BUILDING MISSIONS

* Political mission directed and supported by the Department of Peacekeeping Operations

Map No. 4147(E) Rev. 17   UNITED NATIONS
May 2005

Department of Peacekeeping Operations
Cartographic Section

This chapter details the current status of the most active missions according to region, followed by a discussion on security issues, including nonproliferation, WMD and terrorism.

Africa

Assefaw Bariagaber

Over the last few years, United Nations peace operations in Africa have undergone fundamental changes with respect to their frequency, scope and actor involvement. There are now eight UN peace missions in Africa compared to five a year ago, and only four two years ago. In addition to the number of active operations, the scope of intervention has increased dramatically as well. While the UN withdrew from Somalia and Rwanda in the mid-1990s due to recurring problems it could not handle, the world body has recently shown added resolve, persisting in difficult areas such as Sierra Leone and the Democratic Republic of Congo (DRC). Indeed, the UN's Department of Peacekeeping Operations and Department for Political Affairs successively revised their scope of interventions by increasing force sizes and expanding mission mandates in several areas. The UN bodies, with the help of the Security Council, have enlisted the assistance of various actors in their quest for peace, cooperating with the Economic Community of West African States (ECOWAS) to deal with security threats in Sierra Leone, Liberia and Côte d'Ivoire, and playing a crucial role in organizing a donor conference with the World Bank, where more than $500 million was pledged to help those countries in their post-conflict reconstruction. UN peace operations have also assisted the African Union (AU) in peace efforts in Burundi and the Darfur region of Sudan, where their logistical support had been indispensable. And their joint work with the United Kingdom in Sierra Leone, and with France in the DRC and Côte d'Ivoire has probably saved the peace efforts in those areas from total collapse.

While the UN peace bodies can pride themselves on what they have accomplished, some missions continue to present many problems. There was not much progress in Western Sahara, for example, nor in the border conflict between Ethiopia and Eritrea. The security situation in Darfur, Sudan remains precarious at best, and there is continuing fear than it may spill over into Chad.

With both reasons for optimism and reasons to improve, UN peacekeeping efforts are plowing forward in eight currently active African missions: Burundi, Côte d'Ivoire, Democratic Republic of Congo, Ethiopia-Eritrea, Liberia, Sierra Leone, Western Sahara and, in the deployment stage, Sudan. These missions, described in detail in the following pages, constitute nearly half of the UN's current peace missions around the world.

Burundi

Like Rwanda, its northern neighbor, Burundi has suffered for a long time because of the insidiousness of the Hutu-Tutsi ethnic divide. It is similar to

Rwanda in many respects, including its physical terrain, geographical size, extremely high population density and, above all, its very ethnic composition. Although there have been a series of ethnic-based massacres since the time of Burundi's independence in 1961, a more protracted civil war started only in the early 1990s. This war has left tens of thousands dead and hundreds of thousands seeking refuge in neighboring countries, especially Tanzania. Until recently, the conflict never generated the attention it deserved.

In April 2003, the AU, through its African Mission in Burundi (AMIB), sent some 3,000 African troops to help stabilize the country. On May 21, 2004, the UN took over, establishing the UN Operation in Burundi (ONUB) under Security Council Resolution 1545. ONUB was mandated, with a maximum of 5,650 personnel, to help in the implementation of the Arusha Peace and Reconciliation Agreement of August 28, 2000. This included: monitoring the cease-fire; assisting in election activities; helping re-establish confidence between the various parties; and monitoring the demobilization, disarmament and re-integration of armed combatants.

ONUB was successful in many of its endeavors and, along with the UN Mission in Liberia (UNMIL), is the most successful of the ongoing peace operations in Africa today. It has now completed its deployment throughout the country and the security situation has become visibly stable. Thousands of armed combatants have entered cantonment sites in preparation for relocation and disarmament, and more than 2,000 child soldiers have been disarmed. Thanks to financial support from the European Commission and the UK Department for International Development, ONUB presided over the "pre-disarmament food delivery" to nearly 13,000 former combatants who had assembled in 12 different areas of the country pending demobilization.[3] This has helped prevent continued recruitment by disgruntled parties.

ONUB has also rehabilitated many schools and health facilities, which will serve more than 100,000 people, and provided books and other materials to about 53,000 pupils, and clean water to about 13,500 villagers.[4] Finally, ONUB has been exchanging information on border security with the UN Organization Mission in the Democratic Republic of Congo (*see below*). This collaboration has underscored the regional dimension of the conflict in the Great Lakes region of Africa, as armed combatants frequently cross the borders of one country with impunity to destabilize the other.

It is important to note that many of the armed groups in Burundi have transformed themselves into political parties and are willing to compete for power peacefully. The peace process received a further boost after the Palipehutu-FNL movement laid down arms and negotiated with the government to end violence.[5] Previously, this group had chosen to remain outside the peace process. Similarly, the Forces for the Defense of Democracy have returned to the power-sharing agreement, which has been described as a "breakthrough" for the peace process.[6] With MONUC's mandate still in effect and conditions improving as such, there is now a much better chance for a peaceful end to the conflict. The UN is already thinking beyond the transitional period, particularly after the success of the much-awaited referendum on Burundi's constitution on February 28, 2005.[7]

Côte d'Ivoire

The peace process in Côte d'Ivoire continues to pose difficulties for the UN mission there (UNOCI). Established under Security Council Resolution 1528 in early 2004, UNOCI was mandated to put into effect the January 2003 Linas-Marcoussis Agreement. This agreement called on the government, which controls the south, and the opposition, which controls the north, to cease fire, establish trust and create a "government of national reconciliation." The resolution also authorized French forces to use all means necessary to help UNOCI fulfill its mandate. However, the needed trust has been hard to come by. French forces are regarded as supporters of the opposition, adding difficulties to the peace equation. Attacks by government forces against the opposition and the French forces on November 6, 2004, which the Security Council strongly condemned, are indicative of the less-than-full acceptance of the status quo by the government.[8] In retaliation, French forces launched air attacks on government forces and destroyed the tiny Côte d'Ivoire Air Force.[9]

Alarmed at the deteriorating situation, the Security Council approved Resolution 1572 in November 2004 and imposed an arms embargo on all sides. In a further attempt to contain the situation, Resolution 1584 was adopted on February 1, 2005, strengthening the embargo. The latter document called for "unannounced inspections of all plane cargo holds and transportation vehicles at seaports, airports, airfields, military bases and border crossings." In late 2004 and early 2005, the security situation had deteriorated so much that the UK closed its embassy and ordered British nationals to leave.[10] Thanks to concerted South African efforts, however, the parties have now reached an agreement to end hostilities, settle on the eligibility for the presidency and disarm militias.[11] As of June 2005, both sides had finally agreed to begin disarming.[12]

Despite the difficulties outlined above, UNOCI's presence has been critical in preventing further deterioration of the security situation in Côte d'Ivoire, and in creating a climate conducive to peace. UNOCI has been undertaking joint patrols with government forces and has used its radio station to promote a culture of peace and tolerance. It also helped return civil servants to their former jobs and, through quick impact projects, has rehabilitated educational and health facilities.[13]

As indicated above, the lack of trust between the conflicting parties has remained the main stumbling block. Of special significance is the failure of the government to extend all opposition leaders' eligibility to run for the presidency. Most worrisome, however, is the anti-UNOCI media coverage by supporters of the government. The likelihood of October 2005 elections is increasingly in jeopardy. Meanwhile, the UN has not been able to come up with alternative mechanisms to resolve issues. Third parties, such as South

Africa, may provide a way out of this impasse. In the meantime, UNOCI's mandate is still in effect.

Democratic Republic of Congo

The Democratic Republic of Congo posed the hardest test for UN peace operations in Africa since early 2004. At the time of this writing, the proposed June 2005 elections were very much in doubt and there was general deterioration of the situation on many fronts. This included violent demonstrations against the UN Organization Mission in the Democratic Republic of Congo (MONUC), established by the Security Council in November 1999; the brazen attack and seizure of the towns of Bakuva in the east and Kilwa in the south by RCD-Goma and the Revolutionary Movement for the Liberation of Katanga; the continued fighting between rival militias in Ituri Province and other areas, incorporating the massive civilian displacement and violations of human rights that accompanied the fighting; and the ambush and killing of nine UN troops from Bangladesh in Ituri.[14] Moreover, tension between DRC and Rwanda escalated due to an alleged attack on the latter by Rwandan opposition forces from bases in DRC. MONUC also came under internal attack due to allegations of sexual misconduct and exploitation of women and girls in MONUC-controlled camps.

In short, last year was an *annus horribilis* for MONUC.[15] But the UN did not entirely fail. The organization responded to a series of emergencies with uncharacteristic efficiency. It broadened MONUC's mandate to provide total support for the programs of the Government of National Unity, including disarming irregular forces and advising and assisting the government. Under Security Council Resolution 1565 of October 1, 2004, it: expanded troop deployment by an additional 5,900;[16] destroyed various camps controlled by the Integrationist and Nationalist Front, the group suspected to have carried out the ambush; secured the release of 3,000 "slaves"; and renewed the arms embargo against irregular forces. Also, MONUC and the Congolese National Army mounted joint operations to protect the Walungu area from rebel attacks.[17] With such activities and the much-enhanced Resolution 1565 (2005), MONUC has gradually transformed itself from a neutral party to one in support of the government.

Despite the difficulties outlined above, MONUC continues to be the cornerstone of stability in the DRC. It would be hard to imagine what the security situation would have looked like, especially regarding protection of defenseless civilians, had it not been for MONUC. The mission presided over the repatriation of foreign combatants and their dependents to neighboring countries, organized seminars and workshops to sensitize the population on violations of human rights, including rape and abuse of child soldiers, and disseminated information on national reconciliation through various media outlets. MONUC also contributed to the success of the Burundi mission by sharing information on issues of common concern.

The peace mission in DRC will no doubt continue to present the UN with many challenges, but it may also present it with some opportunities, including serving as a case model for future UN involvement in Africa. The way the UN has managed itself in the DRC conflict seems to indicate that it has learned to act promptly when the stakes are high. UN supporters are likely to reiterate that the UN can do what other states are not able and not willing to do, using MONUC, whose mandate expires in October 2005.

Ethiopia and Eritrea

Of the eight UN missions currently underway in Africa, the peace mission in Ethiopia and Eritrea, officially called the UN Mission in Ethiopia and Eritrea (UNMEE), is the only mission mandated under Security Council Resolution 1312 of July 31, 2000, to monitor a cease-fire agreement along the common border of two universally-recognized sovereign states. The UN held a neutral stance when the mission was initially approved and remains neutral to this day. Unlike other peace missions, where the UN tends to support the government during times of civil unrest, UNMEE represents a "traditional peacekeeping" approach. Because of this, the situation on the ground has remained more or less stable. In fact, Eritrea's decision to lift "some restrictions to UNMEE's freedom of movement" has been a positive development over the last year.[18]

The peace process, however, is not completely on track. UNMEE had hoped to accomplish its mission, including the delimitation and demarcation of the border, by the end of 2003. As of May 16, 2005, however, no end was in sight, mainly because of Ethiopia's refusal to unconditionally accept the Boundary Decision of April 2002. Although Ethiopia has announced its acceptance of the decision "in principle," it still insists on negotiation with Eritrea as a precondition, which Eritrea has steadfastly rejected.

Attempts by Lloyd Axworthy, Secretary-General Kofi Annan's Special Envoy, to break the impasse have not yet borne fruit as Eritrea has seen no prospect for success. Partly due to financial constraints and partly due to the relative stability along the border, the UN has reduced its "sectors" of operation from three to two, and its force size from just over 4,000 military personnel in early January 2003 to around 3,300.[19]

Recent developments are another source of concern. Ethiopia has moved additional troops close to the border in what it called "defensive" positions and Eritrea has re-deployed its forces along the border. The Temporary Security Zone (TSZ) has remained generally calm, although recent killings of Eritrean and Ethiopian armed personnel have alarmed many observers.[20]

Nonetheless, UNMEE continues to provide essential services to those most affected, including many families with farmlands and homes inside the TSZ, who are unable to return home either because they do not have a place to call home or because of mine infestations. In fact, demining has been one of the critical areas in which UNMEE is making a difference. Similarly, it continues to implement quick-impact water, health and sanitation projects, and has conducted workshops on HIV/AIDS awareness.

The Badme region, because of which the war ostensibly started, continues to be the sticking point. Indeed, there may be other regions more expansive and perhaps more strategic than Badme which each country had claimed but lost under the Boundary Decision. However, they did not rise to the level of Badme in their symbolic importance. The UN and other major powers continue to warn that the inevitable cost of a continuing stalemate over this region may well lead to another round of senseless war. In the meantime, the Security Council has extended UNMEE's mandate until September 15, 2005. The stalemate in the peace process strongly suggests a further extension of the mandate when it expires.

Liberia

With nearly 15,000 UN troops, Liberia stands a close second to DRC in terms of the number of UN peacekeeping forces it hosts.[21] But it is much smaller than DRC territorially and although there is some parallel with the conflict in DRC, especially with regard to the massive human rights violations against civilians, the war in Liberia does not have multiple armed groups fighting against one another. Why, then, did the UN intervene with such a large force?

There are two main reasons. First, the conflict in Liberia started in 1989, followed by a larger, crueler war in nearby Sierra Leone in 1991. Both conflicts spilled over into Côte d'Ivoire in early 2002, hitherto an island of stability and prosperity in West Africa.[22] Recognizing the clear regional dimension of the wars in West Africa, the UN approved a larger force not only to stabilize Liberia but also to avert further crossover into other countries. Since early 2004, the missions in Liberia, Sierra Leone and Côte d'Ivoire have been coordinating their activities as never before.

As a result, the UN Mission in Liberia (UNMIL), established under Security Council Resolution 1509 on September 19, 2003, has been successful on many fronts. By early September 2004, an estimated 71,000 combatants had been disarmed, a large consignment of small arms and ammunition had been confiscated and thousands of former combatants had been reintegrated into their communities. Moreover, hundreds of foreign combatants had registered for repatriation to their countries.[23] By March 2005, the number of disarmed ex-combatants stood at just over 101,000, and another 25,600 were in the process of re-integration. Similarly, UNMIL assisted nearly 68,000 internally displaced persons (IDPs) in returning to their homes and, in conjunction with the UN High Commissioner for Refugees (UNHCR) and the World Food Programme (WFP), provided trucks to transport food to about 250,000 IDPs.

In terms of building state capacity in Liberia, UNMIL has been assisting the National Transitional Government (NTGL) in training sessions for prosecutors and law enforcement officials as part of its "rule of law capacity-building initiative" and provided state authorities with the necessary technical support for control of the country's territorial waters. It also has been conducting training sessions to help the Forestry Development Authority guard the timber in the country. Finally, and perhaps more importantly, UNMIL has been providing support for the scheduled October 2005 elections. At the time of this writing, the mission was assisting the National Elections Commission in the preparation of voter registration lists, security detail and election messages.[24] Although UNMIL has been successful in many of its endeavors, some challenges still lie ahead. Continuing instability in nearby Sierra Leone and Côte d'Ivoire are cases in point for this volatile region, plagued by crossover conflicts. There is a critical need to strengthen state authority. The UN has done some of this by assisting in reconstituting the court system, and enhancing transparency and accountability in money management.[25] Similarly, the armed forces of Liberia have a long way to go before they are deemed fully functional, and there still remain armed combatants as well as refugees and IDP's. Recent reports that former President Charles Taylor is working to destabilize the country through his close associates in the country do not help matters. In spite of this, the international community appears determined to go forward. In fact, the peace mission has been extended until September 19, 2005, and will most certainly be expanded further after that point.[26]

Sierra Leone

The UN Mission in Sierra Leone (UNAMSIL) has the distinction of being the only mission in Africa where armed groups held a large number of UN peacekeepers hostage. That was in 2000 when the UK intervened and rescued the mission from probable collapse. At its peak, the number of UN peacekeepers in UNAMSIL reached close to 17,500, making it the largest UN peacekeeping force ever to operate in Africa. Because of the successes it had, especially since the May 2002 elections, the number now stands at less than 4,000. All remaining UN uniformed personnel are likely to withdraw by December 2005, bringing to an end UNAMSIL's mandate. It is expected that a UN political mission will continue to operate thereafter.

In early 2005, there were important developments. The Sierra Leone Truth and Reconciliation Commission finally published its long-awaited report, which both documented the country's "ugly past and [shined] the light on its more promising future."[27] In addition, state authority in Sierra Leone received a much-needed boost when Switzerland donated 260 trucks for its armed forces, and the World Bank and UN Development Programme (UNDP) provided funds to train and enhance the effectiveness of newly elected local authorities. Thanks to stronger state capacity, the black market diamond trading in the country has decreased, enabling the state to collect more revenues from its diamond exporting. Moreover, the UNHCR has officially completed its repatriation program.[28]

With the end of the peace mission in sight, the UN has been focusing more on containing any possible spillover from the conflicts in Liberia and

Côte d'Ivoire. It has been active in inter-mission cooperation, including "sharing of assets among missions; planning on issues pertaining to disarmament, demobilization and reintegration; joint air patrolling; ...and possible establishment of subregional reserve forces."[29] This foresight once again demonstrates that UN missions, particularly among UNAMSIL, UNMIL and UNOCI, are shedding their distinctive individualism in favor of a more integrated subregional approach, much of which is under the aegis of the UN Office for West Africa (UNOWA). UNAMSIL has been the main driving force in this cooperative endeavor. The same type of cooperation has also emerged in the Great Lakes region of Africa, where ONUB and MONUC have started to coordinate their activities. In fact, looking at the geography of existing conflicts one cannot help but notice that, with the exception of the UN mission in Western Sahara, which is described below, the remaining seven African peace missions are currently concentrated in three conflict-prone regions: West Africa, with three peace missions, the Great Lakes and the Horn of Africa, with two missions each. Clearly, the UN has stepped up to the challenge to counter regional diffusion of conflicts with regionally integrated peace missions.

The UN Security Council is determined to hold on to the progress already made in Sierra Leone. At long last, UN perseverance in the face of many disappointments finally paid off, and the UN can look forward to a time when a much-scaled-down political mission will be sufficient to monitor and provide advice so that the infamous past never returns.

Sudan

The UN has been involved in Sudan for less than a year, stepping in after the north and south parties signed a comprehensive peace agreement. The conflict between the central government, based in the north, and the Sudan People's Liberation Movement/Army (SPLM/A), based in the south, has been raging for all but 11 years since 1956, and particularly since the Sharia Law—an Islamic law that regulates marriage, family affairs, and property and inheritance rights—was adopted in 1983. However, the escalating conflict in the Darfur region of the country, which began in early 2003 and the massive violations of human rights that accompanied it (*see Chapter 4 for details*) are what really led the UN to act.

Sudan is a land of extremes. It is the largest country in Africa, with high climatic variations ranging from wet tropical forests in most parts of the south to dry and expansive deserts in most parts of the north. The country is inhabited by two distinct peoples—Arab Muslims in the north and largely African Christians in the south. Some believe that the pronounced difference between the two peoples is more extreme than anywhere else in Africa. Despite the actual or perceived differences, the north and south, hitherto separate administrations under British rule, were brought together a few years before independence in 1956 to constitute what became a sovereign Sudan. Soon after, conflict started.

The SPLM/A bases its reasons for armed opposition on the economic and political neglect of the south by the central government, dominated by northerners, including the absence of infrastructure in the south and the application of the Sharia Law on the entire territory, including the south, which is inhabited by a non-Muslim majority. On the other hand, the government blames the present conflict on the divide and rule colonial policies, Christian missionary activities and outside interference in Sudanese affairs. The conflict intensified after 1983 until it reached a stalemate in early 2000, at which time both the north and the south saw no chance of military victory. The history of past broken agreements and the continuing mistrust, which developed over a period of many years, had made the conflict not amenable to solutions.

In June 2004, under Resolution 1574, the Security Council approved the UN Advance Mission in Sudan (UNAMIS) to prepare for a future UN operation following the signing of the laid out North-South Comprehensive Peace Agreement. The agreement was signed in January 2005, under the auspices of the Inter-Governmental Authority for Development (IGAD)—a regional organization in the Horn of Africa and the Troika countries consisting of the US, UK and Norway. The Council passed Resolution 1590 on March 24 to approve the UN Mission in Sudan (UNMIS). Unfortunately, it took 21 years, two million lives, four million IDPs and about 600,000 refugees to reach this point.[30]

At about the same time the North-South negotiations were being conducted, a fresh conflict started between the Darfur-based Sudan Liberation Movement/Army (SLM/A) and the Justice and Equality Movement (JEM) on one side, and the central government, backed by the Janjaweed Arab militia, on the other. The SLM/A and JEM accuse the government of neglect and marginalization of Darfur because, although Muslim as their northern counterparts, were not Arab. Here, as in the North-South conflict, the issue of "Arabness" has become salient. The government, on the other hand, dismisses this as irrelevant, and views SLM/A and JEM as opportunists who exploited the North-South peace process to extract concessions for Darfur. The conflict increased sharply in scale, intensity and destructiveness in a short period of time. As result, many villages were burnt to the ground; nearly 100,000 were killed;[31] almost 200,000 sought asylum in Chad; and an estimated 1.8 million have been internally displaced.[32] Although the international community has not been able to agree on whether or not genocide has taken place, as the United States has concluded, there is no doubt that human rights violations, which the UN has described as "crimes against humanity," have occurred.[33] For this reason and others, the Security Council turned over the situation in Darfur to the International Criminal Court to prosecute those crimes (*see Chapter 7 for more details*).

Such is the complex nature of the two-pronged war in Sudan. In Darfur, the AU established the ongoing African Mission in Sudan (AMIS), which has been mandated to monitor cease-fire violations agreed upon by the conflicting parties in Abuja, Nigeria. Various countries, including Germany and Canada, have provided financial and logistical support for the AU mission.[34] At present, therefore, UN involvement in Darfur is essentially in support of AMIS.

In the North-South conflict, however, there is no formal AU involvement. As indicated above, the Security Council established UNMIS on March 24, 2005, but only for an initial period of six months. Among other things, UNMIS is mandated to: support the implementation of the peace agreement; monitor and verify compliance with the cease-fire; observe and monitor the redeployment of forces; and assist in the disarmament, demobilization and reintegration program. At the time of this writing, troop deployment was under way and was expected to go smoothly under the leadership of Jan Pronk, who served as SG Annan's Special Representative to the Sudan.

Western Sahara

There has been no change in the dynamics of the conflict in Western Sahara since mid-2004; the UN has been continuing the work it began in 1991 under the mandate of the UN Mission for the Referendum in Western Sahara (MINURSO). Although the oldest of the ongoing peace missions in Africa, MINURSO has been unable to organize a referendum, its main mandate, on the future of the territory and no one knows when this will happen. Meanwhile, Morocco continues to occupy the entire territory and the UN continues to regard Western Sahara as a "non-self-governing" territory whose inhabitants have yet to exercise the right to decide their future. The International Court of Justice recognized this right in a 1975 ruling.[35]

Although it is hard to predict if and when the proposed referendum will take place, the UN has maintained the necessary funding for MINURSO, as its presence has been critical in many areas. MINURSO continues to monitor the cease-fire, which both Morocco and Frente POLISARIO had agreed to in September 1991, regularly conducts ground and air patrols, and helps to dispose of mines and unexploded ordnances. In line with confidence-building measures, it presided over the release and repatriation of 100 Moroccan troops by Frente POLISARIO, organized exchange of family visits where about 1,208 Western Saharan refugees from camps in Tindouf (Algeria) visited relatives in the territory, and established telephone links between the territory and the refugee camps of Laayoune and Awsard.[36] In cooperation with UNHCR and WFP, MUNURSO also organized a donor representative visit, which included the European Commission's Humanitarian Aid Office, the UN Children's Fund and various nongovernmental organizations (NGOs), to draw attention to the need for continued support of the protracted Saharawi refugee situation.[37]

There are now signs that the patience of the parties is wearing thin because of the continued stalemate. As SG Annan noted in an April 2005 report to the Security Council, lately there has been "serious deterioration in compliance" in matters regarding earlier military agreements. For example, the Moroccan Army has been upgrading its radar and surveillance capability, and improving its defense structure. Likewise, Frente POLISARIO has deployed anti-aircraft weapons in some restricted areas, and made repeated incursions into the prohibited buffer strip of the territory.[38] Recent statements by the Frente POLISARIO leadership that a "return to arms" may be "closer than ever" does not augur well for the peaceful resolution of the conflict. The Security Council appears helpless at this moment and has once more extended the mission mandate, this time until October 31, 2005.

Looking Forward

While the UN continues to try to keep the peace in African countries described here, there are emerging security threats elsewhere on the continent, forcing the UN to take on more and more. These include Darfur, where violations of human rights continue to occur despite the UN presence there, and Somalia, which is struggling to reconstitute itself after almost 15 years without a central government (*see the Looming Conflicts section in this chapter*). In fact, in light of continuing violations in Darfur, the UN is under pressure to do what it did in Rwanda—take over the peace process from the AU. Similarly, there are fragile states, where the situation can easily deteriorate into full-scale civil war. These include the Central African Republic and Guinea-Bisssau, where the UN maintains political missions. Given these circumstances, the need for additional peacekeepers is growing—the UN is pressed to bring to a successful end some of the ongoing peace operations before taking on additional security roles elsewhere in Africa and cannot do so without member state support.

There is hope, however. African leaders have now taken African security issues more seriously, as ECOWAS did in Sierra Leone, Liberia and Côte d'Ivoire. ECOWAS also played a crucial role in stabilizing Togo when it imposed sanctions to oppose an unconstitutional transfer of power to the son of the late President, Gnassingbe Eyadema, who ruled Togo for 38 years. Thanks to ECOWAS resolve, successful elections were conducted in April 2005. Similarly, the AU has been instrumental in peacekeeping in Burundi and Darfur, where it has deployed an estimated 2,300 African peacekeeping forces. In all these, the role of regional powers such as South Africa and Nigeria has been crucial; this is expected to continue. The role of the AU and other regional organizations in conflict stabilization in Africa will surely increase in the years to come, especially since the EU, North-Atlantic Treaty Organization (NATO) and others have promised increased funds and logistical support.

Americas

Andreea Florescu

While four of the five new peacekeeping missions deployed in the past year were sent to African countries, one Latin American country warranted the fourth: Haiti. A severe political crisis and renewed violence there led to the establishment of the United Nations Stabilization Mission in Haiti (MINUSTAH) in 2004; it is the fifth peacekeeping operation deployed to the troubled country since 1993. The first stages of MINUSTAH coincided with the departure of the 10-year-old political mission in Guatemala, or MINUGUA. As described in this section, while little if any progress has been achieved in Haiti over the past decade, Guatemala has emerged successfully from nearly four decades of civil strife. Though some deep-rooted problems remain, MINUGUA has been hailed as a model of successful peace-building to be replicated elsewhere.

Haiti

After four years of political impasse and rising levels of violence, the February 2004 resignation of President Jean-Bertrand Aristide plunged Haiti into chaos once more, leading to the establishment, on April 30, 2004, of MINUS-TAH. The new mission took over authority from the Multinational Interim Force that had been created at the beginning of the year as an initial response to the conflict. A transitional government assumed office in March of that year, with the task of restoring order and the rule of law, and preparing the country for elections. The transition period is set to end in September 2006.[1]

Reflecting the increasing complexity of UN peace missions, MINUSTAH was tasked with the traditional mandate of ensuring security, providing support for the reform of the Haitian National Police (HNP), assisting with the disarmament, demobilization and reintegration (DDR) of unlawful armed groups, and with the organization of free and fair elections. In addition, the mission was mandated to support democratic governance and institutional development, and to investigate and prevent human rights abuses, with a particular focus on the situation of women and children.

By May 2005, the mission had reached nearly full deployment strength—6,211 troops and 1,413 civilian police personnel, out of an authorized total of 6,700 troops and 1,622 civilian police.[2] Despite the large number of peacekeepers present in the country, the security situation remained unstable, particularly in Port-au-Prince. HNP and MINUSTAH have been confronting both gangs loyal to President Aristide and yet to be disarmed members of the national army.[3] By May 2005, persistent violence had claimed the lives of five UN peacekeepers, several HNP members and numerous civilians. MINUSTAH forces were directly targeted on several occasions, while two humanitarian trucks were attacked and looted in November 2004.[4] The most disturbing reports signaled attacks against the most vulnerable—women and children.

Despite the security environment, MINUSTAH has been able to train and build HNP's capacity, with help from the Organization of American States and the United States. Mission staff also worked to improve conditions in prisons and orphanages, and conducted awareness-raising campaigns on HIV/AIDS, sexual violence and child protection.[5]

At the beginning of 2005, Interim President Boniface Alexandre announced a national dialogue and reconciliation movement, but disenchanted members of the opposition party, Fanmi Lavalas, have refused to participate. Meanwhile, voter registration and preparations have begun for fall 2005 local and national elections.[6]

Guatemala

The UN Verification Mission in Guatemala (MINUGUA) was deployed in November 1994 to monitor implementation of the Comprehensive Agreement on Human Rights. This agreement was reached by the government of Guatemala and the Unidad Revolucionaria Nacional Guatemalteca (URNG), the two sides to a then-34-year-old internal conflict that killed an estimated 200,000 people, most of them civilians.[7] Upon the signing of the Agreement on a Firm and Lasting Peace in December 1996, the mandate of MINUGUA expanded to include verification in three other areas: indigenous rights, demilitarization and strengthening of civil society, and socio-economic aspects such as agrarian reform and gender issues.[8]

At its peak in 2000, the mission employed a staff of 532 and its allocated 10-year budget totaled $209.7 million. Though small, MINUGUA facilitated significant transformations in Guatemalan society. As outlined in the Secretary-General's August 2004 report to the General Assembly: "the State has ceased to sponsor human rights violations; the military has been reduced and brought under greater civilian control; institutional reform is underway; and democratic and peaceful elections have been held." Key to the mission's success was the fast demobilization, disarmament and reintegration of some 3,000 UNRG combatants and of military units disbanded under the peace agreements. Unlike the situation in Haiti, where the government has yet to put forward a credible and efficient DDR program, it only took one year for the former combatants to demobilize and disarm in Guatemala.[9]

On November 15, 2004, MINUGUA officially closed down, having achieved many "firsts" in UN work in the region: a human-rights related mandate, multi-dimensional peacekeeping and the establishment of truth commissions. Before closing, MINUGUA trained local experts to carry on its work, facilitated government takeover and developed a national database for documenting human rights violations. In January 2005, Guatemala and the UN High Commissioner for Human Rights signed an agreement to establish a UN human rights office.[10]

Looking Forward

Since its deployment, MINUSTAH has helped implement numerous quick-impact projects in the areas of agriculture, education and health to improve the living conditions of the Haitian population in the short-term. But much remains to be done on other fronts. Specifically, SG Annan has expressed concern about the slow progress of aid disbursement as pledged by the international community under the Interim Cooperation Framework with the Government of Haiti (2004-2006).[11] Indeed, Haiti's needs are multifaceted and require a sincere commitment by its political class, as well as by the international community.

As for Guatemala, largely a success story, its struggle for normalcy is not yet over. Structural poverty, crime and lagging institutional, judicial and land reform continue to mar the country. It is hoped that the new human rights mechanisms will curb some of these concerns. According to SG Annan: "The closure of MINUGUA should not be seen as the end of the peace process, but rather as the beginning of a new and necessary phase in which national actors assume full responsibility for monitoring and promoting the goals of the peace accords in the future."[12]

Asia

Ishtiaq Ahmad

The history of UN peacekeeping and peace-building in Asia is nearly as old as the history of the UN itself. It began in 1949, with the establishment of a limited UN peacekeeping mission in Kashmir to mediate between India and Pakistan. Since then, the world body has proactively undertaken a number of peacekeeping and political missions to help nations across the continent move from conflict-driven instability to sustained peace. In recent years, while continuing to play a symbolic peacekeeping role in Kashmir, the UN has contributed remarkably to peacekeeping and peace-building activities in Asia's four other trouble-spots: Tajikistan, Bougainville, Timor-Leste and Afghanistan, as described below.

Afghanistan

The highlight of the UN Assistance Mission in Afghanistan (UNAMA) in 2004 and the first half of 2005 was no doubt the holding of the first-ever democratic presidential elections in Afghan history. On October 9, 2004, more than 10 million Afghan citizens went to one of 25,000 polling stations across the country to pick one of 18 candidates to be their elected leader. On November 3, Afghan Interim President Hamid Karzai was officially declared the winner, giving him a five-year mandate to try to steer the country out of a quarter-century of civil war and strife. The announcement was made by officials of the Joint Electoral Management Body (JEMB), an UNAMA-supervised Afghan agency that organized the election, after a team investigating allegations of election-day voting fraud concluded that the irregularities that existed were insufficient to overturn Mr. Karzai's commanding lead.[1]

Despite the fact that warlord factions were threatening voters, candidates and political organizers in the months preceding the election, according to Human Rights Watch,[2] the JEMB-supervised registration process ended extraordinarily well. At least 10.3 million Afghans enrolled to vote, with women comprising more than 4.2 million, or 41 percent of the total. More than two million Afghan refugees living in Pakistan and Iran also registered to vote.[3] JEMB made extensive arrangements to smoothly conduct the elections, including the establishment of 25,000 polling stations and 100,000 voting screens, as well as the training of 115,000 polling officials, and the appointment of 5,000 independent domestic observers and 70,000 members of political parties to monitor polling stations. Some 300 donkeys also acted as a logistical support system to transport election material across Afghanistan's mountainous reaches.[4]

On December 7, 2004, Mr. Karzai was inaugurated as president, together with his two vice presidents, Ahmad Zia Massoud and Abdul Karim Khalili. The formation of a new 27-member cabinet, which took almost two months, was announced on December 23. President Karzai sought to ensure an ethnic balance in the Cabinet, resulting in 10 Pashtuns, eight Tajiks, five Hazaras, two Uzbeks, one Turkmen and one Baloch. Three of the chosen ministers were women.[5]

Preparations for the September 18, 2005 elections, to vote in the 249-seat lower house of Afghanistan's Parliament, called the *Wolesi Jirga*, and provincial councils, began soon after the presidential election. (The upper house, the *Meshrano Jirga*, was to be elected indirectly by provincial and district councils, with a third of the seats distributed by the Afghan president.) On January 24, 2005, President Karzai established the Independent Electoral Commission (IEC), consisting of six men and three women, representing seven different ethnic groups, to establish the electoral framework. Other key decisions made by the government had to do with the definition of the electoral system, demarcation of electoral district boundaries, definition of criteria to determine provincial population figures in order to allocate seats in the *Wolesi Jirga* (a national census would not be completed until 2007), and participation of refugees and nomads in the parliamentary and local elections.[6]

Parliamentary and provincial council elections were expected to be a more significant event in Afghanistan's post-Taliban history because a real transfer of local power was at stake. By March 18, 2005, 51 parties had been registered by the Ministry of Justice and 32 applications were under consideration.[7] The response to the candidate nomination process for the *Wolesi Jirga* and Provincial Council elections, which began on May 1, had also been enormous. Within three days of its initiation, 150 candidates across the country had submitted their applications.[8]

Although election processes are underway, the Security Council extended UNAMA's mandate in March for another year to ensure sustainable peace and stability.

Afghan Drug Trafficking: A Sign of Hope amid a Continuing Problem

The illicit narcotics industry continued to dominate Afghanistan's economy during the past year, even though poppy cultivation did decline for the first time since the toppling of the Taliban regime in

2001. Drug trafficking generated income equivalent to an estimated 60 percent of the legal gross domestic product, an increase of 35 percent from 2003, and 87 percent of the global supply. According to the 2004 Afghanistan Opium Survey produced by the UN Office on Drugs and Crime (UNODC), land being used for poppy cultivation during the year reached 131,000 hectares, up 64 percent from 2003, and a dramatic increase from the 8,000 hectares cultivated in 2001. The survey stated that poppies were being planted in all of the Afghan provinces.[9]

The findings of the survey led to the UN announcement of drug trade—and not the risk of a resurgent Taliban—as the main threat facing Afghanistan. Afghanistan's Counter-Narcotics Directorate was soon elevated to a full ministry and in December 2004, the President convened a National Counter-Narcotics *Jirga*, which was attended by regional governors, security officials, elders, tribal and religious leaders from all Afghan provinces. *Jirga* participants pledged to use their political, religious and social influence to combat cultivation, production and smuggling of illegal narcotics.[10]

As soon as the new Afghan cabinet was sworn in, it began addressing legal and judicial requirements to support counter-narcotics interdiction operations. A new law on money-laundering was adopted in December 2004. Moreover, a Counter-Narcotics Criminal Justice Task Force—composed of 85 specialist investigators, prosecutors and judges and assisted by the United Kingdom, United States, Canada and Norway—was created to fast-track counter-narcotics cases within the criminal justice system.[11]

In January 2005, UNODC Executive Director Antonio Maria Costa met President Karzai to pave the way for warrants to be issued for drug traffickers, based on international treaties.[12] And in February, the Afghan government and the UK, the lead nation on counter-narcotics activities, launched the 2005 Counter-Narcotics Implementation Plan. With almost 60 percent of Afghanistan's opium produced in the provinces of Badakhshan, Helmand and Nangarhar, the new plan initially concentrated Afghan and international efforts on eradication of poppy and the creation of alternative livelihoods in those provinces, as well as Kandahar. For its part, the US pledged $780 million for counter-narcotics efforts, which were to concentrate on eliminating poppy cultivation at the level of the individual farmer.[13]

In a welcome departure from recent past, the renewed Afghan and international commitment to combat drug trafficking has already led to a decline in poppy planting in areas where production had been traditionally high. A rapid assessment survey carried out jointly by UNODC and the Afghan Ministry of Counter-Narcotics in February found that farmers were growing fewer opium poppies in early 2005 than the year before, and that overall output was expected to drop for the first time since 2001.

The Security Council welcomed the efforts of the Afghan government to implement its national drug control strategy adopted in May 2003, including through the launch in February of the 2005 Counter-Narcotics Implementation Plan. It urged the government to take decisive action to stop the processing and trade of drugs and to pursue the specific measures set out in the plan.[14]

Amid these hopeful signs, the fight against opium production still faces numerous challenges. Afghan farmers grew poppies because they were more profitable than other crops and had greater resistance to poor weather. The income from poppy cultivation was 12 times greater than what a farmer could earn by growing wheat. Poppy-growing farmers have complained that they have not received assistance in finding an alternative crop.

In January, more than 30 local and international nongovernmental organizations working in Afghanistan—including CARE, Mercy Corps and Oxfam—criticised the US-led initiative on targeting individual producers of opium. They argued the new plan could hurt individual farmers and would do little to punish those drug traders at middle and higher levels (e.g., warlords, provincial governors, army officials). They urged instead that the US focus its counter-narcotics effort on creating an alternative livelihood for farmers.[15]

Like the narcotics situation, the security environment in Afghanistan has relatively improved as well, barring a couple of instances of kidnapping of UN and NGO officials that received much media publicity. In addition, insurgent forces struck a few targets of the government, International Security and Assistance Forces (ISAF) and coalition forces. Factors that contributed to relative improvement in the security environment from the past year, among others, included significant progress made in the disarmament, demobilization and reintegration program; the increased strength and quality of the Afghan National Army and Afghan National Police; the expansion of ISAF beyond Kabul in northern and northeastern Afghanistan; and growing public support of the new president and government, an outcome of electoral successes.

The first important success in the DDR program became visible in December 2004 when, for the first time since its start in 2003, all units in the entire region of Afghanistan were declared disarmed.[16] According to Secretary-General Kofi Annan's March 18 report on Afghanistan, the country had indeed passed a new landmark in its demobilization efforts after two decades of war and factional conflict. More than 43,700 troops from the militia forces had been disarmed—almost half of them over the previous six months. Of that number, nearly 39,000 had been demobilized. Under the Afghan New Beginnings Program, supported by Japan and supervised by the UN Development Programme, some 37,806 of those demobilized had started their reintegration programmes, including 46 percent in agriculture and 28 percent in vocational training such as carpentry. The second element of the DDR program, the cantonment of heavy weaponry, also exceeded expectations. By March, some 8,600 serviceable heavy weapons had been cantoned in six of the eight targeted regions, twice the total number of heavy weapons that were originally surveyed.[17]

As for progress in security sector reforms, as pointed out in SG Annan's report, the training of the Afghan National Army continued to make progress, with the US, assisted by France, acting as lead nation. By March, the size of the Afghan National Army had been expanded to approximately 22,000 soldiers and officers. The training schedule was accelerated so as to enable the Afghan National Army to reach its target of 70,000 troops by December 2006. In February, the German-led and US-assisted program of building the Police had trained 53,400 personnel, including 17,705 officers and 35,695 non-commissioned officers and patrolmen.

NATO also partially fulfilled its commitment to increase the strength of ISAF and expand its operations beyond the Afghan capital. With an increased strength of nearly 9,000 peacekeepers, ISAF provided an essential contribution to the security of Kabul, and the northern and northeastern regions. In late March, ISAF assumed an additional role for security through a staged transfer of responsibility from the coalition Provincial Reconstruction Teams (PRTs) in western Afghanistan. In March, as per the Secretary-General's report, there were 17 operational PRTs, and seven new teams were to be established by August 2005.

An expanded ISAF was certainly in a position to provide greater security in the lead up to the parliamentary elections by extending the writ of the central government to a portion of the Afghan hinterland, where 80 percent of the people lived. However, since the insurgency was confined mostly to southern and eastern Afghanistan, the real challenge for NATO was to extend ISAF operations to these more troublesome regions in accordance with the SC resolution of October 2003.

While security moved forward, the pace of judicial reforms remained rather slow last year. Supported by UNAMA and other UN agencies, the Judicial Reform Commission continued to suffer from a lack of clarity in its mandate and a lack of capacity to lead justice reform. In view of that, the Afghan government started reviewing a draft decree to devolve the functions of the commission to the three permanent national judicial institutions: the Supreme Court, the Attorney-General's office and the Ministry of Justice. The Consultative Group for Justice resumed its work during the year. UNAMA trained over 450 judges and prosecutors under a 16-month training program for Afghan judiciary. With support from UNDP's technical advisers, the Ministry of Justice and the Attorney-General's office made significant progress in the implementation of the government's public administrative reform program. There was also progress in the preparation of essential draft legislation for the administration of justice at advanced levels (organization of the courts of law, organization of the Attorneys' Prosecutor's Office) and other draft legislation, such as the juvenile justice code, was before the cabinet.[18]

Finally, developments on the reconstruction front occurred. In January 2005, the UN Country Team developed the UN Development Assistance Framework, which provided an analysis of how the UN system could improve its response to the priorities identified by the Afghan government and the Millennium Development Goals. On February 21, Afghanistan's first national human development report, entitled "Security with a Human Face," was launched. Written by an independent group of Afghans, the report was meant to help both the Afghan government and its international partners in their joint efforts to rebuild the devastated nation.[19] Among others, an important recommendation in the report was to address the link between poverty reduction, democracy and conflict prevention in order to lay the foundation for sustained economic growth and stability in Afghanistan. The report urged the international community to take a long-term view of Afghanistan's development.

Bougainville

At the time of this writing, the UN Observer Mission in Bougainville (UNOMB) was expected to conclude its operation by June 30, 2005, following the holding of presidential and parliamentary elections to establish the first autonomous government in Bougainville, hitherto an integral province of the South Pacific archipelago Papua New Guinea. "With the establishment of the Bougainville Government, the political role of the UN in the peace process will have been successfully completed," declared the Secretary-General in his March 30 report to the Security Council.[20] The polls, held between May 20 and June 2, elected a president and a house of representatives, comprising 33 members, along with three elected women and three elected former combatants.

Since January 1, 2004, UNOMB had successfully overseen the peace efforts of the National Government of Papua New Guinea and the Bougainville parties regarding weapons disposal and ensuring the parties' compliance to it, as well as the making of a constitution and its successful implementation through elections. As of March 30, UNOMB had destroyed most of the 2,014 weapons originally placed in containers in accordance with the weapons disposal plan. The National Court also resumed its hearings in Buka, the capital, for the first time in four years to try a backlog of cases that had accumulated since then. UNOMB was instrumental in persuading the Mekamui Defense Force (MDF), led by Francis Ona in the "no-go" zone, not to disrupt the elections. In March, it facilitated two meetings between MDF leaders and officials of the Provincial Administration of Bougainville to initiate the process of reconciliation between Francis Ona and President of the Bougainville People's Congress Joseph Kabui.[21]

MDF and two other Bougainville combatants had agreed to a cease-fire in 1998 after 10 years of independence war with the National Government of Papua New Guinea, resulting in the 2001 Bougainville Peace Agreement under the auspices of UN Political Office in Bougainville (UNPOB), UNOMB's predecessor.

Insofar as Bougainville's post-election scenario was concerned, besides the MDF boycott of the political process, the autonomous government is expected to confront significant post-conflict peace-building challenges concerning rehabilitation and recovery, which call for speedy delivery and decision-making mechanisms. It also requires the continued assistance of UN agencies, particularly UNDP and the donor community.

India-Pakistan

The peace process between India and Pakistan achieved remarkable progress since early 2004 as both sides began adopting confidence-building measures that could facilitate the settlement of the more than half-a-century-old Kashmir dispute. The UN Military Observer Group in India and Pakistan (UNMOGIP), the oldest UN peacekeeping operation in Asia, gained renewed significance in its mission to monitor the line of control in the disputed region, and to investigate and report its findings to UN headquarters.

UNMOGIP was established in 1949 to supervise the cease-fire between the two countries in the disputed state of Jammu and Kashmir. The dispute led to two of the three wars between India and Pakistan since independence in 1947 and brought them close to a potentially nuclear conflict in 1999 and 2002.

It was the historic January 2004 agreement between leaders of India and Pakistan in Islamabad to start a "composite dialogue" that set the pace for successive initiatives on Kashmir. Each side initially made unilateral moves, with Pakistani President Pervez Musharraf proposing in October 2004 demilitarization and joint administration of Kashmir by the two nuclear-capable nations. In November, India began to withdraw some of its troops from the portion of Kashmir under its administration.[22]

On February 16, 2005, the peace process received further impetus when the foreign ministers of the two countries agreed in Islamabad to start a landmark bus service across the line of control between Srinagar, the capital of Indian-administered Kashmir, and Muzaffarabad, the capital of Pakistan-administered Kashmir. On April 7, the bus service resumed as scheduled, reuniting Kashmiri families divided ever since India and Pakistan fought their first war over the territory in 1947.[23]

On April 18, 2005, in a move widely termed as "cricket diplomacy," President Musharraf and Indian Prime Minister Manmohan Singh, standing on the sidelines of a cricket match between Indian and Pakistani teams in India, declared that the peace process was now "irreversible." In their joint statement, the two leaders agreed to set up a joint business council to improve trade; launch a rail link between the Indian state of Rajasthan and the Pakistani province of Sindh by January 2006; increase the frequency of the bus service across divided Kashmir; allow trucks to use this route to promote trade; open a new bus link between Poonch in Indian Kashmir and Rawalakot in Pakistani Kashmir; reopen consulates in Mumbai (Bombay) and Karachi by the end of the year; and begin a bus service between Amritsar and the Pakistani city of Lahore.[24] SG Annan welcomed the joint statement, encouraged, in particular, by their declaration that the dialogue had become "irreversible."[25]

Despite such significant initiatives, both sides remained far apart on finding a final solution to Kashmir. India was unwilling to accept a redrawing of boundaries in the disputed region; Pakistan contended the line of control could not be made a permanent border.[26] The expansion of transport and trade links between the two parts of Kashmir was expected to at least help the two countries find some middle ground.

Moreover, as India and Pakistan moved forward in transforming the heavily militarized frontline dividing Kashmir into a "soft border," there remained a potential risk of militants stoking the insurgency in Indian-controlled Kashmir and upsetting the process. For their part, however, the leaderships of the two countries seemed committed not to let militant attacks impede the peace process. In their April 18 joint statement, President Musharraf and Prime Minister Singh jointly condemned the April 6 grenade attack by Kashmiri militants to kill passengers on the inaugural bus service. This was a radical departure from the past, whereby India would accuse Pakistan of sponsoring militancy in Kashmir and Pakistan would deny involvement in it.

The SG also strongly condemned the attack on a Srinagar compound housing the bus passengers, hoping "the bus service will begin as planned, and that it can help pave the way for additional confidence-building arrangements followed by substantive agreements on all outstanding issues, including the issue of Jammu and Kashmir."[27]

An essential hedge against militant attempts to subvert the India-Pakistan peace process over Kashmir could be a proactive monitoring of the line of control. UNMOGIP could play an important part in this context if its operational strength and scope were expanded. However, such a role could not be visualised in view of its extremely limited strength of some 45 unarmed military personnel drawn from nine countries under the command of a chief military observer.[28] Pakistan has long pressed for increasing the UN peacekeeping commitment in Kashmir, given the dispute's potential to cause nuclear disaster in South Asia.

UNMOGIP is every year periodically headquartered in the Pakistani city of Rawalpindi, where its movement is restricted by Indian authorities. However, while charting the path to peace in Kashmir jointly with Pakistan, India could be more accommodating of international input in settling the dispute. An expanded UNMOGIP could play a crucial role by coordinating its monitoring efforts with the military personnel of India and Pakistan so as to prevent any act of terrorism by Kashmiri militants across the line of control. Such a role on the part of UNMOGIP could continue until the Kashmir dispute was resolved amicably to the mutual satisfaction of the Kashmiri people as well as India and Pakistan.

Tajikistan

Another UN peace-building mission that recently ended its mandate was the UN Tajikistan Office of Peace-building (UNTOP), which had worked closely with the parties to the 1997 General Agreement on the Establishment of Peace and National Accord since June 2000. Its efforts to consolidate peace and national reconciliation through promoting the rule of law, strengthening democratic institutions and building national capacity in the area of human rights eventually led to the holding of February 27, 2005, elections for Tajikistan's lower house of parliament. President Emomali Rakhmanov's People's Democratic Party won a landslide victory.[29] However, the country's opposition parties, particularly the Islamic Renaissance Party, as well as the Election Observation Mission of Organization of Security and Cooperation in Europe (OSCE), accused the government of manipulating the political process.

At a news conference on February 28, head of the OSCE Observer Mission Peter Eicher said: "The 27 February elections in Tajikistan failed to meet many key OSCE commitments and other international standards for democratic elections.... Despite some positive aspects of the election process, including a few elements that showed improvement over previous elections, large-scale irregularities were evident, particularly on election day."[30] Among the irregularities listed by the OSCE Mission were a failure to include representatives of opposition parties in all district election commissions and the inclusion of many members of the ruling party in senior positions in those district election commissions.

Four of the five opposition parties competing in the elections also signed a petition on February 28, complaining about widespread violations and calling for the elections to be declared invalid. However, the use of the legal system to resolve controversial election results represented a sign that the Islamist opposition was willing to challenge the government in court rather than in other, extra-legal ways. The improvement in the security situation since the last election in 2000 was also an encouraging sign.[31]

For UNTOP and its predecessor, the UN Mission of Observers in Tajikistan (UNMOT), the task of consolidating political peace in the former Soviet republic was complicated by the struggle for political power between the ruling ex-communist political elite and the Islamist opposition invigorated by a regional wave of Islamic extremism.

On June 1, UNTOP ended its mission in Tajikistan, leaving the peace-building responsibility to the UN Country Team and the OSCE, which had assisted the two UN missions since 1997. An important challenge for both would be how to co-opt the Islamist opposition in the political process without letting the ruling party manipulate it further so as to pave the way for a fairer presidential election in 2006. Central Asia's democratic upsurge, with its anarchic undertones as visible in Kyrgyzstan and Uzbekistan, could impact the international role in consolidating political peace in Tajikistan in the post-UNTOP period.

Timor-Leste

In the history of UN peacekeeping in Asia, Timor-Leste could qualify as a major success story. Southeast Asia's newest nation has moved from a peacekeeping into a peace-building phase as the mandate of UN Mission of Support in East Timor (UNMISET) ended on May 20, 2005, with the establishment of the UN Office in Timor-Leste (UNOTIL)—a one-year follow-up mission to last until May 20, 2006. The April 28 Security Council resolution establishing UNOTIL noted that the country's emerging institutions were still in the process of consolidation and that further assistance was required to ensure sustained development and strengthening of key sectors, mainly rule of law, including justice, human rights and support for the Timor-Leste police and other public administrators.[32]

UNMISET had assisted Timor-Leste since independence from Indonesia in May 2002 in strengthening its political institutions and national security. East Timor, renamed Timor-Leste at independence, was a Portuguese colony before Indonesia took it over in 1976 and ruled it repressively for 23 years.

Despite its limited strength, as compared to the UN Transitional Administration in East Timor (UNTAET) whose mandate ended at independence, UNMISET played an important role in turning over responsibility for key tasks to East Timorese. Its major contributions included developing the public administration's legislative and regulatory capacity, broadening the Serious Crimes Unit's investigating capacity, establishing a national police force and enabling Government Security Agencies to handle security matters by themselves.

As a special political mission to help Timor-Leste move further toward governmental self-sufficiency and self-reliance, UNOTIL was tasked to support the development of critical state institutions by providing up to 45 civilian advisers; support further development of the police through the provision of up to 40 police advisers; and bolster the development of the Border Patrol Unit with as many as 35 additional advisers, 10 of whom may be military advisers. UNOTIL would also offer training in observance of democratic governance and human rights by providing up to 10 rights officers and review progress on those fronts.[33]

On February 18, 2005, SG Annan also announced the composition of an independent commission of experts, which was to be sent to Timor-Leste and Indonesia to review the serious crimes accountability processes.[34] This was in response to a 2004 decision by the Indonesian Appeals Court to overturn convictions of Indonesian officials for serious crimes during the anti-independence violence in 1999. The commission is also assisting the Truth and Friendship Commission, which Indonesia and Timor-Leste agreed to establish in December 2004, and began talks on the demarcation of Timor-Leste's border with Indonesia's West Timor region. Insofar as the delimitation of Timor-Leste's maritime border with Australia was concerned, negotiations have been underway between the two countries since September 2004 over the disputed oil and gas fields in the Timor Sea.

Timor-Leste's lingering economic woes, often a cause of domestic public uproar, might complicate UNOTIL's task of handing over government responsibility to the country's leadership. Given that, on April 25, the SG called on the international community to help Timor-Leste in achieving sustainable development.[35] In its resolution of April 28, the Security Council—while underlining that the UN assistance to Timor-Leste should be coordinated with the efforts of bilateral and multilateral donors, regional mechanisms, NGOs, private sector organizations and others—encouraged the Secretary-General's Special Representative in Timor-Leste to establish and chair a consultative group, made up of those stake-holders, that would meet regularly for that purpose.[36]

Looking Forward

With the end of missions in Bougainville and Tajikistan, and Timor-Leste's transition from a peacekeeping to peace-building phase, it is likely that the 60th General Assembly will focus on the India-Pakistan peace process as well as the electoral accomplishments in Afghanistan. As always, it will be interesting to see what new overtures over Kashmir the leaders of India and Pakistan make on the sidelines of the session. The debate inside the General Assembly may, however, be dominated by UNAMA's success in holding the presidential polls in Afghanistan and its contributions in the run-up to the first-ever parliamentary elections in Afghan history in September 2005, coinciding with the 60th anniversary of the world body. Pursuant to Resolution 59/112 AB of December 8, 2004, the Assembly is expected to discuss the situation in Afghanistan and its implications for international peace and security. The Assembly will also take into consideration efforts by the international community to restore peace and normalcy to the country and the issue of emergency assistance dedicated to the country's reconstruction.

Europe

Espen Barth Eide, Pernille Rieker

The significant surge in "blue helmet" peacekeeping that has taken place elsewhere on the globe is not reflected in Europe. While three United Nations peacekeeping operations remain on the continent, the general trend is that peacekeeping in Europe is becoming regionalized, that is, regional, multilateral operations are managing the operations in place of, or in conjunction with, the UN peace bodies. This is indeed quite logical. After all, Europe is the world's most institution-rich region, and the European integration process fundamentally transforms relations between members and non-members of the European Union. Enlargement of both the EU and NATO toward the east and south, and the establishment of partnership agreements with countries that are currently not ready for EU membership, has also contributed to an "all-European" political dynamic. In fact, the EU has taken over a number of peacekeeping responsibilities, as has NATO. In addition, the Organization of Security and Cooperation in Europe has gotten involved in peace efforts, monitoring and working in political missions in 16 countries, practically all of them in the Balkans or the post-Soviet area.

None of this is bad news for the UN. Chapter VIII of its *Charter* underlines the important role of "regional arrangements." Former Secretary-General Boutros Boutros-Ghali argued in the early 1990s that Europe itself, rather than the UN, should stand up to the emerging challenges in the Balkans. The initial track record of regional involvement was low, and the UN was forced to take most of the responsibility of crisis management in the Balkans for the first half of the 1990s. Since then, however, "outsourcing" has become commonplace, not the least in Europe. With the sole exception of the NATO-led war over Kosovo in 1999, all multilateral peace efforts in Europe, that were led by the EU, NATO, OSCE, the Council of Europe or for that matter the (now defunct) West European Union, have taken place with express or implicit endorsement from the UN. The challenge today relates to developing meaningful partnerships, making sure that high standards are employed in all types of operations, and that all peacekeeping and peace-building efforts are geared toward commonly defined aims.

The UN is still directly engaged, however, in three operations in Europe: Cyprus, Georgia and Kosovo. Discussed below, each one is closely related to European regional organizations and political processes.

Cyprus

The UN Peacekeeping Force in Cyprus (UNFICYP) was established in 1964 to prevent the resumption of fighting between Greek Cypriot and Turkish Cypriot communities over the island's territory. In the absence of a political settlement, UNFICYP's mandate has been periodically extended since 1974 for six-month periods.

An intensive effort was undertaken between 1999 and early 2003 to resolve problems between the two groups. It would have allowed a reunited Cyprus to sign the Treaty of Accession to the European Union on April 16, 2003. The proposed Foundation Agreement in "The Comprehensive Settlement of the Cyprus Problem" as finalized was submitted to separate simultaneous referenda on April 24, 2004. It was rejected by the Greek Cypriot electorate by a margin of 3 to 1, and approved by the Turkish Cypriot electorate by a margin of 2 to 1. It therefore did not enter into force and only the Greek Cypriot part of the island became a member of the EU in May 2004.

Following a review of UNFICYP's in September 2004, the Secretary-General recommended that the mission again be extended until June 2005.[1] The aim was to foster conditions conducive to a comprehensive settlement.

SG Annan also proposed a more mobile and efficient concept of operations and recommended that the military component of the mission be reduced from 1,224 to 860, and that the deployment of 45 UNFICYP civilian police be increased to 69.[2] On October 22, the Security Council, by Resolution 1568, endorsed the Secretary-General's recommendations.

During the first half of 2005, there have been some interesting changes on the Turkish Cypriote side. Mehmet Ali Talat, the leader of the Turkish Cypriot community, who was elected on April 17 to the post of president with a 56 percent majority vote, has vowed to resume peace talks with the Greek Cypriot government and to "reach and safeguard a solution to the Cyprus problem."[3] Mr. Talat, who succeeds Rauf Denktash, the founder of the breakaway Turkish Cypriot state, also has called on the EU to "strongly support Turkish Cypriots" and declared his readiness to meet Greek Cypriot President Tassos Papadopoulos. The leaders of the Greek Cypriot community welcomed the change in leadership. Following Mr. Talat's victory, the European Commission stated that it now expected UN-brokered talks leading to a comprehensive solution to the Cyprus issue to resume.[4]

Georgia

When Georgia gained independence from Russia in 1991, two republics within its borders began their own struggle for independence. The bloodiest revolt was in Abkhazia (the other was in South Ossetia), where a war between 1992 and 1993 left 10,000 people dead. The UN Observer Mission in Georgia (UNOMIG) was established in August 1993 to negotiate peace, monitor the most recently negotiated cease-fire agreement and oversee the Commonwealth of Independent States (CIS) peacekeeping force. It comprised mostly Russian soldiers and contributed to safe conditions abetting the return of refugees and internally displaced persons.

Over the years, the Secretary-General and his successive special representatives, with support from representatives of the Russian Federation, OSCE and the "Group of Friends" of the Secretary-General (France, Germany, the Russian Federation, the United Kingdom and United States) have promoted the stabilization of the situation and the achievement of a comprehensive political settlement. Such a settlement would focus on the future political status of Abkhazia within the state of Georgia and the return of refugees and displaced persons. To date, few substantial results have been achieved.[5]

Acting on the Secretary-General's recommendation, the Security Council extended the mandate of UNOMIG in July 2004 via Resolution 1554 for a period of six months (it was then extended again until summer 2005). While reaffirming the independence and territorial integrity of Georgia and the necessity to define the status of Abkhazia within Georgia, the Council deeply regretted the continued refusal of the Abkhaz side to agree to a discussion on the substance of the "Basic Principles for the Distribution of Competences between Tbilisi and Sukhumi."[6] The Council called on the parties to spare no efforts to overcome their ongoing mutual mistrust and underlined that negotiations toward a lasting political settlement acceptable to both sides would require concessions from both sides. The Council further called on the Georgian side to provide comprehensive security guarantees to allow for independent and regular monitoring of the situation in the upper Kodori Gorge by joint UNOMIG and CIS peacekeeping force patrols.

Reporting to the Security Council on October 18, 2004, SG Annan said that the Georgian-Abkhaz peace process had come perilously close to a standstill. While his special representative was still in close and frequent contact with both sides, the parties themselves had not met at the political level since July, and even the regular working level contacts were suspended. In his January 2005 report, he added that 2004 had not been an easy one for the Georgian-Abkhaz peace process. While the parties came together during the course of the year on some substantive issues, efforts to advance a dialogue encountered serious challenges. Renewed tension in the conflict zone led to a chain of events that brought all contacts between the two sides to a halt and over the past five months, the mission's main efforts focused on finding ways to re-establish dialogue and avoid regression.[7]

President Mikheil Saakashvili's announcement of a peace initiative in January 2005 was a positive step toward the peaceful resolution of the Georgian conflict. But without immediate and visible steps to back up President Saakashvili's words—beginning by seriously addressing the refugee and displaced persons issue in order to build some mutual confidence before plunging directly into status questions—there is a real danger that Georgia and South Ossetia could blunder into another military clash.[8]

The UN is not the only international organization operating in Georgia. The EU and OSCE are also present and the three operations work in close cooperation. While the OSCE mission has been in place since 1992 to assist the government with conflict settlement, democratization, human rights and the rule of law, the EU mission is more recent, initiated in 2004. In response to an invitation from Georgia, the EU decided in June 2004 to send the EU's first ever European Security and Defense Policy Rule of Law Mission to Tbilisi for one year until July 2005. The mission has a 2 million Euro budget and eight senior prosecutors and judges from eight member states (Italy, Latvia, Lithuania, Sweden, Germany, The Netherlands, Poland and Denmark). Its objectives are to help Georgia devise and implement reform of its criminal judicial system.[9] Following 10 months of cooperation with EU judicial experts, on May 18, 2005, the government presented the first draft of its national strategy for handling criminal cases and the findings are being pursued by a high-level government working group.

Kosovo

Long-simmering tensions in Kosovo were left untouched when most other conflicts in the Balkans were terminated by the Dayton (Bosnia and Herzegovina) and Erdut (Croatia) agreements in 1995. The non-violent resistance to Serbian rule in Kosovo, which was gradually substituted by armed resistance from 1997 and massive Serbian military repression from 1998, led to the NATO-led war over Kosovo in spring 1999.[10] Although NATO's military intervention lended tactical support to the Kosovar Albanian army, the international community was not ready to grant full independence to Kosovo when the war ended in 1999. Instead, Kosovo remained a part of Serbia. It was to be run by a UN-led transitional administration underpinned with a NATO-led peacekeeping force until a final decision on the province's status could be found.

On June 10, 1999, the Security Council passed Resolution 1244, which authorized the UN Interim Administration Mission in Kosovo (UNMIK) to begin the long process of building peace, democracy, stability and self-government in the shattered province. UNMIK is unique in that several organizations have come in to help under the UN umbrella. The OSCE and EU have their defined responsibilities as "pillars" of UNMIK (OSCE for institution-building, the EU for economic reconstruction and development).[11] The NATO-led Kosovo Force (KFOR) is responsible for establishing and maintaining security in Kosovo, including public safety and order, verification and, when necessary, enforced compliance with the agreements that ended the conflict.

Well over 90 percent of the inhabitants of Kosovo are Kosovar Albanian, and practically all Albanians support full independence for Kosovo. The small remaining Serb and Roma communities are equally skeptical of independence, which they fear will deteriorate the situation of the minorities in Kosovo. Tensions have been particularly strong over the divided town of Mitrovica where Serbs live in the northern part and Albanians live in the southern part. Kosovo's future status also figures heavily in Serbian politics. Serbian nationalists see Kosovo as the cradle of Serbian civilization, and the current reform-minded government in Belgrade has to tread a fine line between accommodating international demands and maintaining sufficient support at home. Likewise, other neighboring states (Albania, Macedonia and Bulgaria) have their own strong perspectives on the future of the province.

Kosovo's future, in fact, is the main remaining political problem for UNMIK. Successive Special Representatives of the Secretary-General have tried to resolve tensions by following a "standards before status" policy. The argument had been that the Albanian majority and the embryonic self-government first have to demonstrate their commitment to democratic rule, respect for human rights and protection of minorities before advances toward autonomy or independence could be undertaken.[12]

Violence erupting in March 2004 led to 19 deaths and several thousands fleeing their homes. International personnel, installations and equipment were targeted on a much higher scale than in any previous incident, and KFOR proved largely unable to protect key Serb landmarks and population clusters. The violence seems to have been triggered by a combination of increasing unease with the slow pace toward independence and frustration related to the 60 percent unemployment rate. In any case, the violence was a wake-up call for UNMIK and the international community about Kosovo, illustrating that the status issue could not be set aside for much longer. General elections were held in the province on October 23, 2004. They occurred peacefully, but the turnout was low on the Serb side.[13] President Ibrahim Rugova was reelected, and a new government was formed between his Democratic League of Kosovo party and Ramush Haradinaj's Alliance for the Future of Kosovo party. Hashim Tachi and his Democratic Party of Kosovo was left out of this coalition. Following elections, the Secretary-General's Special Representative Soren Jessen-Petersen handed over more power to the provisional government.

On March 8, 2005, Mr. Haradinaj was indicted by the International Tribunal for the former Yugoslavia; on March 9, he voluntarily left office and traveled to the Hague for prosecution, arguing that he was ready to defend his case before the Court. Since Mr. Haradinaj is seen both as a "war hero" and a popular contemporary politician by many Albanians, renewed tensions and street violence was expected, but did not occur. At least in part, this seems to be the result of better preparations by the international community as well as reconciliatory statements by Mr. Haradinaj and other Kosovar Albanian leaders who recognize that 2005 is a critical year on the road to a final status for the province. It has become clear to most parties involved that the long-term reconciliation and stabilization of both Kosovo and the Balkans in general require that war crimes be prosecuted regardless of which side of the various conflicts committed them.

In April 2005, Serbian President Boris Tadic made a proposal to meet President Rugova to start talks about Kosovo's future, but Mr. Rugova refused. Despite this setback, there is reason to believe that progress will take place over the next few years. In June 2005, the Security Council appointed Ambassador Kai Eide as a "review envoy" that will prepare the steps toward such progress.[14]

A four-stage plan, as suggested by the International Commission on the Balkans in spring 2005 seems to be a likely option. Here, the first stage is Kosovo's *de facto* separation from Serbia. The second stage is "independence without full sovereignty," meaning that Kosovo would be recognized as independent but with international community (UNMIK) veto over aspects of human rights and minority issues. This stage also involves continued UN or, if transferred, EU protection. The third stage is "guided sovereignty," in which Kosovo becomes a candidate for EU membership and the international "veto" is removed. Finally, "full and shared sovereignty for Kosovo within the EU" would occur. The last stage is most likely only to occur sometime into the next decade, however.

Outsourcing Peace Missions: The EU Example

As described in this section, there is an ongoing trend toward outsourcing peace operations in Europe from the UN to various regional organizations. The European Union, in particular, has shown considerable capacity to use international regimes (i.e., international norms, arrangements, agreements and laws designed to minimize security threats and promote cooperation) in the service of long-term structural conflict prevention. Until recently, this capacity has been primarily in the economic sphere and in regions close to the EU's territory. The most important tool has been the offer of membership in the EU itself, which stimulates nation candidates to make significant structural adjustments in areas identified by the EU as important to conflict prevention, notably rule of law and democratic institutions.

The EU has taken a strategic approach to the Western Balkans since 1999, when it put into place the Stabilization and Association process pursuant to which membership becomes a possibility. Croatia and Macedonia signed such agreements in 2001 and 2002, respectively, and both have now applied for EU membership; Albania has been negotiating a Stabilization and Association Agreement since early 2003; and Bosnia and Herzegovina is in the process of undergoing a feasibility study on whether it is ready to negotiate an agreement. Progress for Serbia and Montenegro along this track has been blocked for some time by the difficulties of implementing economic harmonization between the states' two constituent republics.

A new set of questions is emerging around how to expand this peace belt into troubled areas such as the South Caucasus. The European Commission's Wider Europe/New Neighborhood initiative, which the Thessaloniki Summit endorsed in June 2003, must be seen in this context.[15] Increasingly referred to as the European Neighborhood Policy (ENP), the initiative, like enlargement, promotes peace-building indirectly by promoting standards and values seen as contributory to conflict prevention and stabilization. In the beginning, ENP was oriented toward Morocco, Tunisia, Jordan, Israel, Palestine, Ukraine and Moldova, but at the European Council in June 2004, EU foreign ministers accepted a commission proposal to include Armenia, Azerbaijan and Georgia.[16]

Due to its multi-functional nature, the EU controls most of the instruments necessary to conduct preventive diplomacy, from enquiry and mediation to judicial settlement. The practice of appointing EU Special Representatives for trouble spots is also increasingly frequent. However, the EU still seems to have room for improvement when it comes to the coherent application of all these measures under one overall policy.[17]

In 2003, the EU's crisis management capacity became operational. It started with the takeover of the UN police mission in Bosnia in January and was followed by replacing NATO in Macedonia; the latter launched the first EU military peacekeeping operation (Concordia). Both operations must be seen as first steps toward assuming increasing operational responsibility in the Balkans.

Other European Peace Operations

In addition to the UN's three ongoing operations in Europe, two other peace operations are being managed largely by regional organizations: Bosnia and Herzegovina, and Macedonia. Despite a somewhat problematic start, the EU has now become the key actor in these two countries and is replacing both the UN and NATO.

Bosnia and Herzegovina

While the history of European Union involvement in Bosnia and Herzegovina is littered with good intentions, such as its police mission and stabilization force, the EU is still viewed with considerable suspicion in the country due to its perceived failure to act unanimously and decisively during the war during the early 1990s. The EU is now conducting a range of policies to promote peace-building and stability. All in all, it has committed 2.5 billion Euros to Bosnia and Herzegovina since 1991 and an agreement on the opening of negotiations with the country in the form of a Stabilization and Association Agreement is expected by the end of 2005.[18]

The replacement of the UN-led International Police Task Force (IPTF) on January 1, 2003 by the EU Police Mission marked a step in the assumption by the EU of greater responsibility for Bosnia and Herzegovina's security. The police mission is built on the success and achievements of IPTF, which have included implementation of a ranking system, control and public oversight, and implementation of laws establishing cooperation between Bosnia and Herzegovina in law enforcement agencies. The EU Police Mission is to help Bosnia and Herzegovina authorities develop local police forces that meet the highest European and international standards and to ensure that sustainable institutional structures are in place by the end of its mandate in December 2005.[19]

On July 9, 2004, the Security Council further increased the EU's role in the country with Resolution 1551. The resolution welcomed the EU's intention to launch its own mission, with a military component, in the country. Called Althea, the operation is replacing NATO's Stabilization Force and is implemented within the "Berlin plus" arrangements on EU-NATO cooperation. While NATO brought its Stabilization Force to a conclusion in December 2004, it still maintains a military headquarters in the country. In fact, it provides planning, logistic and command support for the EU-led operation and carries out a number of specific tasks related to reforming the government's defense structures. In addition to the EU and NATO, the OSCE is present in Bosnia and Herzegovina, helping the country to rebuild itself as a multi-ethnic, democratic society. The OSCE mission has established programs to promote the development of democratic political institutions at all levels and work in close cooperation with the EU and NATO.

Macedonia

In 1993, still at an early stage in the conflicts in the Balkans, the UN Protection Force (UNPROFOR) deployed a preventive peacekeeping force in the

Former Yugoslav Republic of Macedonia. There was substantial fear at the time that the sequence of conflicts that had begun in Slovenia in 1991, spread to Croatia that autumn and to Bosnia in 1992 would spill over further into Macedonia. The established UN Preventive Deployment Force in Macedonia (UNPREDEP) worked closely with the OSCE's Spillover Monitoring Mission. UNPREDEP was the first peacekeeping force deployed before the outbreak of an eventual conflict, and whether it was due to UNPREDEP or not, the fact is that war was avoided in Macedonia until the force's withdrawal in 1999.[20]

After the Kosovo war, signs of a potential civil war alarmed the international community, but effective mediation from both NATO and the EU led to the Ohrid agreements, which reconciled the (Macedonian) Albanian and Macedonian Slav actors sufficiently to avoid further violence. NATO stepped into the void left by UNPREDEP's withdrawal, and in March 2003, the EU took over NATO's operation, which then became the EU's first military operation ever (Operation Concordia). This operation, launched with NATO assets, was to secure the environment to allow the Macedonian government to implement the "Ohrid Framework Agreement." This amounted to confidence-building, providing emergency evacuation for international monitors, and advising and coordinating border security. Twenty-seven states, including 14 non-EU members, sent 350 soldiers. The original six-month mandate was extended to December 15, 2003, when it was superceded by an EU police mission for another year; it was further extended for one year in December 2004.[21]

Today, NATO remains committed to helping the Former Yugoslav Republic of Macedonia to become fully integrated in Euro-Atlantic structures and therefore maintains a Senior Civilian Representative and a Senior Military Representative. In addition, OSCE is working on monitoring, police training and development, and other political activities related to the implementation of the Ohrid Framework Agreement.

Looking Forward

While the UN still has the responsibility for three important operations in Europe—UNFICYP in Cyprus, UNOMIG in Georgia and UNMIK in Kosovo—regional organizations are becoming increasingly important in providing peace and security in Europe's trouble spots. The EU, in particular, is gradually replacing both the UN and NATO in the Balkans and is now starting to engage in other parts of the continent, such as Georgia and perhaps soon, in Moldova.[22] As these changes occur, one challenge will be to improve coordination between the different organizations and actors in order to make the peace operations as efficient as possible.

While the EU operations referred to above are all test cases for the EU's crisis management capacity, they also represent an important test for cooperation between the UN and regional organizations.[23] This approach fits well with the UN Secretary-General's own thinking in his March 2005 report *In Larger Freedom: Toward Development, Security and Human Rights for*

All, in which he states: "Time is now ripe for a decisive move forward: the establishment of an interlocking system of peacekeeping capacities that will enable the United Nations to work with relevant regional organizations in predictable and reliable partnerships." [24]

The Middle East and Iraq

Jean Krasno

Events in the Middle East since 2004 have been full of surprises, some signaling hopeful outcomes for the future and others reflecting the same violence and hardened positions of the past. Elections took place in Iraq on January 30, 2005 to form a Transitional National Assembly amidst doubt and violence; the sudden death of Palestinian leader Yasser Arafat ended an era and opened the door to new peace talks; Syrian troops that had been in Lebanon since 1978 were, within a few short months, pressured to leave Lebanon and return to Syria; and finally, there was a small hint that democracy might be spreading to the Arab world. The United Nations in one way or another was involved in all these events. The following section outlines the organization's peace efforts in each.

Iraq

The United Nations Assistance Mission for Iraq (UNAMI) was established in 2003, but after the bombing of UN headquarters in Baghdad in August of that year killed UN Special Representative of the Secretary-General for Iraq Sergio Vieira de Mello, everything was moved to Amman, Jordan. UNAMI's task has been to coordinate the work of the UN and its agencies in carrying out projects inside Iraq. It has 11 clusters, including education, food distribution, refugees and displaced person assistance. But one of the most important and active clusters in 2004 and early 2005 was cluster 11, focusing on electoral support. In February 2004, the UN sent an assessment team led by Ambassador Lakhdar Brahimi to report on the feasibility of holding elections in Iraq to form a Transitional National Assembly. The assembly, in turn, would form a legitimate government and write Iraq's new constitution. As a result of Amb. Brahimi's positive report, elections were scheduled for January 2005.

While UNAMI worked to get Iraq ready for elections, as detailed below, the UN Security Council passed Resolution 1546 on June 8, 2004, endorsing the formation of an Interim Government of Iraq to take over from the Iraqi Governing Council that had been hand-picked by the US-led Coalition Provisional Authority (CPA). The handover was to take place on June 30, 2004, but to preempt any disruption by insurgent forces, CPA Chief Paul Bremer quietly left Baghdad two days ahead of schedule, handing power over on June 28 to the interim government led by Prime Minister Ayad Allawi and President Ghazi al-Yawar. The two were to lead the government until elections were held some six months later. To fill the vacuum left by the departure of Paul Bremer, the US named former ambassador to the UN, John Negroponte, the US ambassador to Iraq. (In April 2005, Amb. Negroponte was confirmed as the new US National Intelligence Director and was expected to be replaced by Zalmay Khalilzad, former US ambassador to Afghanistan.)

Shortly after the Brahimi report was presented to and accepted by the Security Council in February 2004, the UN was back in Iraq conducting a behind-the-scenes needs assessment to facilitate the creation of election procedures, set up a process to select a national electoral commission that would be independent and Iraqi-owned, and assist in the creation of a transitional legal framework for holding the elections. The team was made up of experts from the UN's Electoral Assistance Division, headed by Carina Perelli. With some 50 staff working on the elections, with around 25 in Iraq, the team created a training structure that resulted in more than 120,000 Iraqis managing the ballot boxes on January 30, 2005.

Since there was no UNAMI headquarters in Baghdad and since most Iraqis had not heard of UNAMI, the electoral team was known simply as "the UN" on the ground. Staff wore Kevlar helmets and vests, and were heavily guarded by armed CPA military personnel as they moved around the country. With the security situation fragile at best and deadly at worst, the electoral team had to work all over Iraq while maintaining a low profile. If any of them had been killed, one team member said, the UN would have pulled all of them out, along with their expertise.

The UNAMI team had only eight months to meet the tasks at hand. Iraq, under Saddam Hussein, had held elections but they were not considered "free" or "fair." The new process had to have immediate credibility or it would fail. UNAMI staff established the Independent Electoral Commission of Iraq (IECI); determined the basis for a census count to establish a voter roster and database for voter registration (an accurate base did not exist); and worked with nongovernmental organizations to train Iraqis to administer elections and monitor the voting process. All parties involved wanted the elections to be completely Iraqi-run, and the elections were, but not without huge input by UN experts.

The UNAMI team created a unique process to form a national electoral commission that was selected in a truly independent manner. First, the team developed a 17-page application form for candidates; this provided a full body of background information on each individual and also helped to deter those not completely serious about running. By deadline, the team had received around 2,000 applications that were then taken out of harm's way to Amman to be scanned and entered into a database. A vetting team then approved a short list of about 25 candidates. To make the process more independent, a panel of international experts was called in to review the list and select a top group of 14. Nowhere on the application were people asked to identify their ethnic group. According to one team member, it was important that the commission be made up of "Iraqis" representing their country, not members of competing ethnic groups such as the Sunnis, Shias or Kurds. The Iraqi Governing Council had agreed to the process and when presented with the list of names, did not know any of them. This demonstrated that the process had been independent and not influenced by the Council, which was handpicked by the CPA.

While the selection of the commissioners was underway, the UN team established a base for voter registration. Iraq has a population of about 25 million people. However, 40 percent are under age 14. UNAMI staff determined that the best existing Iraqi database to work with was the system that Iraq kept for allotting food and medical rations to the Iraqi people. There was a ration card for each family containing birth dates and addresses. It was not perfect as some Iraqis had kept people on the list even though they had died in order to be rationed more supplies. Regardless, the UN began with this as a database, publishing it for each community so that corrections by families could be made to the electoral administration. Ultimately, there were 14.2 million records of eligible voters (most likely an inflated figure since no one was excluded unless a family member took them off the list). The possibility of people voting more than once using these dead records was excluded by the use of ink, in which each voter's finger was dipped before casting a vote. On January 30, 2005, 8.5 million Iraqis voted, giving approximately 60 percent turnout. It should be noted that there were actually 20 elections going on that day to cover other national and provincial elections.[1]

The elections were based on a nationwide proportional voting procedure by party, although individual candidates could put forward their own names for the ballot. The threshold level for forming a party was set very low, requiring only 500 signatures on a petition. The total number of seats in the assembly was preset at 275, so the party or candidates with the most votes took the proportional number of seats to add up to 275. The purpose of this plan was to create national rather than regional parties that would contribute to geographic differences and offer more opportunities to smaller entities. One drawback to this structure is that the national assembly is somewhat fractured; the aggregation of policy will have to happen in the assembly rather than at the party level. This has been clearly evident in the difficulties the newly elected leaders had in forming the current Iraqi government.

In February 2005, with the transitional assembly set up but no actual government in operation, Secretary-General Kofi Annan's Special Representative for Iraq Ashraf Qazi (named in July 2004 to replace Sergio Vieira de Mello) met with Iraqi leaders across the political spectrum to try to overcome impasses in selecting new leaders. By early April, the top leaders were announced: Prime Minister and Head of State Ibrahim al-Jaafari (a Shia of the United Arab Alliance party); President Jalal Talabani (a Sunni Kurd of the Kurdistan Alliance); Vice President Sheikh Ghazi al-Yawar (a Sunni of the Iraqis Party); and Vice President Adel Abdul Mahdi (a Shia of the United Iraqi Alliance). The speaker of the National Assembly, Hajim M. al-Hassani, oversees a diverse body of 275 seats: 140 held by the United Iraqi

Alliance (Shia); 75 held by the Kurdistan Alliance (Kurdish); 40 held by the Iraqi List (a diverse collection of smaller Shia parties); and 20 other assembly members of varied group affiliation. No single party has the two-thirds majority needed to pass the constitution, so the assembly will have to reach across party lines to form a consensus.

Because of the delay in choosing these leaders, tensions built and insurgent attacks mounted over the first half of 2005 as Iraqi citizens waited for a full government to be formed. US Secretary of State Condoleezza Rice and Vice President Dick Cheney made calls to Baghdad urging the assembly to reach a decision. By May 3, a new cabinet was sworn in but seven Iraqi posts remained unfilled. Still missing were the defense and oil ministers, two important positions. They were named a week later: the new defense minister, a Sunni, Sadoon al-Dulaimi, and oil minister, a Shia, Ibrahim Bahr al-Uloum. Only a few days before the swearing-in ceremony, a female member of the assembly was shot to death in front of her home in Baghdad. The new Iraqi government, at the time of this writing, appears to have failed to reach out in a credible manner to the Sunni Arab minority, a failure that could very well garner support for insurgent resistance.

The surge in attacks was not surprising. Violence in Iraq has persisted since the 2003 war. More than 1,700 Americans have lost their lives, and estimates of Iraqi civilian deaths are in the thousands. An independent group keeping count of Iraqi civilian deaths by adding up those accounted for in the news each day have an estimate on their website (www.iraqbodycount.net) that reached some 24,000 in May 2005. According to the site, some 600 of the more than 800 who died during the fighting in Falluja were civilians and half of those were women and children. A much larger in-country study conducted by the Bloomberg School of Public Health at Johns Hopkins University determined that by October 2004, at least 100,000 Iraqi civilians had died from attacks since the March 2003 war.

General Richard Myers in a Pentagon news briefing on April 26, 2005, stated that during the period right before the elections and during the battles at Falluja and Najaf, insurgent attacks spiked. After elections, attacks went down to about 40 per day. But in April 2005, attacks surged again, climbing to levels of the previous year at about 50 to 60 attacks a day. All in all, 2004 and early 2005 have been full of kidnappings, gruesome beheadings, scorched bodies and news-breaking stories of torture at the hands of the Americans in the prison at Abu Ghraib.[2]

Even though Gen. Myers claimed that there were 159,000 trained Iraqi soldiers and, as reported, still some 138,000 American troops plus a few thousand from other coalition countries in Iraq, the situation is still not secure. While the US has not yet mentioned a withdrawal date, it will certainly depend on the status of violence in the country and the capability of the Iraqis to provide security on their own. In mid-May, the US launched an aggressive offensive in western Iraq along the Syrian border to stop military equipment and fighters from coming over the border into Iraq. However, a search for the most wanted terrorist, Abu Musab al-Zarqawi, had still not produced results.

Overall, the formation of a stable Iraqi government has been faced with agonizing delays but has been important in forming a consensus toward a new constitution for the fledgling democracy. As of June 2005, the UN was waiting for the new Iraqi government to request further assistance in this matter. There are still a number of things to be done for which Iraq will need the UN's help, such as establishing electoral articles within the constitution and how citizenship will be determined. If all goes according to schedule, the constitution is supposed to be ready before the General Assembly opens its 60th session in fall 2005 with an Iraq-wide constitutional referendum by mid-October 2005, and final elections to form a government by December 2005.

Before leaving this discussion, it is important to note that important questions have been raised concerning the original motivation for the US-led war in the country in 2003. In 2004, both the David Kay report and the Charles Duelfer report (*see the Disarmament section of this chapter for further details*), stated that there were no weapons of mass destruction found in Iraq. Both Mr. Kay and Mr. Duelfer participated in the UN inspections led by UNSCOM, UN Special Commission for Iraq, and the UN's International Atomic Energy Agency (IAEA) and are considered credible authorities on WMD. Claims by the Bush administration that Iraq had been involved in the attacks on September 11, 2001 were also refuted by the 9/11 Commision's report in 2004.

Securing oil production in the region, perhaps a more plausible motivation for the US-led war, has met a number of obstacles as Iraqi oil production has failed to reach capacity set goals. Oil has indeed played a high profile role in Iraq, particularly recently with the controversy over the Oil-for-Food Programme. It was already apparent in 1991 that economic sanctions were taking a toll on the Iraqi people; an oil-for-food plan was proposed at that time. However, as Mr. Duelfer points out in his report, Saddam Hussein did not take up the offer until 1996 when the economy appeared to be in real trouble. At that time, Iraq was allowed to sell oil under UN auspices in order to create enough revenue to purchase needed humanitarian items. The program involved huge numbers of contracts with companies all over the world both in purchasing the oil and in supplying the goods to be delivered into Iraq. The UN clearly became overwhelmed by the enormity of the task as the organizational structure became inadequate. Suggestions of mishandling of funds led to the appointment by the Secretary-General of a commission led by Paul Volcker to investigate the entire program. What has been frustrating about the reporting on this issue has been the constant confusion by the media between problems within the program and the oil that Saddam Hussein was selling illegally on the black market. Lists of companies, as Mr. Duelfer points out, knowingly bought oil from Saddam Hussein, circumventing the UN's efforts to keep sanctions in place. Keeping the spotlight on the UN may be a strategy to shift the blame and keep the focus away from the culpability of these firms. Hopefully the final installment of the Volcker report, due in summer 2005, will clear up this confusion. (*See Chapter 4 for further details*.)

In conclusion, no WMD, no link to September 11th, high levels of continued violence, higher gas and oil prices, and very uneven but measured progress toward democratization are the issues surrounding Iraq. Whatever the motivation to go to war, Iraq must be stabilized before US and other troops can go home. The new constitution will have to form some kind of power-sharing arrangement among the major stakeholders in Iraq. Building that consensus will not be easy and the more the UN can play a mediating role, the better. The UN will also need to assist Iraq, as it did in the January elections, to organize a constitutional referendum and general elections by the end of 2005. If the new Iraqi government can sustain consensus, this schedule is feasible. UNAMI continues to operate out of Amman; Security Council resolution 1557 of August 12, 2004, extended its mandate for 12 months until August 2005. However, the security situation is still extremely serious and it will be difficult for UN personnel and Iraqi leaders to have freedom of movement in order to meet and function, at least at the time of this writing. Only then can the Iraqi people have their needs met, needs that go beyond the writing of a constitution to cover healthcare, jobs and solutions to other day-to-day problems.

Lebanon

In September 2004, the Security Council passed Resolution 1559 calling for the "political independence of Lebanon under the sole and exclusive authority of the Government of Lebanon throughout Lebanon." The resolution went on to say that the UN "calls upon all remaining foreign forces to withdraw from Lebanon" and affirms the UN's support for "free and fair" upcoming presidential elections.[3] The withdrawal of Syrian forces from Lebanon along with Hezbollah militia fighters is something that many had hoped would happen for years, but in the face of Syrian intransigence, no movement seemed possible. Some 14,000 Syrian troops were deployed in Lebanon as part of a Syrian force that had been there since the Lebanese civil war of 1975-1990, initially to assist its smaller neighbor to stabilize the peace. But Syria's presence was increasingly seen as domineering and repressive. Plus, Syria's support of Hezbollah, combined with neighboring Iran, posed a constant threat to Lebanon.

International reaction to Syria's interference in Lebanon was spurred when the Syrian government of Bashar al-Assad engineered a Lebanese constitutional change by ramming legislation through the Lebanese parliament that would have allowed the Syrian-backed prime minister to serve an additional term. France joined the US in sponsoring Resolution 1559 in a rare show of rapprochement between the two major powers since their angry split over the 2003 Iraq war. The Security Council renewed its demands on January 28, 2005 via Resolution 1583, which extended the mandate of UNIFIL, the UN Interim Force in Lebanon, and reiterated its strong support for the "political independence of Lebanon." UNIFIL was established in 1978 after Israeli forces entered Lebanon in response to years of cross-border skirmishes with the Palestinian Liberation Organization. It was meant to be an "interim" force but has stayed due to insecurities in the area. After the Israeli withdrawal from the south Lebanon security zone a few years ago, UNIFIL moved into the south and now patrols the area of Lebanon bordering Israel. Its troop strength is about 2,000 from seven countries and it is assisted by some 50 UNTSO (*see details below*) military observers.

Pressure intensified for Syrian withdrawal after the February 14, 2005, assassination of the very popular former Lebanese Prime Minister Rafik al-Hariri in Beirut which many blamed on Syria. The assassination sparked massive anti-Syrian protests throughout the city that continued for weeks. With increasing pressure from the international community to withdraw his forces, Mr. Assad appealed to Arab leaders for support but was rebuffed by the Saudis and others. By the end of March 2005, the pro-Syrian Prime Minister of Lebanon, Omar Kasami, resigned, clearing the way for opposition leaders to ensure nationwide elections by the end of May.[4] While the rest of the world watched in total amazement, the last Syrian troops pulled out of Lebanon on April 26, 2005, ending 29 years of Syrian presence in Lebanon.[5] No one thought it would ever happen, let alone so quickly. The UN immediately dispatched a team to verify the withdrawal, called for under Resolution 1559, and by May 23, Secretary-General Annan announced that all Syrian troops had gone. Concerns remained, however, over the continued presence of armed Hezbollah militias, particularly in the south. Under mounting pressure, Syrian President al-Assad broke ties with the US and has called for a Ba'ath Party Congress to be held in mid-June.[6]

On April 7, the Security Council voted unanimously to authorize an international investigation into the assassination of Rafik al-Hariri and the UN prepared the groundwork for setting up the investigative commission. Mr. Hariri's 37-year-old son, Saad al-Hariri, has taken up the leadership of the opposition party with the support of his family. He has been involved in the family's multi-billion-dollar business and is well trusted. With the popular sympathy over the assassination of his father, and the family's wealth and international connections, he will most likely win a seat in the parliamentary elections. In an interview on *CNN* in April 2005, Saad al-Hariri said he has "full confidence in the UN process."

The UN investigation will assist Lebanese authorities and hopefully report on the situation before fall 2005 to maintain its timeliness and credibility. In the meantime, UNIFIL will continue to monitor the southern border area. The disarmament of Hezbollah fighters is still a pressing issue.

Israel-Palestine

The last several months of 2003 witnessed the continuation of Palestinian *intifada* attacks and Israeli retaliation. In October 2003, the Security Council reached a stalemate when the US refused to go along with a condemnation of Israel's "security wall" on the grounds that the related reso-lution failed to also condemn the attacks against Israel which led to the building of the wall. Responding to the Security Council's inability to act on the matter, the UN General Assembly voted to request that the Internation-al Court of Justice (ICJ) in the Hague provide an Advisory Opinion. The court accepted the request and by July 2004, issued a majority opinion (14 to 1) declaring the "Wall in the Occupied Palestinian Territory" to be illegal (*see Chapter 7 for further details*). The decision, however, failed to say any-thing about the parts of the wall built within the state of Israel as deter-mined before the 1967 war. The opinion seemed to have had some impact on the construction of the wall, which went through some alterations in anticipation of the ICJ ruling and Israel's own Supreme Court rulings on the matter. Nevertheless, many Israelis see the wall as an important part of Israel's security strategy and claim that the reduction in suicide bombings is due in part to the wall.

Back in spring 2003, there was an international effort to reinvigorate negotiations on a peaceful settlement of the Israeli-Palestinian conflict. Rus-sia, the UN, US, and EU formed a group called the "Quartet," which released a plan in June 2003 titled "the Roadmap." The quartet described the plan as a performance-based roadmap with timelines and target dates that would prepare the region for a two-state solution—achieved only through an end to violence and terrorism. However, the plan was relegated to the back burner as disagreements and violence continued. Then, a door opened. The death of Yasser Arafat in November 2004, while a sad event for many Palestinians who had followed his leadership for 40 years, presented an opportunity for others to open up the peace process. Israel had long complained that Arafat was either unwilling or unable to reign in suicide bombings and other attacks against Israeli citizens and hoped there might be a new leader for the Palestinian people whom they could consider a partner for peace. Palestinian elections in January 2005, assisted by the UN, produced Mahmoud Abbas as the new president of the Palestinian Authority. Hope for a new dialogue was awakened when Egypt stepped forward to assist in peace talks.

A summit between Israeli President Ariel Sharon of Israel and Mah-moud Abbas was held in Egypt on February 8, 2005. The two leaders declared an end to all hostilities. President Sharon renewed his commitment to the Roadmap, which proposed the creation of an independent Palestinian state. Reaching across the table, the two men shook hands to confirm an agreement that would result in statehood for the Palestinian people and an end to the more than four-year *intifada*. Significantly absent from the talks, however, were groups such as Hamas. It was not clear if Mr. Abbas would be able to control these groups or even members of his own Fatah party. President Sharon promised to stop military activity and to pull all troops and the approximately 9,000 settlers from Gaza by summer 2005. In return, Mr. Abbas was expected to crack down on and deter breaches of the cease-fire.[7]

The next few weeks were tense as President Sharon faced both opposition from the far right and from within his own party. However, on March 29, 2005, in a vote of 58 to 36 (with one abstention), the Israeli parliament, the Knesset, passed the $62 billion state budget, paving the way for his plan to remove all the settlements in Gaza and four in the West Bank. The settlers organized a resistance and personal security around Sharon was tight, demonstrating an unstated fear of a repeat of the assassination of Yitzak Rabin by an Israeli after the Oslo Accords.[8]

President Sharon appeared to be making plans unilaterally rather than waiting to negotiate with his Palestinian counterpart. Pressured by his own Supreme Court, he moved the separation wall much closer to the pre-1967 boundaries set by the 1949 armistice, referred to as the "green line." While plans were underway for the Gaza pullout, Israel continued to build settlements on eight percent of West Bank land just inside the new wall. But this was down to about one half of what Israel was claiming in summer 2004.

By spring, the cease-fire seemed to be solidifying. Attacks were down considerably and Mr. Abbas had named three new security chiefs to head the three main security agencies in the Palestinian Authority. Israel had released 500 of the 900 Palestinian prisoners promised at Sharm el-Sheikh. Then violence erupted again when Palestinians fired Qassam rockets, hitting the Israeli town of Sederot on May 5. President Sharon responded by withholding the release of the remaining 400 prisoners until the Palestinian Authority gained greater control of the militants. This looked more difficult for Mr. Abbas after Hamas' strong showing in municipal elections held in early May. There are concerns that Hamas might win legislative elections scheduled for mid-July 2005. The Islamic resistance group in the past has expressed its commitment to destroy Israel and this has caused great concern for the entire peace effort.

The US and Secretary of State Condoleezza Rice have kept their distance from the peace process, preferring to leave it to the parties and to Egypt as the regional mediator. But the US House of Representatives did not appear to be cooperating when it voted not to allot the $200 million President Bush had requested to go directly to the Palestinian Authority to support reforms.

Two long-term UN peacekeeping operations, UNTSO and UNDOF, in the Middle East have had their mandates extended until summer 2005 when they again, most likely, will be extended for the normal six month period. UNTSO, the UN Truce Supervision Organization, was the first to be created in 1948 to observe and report on any breaches to the truce agreement between Israel and Arab countries. UNTSO continues its work observing the situation from its headquarters in Jerusalem and assists the other peacekeeping operations in the area, particularly when they need additional personnel. UNDOF, the UN Disengagement Observer Force, was established in 1974 after the 1973 War to observe and monitor the Golan Heights, an area occupied by Israel after clashes with Syria. The area has been peaceful and the cease-fire has been successful. But people in the area have been cut off for years from family members and economic ties in Syria. A few months ago, a symbolic breakthrough was made when farmers in the Golan Heights were allowed to sell their apples across the border in Syria, opening the possibility of economic relations.

Looking Forward

As usual in the Middle East, there is uncertainty. But events over 2004 and most of 2005 hold more hope than in the past several years. What is new for the Middle East in calculating what might come next depends, in part, on the outcome of several upcoming elections, which to a much greater extent are expected to be more "free and fair" than in the past; in some cases, they are happening for the first time. Beyond elections, hopes for greater stability in Lebanon are more certain as it gains its long-awaited independence. In Iraq, the main concern is the security situation and whether or not Iraq will hold together. Credible participation by Sunnis and Kurds along with the Shia majority is key to achieving Iraqi unity. And in Israel, the pullout of Gaza to take place in August 2005 will inevitably be tense. For the near future, the security wall will stay with some modifications until a new Palestinian state is formed and attacks have completely ceased over a period of some years.

Looming Conflicts

Micky Hingorani

Nepal

In addition to suffering from a nine-year insurgency by Maoist rebels intent on overthrowing Nepal's constitutional monarchy, the citizens of this besieged mountain country are living in an increasingly repressive state. On February 1, 2005, King Gyanendra seized power and declared a state of emergency. This event curtailed constitutional freedoms, including those of expression, press and assembly.[1] The King purportedly executed the military-backed coup because he believed the government had not acted effectively enough to protect Nepal from Maoist rebels. Despite his declared reasons, King Gyanendra's actions will likely exacerbate the problems of this already tense country, which has lost approximately 11,500 lives over the past decade.[2]

The Maoists, with an estimated force of 10,000 to 15,000 fighters, have been striving to end Nepal's constitutional monarchy and replace it with a Marxist republic.[3] As a response to the King's recent actions, they have launched a series of roadblocks and general strikes. They have used increasingly brutal tactics to intimidate the civilian population, including executions and the burning of villages.[4]

The Royal Nepalese Army (RNA) has done little to endear the support of the public, despite claims to work for "hearts and minds." Instead, it has engaged in summary executions, torture and "disappearances," revoked *habeas corpus*, imprisoned journalists, barred the travel of intellectuals and human rights observers, and stifled political protest.[5]

As the conflict continues to rage, the army claims to have inflicted significant damage on the rebel forces, striking deep into their rural stronghold.[6] As of May 2005, the King's imposed state of emergency had been lifted, though it remains unclear how this will effect the situation on the ground. Maoist rebel leaders appear to be arguing internally over peace talks with the government.[7] With neither side of the conflict having the strength to win militarily,[8] it is now incumbent upon the international community to press hard for peace negotiations and the restoration of democracy by King Gyanendra.

Somalia

Somalia is inching toward having its first functioning government since 1991, but many problems remain. Currently underway is the 14th attempt to install a central government since a number of militias combined forces to oust then-dictator Mohamed Siad Barre before turning on one another. The aftermath has been filled with violence between the forces of opposing warlords, each controlling small fiefdoms across the ravaged country. Estimates report that approximately 500,000 people have died in the fighting and three quarters of a million have been forced from their homes.[9]

Strangely, the first challenge faced by the Transitional Federal Government is to safely enter its own country. Interim Prime Minister Ali Mohammed Gedi only first visited the Somali capital, Mogadishu, at the end of April 2005 due to previous security concerns,[10] and the transitional government itself, including President Abdullahi Yusuf Ahmed, is working in exile in Nairobi, Kenya. They require a peacekeeping force before they can begin working within Somalia. Although President Yusuf originally called for 20,000 international peacekeepers to make up this force, he has managed to secure only 6,800. If 20,000 troops were allotted, many soldiers would need to come from neighboring countries, including Ethiopia, which has a history of fomenting discontent in Somalia. During discussions on the matter, a brawl broke out in the Somali Parliament, echoing public sentiment that has led to three demonstrations in Mogadishu.[11]

Regardless of where the African Union troops come from, Somalia is proving exceedingly xenophobic. A Muslim cleric issued a fatwa against foreigners and there are rumors of a $5,000 reward for killing one. In February 2005, a *BBC* producer was killed in Mogadishu and bombs, apparently aimed at AU soldiers, exploded, killing a bystander.[12]

President Yusuf and members of his government must convince ordinary Somalis, who are often fervently loyal to their clans,[13] of the merits of centralized government. So far, there has been little substantive administrative discussion regarding how the new government would function, including controlling revenue, working with warlords outside the transitional government and dealing with the regions of Somalia which have declared independence.[14] Despite all its problems, the Transitional Federal Government represents new hope for peace and order in a country grown accustomed to daily violence by the warlord's militias. It could use, however, significant outside help, starting with troops.

Uganda

In late 2004, Ugandan President Yoweri Museveni extended offers of a cease-fire to the Lord's Resistance Army (LRA), a rebel group that has been fighting the government since 1986[15]. Known for their brutality and tendency to abduct and draft children into war, LRA is led by Joseph Kony[16]. Although the violence has displaced an estimated 1.8 million people and insurgents have abducted approximately 20,000 children over the past 19 years, President Museveni described LRA as a "crushed force" now numbering around 250[17]. Attempting to halt the violence via negotiations is former Ugandan State Minister Betty Bigombe. A more effective counter-insurgency by the Ugandan army and an investigation by the ICC have aided her efforts[18], as has Sudan's reduced assistance to LRA[19]. Unfortunately, rebels are not reciprocating attempts at peace. The group renewed attacks on civilians in Gulu in late April 2005[20], and the conflict now has the potential to spread as LRA leaders have retreated into southern Sudan[21]. Because President Museveni's cease-fire did not address Kony's concern over the security of LRA leaders after conflict resolution, he must now put forward a plan for peace with safety guarantees[22]. Until then, it may be up to the international community to put pressure on LRA, and to encourage the President not to lose patience in the peace process moving forward.

Disarmament and Weapons of Mass Destruction

Rebecca Johnson

The last few years have been difficult for nonproliferation and world security. Despite the fact that the term "WMD" entered public discourse, there was little agreement about the nature or probability of nuclear, radiological, chemical or biological weapons threats and what to do to minimize them. North Korea became the first state to withdraw from the Treaty on the Non-Proliferation of Nuclear Weapons (NPT) while Iran continued to duel with the United Nations International Atomic Energy Agency and the "EU-3" foreign ministers of France, Germany and the United Kingdom over its fuel cycle ambitions. Libya returned to compliance with the NPT, and its accession to the Chemical Weapons Convention (CWC) and Comprehensive Test-Ban Treaty (CTBT) have been widely welcomed. The most notable security benefit of Libya's policy change was the exposure of a long-suspected black market in nuclear technology, materials and equipment run by Dr. Abdul Qadeer Khan. While his exposure crippled the network, there are continuing concerns about what he may have supplied to Iran. Much more must be done to ensure that his commercial partners from countries like Germany, Malaysia, South Africa and the UK are closed down as well.

The UN General Assembly's First Committee on disarmament and international security adopted 52 resolutions at its 59th session and took three decisions in votes that were subsequently confirmed by the full Assembly, providing a comprehensive window on recent developments and positions. While it would be incorrect to portray current US policies as the sole obstacle, they have contributed greatly to the problems that have paralyzed the Conference on Disarmament (CD) and the UN Disarmament Commission (UNDC). They have also delayed entry into force of the CTBT and negotiations to ban the production of fissile materials for weapons purposes as well as multilateral talks to prevent the deployment or use of weapons in and from space.

The First Committee meeting took place just after Charles Duelfer, a former UN weapons inspector, published the concluding report of the Iraq Survey Group in September 2004. Established by the US, the survey group's mission was to find the WMD that the US-led coalition had used as its justification for going to war. After 18 months of unfettered access under the auspices of the US-led occupation forces, the survey group concluded that Iraq could not have posed a WMD threat in 2002-2003. In essence, it confirmed the assessment made by the UN Monitoring, Verification and Inspection Commission (UNMOVIC) in February 2003. In some of its less-publicized insights, the Duelfer Report has potentially far-reaching consequences for the proliferation challenges facing the world, but these have yet to receive the attention they deserve.

Two further developments illustrate the challenges posed to the General Assembly as it heads into its 60th session in fall 2005: the adoption of Resolution 1540 on WMD and the divided NPT Review Conference that took place in May 2005. Intended to "enhance coordination of efforts on national, subregional, regional and international levels," Resolution 1540 placed responsibilities on states to join and strengthen various conventions to thwart terrorism and to enact consistent national legislation to prevent illicit trafficking in WMD-related materials and technologies. With its focus firmly on terrorists and non-state armed groups, Resolution 1540 was prompted partly by concerns raised about the legality and legitimacy of the controversial Proliferation Security Initiative (PSI), in accordance with which a group of states agreed to coordinate policing and intelligence, and exercise powers of search and seizure on suspected vessels and their cargoes. Resolution 1540 goes significantly beyond PSI because it clearly embeds national and plurilateral actions in the "multilateral treaties whose aim is to eliminate or prevent the proliferation of nuclear, chemical or biological weapons." Adopted under Chapter VII of the UN *Charter*, Resolution 1540 reinforces the necessity for multilateral legal regimes and national, plurilateral or regional measures to be made mutually consistent and security-enhancing. This goes some way toward the unifying approach taken in the reports from the High-level Panel on Threats, Challenges and Change, and from the Secretary-General, but there remain many challenges to integrating the different levels of action in ways that will be effective and acceptable to the vast majority of states.

Such contradictions were most apparent at the NPT Review Conference, which failed to agree on any substantive recommendations for furthering the objectives and implementation of the nuclear nonproliferation regime. Attended by 153 of the 188 NPT parties in good standing, the conference became mired in procedural wrangling over its agenda and working groups, as a few countries, most notably the US and Iran, sought to avoid any outcome that would constrain their own nuclear options.

In treaty terms, the failure in 2005 to adopt further substantive recommendations means that agreements obtained in the review conferences of 1995 and 2000 still stand as the benchmarks for measuring progress and promoting compliance. Politically, however, the fact that the majority of states failed to stand up to the few naysayers sends a dangerous message to would-be proliferators and the states that possess nuclear weapons, inside and outside the treaty. A number of states are already reasserting their criticisms of the decision to extend the NPT indefinitely in 1995. They point to the continued role accorded to nuclear weapons in the military doctrines of the major powers, and castigate inadequate progress in fulfilling commitments to disarmament. The bottom line is that, if the military utility and security value of nuclear weapons continue to be evoked at a high level by some states, the have-nots will lose confidence that the nonproliferation regime can meet their security needs.

Weapons Security and Regimes

Fear of mass-destruction terrorism increased in salience after September 11, 2001, leading to more concerted attention on controlling and preventing access to WMD-usable materials, especially nuclear materials. To assess the relevance of the nonproliferation and disarmament regimes, it is important to understand the real and perceived WMD-related threats to international security: from non-state actors; trade and black market procurement; clandestine weapons programs in certain states; and states seeking to hedge bets, especially for developing nuclear weapon options under the guise of NPT-permitted nuclear power programs. In addition, there are the problems of reducing and eliminating existing weapons and programs. While there are abiding dual-use, technical and environmental problems involved in getting rid of stocks of chemical and biological weapons, the problem of continued possession and acquisition is most acute with regard to nuclear weapons. The NPT-based regime recognizes five nuclear weapon states (China, France, Russia, UK, US), whose military doctrines and policies continue to associate high levels of military, security or political power with nuclear weapons. In addition to North Korea and Iran, whose nuclear power programs have recently caused serious proliferation concerns, three non-NPT states—India, Pakistan and Israel—have ongoing nuclear bomb programs, with estimated arsenals ranging from 30 to 200 deliverable nuclear weapons. Since 1998, India and Pakistan have openly declared their nuclear programs, while keeping actual capabilities secret. For regional and geostrategic reasons, Israel has maintained a deliberate policy of nuclear ambiguity and opacity.

Lessons from the Iraq War

In seeking legitimacy for invading and occupying Iraq in 2003-2004, the US-led coalition portrayed Saddam Hussein's regime as posing an imminent WMD threat. However, as the Duelfer Report and others have now illustrated, though Saddam Hussein may not have abandoned his earlier aspirations, Iraq had never succeeded in acquiring nuclear weapons, and by 2002, did not have militarily significant chemical or biological weapons or any ongoing production programs.

Unlike the more cautious US National Intelligence Estimates of previous years, none of the key findings on Iraq in October 2002 estimates were accurate, with the exception of the assessment that Saddam Hussein was unlikely to transfer any weapons to terrorist groups. The significant, clandestine programs uncovered in 1991 had in fact been dismantled and destroyed, largely through the seven years of IAEA and UNSCOM (UN Special Commission) efforts, oversight and pressure. Though this is what Iraq had claimed in its December 7, 2002 "Full and Complete Disclosure" of its WMD programs mandated by the UN, there had been a rush to judgement and disbelief. US officials dismissed Dr. Hans Blix, head of UNMOVIC, when he reported to the Security Council in February 2003 that UNMOVIC inspections in the months leading up to the war had drawn a blank, despite having checked out locations identified by US and UK intelligence.

Several important lessons can be drawn from the Iraq experience: the impossibility of proving a negative; the fallibility of information and the dangers of manipulating intelligence; the difficulties of ascertaining the intentions and tactics of non-democratic leadership; and the countervailing roles that strategic opacity may play for domestic and international audiences. This is not the place to analyze the policies of the US and UK, but in considering the lessons for the UN, two perspectives offer contrasting but linked emphases. First, the limited usefulness of "forceful prevention": Iraq's substantial nuclear program, as exposed in 1991, suggested that the Israeli bombing of the Osirak reactor in 1981 might have bought a little time, but that "such short term fixes simply allow proliferators to learn, adapt and make their programs even more hidden and resilient." Second, despite the apparent diminishing returns of containment, the IAEA, UNSCOM and UNMOVIC, combined with increasingly targeted "smart" sanctions against Saddam Hussein's regime had been more effective than realized in shutting down Iraq's WMD programs and preventing their regeneration after inspectors were forced to leave in 1998.[1]

INTELLIGENCE

One of the most publicly humiliating lessons of the Iraq war concerned the intelligence presented by the governments of the US and UK. Following the US's 9/11 Commission's detailed investigation into intelligence failures in the lead-up to the September 11, 2001 attacks, the US Senate Committee on Intelligence concluded that there was no credible evidence to support the claims that Iraq had stockpiles of biological and chemical weapons or was close to having a nuclear weapon.[2]

As noted by Joseph Cirincione of the Carnegie Endowment for International Peace, "the report discusses in intense detail how the intelligence community misrepresented and misjudged information about Iraq's" suspected weapons programs: "[O]fficials in both the United Kingdom and the United States used these faulty intelligence findings to make the case that war was the only answer." Mr. Cirincione added that the Senate report avoided faulting the administration for bending the intelligence to support that policy. The report instead lays blame on poor organization of the intelligence agencies and bureaucratic problems.[3]

In February 2004, shortly after President Bush set in motion the Senate inquiry, UK Prime Minister Tony Blair announced a high-level bipartisan committee, headed by Lord Butler of Brockwell, to investigate the intelligence on WMD programs and trade. The brief included consideration of discrepancies between the intelligence about Iraqi WMD gathered and presented before the invasion and the findings of the Iraq Survey Group. Published in July 2004, the Butler Report was dressed in a peculiarly British language of diplomatic euphemisms, but left little doubt about its critical conclusion that unreliable sources and "overheated," politically directed analysis had produced false intelligence.[4]

SURVEYS AND REPORTS

By the time the reports from Lord Butler and the US Senate were published, it was clear that the Iraq Survey Group would not turn up any significant evidence of WMD programs, despite having some 1,200 British and American experts in nuclear, chemical and biological weapons-related issues, and unlimited access to anywhere they wanted to go in Iraq. In his interim report in October 2003, David Kay, the head of the survey group before Mr. Duelfer took over, referred to remnants of programs, including a clandestine network of laboratories with equipment suitable for continuing chemical and biological weapons research, but no weapons or evidence of ongoing programs. On September 30, 2004, the final findings of the group were published.

The report analyzes the value accorded to WMD by Saddam Hussein's regime and notes that, until the war, their experience had been "positive": missiles and chemical weapons had tipped the balance in the war with Iran without attracting strong Western condemnation, and they believed that Iraq's chemical and biological weapons capabilities had deterred the US,

Israel and Coalition forces from taking the first Gulf War all the way to Baghdad after ousting Iraqi forces from Kuwait in 1991. WMD "demonstrated its worth to Saddam... [and] he purposely gave an ambiguous impression about possession as a deterrent to Iran." Summarizing Saddam Hussein's WMD ambitions, the Duelfer Report acknowledged the "excruciating dilemmas...[and] chronic, systemic fear on the part of the best and the brightest" of Iraq's scientists and intellectual elite. He concluded that, with the overriding objective of ending international sanctions and constraints, Saddam Hussein decided to dispense with WMD as "a tactical retreat in his ongoing struggle." Consequently, Iraq had not produced new WMD and there was no proof of any bioweapons stocks since 1991, though "some production capacity that Baghdad thought could be passed off as serving a civilian function was retained." Iraq's WMD programs had thus been allowed to decay almost completely since the end of the first Gulf War and there were no deployable WMD of any kind as of March 2003, when the US went to war.[5]

The Duelfer Report contained important insights into how Western cultural ignorance and assumptions contributed to intelligence mistakes. US policy and actions with regard to Iran and North Korea suggest these lessons have not yet been adequately absorbed. It is also clear that Saddam Hussein made his own mistakes as he sought to use the WMD card in his power plays and efforts to get sanctions lifted. With regard to US intelligence failures, Mr. Duelfer noted that "The key [Iraqi] Regime figures in the WMD area had a much better understanding of how the West viewed their programs than the other way around.... The Regime, drawing on the experience of the 1990s with the UN and given the priorities to which it subscribed, scrambled the types of signatures they knew we would be searching for. This contributed to the difficulty in verifying what happened to Iraq's WMD."[6]

WMD Regimes Today

Three fundamental treaties govern the prohibition of biological and chemical weapons and the nonproliferation of nuclear weapons. There are several related multilateral, bilateral and Security Council instruments that reinforce or extend the treaty provisions. The use of chemical and biological weapons in war was prohibited in 1925 via the *Geneva Gas Protocol* as a result of universal abhorrence at their effects on World War I soldiers. It took some 45 years before the US decided to halt production of its biological weapons programs and persuaded the then-Soviet Union and others to negotiate the 1972 *Convention on the Prohibition of the Development, Production and Stockpiling of Bacteriological (Biological) and Toxin Weapons and on their Destruction* (BWC). The treaty, which entered into force in 1975, prohibited the development, production, stockpiling or acquisition of biological and toxin weapons and required the destruction or conversion of such weapons or delivery means. While the BWC, which currently has 153 states parties, broke new ground in establishing a non-discriminatory prohibition regime, making no distinction between states with existing biological weapons programs and those without, it contained no provisions for monitoring or verifying compliance. The end of the Cold War provided the opportunity to negotiate a verification protocol, but in 2001, after six years of painstaking technical and diplomatic work, negotiations collapsed without agreement.

One of the principal beneficiaries of the initial post-Cold War enthusiasm for multilateral arms control was the *Convention on the Prohibition of the Development, Production, Stockpiling and Use of Chemical Weapons and on their Destruction*, more usually called the *Chemical Weapons Convention* (CWC), which was concluded by the CD in 1992. In this case, the political conditions, given urgency by Iraq's development and use of chemical weapons, enabled governments to apply a comprehensive approach to chemical weapons threats by establishing a non-discriminatory prohibition regime that required all the existing chemical weapons arsenals to be verifiably dismantled and destroyed. The CWC entered into force in 1997 with the most fully-defined and intrusive verification regime ever developed. There are currently 167 states parties.

Although the very first resolution passed by the UN in 1945 was a call for nuclear disarmament, the first treaty addressing nuclear weapons was the 1963 Partial Test-Ban Treaty (PTBT) which prohibited nuclear testing in the atmosphere, under water and in outer space. The NPT followed in 1968, shortly after the Tlatelolco Treaty. Pushed forward by Mexico, the Tlatelolco Treaty was the very first agreement aimed at creating a regional nuclear weapon free zone, in this case for Latin America and the Caribbean. Over the next 30 years, such nuclear weapon free zone treaties were negotiated for the South Pacific, Africa and southeast Asia. Various bilateral arms control agreements between the US and Soviet Union were lined up during the 1970s and 1980s, including two threshold testing limitations, the SALT and START agreements, the 1972 Anti-Ballistic Missile Treaty (ABM), and the 1987 Intermediate Nuclear Forces Treaty (INF).

During the Cold War, the arsenals of the five NPT nuclear powers continued to grow in size. While the majority of countries joined the NPT as non-nuclear weapon states, contributing to a widespread acceptance of the nonproliferation regime's norms and rules, several states—notably India, Israel, Pakistan and South Africa—pursued nuclear weapons programs outside the treaty. With its political transformation and the end of apartheid, South Africa renounced its nuclear program, worked closely with the IAEA to dismantle its facilities, and joined the NPT in 1991; China and France finally acceded to the treaty in 1992.

Biological and Chemical Weapons

During the 20th century, some 30 countries had research and development programs for biological and/or chemical weapons. Many had been discontinued by the time states acceded to the BWC, though there is evidence that some countries continued with development and even weaponization programs until the early 1990s. It is difficult to make assessments of existing holdings, in part because of the diffusion of many dual-use materials and technologies, but the number of states pursuing biological and chemical weapons has greatly diminished. Instead, focus has switched to terrorists and non-state groups, for whom such weapons are thought to be increasingly attractive.[7]

There are three basic types of chemical weapons: the first is highly potent, with mass-death effects; the second is battlefield munitions, such as mustard gas, of marginal significance now; and third, the so-called "non-lethal" weapons that rely on toxic effects and irritants. This latter category is prohibited from international use but not covered by the CWC if used domestically, for example by police to control demonstrations. An example of recent use was the Moscow theatre siege, in which the Russian authorities' use of a narcotic gas believed to be a derivative of fentanyl asphyxiated and killed twice as many hostages as terrorists. Recent studies have argued that such weapons should not be classified as "non-lethal," and that their domestic use should be prohibited in conformity with the international prohibitions under the CWC.

Biological weapons fall into three main categories as well: bacterial organisms, such as those that cause anthrax, plague and tularemia; viruses, such as cause smallpox or hemorrhagic disease; and toxins such as botulinum or ricin that poison or incapacitate humans. Biological warfare is banned under international law, so any intentionally aggressive use of biotechnology, whether by a state or non-state actor would be an act of terrorism. Unlike chemical weapons, which have a limited range and fewer delivery options, biological weapons are of accelerating concern. Providing the treaty regime remains strong, it is unlikely that states will invest heavily in biological weapons, as opposed to biodefense programs, but the technologies are similar, so defenses can be quickly adapted to offensive uses, with the potential for devastating effects.

The chemical weapons prohibition regime is the strongest in existence, overseen by the Organization for the Prohibition of Chemical Weapons, and is regularly endorsed by consensus in the General Assembly. The CWC has been largely successful in embedding the norm against chemical weapons acquisition, production and use, and in promoting information exchange on best practices for destroying chemical weapons. However, there are persistent difficulties with regard to the speed and environmental consequences of the destruction of the chemical weapons arsenals built up during the Cold War. While more than 40 percent of US stockpiled munitions have been destroyed, the figure for the destruction of the agent-tonne stockpile is less than 30 percent, and the US General Accounting Office has reported that it will be at least 2012 before the US chemical weapons stockpile is completely destroyed. US delays are partly due to the need to pay attention to environmental and safety concerns. The figures for Russia are much worse, with only 25 percent of their massive stockpiles destroyed to date. Though Russia receives assistance under US and EU cooperative threat reduction programs, the level of funding and assistance continue to be a major factor in delays. In addition to Russia and the US, efforts are underway to destroy stockpiles held by Albania, India, Libya and South Korea, while concerns remain about hidden stockpiles in countries such as North Korea and Syria.[8]

Notable positive developments include the First Review Conference of States Parties to the CWC in 2003, Libya's decision to abandon its chemical weapons program and sign the treaty, and as noted earlier, Security Council Resolution 1540, which requires that states extend the convention's objectives and provisions to people, commercial entities and non-state groups. The 2003 review conference resulted in a political declaration and a consolidated review document that identified areas needing improvement, largely focusing on promoting universality, implementation, distribution and scope of chemical industry inspections, stockpile destruction and administration.

There is much less optimism to report with regard to the BWC. Following the failure of states parties to adopt the verification protocol, the 2001 review conference had to be suspended for a year. By the time it reconvened in 2002, it was clear that the protocol, at least as negotiated, was dead. The review conference was able only to adopt a decision to hold annual expert and political meetings of states parties until the Sixth Review Conference in 2006. The focus of the 2004 meeting focused on enhancing international capabilities for responding to suspected or actual biological weapons threats or attacks. It also emphasised the importance of early detection and immediate and effective response, and encouraged further cooperation between national institutions, emergency services and international organizations.[9]

Though there is recognition that addressing biological weapons requires multilayered approaches, some states have now rejected or abandoned hope of strengthening international cooperation to ensure compliance and verification under the treaty. While some still try to revive the verification protocol, others now want to move on and build bridges between collective, treaty-based mechanisms and national-coercive approaches to prevent biological weapons acquisition. Dissatisfaction with the current state of affairs is clear from the debate on biological weapons held during the 2004 First Committee session. A large number of states called for strengthening the norms against biological and chemical weapons through the BWC and CWC, particularly in light of the threat of terrorism, and for greater adherence to these regimes. Many specifically stressed the importance of strengthening the BWC through universalization and agreed verification mechanisms.

A number of solutions have been proposed by nongovernmental practitioners and academics. Some emphasize strengthening the UN's capacities to build on the lessons and institutional capabilities of UNMOVIC. Others focus on developing codes of conduct, ethics and accounting for scientific and medical research, as well as increasing worldwide awareness of the dangers at stake. In this regard, there is general support for Resolution 1540.[10]

Nuclear Weapons

When representatives of the states party to the Nonproliferation Treaty and thousands of civil society representatives gathered in New York for the seventh review conference of the NPT in May 2005, there was little expectation that the conference would be successful. In a deteriorating political climate characterized by US intransigence and international failures to address the different compliance challenges posed by North Korea and Iran, they faced six key challenges: institutional weaknesses for implementing the treaty and ensuring compliance; making withdrawal from the treaty more difficult; inadequate progress on nuclear disarmament, including the failure to bring the CTBT and fissile materials ban into effect; the role of nuclear weapons in military doctrines, which continues to impede further and deeper progress toward disarmament; the relationship between the nuclear fuel cycle and acquisition of nuclear weapons; and enhancing the safety and security of weapons, materials, technology and facilities to prevent accidents, use or any terrorist acquisition.

In his opening address to the conference on May 2, Secretary-General Kofi Annan called on the states to strengthen confidence in the integrity of the NPT, work out how to address violations and withdrawals, and make compliance measures more effective. In this regard, he called for the *Model Additional Protocol* to be universalized and made the new standard for verifying compliance. He called for nuclear threats to be reduced not only with regard to states, but also non-state actors. SG Annan commended IAEA Director-General Mohamed ElBaradei for working to advance consensus on how to manage the fuel cycle. Addressing some of the specific issues on the NPT table, he also recommended prompt negotiation of a fissile materials ban, early entry into force of the CTBT (pending which the moratoria on nuclear testing should be reconfirmed), de-alerting of all nuclear weapons, and further irreversible reductions in warheads. He concluded, "But you must go further. Many states still live under a nuclear umbrella, whether of their own or an ally. Ways must be found to lessen, and ultimately overcome, their reliance on nuclear deterrence."

The Secretary-General may have correctly identified the major challenges, but the NPT states parties failed to rise to them. Far from building on past agreements, the 2005 review conference failed to adopt any kind of decisions or recommendations for furthering progress in the vital security issues of nuclear nonproliferation and disarmament, and they did not address sensitive issues such as proliferation-prone technologies in the fuel cycle and disincentives for states considering withdrawal from the treaty.

THE NONPROLIFERATION TREATY

Described frequently as the "cornerstone" of nonproliferation, the NPT is a product of nuclear hopes and fears arising out of Cold War political relations. While many characterize the treaty as having three pillars—nonproliferation, nuclear disarmament and "peaceful" uses of nuclear energy—

the treaty is more usefully considered in terms of its two core bargains between nuclear haves and have-nots: the renunciation of nuclear weapons in return for nuclear disarmament, and access and assistance for developing nuclear energy for non-military purposes.

In fact, the NPT most clearly reflected the strategic interests of the major powers in its primary emphasis on preventing horizontal proliferation, tempered by a weak Article VI commitment to end the arms race and pursue nuclear disarmament. Under Article III, safeguards were required of acceding non-nuclear weapon states, but there was a total absence of any parallel monitoring for the five defined nuclear weapon states, though they came in time to accept some voluntary inspections. The early hope that nuclear energy would provide cheap, safe, clean energy for future generations was reflected in the language of Article IV, which promised facilitation and participation in the "fullest possible exchange" of nuclear technology and materials as an "inalienable right," subject to conformity with Articles I and II, which prohibited weapons acquisition by and transfers to non-nuclear weapon state parties. In addition to insisting that the nuclear powers make some kind of commitment to disarmament, several states with ambitious nuclear programs insisted that the original treaty remain in force for an initial period of only 25 years, requiring a further decision if it were to be extended beyond that.

By the end of the 1990s, no one seriously challenged the relationship between disarmament and nonproliferation where biological and chemical weapons were concerned. By contrast, the strategic and political roles assigned to nuclear weapons made it much harder for the nuclear weapon states to accept that the progressive elimination of their own nuclear arsenals might likewise be a prerequisite for effective nonproliferation. In 1995, the importance of disarmament for nonproliferation was reinforced when NPT states adopted decisions on Principles and Objectives for Nuclear Nonproliferation and Disarmament and strengthening the NPT's review process as integral parts of a package of decisions to extend the treaty indefinitely. The paragraphs on disarmament specified the CTBT and ban on fissile material production already in the pipeline, and then tailed off into fudged references to "the determined pursuit...of systematic and progressive efforts to reduce nuclear weapons globally, with the ultimate goal of eliminating those weapons." This was as generalized as they could get away with, but nevertheless an improvement on the vagueness of the NPT's Article VI.

THE COMPREHENSIVE TEST-BAN TREATY

The CTBT was identified as a priority in the preamble of the NPT. After many failed initiatives, it was finally negotiated in the CD from 1994 to 1996, adopted by the UN General Assembly and opened for signature on September 24, 1996. Prohibiting all nuclear weapon test explosions and any other nuclear explosion, the CTBT's entry into force was made a high priority in decisions agreed by NPT states parties at the review conferences of 1995 and 2000.

At the time of the review conference in May 2005, the CTBT had 175 signatures and 121 ratifications, including 33 of the 44 ratifications necessary for the treaty to enter into force. Among those necessary for entry into force, India, Pakistan and North Korea have never signed. In 1999, due to ideological opposition and political mismanagement, the US, which had been the first to sign in 1996, failed to achieve the necessary two-thirds majority in the US Senate for ratification. Since 2001, the Bush administration has broken with tradition and prevented consensus on the General Assembly resolution supporting the CTBT.

In 2004, General Assembly Resolution 59/109 on the CTBT was overwhelmingly adopted with 177 votes in favor. There were only two votes against: the US and the tiny Pacific island of Palau, a US protectorate no longer in a position to make independent decisions. Four states abstained on the resolution: Colombia, India, Mauritius and Syria. India has not signed the CTBT and opposed its adoption by the General Assembly in 1996. Since conducting a series of underground nuclear tests in 1998, India has declared a moratorium on testing, and says that it would not prevent entry into force, a position designed to distract from the fact that it has not yet signed the treaty. Colombia explained that it supports the CTBT but has a constitutional problem about payments to the CTBT prior to entry into force and so abstained to draw attention to this. Syria complained that the CTBT did not enshrine security assurances against the use or threat of nuclear weapons to non-nuclear weapon states and that it did not refer to the development of new types of nuclear weaponry but "confines itself to banning only explosions." Israel, Pakistan and China have not yet ratified the CTBT, but all three voted in favor of the resolution. Though Pakistan followed India in May 1998 with a series of nuclear tests, it now abides by a moratorium, as does China.[11]

THE CONFERENCE ON DISARMAMENT AND FISSILE MATERIALS NEGOTIATIONS

A treaty banning the production of highly enriched uranium and plutonium for weapons purposes was the second disarmament priority agreed in 1995 and enshrined in the principles and objectives adopted as part of the NPT extension decision. Like the CTBT, this has run into political trouble and looks further away than ever. On the arms control agenda since 1946, a fissile materials ban was regarded as an essential step for preventing further enlargement of nuclear arsenals. It proved impossible to take forward during the years of US-Soviet arms-racing, but once the Cold War ended, new opportunities arose. On the basis of a consensus General Assembly resolution in 1993, the CD agreed on a mandate to negotiate a basic cut-off treaty to prohibit future production. Because the major nuclear powers are awash with fissile materials from dismantled nuclear warheads, a cut-off treaty has diminished in its disarmament value but would play an important role in constraining smaller arsenals, such as China, and the *de facto* weapon possessors. Four of the nuclear weapon states—France, Russia, the UK and US— have declared and abided by a moratorium for more than 10 years.

Adopted by the CD shortly before the 1995 NPT Review and Extension Conference, the Shannon mandate (so-called after the Canadian ambassador responsible for getting agreement) specifies "a non-discriminatory, multilateral and internationally and effectively verifiable treaty banning the production of fissile material for nuclear weapons or other nuclear explosive devices."[12] However, negotiations never got properly underway in the CD. Though the desire by many states to have negotiations on these two issues was genuine, procedural linkages were also used to camouflage reluctance about the fissile material ban by countries such as Pakistan and China. Israel's reluctance was also exposed in 1998 when it briefly held out against consensus on a work program after US leverage had brought Pakistan and India on board. Though US leadership managed to get negotiations started at that time, they fell victim to the CD's rigid application of the rule of consensus the following year, which forestalled adoption of a work program in 1999 and for every year thereafter.

In an apparent breakthrough late in 2003, China, which had been holding out for a parallel commitment to negotiations on preventing an arms race in outer space, was persuaded to support a proposal from five senior ambassadors for balancing the conference work program without committing to space negotiations as such. All eyes were then on the US, which continued to oppose the five ambassadors' proposals. More recently, on July 29, 2004, a new obstacle was introduced when Jackie Sanders, US Special Representative of the President for the Nonproliferation of Nuclear Weapons, told the CD that following an internal, interagency review, the US had come to the conclusion that effective verification of a cut-off treaty was "not achievable." She appeared to call for the much-delayed negotiations to proceed on these new terms.[13] Three months later, the US refused to go along with consensus on a fissile material ban resolution in the First Committee based on the language of previous resolutions that reiterated the Shannon mandate.

The vote on General Assembly Resolution 59/81 was 179 in favor, with two "no's" (the US and Palau) and two abstentions (the UK and Israel). Israel, which has long been reluctant about a fissile material ban, underscored the wider political issues. Viewing the treaty "in both regional and global contexts," Israel's representative said that "issues related to nuclear disarmament can be dealt with only after achieving lasting relations of peace and reconciliation...[and] overall regional security and stability." In an oblique reference to Iran, Israel noted recent developments with regard to "the misuse and un-checked dissemination of nuclear fuel cycle capabilities" and argued that "an overall priority in nonproliferation should be assigned to developing a new effective nonproliferation arrangement pertaining to the nuclear fuel cycle." The UK's abstention angered fellow EU members, the rest of whom voted in favor. It does not, however, signify a change of heart on the concept of a fissile materials ban so much as a pragmatic repositioning to harmonize with US views.[14]

The US position, taken in the context of the long impasse at the CD and the post-September 11 security goals exemplified by Resolution 1540, suggest that the fissile material ban may need to be rethought. To be truly relevant now, there needs to be a treaty or set of interlocking agreements or instruments to prevent the production, sale, use and transportation of weapons-usable nuclear material, and to close this path permanently to nuclear armaments, proliferation and terrorism.[15]

CURRENT NUCLEAR WEAPONS HOLDINGS

The fall of the Berlin Wall made it possible for the four nuclear powers most directly involved in Cold War nuclear rivalries to undertake deep reductions in their respective arsenals. But even as they claimed credit for cutting the number and types of their nuclear forces, Russia, France, the US and UK continued to emphasize the importance of their nuclear "deterrents" for security. China, the last to weaponize, quietly carried on with its program of nuclear modernization, while periodically calling for the "complete and thorough prohibition and destruction of nuclear weapons" and a multilateral agreement on no-first-use. At the time of writing and despite deep cuts since 1987, these five states account for some 16,000 deployed nuclear weapons, most still in the US and Russian arsenals, and around 14,000 additional warheads in storage. There are also up to 480 tactical nuclear weapons owned by the US but deployed under NATO nuclear sharing arrangements on the territory of the UK and five non-nuclear weapon states party to the NPT: Belgium, Germany, Italy, The Netherlands and Turkey.[16]

The test-ban and nonproliferation regimes took a heavy blow in May 1998, when India and Pakistan conducted five or six underground nuclear explosions each and then sought acceptance as nuclear weapon states. Despite strong opposition from NPT states, especially in the Middle East, Israel has continued to maintain a policy of nuclear opacity and refuses to confirm or deny whether it has nuclear weapons.

Table A: Deployed Nuclear Forces

COUNTRY	STRATEGIC	NON-STRATEGIC	TOTAL
China	282	120	402
France	348		348
India			~30-40
Israel			~80-200
Pakistan			~30-50
Russia	4,422	3,380	7,802
UK	185		185
US	5,886	1,120	7,006
Total			**~16,033**

Source: SIPRI Yearbook 2004, Stockholm
International Peace Research Institute, 2004.

NUCLEAR DISARMAMENT

In 2000, the New Agenda Coalition of seven non-nuclear weapon states (Brazil, Egypt, Ireland, Mexico, New Zealand, South Africa and Sweden) worked with civil society to develop the ideas, teamwork and strategies that enabled the NPT Review Conference in May 2000 to adopt a substantive set of agreements. Known now as the "Thirteen Steps," the NPT 2000 plan of action on nuclear disarmament included a ground-breaking "unequivocal undertaking by the nuclear weapon states to accomplish the total elimination of their nuclear arsenals." A number of steps were specified: entry into force of the CTBT; negotiations on a fissile materials treaty; deeper cuts and further unilateral reductions in nuclear arsenals; deeper reductions in non-strategic nuclear weapons; irreversibility; increased transparency and confidence-building measures; reduced operational status and a diminished role for nuclear weapons; negotiations involving all the nuclear weapon states; and verification to build confidence in the implementation of agreements. If these commitments were implemented, they would necessitate: deeper quantitative reductions in numbers of warheads and delivery systems; no replacement of obsolete, dismantled or withdrawn nuclear weapons or systems; the progressive transfer of nuclear infrastructure from research, design, production and refurbishment of nuclear warheads and delivery systems to safe and secure dismantlement with enhanced verification capabilities.

Such changes in policy have not occurred. The only positive, albeit meager, development in arms control since 2000 has been the 2002 Moscow (Strategic Offensive Reductions-SORT) Treaty between the US and Russia. With a target date of 2012, this would still leave the two largest arsenals with more than 2,000 deployed strategic nuclear weapons, which may be on hair-trigger alert, as well as thousands of tactical and strategic nuclear weapons in storage.

THE NPT HOLDOUTS: INDIA, ISRAEL AND PAKISTAN

India, Israel and Pakistan have developed nuclear weapons since 1970, remaining firmly outside the NPT. Even so, the world was shocked in May 1998 when India conducted a series of five underground nuclear weapon tests and declared itself a nuclear weapon state. Pakistan followed within weeks, surprising India with the alacrity with which it managed to conduct six underground nuclear tests in Southwest Baluchistan, close to the border with Iran. Within a couple of weeks after Pakistan's tests, the P-5 met in emergency session and then pushed through Security Council Resolution 1172. The G-8 also issued a high-level communiqué, arguing that the tests had worsened India and Pakistan's security environment, damaged their prospects of achieving sustainable economic development, and undermined global efforts toward nonproliferation and nuclear disarmament. Sanctions, particularly covering military goods, were imposed by a number of states, including Japan and the US.

In the next two years, India and Pakistan, who had fought at least three wars over the region of Jammu and Kashmir in as many decades, engaged in two further episodes of border warfare, this time with the dangerously unstable addition of nuclear brinkmanship. Despite some overblown threats and rhetoric, they managed to pull back from the brink. Following the Lahore Summit agreement to notify each other about nuclear testing, they have each undertaken a moratorium to refrain from testing. Alongside the recent adoption of important confidence-building measures relating to travel and communication between the two countries, India and Pakistan have also inaugurated a hotline between senior civil servants to "prevent misunderstandings" and each has tightened up national command and control over the weapons.

As the security environment appeared to stabilize, international criticism faded and sanctions were quietly dropped. As part of its "war on terrorism," the US offered both India and Pakistan the opportunity to become politically and militarily rehabilitated without giving up their nuclear weapons. Most recently, the Bush administration appears set to sell fighter aircraft to both sides and the US and others are looking at ways to circumvent the Nuclear Suppliers Group's restrictions and conduct nuclear trade, at least with India, purportedly for solely non-military purposes. In the past couple of years, there have been signs that the P-5 would prefer to accommodate India and Pakistan as if they were nuclear club members, provided that they not engage in trafficking with non-nuclear weapon states. While India is already gaining some acceptance as a "responsible" nuclear power, this will be very difficult for Pakistan unless it is willing to come clean over the A.Q. Khan network and demonstrate greater physical and political controls and protection of nuclear materials and technologies.

Israel is in a rather different position. Although the revelations of Mordecai Vanunu in 1987 led to estimates of an Israeli arsenal of some 80 to 200 nuclear weapons, Israel has steadfastly maintained a formal position that it will "not be the first to introduce nuclear weapons into the Middle East." Unlike India and Pakistan, Israel does not seek recognition or status as a nuclear power and does not discuss nuclear doctrine or policy. As the only country in the Middle East that has not joined the NPT, however, Israel's nuclear program is under constant diplomatic attack from its Arab neighbors and Iran. The NPT review conferences of 1995 and 2000 almost foundered on this issue, with the consequence that, in 1995, Russia, the UK and US agreed to co-sponsor a resolution on the Middle East, which called for "a Middle East zone free of nuclear weapons as well as other weapons of mass destruction." This resolution has become the basis for demands ever since, and was an important reason why Egypt opposed an agenda for the 2005 review conference that did not put deliberations in the context of the agreements from 1995 and 2000.[17]

Most analysts accept that Israel, India and Pakistan will not give up their nuclear weapons and join the NPT except in the context of nuclear disarmament, but this poses a problem for governments, since it is impossible to imagine the NPT being amended to admit three additional nuclear weapon states. This question lies at a very sensitive interface between treaty law, pragmatic politics and the dynamics of proliferation, as illustrated by the contentious issue of security assurances. The non-nuclear weapon states, which push for the nuclear weapon states to give them unconditional guarantees not to target them with a nuclear attack, might, for security reasons, want similar assurances from India, Israel and Pakistan, but they don't ask for this because they also fear that such an arrangement would codify an unacceptable nuclear weapon status for the three opt-outs.

NORTH KOREA

Following concerns about the nuclear program of the Democratic People's Republic of Korea (DPRK, or North Korea) in the early 1990s, the Agreed Framework between the US and North Korea was adopted in 1994, with the support of China, Russia, South Korea, Japan and the rest of the international community. The agreement, which imposed a freeze on North Korea's nuclear program, including the reprocessing of plutonium from nuclear waste, in return for other kinds of energy assistance, was intended to give Pyongyang the incentives to back away from proliferation-prone nuclear technologies, but it ran into many problems. The current crisis was set in motion when North Korea was identified by President Bush as part of "an axis of evil" in his January 2002 State of the Union speech. Soon after, in October 2002, US officials accused North Korea of pursuing a uranium enrichment program. North Korea subsequently expelled IAEA officials and their equipment from the country and, in January 2003, announced its withdrawal from the NPT.

Several rounds of seemingly fruitless "six party talks" have been held among China, Japan, North Korea, Russia, South Korea and the US. Instead of meaningful diplomacy, however, the US and North Korea seem to use the talks as a platform to reiterate their publicly stated positions and make thinly-veiled insults against the other's leaders. In February 2005, North Korea announced that it was suspending its participation in the talks and claimed to have "manufactured nukes" for "self-defence to cope with the Bush administration's ever more undisguised policy to isolate and stifle the [North]." Though it remains unclear whether North Korea has actually developed any deployable nuclear weapons, its actions and rhetoric present a profound challenge that the international community appears unable or unwilling to address.[18]

North Korea poses a fundamental challenge for the nonproliferation regime on two levels. As the first state to withdraw from the NPT when confronted over its non-compliance, the defection has exposed the political and institutional inadequacies of the treaty and the Security Council, to whom the issue was referred. The second challenge has to do with the deterrence value attached to nuclear weapons in North Korea's adversarial relationship with the US: there is a nonproliferation cost as some have drawn the conclusion that Kim Jong Il has gained credibility through convincing the US it has deliverable nuclear weapons, whether or not any have actually been manufactured. The failures of the 2005 review conference have compounded the impasse, with states parties unable to agree whether to treat North Korea as having left the NPT or as being in serious non-compliance with the treaty. The conference failure also meant that there was scant discussion of innovative proposals from the EU, Canada and others on withdrawal and strengthening the NPT states parties' powers to deter states from violating or withdrawing from their nonproliferation obligations. The international community has missed many opportunities to deal with these questions, and as time passes, it becomes more difficult to do so without the use of force.

IRAN

The crisis over Iran's nuclear fuel cycle program formally dates back to August 2002, when opponents of the current Iranian regime publicized information about two undeclared nuclear facilities, as well as various front companies involved in purchasing nuclear materials and equipment. The facilities, which had not been declared to the IAEA as required in Iran's safeguards agreements under the NPT, comprised a plant for heavy water production near Arak, and an underground gas centrifuge uranium enrichment plant near Natanz, still under construction. Also of concern is a uranium conversion plant at Esfahan. As the US and Iran ratcheted up rhetorical attacks on each other, the foreign ministers of France, Germany and the UK stepped in and brokered a deal with Iran in October 2003. Iran submitted additional information to the IAEA on past nuclear activities, acknowledging for the first time that it had carried out undeclared enrichment and reprocessing experiments that dated back to the early 1990s. In return for Iranian promises of full cooperation with the IAEA, the EU-3 blocked US efforts to refer Iran to the UN Security Council.

The November 2003 IAEA Board of Governors meeting adopted a resolution that welcomed the October agreement and encouraged Iran to implement its commitments fully. On December 18, 2003, Iran signed the *Additional Protocol*, with the consequence that the IAEA again gave Iran more time to resolve past safeguards violations and implement the protocol. During 2004, as the US became increasingly bogged down in Iraq, the agreements with Iran began to unravel, and Iran once more asserted its rights under the NPT to develop the full fuel cycle for peaceful purposes. As the US again pushed the IAEA to refer Iran to the UN Security Council, the EU-3 re-started its negotiations with Iran. These resulted in the Paris Agreement of November 15, 2004, whereby Iran agreed to suspend its uranium conversion and enrichment plans in return for EU support, for example in joining the World Trade Organization. While the US and EU are pushing for Iran to halt such plans permanently, Iran has emphasised that it agreed to the suspension solely as a temporary confidence-building measure. Claiming that it has as much a right as any other country to carry out programs such as uranium conversion and enrichment, Iran evokes Article IV of the NPT, which refers to the development of nuclear energy as an "inalienable right," though it must be carried out in accordance with the nonproliferation obligations in Articles I and II, as well as the safeguards required under Article III.

Specifically, Iran points to Japan's full fuel cycle program and expresses a desire and willingness to emulate Japan, including hosting permanently stationed IAEA monitors at its nuclear facilities in order to reassure the international community of its peaceful intentions. Indicative of this approach is Iran's statement to the NPT review conference. Dr. Kamal Kharrazi, minister of foreign affairs, declared that Iran "is determined to pursue all legal areas of nuclear technology, including enrichment, exclusively for peaceful purposes."[19]

NPT states parties reached an impasse on this issue for several reasons. The issue of non-discrimination is a litmus test for many countries, who are wary of imposing additional restrictions on the nuclear programs of non-nuclear weapon states when the nuclear powers have no such restrictions and only voluntary safeguards. Application of the principle of non-discrimination, however, would require that the reprocessing and enrichment programs of countries such as Japan and Brazil would have to be suspended along with Iran's. Iran participated in the 2005 NPT review conference determined to prevent any agreements on restricting the fuel cycle or singling out of Iran for criticism. Like the US and Egypt, who had their own reasons, Iran deployed procedural tactics to block substantive negotiations; at the same time, in a worrying echo of India's rhetoric in the years before its May 1998 nuclear tests, Iran sought to deflect attention from its own activities by taking the moral high ground on lack of progress on disarmament and universality.

Space Weapons and Security

Since September 11, the US has attempted to focus worldwide attention on the threats from ballistic missile-delivered WMD. Though ballistic missiles are only one—and by no means the most likely—delivery method for WMD, the fear of such attacks fuels the US drive to develop missile defenses in a multi-tiered architecture based on land, sea, air and even to develop weapons for use from platforms orbiting the Earth in outer space.

In addition to communications, banking and entertainment, the world now relies on outer space for important security and development purposes from meteorology to environmental monitoring. Yet proponents of weaponizing space are prepared to put these civilian uses and benefits at risk, arguing that space weapons are essential to protect space assets from a preemptive attack and that whomever controls space will obtain an unassailable military and commercial dominance on Earth.

There are already a number of international treaties and instruments with jurisdiction over space activities, but they do not adequately cover the challenges posed by space-based weapons and ballistic missile defense. None of the existing legal instruments unequivocally prevents the testing, deployment and use of weapons other than nuclear, chemical and biological, in outer space. Nor does any relevant legal instrument cover the use of force or threat of use of force against a country's assets in outer space. The placement of nuclear weapons in space is prohibited under the 1967 Outer Space Treaty, but nuclear-warheads on ballistic missile defense interceptors launched from the ground into space are not prohibited. Russia continues to deploy nuclear interceptors on its ageing Galosh defense system around Moscow, and it now appears that the Bush administration wants to revisit past US decisions not to use nuclear interceptors for this purpose.

As US policies and administration statements have heightened concerns about the weaponization of outer space, civil society and several states have put forward proposals for making progress on this issue. In 2001, at a major international conference held in Moscow, the Acronym Institute put forward a strategy for a comprehensive-incremental approach to build a space security regime, comprising negotiations to prohibit the deployment of weapons in and from outer space, ban the use of anti-satellite weapons and develop a code of conduct for the peace-supporting, non-offensive and non-aggressive uses of space. The complementarity and necessity of linking these three components has since become widely accepted, although other governments and NGOs prioritize different aspects in their advocacy. Washington-based groups, notably the Henry L. Stimson Center, have worked with technical and legal experts, military and civilian space users to draft a code of conduct for outer space as well. The key provisions forbid simulated attacks, flight-testing of anti-satellite weapons, the deployment of space weapons and of weapons in anti-satellite mode, and the harmful use of lasers.[20]

In 2002, the governments of Russia and China co-sponsored a CD working paper with a draft treaty on preventing the deployment of weapons in outer space. Russia and China have since circulated CD discussion papers on legal, institutional and verification-related issues and promoted wider discussions with governments and civil society experts. In addition, Canada, working with several NGOs, has developed a Space Security Index which monitors trends and annual developments with regard to eight space security indicators ranging from the space environment and commercial uses to space-based strike weapons. The US Administration and Congress, meanwhile, are deeply divided about the security benefits, risks, costs and technical feasibility of weaponizing space. With so many initiatives on the table for alternative approaches to space security, it is imperative that the international community discuss these important issues. If the CD remains deadlocked, pressure will mount for experts groups, and negotiations to be convened under different auspices.

Conventional Weapons

While the potential devastation that could be wrought by weapons of mass destruction is appalling to contemplate, the actual killings and maimings that are caused daily by landmines, small arms and so-called light weapons continue to devastate lives, families and economies around the world. In the past year, three issues have come to the fore in this arena: marking and tracing small arms and light weapons; addressing the dangers of man-portable air defense systems, otherwise known as MANPADS; and inclusion of explosive remnants of war as Protocol V of the *Convention on Certain Conventional Weapons* (CCW). Other issues likely to be taken up in the near future are addressing the arms brokers and ammunition stockpiles.

SMALL ARMS AND LIGHT WEAPONS

A major breakthrough on small arms and light weapons occurred in July 2001, when the UN negotiated and agreed on Programme of Action to Prevent, Combat and Eradicate the Illicit Trade in Small Arms and Light Weapons in All Its Aspects.[21] Since then, there have been a variety of regional initiatives, notably in Africa, the Americas and Europe. The Organization of American States, South African Development Community and Nairobi Secretariat on small arms and light weapons in the Great Lakes have concluded legally binding instruments aimed at curbing the illicit trade in small arms. The Economic Community of West African States is currently converting its moratorium on small arms manufacture and transfers into a legally binding convention. Most recently, the Andean Community of Bolivia, Colombia, Ecuador, Peru and Venezuela has taken forward one of the most advanced regional initiatives for limitation, control and transparency of conventional armaments, including confidence-building measures and verification. In addition, 12 sub-regional organizations have identified focal points responsible for implementing the plan of action on small arms.[22]

The Programme of Action identified actions to be undertaken nationally and on the regional and global levels. Among its many provisions, the program refers to the need for effective national legislation and regulation on small arms and light weapons, and making illicit possession and production a criminal offense. It also aims to keep track of officially-held arms. More than 100 countries have submitted reports on these measures to date.[23]

In June 2004, a two-week open-ended working group was convened under the auspices of the Programme of Action to negotiate an international instrument to enable states "to identify and trace, in a timely and reliable manner, illicit small arms and light weapons." The goal of this initiative is to have information on all legally-produced arms in order to facilitate the identification and tracing of illicit small arms and light weapons, so that if a weapon turns up in commission of a crime, or in a war zone or country under UN sanctions, it will be easier to find out how it was diverted from the legal to illegal trade. Following a debate in the First Committee on disarmament and international security, during which these issues were raised, the small arms and light weapons resolution in 2004 was adopted by consensus.

Signaling their intention to put a resolution on ammunition before the

General Assembly in the near future, Bulgaria, France, Germany and The Netherlands won consensus for a draft decision to place the issue of "Problems arising from the Accumulation of Conventional Ammunition Stockpiles in Surplus" onto the agenda of the 60th General Assembly. Though there was no resolution in 2004 on arms brokers, the ground is clearly being laid with calls from the International Committee of the Red Cross, Norway and the Caribbean Community countries for the First Committee to establish an expert panel "to develop proposals for an international system of controls on arms brokers."

MANPADS

The UN Register on Conventional Arms, covering imports and exports of major conventional weapons, is now in its 12th year. In 2004, in response to concerns about the terrorist potential of man-portable air defense systems or MANPADS, the register was expanded for the first time to include "large caliber artillery systems" from 100 mm to 75 mm. Mobile and easily acquired in the black market, MANPADS are shoulder-launched surface-to-air missiles with heat-seeking sensors, designed to follow the heat of a jet engine's exhaust to its source. They are capable of shooting civilian as well as military aircraft out of the sky.

In conjunction with the register's expansion, Australia co-sponsored a resolution in the First Committee, calling for "effective and comprehensive national controls on the production, stockpiling, transfer and brokering" of MANPADS. The resolution, which was adopted by consensus, encourages states to enact or improve legislation, regulations and practices, as well as encouraging "initiatives to exchange information and to mobilize resources and technical expertise" to assist states in combating unauthorized use and transfer of MANPADS.[24]

LANDMINES

As with small arms and light weapons, some of the strongest initiatives on landmines are occurring in Africa and Asia. Forty-eight African states within the African Union, for example, adopted in September 2004 a Common African Position on Anti-Personnel Landmines. The fundamental treaty banning landmines is the *Convention on the Prohibition of the Use, Stockpiling, Production and Transfer of Anti-Personnel Mines and on Their Destruction*, more usually called the Mine-Ban or "Ottawa" Treaty. Opened for signature in 1997, the Mine-Ban Treaty to date has 144 states parties. In 2004, the General Assembly resolution supporting it received 157 votes in favor. No one voted against, but 22 countries who are non-signatories to the treaty, abstained.

The Nairobi Summit for a Mine-Free World, the first review conference for the Mine-Ban Treaty, took place in late 2004 with high-level participation. It adopted an action plan for the next four years, entitled "Ending the suffering caused by anti-personnel mines: Nairobi Action Plan 2005-2009." This committed parties to the pursuit of universal adherence and to substantial political, financial and material commitments to ensure full compliance with the treaty, including the expeditious and timely destruction of all stockpiled anti-personnel mines, meeting deadlines for clearing mined areas, assistance, enhanced care, rehabilitation and reintegration efforts, transparency and effective information exchange.[25]

EXPLOSIVE REMNANTS OF WAR

In another important development to reduce the indiscriminate maiming of civilians by weapons left over from long-finished conflicts, the *Convention on Certain Conventional Weapons* recently negotiated a new protocol covering explosive remnants of war. Protocol V, according to the International Committee of the Red Cross, does not prohibit or restrict any conventional weapons in particular, but does establish a framework for states to minimize the dangers of unexploded or abandoned ordnance. The protocol also encourages generic measures to prevent munitions from becoming explosive remnants of war. A noteworthy limitation of the protocol, however, is that it only applies to future conflicts. Furthermore, there are many qualifiers in the protocol text such as "where feasible" that may weaken its effectiveness. Protocol V is expected to enter into force in 2006.[26]

Terrorism

Many security analysts believe that the dramatic and catastrophic impact of using nuclear, chemical or biological weapons is within the aspirations—if not yet the grasp—of dedicated terrorist groups such as Al Qaeda. Within three weeks of the September 11, 2001 attacks on the US, the Security Council passed Resolution 1373, which requires UN member states to, among other things: deny financial support, safe havens or support for terrorist groups; share information with other governments on any people or groups practicing or planning terrorist acts; criminalize active and passive assistance for terrorism; and become party as soon as possible to the relevant international conventions and protocols relating to terrorism. Resolution 1373 also created the Counter-Terrorism Committee (CTC) to monitor its implementation. Though its objectives are laudable and its coverage ostensibly global, the CTC has run into political difficulties including problems over defining a terrorist, sovereignty, and the special interests of the arms manufacturers and bankers who hold inordinate sway over the policies of many governments.

With the CTC badly in need of revitalization, the UN in 2004 took several further measures to impose legal obligations on states to deal with terrorism. As noted, Resolution 1540 requires states to apply the provisions of WMD treaties to non-state actors and authorizes coercive military force to prevent trafficking in WMD-related technology and goods. In October 2004, the Council adopted Resolution 1566, which called upon member states to become party to relevant conventions against terrorism and established a working group to consider practical measures and procedures for, among other things, preventing terrorists' movement, freezing their assets and compensating victims.[27] Most importantly, this resolution gave renewed impetus to efforts begun in 1996 to achieve a comprehensive convention on international terrorism and conclude the draft convention on nuclear terrorism. Finalized in April 2005, the *International Convention for the Suppression of Acts of Nuclear Terrorism* addresses threats from the unlawful acquisition of nuclear materials to make nuclear weapons or radiological dispersal devices (i.e., the so-called "dirty bombs" designed to ignite nuclear waste and spread contamination). This convention will be opened for signature on September 14, 2005. In addition, institutions such as the International Maritime Organization have been negotiating specific protocols relating to terrorism and WMD-related materials in conventions dealing with maritime safety and security.[28]

To address terrorism effectively, general and specific approaches are necessary, with stronger action on all three levels: choking off supply, reinforcing the regimes, and addressing (but not pandering to) those aspects on the demand side that are linked with perceptions of injustice, discrimination or insecurity. Proliferation and terrorist acquisition may be slowed by supply-side denial of access to nuclear technologies and materials, imposed by the dominant supplier states, backed up by coercive military force, as sanctioned by the PSI, Resolution 1540, export controls and the G-8 initiatives. But such approaches only go some way toward prevention. Without equal attention to the causes of terrorism and the drivers of proliferation, supply-side initiatives run the risk of pushing the problem further underground, where it is even more difficult to monitor or constrain.

Looking Forward

The 2005 Nonproliferation Treaty Review Conference failed because a small number of governments put their narrowly defined self-interests above the imperatives of international security. In particular, by attempting to hold open their own nuclear options, states prevented the wider international community from adopting measures to strengthen the nonproliferation regime. This failure will not cause immediate proliferation, but it is the symptom of a deeper sickness in international relations that may result in greater instability as more countries hedge their bets. Without regimes, which embed norms, principles, good practices and the rules of international law, it will be much harder to gain global acceptance for measures to counter terrorism and proliferation. It will also be more difficult to sustain the coalitions of the willing required for the Proliferation Security Initiative, Resolution 1540 and other legislation in the long run. A comprehensive approach needs to be consensual and offer greater security and other incentives, with regional as well as national and international measures put in place. Disarmament, if progressively pursued with effective monitoring, verification and elimination and disposal of weapons and materials, can do much to reduce nuclear threats (as accepted in the parallel WMD cases of biological and chemical weapons) and keep dangerous materials out of the hands of those who might be tempted to use them. Delinking disarmament from nonproliferation narrows the zone of political, technical, legal and physical options within which effective policies can be developed against both terrorism and proliferation.

To enhance security, the world needs less military expenditure, and more support for cooperative threat reduction approaches, such as that established by the US-led Nunn-Lugar programs in former Soviet states. Global threat reduction strategies, combined with poverty alleviation and disarmament, demobilization and reintegration of ex-combatants, have moved up the agendas of the G-8, European Union and Non-Aligned Movement, and will need to be taken forward by all countries. Such strategies—and the action plans that build on them—show a general understanding of the multilayered nature of the security challenges and proliferation arising from failed states and armed groups of terrorists or militia. But if the world is to avoid a nuclear or bioweapons catastrophe, governments must be more willing to address their own roles in contributing to arming combatants and fueling proliferation aspirations and capabilities.

Commentary:
Is Democracy in the Middle East Spreading?

Jean Krasno

The Bush administration's stated purpose for the war in Iraq, now that no weapons of mass destruction have been found, has been to spread democracy to the Middle East. To some extent, there is evidence that steps toward democratization are slowly being taken.

Elections took place in Saudi Arabia in February 2005 for the first time with assistance from the United Nation's Electoral Assistance Division. And in May 2005, the 64-member Kuwaiti National Assembly, which is all male, reversed its decision not to allow women to vote or participate in city council elections, giving them the right to vote and run for election by 2007. With this decision, Kuwait, whose parliament holds more power than many in other Muslim countries and who does have one of the few women ambassadors to the UN, Nabeela Abdulla al-Mulla, now joins Oman, Qatar and Bahrain in allowing women to vote in elections. Palestinian Authority elections and elections in Lebanon free of Syrian influence are also important steps.

Egyptian President Hosni Mubarak proposed amending his country's constitution to allow opposition candidates to run for president in the upcoming September 2005 election instead of only being able to vote "yes" or "no" on a single candidate chosen by parliament. At first, this seemed like a real step forward in democratizing Egypt's closed political system, but very tough hurdles have been proposed that would block most candidates from running (e.g., a candidate must be either a member of an official party's leadership council or be approved by parliament). Some have claimed that this amendment simply allows the president to choose who might challenge him in the election.

Despite some movement toward democratization in the region, the recent, third Arab Human Development Report produced by the UN Development Programme describes the Arab world as having an "acute deficit of freedom and good governance." The report states that today's Arab state is "a black hole, which converts its surrounding social environment into a setting in which nothing moves and from which nothing escapes." Arab society is bound by strict tradition and an educational system that instills submissiveness, not creative thought and questioning, the report argues. If democracy is to take a firm hold, economic development and social-political development must go hand-in-hand.

Thomas Friedman, a *New York Times* columnist and Middle East expert, heralds the report as a major step in coming forward with an in-depth analysis of the true political situation in the Arab world. "Read this report and you'll also understand why part of every Arab hates the US invasion of Iraq—and why another part is praying that it succeeds," he wrote in an April 2005 article.

Efforts at democratization in much of the Arab world appear cosmetic, but steps toward "free and fair" elections within the region, along with international pressure, just may embolden Arab democracy-seekers to take up a "desert flower" revolution.

Endnotes

Africa

1. The term "weapons of mass destruction" is applied to nuclear, chemical, biological and radiological weapons, although these weapons differ greatly in their modes of production, acquisition and likely delivery, in the probable scale and devastation of their effects, and in the nature and quality of the international legal regimes established to prevent their acquisition and use.
2. Peacekeeping missions, which focus on maintaining or restoring international peace and security, are deployed with the full consent of the parties involved and only after a cease-fire has been issued; they do not have enforcement powers but do involve military personnel. Political and peace-building missions support peacekeeping missions through reconciliation and negotiation between parties and ensure that conflict does not reignite by implementing development activities.
3. UN Document S/2004/90 (2004).
4. UN Document S/2005/149 (2005).
5. ONUB Press Release (2005), ONUB/PIO/PR/60/2005.
6. "'Breakthrough' for Burundi Peace," BBC News, May 11, 2005.
7. ONUB Press Release 52 (2005).
8. UN Press Release SC/8239.
9. "Families of French Soldiers to Leave Ivory Coast," Reuters, May 10, 2005.
10. "Britons Told to Leave Ivory Coast," BBC News, April 1, 2005.
11. "Ivory Coast Foes Agree Ceasefire," BBC News, April 6, 2005.
12. "Deal in Ivorian Disarmament Talks," BBC News, May 14, 2005.
13. UN Document S/2005/186 (2005).
14. UN Document S/2005/167 (2005).
15. "UN Reforms Aim to End Sexual Abuse by Peacekeepers," Reuters, May 10, 2005.
16. As of March 31, 2005, according to the UN Department of Peacekeeping Operations website (DPKO).
17. "The UN Gets Tougher," Economist, March 12, 2005. / UN Document S/2004/1034 (2004).
18. UN Document S/2005/142 (2005).
19. UN Document S/Res/1560 (2004). / DPKO website.
20. "Eritrean Militiaman Shot on Tense Ethiopian Border," AlertNet, May 5, 2005.
21. UN Document S/2005/177 (2005).
22. "Rebuilding Failed States: From Chaos, Order," Economist, March 5, 2005.
23. UN Document S/2004/725 (2004).
24. UN Document S/2005/177 (2005).
25. Ibid.
26. UN Document S/Res/1561 (2004).
27. ECOSOC Press Release 6140 (September 27, 2004).
28. UN Document S/2004/965 (2004).
29. UN Document S/2005/135 (2005).
30. UN Document S/2004/453 (2004).
31. "Annan Demands Darfur Resolution," BBC News, March 8, 2005.
32. AFR Press Release, October 22, 2004.
33. "Canadian Troops Head to Sudan," Cnews, February, 10, 2005.
34. "More African Troops Go to Darfur," BBC News, December 16, 2004.
35. "Regions and Territories: Western Sahara," BBC News, March 30, 2005.
36. UN Document S/2004/827 (2004).
37. UN Document S/2005/254 (2005).
38. Ibid.

Americas

1. UN Document S/RES/1542 (2004). / UN Document S/2004/698 (2004).
2. UN Document S/2005/313 (2005).
3. "As UN Nears Full Troop Strength in Haiti, Lull in Violence Is Reported," UN News Service, December 23, 2004.
4. UN Documents S/2005/313 (2005), S/2004/908 (2004) and S/2005/124 (2004). / "Calm Returning to Troubled District in Haitian Capital, UN Mission

Says," *UN News Service*, November 4, 2004.

5. Ibid. / UN Documents S/2004/698 (2004), S/2004/908 (2004).

6. UN Document S/2005/313 (2005).

7. "In Final Report, Annan Hails UN Mission in Guatemala as Model of Success," *UN News Service*, April 14, 2005,

8. UN Document A/59/307 (2004).

9. Ibid. / "UN Mission to Guatemala Signs

off with Warning about Racism and Inequality," *UN News Service*, September 30, 2004. / UN Document A/59/746 (2004).

10. "UN, Guatemala Sign Agreement to Open Human Rights Office," *UN News Service*, January 11, 2005.

11. UN Document S/2005/313 (2005).

12. SG's Message to the Closing Ceremony of MINUGUA, November 15, 2004.

Asia

1. Keith B Richburg, "Karzai Officially Declared Winner," *Washington Post*, November 4, 2004.

2. "The Rule of the Gun: Human Rights Abuses and Political Repression in the Run-Up to Afghanistan's Presidential Election," *Human Rights Watch*, September 29, 2004.

3. "More than 10.3 Million Afghans Enrolled to Vote as Registrations Close," *UN News Center*, August 23, 2004.

4. "Using Officials and Donkeys, Afghans Prepare for Historic Presidential Vote," *UN News Center*, September 30, 2004.

5. UN Document S/2005/183 (2005).

6. Ibid.

7. Ibid.

8. *UNAMA* Press Release (2005).

9. Peter Willems, "Business is Booming," *Al-Ahram Weekly*, December 8, 2004.

10. UN Document S/2005/183 (2005).

11. Ibid.

12. "UN's Top Counter-Narcotics Official Calls for International Arrest Warrants against Afghan Drug Traffickers," *UN News Center*, January 30, 2005.

13. "Up to 5,000 British Troops Sought for Afghanistan Drugs Crackdown," *Independent*, December 5, 2004.

14. UN Document SC/8341 (2005).

15. "Relief Groups Criticise Anti-Drug Program," *Radio Free Europe/Radio Liberty website*, February 1, 2005.

16. "Afghan Demobilization Marks Milestone with One Whole Region Disarmed: UN," *UN News Center*, December 16, 2004. / "Second Region in Afghanistan Now Disarmed, UN Announces," *UN News Center*, February 13, 2005.

17. UN Document S/2005/183 (2005).

18. Ibid.

19. Ibid. / "Afghanistan's Future Holds Promise and Peril," *UNDP website*, February 21, 2005.

20. "UN Mission in Bougainville Scheduled to End on 30 June, after Elections," *UN News Center*, March 30, 2005.

21. UN Document S/2005/204 (2005).

22. "Timeline: Steps to Peace in South Asia," *BBC News*, April 15, 2005.

23. "India and Pakistan: All Aboard?" Economist, February 17, 2005/ "Bus Aids Kashmir's Road to Peace," *BBC News*, April 7, 2005.

24. "Rivals Say Peace "Irreversible," *BBC News*, April 18, 2005.

25. UN Document SG/SM/9826 (2005).

26. Simon Denyer, "India, Pakistan Cricket Diplomacy No Game It's Real," *Reuters*, April 19, 2005.

27. UN Document SG/SM/9806 (2005).

28. In August 2004, the SG appointed Maj. Gen. Guido Palmieri of Italy as the new Chief Military Observer of UNMOGIP. / UN Document SG/A/889 (2004).

29. "Tajik Ruling Party Wins Elections," *BBC News*, February 28, 2005.

30. "OSCE: Tajik Elections Fall Short of Standards," *Radio Free Europe/Radio Liberty website*, February 28, 2005.

31. Ibid.

32. UN Document SC/8371 (2005).

33. UN Document SC/8371 (2005).

34. "Annan Names Experts to Probe Impunity in Independence Violence in Timor-Leste," *UN News Center*, February 18, 2005.

35. "Annan Calls on Donors to Help Timorese Build a Better Future," *UN*
News Center, April 25, 2005.

36. UN Document C/8371 (2005).

Europe

1. UN Document S/2004/756 (2004).

2. "In Reorganization of UN Mission in
Cyprus, Annan Recommends Cut in
Troops," *UN News Center,* June 17, 2005.

3. "Pro-unification Talat Wins Northern
Cyprus Vote," *EurActive website,* April
18, 2005.

4. "Turkish Cypriot PM Wins Election,"
BBC News, February 21, 2005.

5. DPKO website.

6. Tiblisi is the capital of Georgia; Sukhumi is the capital of Abkhazia.

7. DPKO website.

8. "Georgia–South Ossetia: Refugee Return
the Path to Peace," *ICG,* April 19 2005.

9. "European Security Review," *ISIS*
Europe, July 23, 2004.

10. Noel Malcolm. Kosovo: A Short History.
(London: Papermac, 2002). / Tim Judah.
Kosovo–War and Revenge. (New Haven
and London: Yale University Press, 2002).

11. UNMIK website.

12. "Foes of Multi-ethnic Democracy Still
Threaten Kosovo's Progress–UN Envoy,"
UN News Center, June 17, 2005.

13. "Annan and UN Envoy Hail Success of
Weekend Elections for Kosovo Assembly," *UN News Center,* June 17, 2005.

14. *UN Daily News,* June 3, 2005.

15. Presidency Conclusions, Thessaloniki
European Council, June 19-20, 2003.

16. Presidency Conclusions, Brussels
European Council, June 17-18, 2004

17. Rieker, Pernille and Ulriksen Stale. En
annerledes supermakt. Sikkerhets og
forsvarpolitikken i EU (NUPI, Oslo,
2003).

18. "EU Crisis Response Capability Revisit-
ed," ICG, January 2005.

19. "The EU Police Mission in Bosnia and
Herzegovina," *International Peacekeeping No. 11,* 2004.

20. "An Ounce of Prevention: Macedonia
and the UN experience in preventive
diplomacy," *USIP,* 2003.

21. EU Police Mission website.

22. A peacekeeping operation in Moldova
has been under consideration at various times during 2003 and 2004 but
not implemented due to difficulties
reaching agreements with Russia,
which has maintained military presence there since the break-up of the
Soviet Union.

23. "EU-UN Partnership in Crisis Management: Development and Prospects,"
International Peace Academy, June 2004.

24. In Larger Freedom Report, para 112.

The Middle East and Iraq

1. The information herein was collected
through interviews with members of
the UN Electoral Assistance Division in
New York.

2. US Department of Defense website. /
New York Times, May 5, 2005.

3. Hassan M. Fattah, "Syria Under Pressure: Worse Trouble May Lie Ahead,"
New York Times, March 3, 2005.

4. Dexter Filkins, "Pro-Syrian Premier
Expected to Resign in Lebanon Today,"
New York Times, March 30, 2005.

5. Hassan M. Fattah, "Last Syria Force

Leaves Lebanon," *New York Times,* April
27, 2005.

6. Kristin Dailey, "UN Verifies Total Syrian
Withdrawal from Lebanon," *The Daily*
Star, May 24, 2005. / "Syria Arrests
Many and Stops Cooperating with US,"
SyriaComment website, May 24, 2005.

7. "The day that peace broke out?" *Economist,* February 11, 2005.

8. Steven Erlanger, "Sharon Clears Final
Hurdle in Gaza Pullout Plan's Path: Key
Vote Avoids Collapse of Government,"
New York Times, March 30, 2005.

Looming Conflicts

1. "Feudal follies," *Economist*, February 3, 2005.
2. "Nepal's Army Launches Massive Attack Against Rebels to Regain Lost Ground," *AP*, April 25, 2005.
3. "Who are Nepal's Maoist Rebels?" *BBC News*, August 17, 2004.
4. "Nepal: Dealing with a Human Rights Crisis," *ICG*, March 24, 2005.
5. Ibid.
6. "Nepal Army Claims another Big Victory over Maoist Rebels," *Agence France Presse*, April 14, 2005.
7. "Rebel Leaders Admit Rift," *BBC News*, May 1, 2005.
8. "Nepal: Q&A," *BBC News*, April 30, 2005.
9. "Yusuf the uniter?" *Economist*, February 17, 2005.
10. "Somali PM asks warlords to cooperate during maiden visit to Mogadishu," *Agence France Presse*, April 29, 2005.
11. "As Its Lawmakers Squabble Abroad, Somalia Suffers," *Los Angeles Times*, March 23, 2005.
12. Ibid.
13. Ibid.
14. "Somalia: Continuation of War by Other Means?" *ICG*, December 21, 2004.
15. "Face to face with the Lord's Resistance," *The Globe and Mail*, April 27, 2005.
16. "Darfur, Southern Sudan and Northern Uganda: The Quest for a Comprehensive Peace," Woodrow Wilson International Center for Scholars.
17. "Uganda's Invisible War," *BBC News*, October 22, 2004.
18. Ibid.
19. "Peace in Southern Sudan, Is the Only Hope for the Same in Northern Uganda," *New Vision*, June 30, 2004.
20. "Ugandan Rebels Show Door to Peace Closing Fast," *Reuters*, May 1, 2005.
21. "Ugandan Rebels Recruiting Sudanese Children, Religious Leaders Say," *BBC News*, April 29, 2005.
22. "Shock Therapy for Northern Uganda's Peace Process," *ICG*, April 11,

Editor's Note: Much of the information in the peacekeeping sections of this chapter comes from the UN Department of Peacekeeping Operations and the UN Department of Political Affairs.

Disarmament & Terrorism

1. Cyrus Samii, "Managing Nuclear Threats after Iraq," *International Peace Academy, UN University, Ritsumeikan University and Ritsumeikan Asia Pacific University*, February 2005.
2. Report on the US Intelligence Community's Prewar Intelligence Assessments on Iraq, *US Senate Select Committee on Intelligence*, July 2004.
3. Joseph Cirincione, "Two Terrifying Reports: The US Senate and the 9/11 Commission on Intelligence Failures Before September 11 and the Iraq War," *Disarmament Diplomacy*, July-August 2004. / Ibid.
4. Robin Cook, *The Independent*, July 15, 2004.
5. Charles Duelfer, Letter to US Congress transmitting the Comprehensive Report of the Special Adviser to the Director of Central Intelligence on Iraq's WMD, September 23, 2004.
6. Duelfer Report.
7. Monterey Institute for International Studies, Center for Nonproliferation Studies website.
8. Richard Guthrie, John Hart, Frida Kuhlau and Jacqueline Simon, "Chemical and Biological Warfare Developments and Arms Control," *SIPRI Yearbook 2004*, Stockholm International Peace Research Institute, 2004.
9. Jez Littlewood, "Substance Hidden under a Mountain of Paper," *Disarmament Diplomacy*, October-November 2003. / UN Press Releases (August 2,

2004 and December 13, 2004).

10. Nicholas A. Sims, "Nurturing the BWC: Agenda for the Fifth Review Conference and Beyond," *CBW Conventions Bulletin*, September 2001. / Trevor Findlay and Angela Woodward, "Enhancing BWC Implementation: A Modular Approach," WMD Commission Research Paper 23, 2004.

11. This section is drawn from the author's publications on the CTBT and contemporaneous notes of the First Committee discussions and explanations of vote, November 2004. *See* also: Rebecca Johnson, "2004 UN First Committee: Better Organised, with Deep Divisions," *Disarmament Diplomacy*, April-May 2005.

12. UN Document CD/1299 (1995).

13. Arms Control Association Press Release (July 30, 2004).

14. Rebecca Johnson, "2004 UN First Committee: Better Organised, with Deep Divisions," *Disarmament Diplomacy*, April-May 2005. / UN DDA website.

15. Jean du Preez, "The Fissban: Time for Renewed Commitment or a New Approach?" *Disarmament Diplomacy*, April-May 2005.

16. Hans Kristensen, "U.S. Nuclear Weapons in Europe," *Natural Resources Defense Council*, 2005.

17. Author's conversations with Egyptian diplomats, New York, May 2-27, 2005. Also see NPT reporting at Acronym Institute website.

18. Nicola Butler, "Slow Road to Nowhere: North Korea and the Six Party Nuclear Talks," *Disarmament Diplomacy*, April-May 2005. / "DPRK FM on Its Stand to Suspend Its Participation in Six-party Talks for Indefinite Period," *KCNA*, February 10, 2005.

19. Kamal Kharrazi, "General Debate Statement to the 2005 Review Conference of States Parties to the NPT," May 3, 2005.

20. Rebecca Johnson, "Missile Defence and the Weaponization of Space," *ISIS Policy Paper*, January 2003. / Michael Krepon, Christopher Clary, "Space Assurance or Space Dominance?" *The Henry L. Stimson Center*, 2003.

21. General Assembly Resolution 50/70B (1995).

22. UN Document S/2005/69 (2005).

23. Elli Kytömäki and Valerie Yankey-Wayne, "Implementing the United Nations Programme of Action on Small Arms and Light Weapons," *UNIDIR*, 2004.

24. General Assembly Resolution 59/90.

25. UN Document APLC/CONF/2004/5 (2005).

26. General Assembly Resolution 59/107 (2004).

27. Security Council Resolution 1566 (2004).

28. UN Document A/60/37 (2005).

Chapter 3

Development: Meeting the Millennium Challenge

Roger Coate, Gail Karlsson

We have the opportunity in the coming decade to cut world poverty by half. Billions more people could enjoy the fruits of the global economy. Tens of millions of lives can be saved. The practical solutions exist. The political framework is established. And for the first time, the cost is utterly affordable. Whatever one's motivation for attacking the crisis of extreme poverty—human rights, religious values, security, fiscal prudence, ideology—the solutions are the same. All that is needed is action.
—UN Millennium Project Director Jeffrey D. Sachs and Contributing Authors
*Investing in Development: A Practical Plan to Achieve the
Millennium Development Goals,* January 2005

"**D**evelopment," at least as we conceive of it today, was not on the forefront of the agenda when American and British post-World War II planners were mapping out their grand scheme for a new world order. This new order was to be based on norms and principles of liberalism melded together with those of the Westphalian state system, in which states are the principal actors in the international arena. The United Nations was therefore designed as a system of international institutions and member states that would serve as a foundation for promoting and sustaining the conditions necessary to ensure lasting peace and economic prosperity. Today, these conditions are set out to be achieved via the eight Millennium Development Goals, agreed to by all 191 UN member states in 2000. But before discussing the details of these goals, it is important to understand how the UN got involved in development issues in the first place.

Looking Back

Roger Coate

The United Nations itself was only one of a family of international bodies designed to coordinate, assist and monitor global development. In fact, it emerged fourth after the Food and Agricultural Organization (FAO) was established in 1943, and the International Bank for Reconstruction and

Development (World Bank) and International Monetary Fund (IMF) were set up in 1944. The UN was created in 1945 at the same time as the UN Educational, Scientific and Cultural Organization (UNESCO). These organizations, plus the International Trade Organization, which failed to materialize (*see Chapter 6 for details*), were to play complementary roles in building the conditions necessary for promoting peace, democracy and a stable, liberal world economic order.

The UN body was given only a limited role in promoting such development. The principal UN organs, including the Economic and Social Council (ECOSOC), were not seen as having a major operational role in advancing development, but rather as legitimating and coordinating development.

The General Assembly was established as the principle organ overseeing issues before the UN's member states and its Second Committee was made specifically responsible for economic development issues. However, in recent decades, the most important work in the development field has taken place in UN-sponsored conferences and special sessions of the Assembly. ECOSOC, comprised of regional and functional commissions that address nearly all development issues, was delegated the responsibility for promoting and coordinating the UN's development-related work.

The UN's early operational work in the development field began with the UN Expanded Programme of Technical Assistance set up to "create national infrastructures that would provide the basis for economic growth led by the private for-profit sector." During the 1960s, development activity began to focus more and more on persistent income inequalities between developed and developing countries.[1] An important benchmark was the establishment of the UN Conference on Trade and Development (UNCTAD) in 1964. And in 1965, the UN increased its technical assistance role to the poorer countries by creating the UN Development Programme (UNDP). Over the years, UNDP has grown to become the UN's largest source of development assistance and coordinator of the UN's development work. UNCTAD, which celebrated its 40th anniversary in 2004, continues in its role of integrating least developed countries into the UN's trade and development framework.

Building on the work of the UN's first three development decades (1960s-1980s), a number of major international conferences in the 1990s transformed and focused the global development debate. From these conferences, a more-or-less coherent programmatic framework for development emerged, which contained a consensual set of goals and objectives. These goals found their way into the Secretary-General's Millennium Report and subsequently the UN *Millennium Declaration*,[2] which was adopted unanimously by heads of state and governments at the Millennium Summit in 2000.

The Goals at Stake

The Millennium Development Goals (MDGs) themselves are specific goals with associated targets and indicators that serve to guide the UN's development efforts for eradicating poverty and associated social ills by the year 2015. The overall MDG process represents a strategic vision for mobilizing the international community for action. More specifically, the strategy is organized around eight main development goals and 18 related targets, as depicted in Table A.

Table A: The Millennium Development Goals and Targets

GOAL 1: ERADICATE EXTREME POVERTY AND HUNGER

Target 1 Halve, between 1990 and 2015, the proportion of people whose income is less than $1 a day

Target 2 Halve, between 1990 and 2015, the proportion of people who suffer from hunger

GOAL 2: ACHIEVE UNIVERSAL PRIMARY EDUCATION

Target 3 Ensure that, by 2015, children everywhere, boys and girls alike, will be able to complete a full course of primary schooling

GOAL 3: PROMOTE GENDER EQUALITY AND EMPOWER WOMEN

Target 4 Eliminate gender disparity in primary and secondary education, preferably by 2005, and to all levels of education no later than 2015

GOAL 4: REDUCE CHILD MORTALITY

Target 5 Reduce by two-thirds, between 1990 and 2015, the under-age-five mortality rate

GOAL 5: IMPROVE MATERNAL HEALTH

Target 6 Reduce by three-quarters, between 1990 and 2015, the maternal mortality ratio

GOAL 6: COMBAT HIV/AIDS, MALARIA AND OTHER DISEASES

Target 7 Have halted by 2015 and begun to reverse the spread of HIV/AIDS

Target 8 Have halted by 2015 and begun to reverse the incidence of malaria and other major diseases

GOAL 7: ENSURE ENVIRONMENTAL SUSTAINABILITY

Target 9 Integrate the principles of sustainable development into country policies and programs and reverse the loss of environmental resources

Target 10 Halve, by 2015, the proportion of people without sustainable access to safe drinking water

Target 11 By 2020, to have achieved a significant improvement in the lives of at least 100 million slum dwellers

GOAL 8: DEVELOP A GLOBAL PARTNERSHIP FOR DEVELOPMENT

Target 12 Develop further an open, rule-based, predictable, non-discriminatory trading and financial system (includes a commitment to good governance, development and poverty reduction—both nationally and internationally)

Target 13 Address the special needs of the least developed countries (LDCs) (includes tariff and quota-free access for LDC exports; enhanced program of debt relief for heavily indebted poor countries [HIPC] and cancellation of official bilateral debt; and more generous official development assistance [ODA] for countries committed to poverty reduction)

Target 14 Address the special needs of landlocked countries and small island developing states

Target 15 Deal comprehensively with the debt problems of developing countries through national and international measures to make debt sustainable in the long term

Target 16 In cooperation with developing countries, develop and implement strategies for decent and productive work for youth

Target 17 In cooperation with pharmaceutical companies, provide access to affordable, essential drugs in developing countries

Target 18 In cooperation with the private sector, make available the benefits of new technologies, especially information and communications

Source: "About the Goals," UN Millennium Development Goal website, 2004

A UN system-wide strategy has been designed for mobilizing support and monitoring progress toward achieving the MDGs. The strategy has four main components: the Millennium Project, Millennium Campaign, Millennium Development Goal Reports, and country-level monitoring and operational country-level activities. The Millennium Project was tasked with identifying the operational priorities, organizational means of implementation and financing structures necessary to achieve the MDGs. The project is directed by Columbia University Professor Jeffrey Sachs, who serves as special adviser to the Secretary-General. Ten expert task forces were set up to carry out the needed research. The project's interim report (hereafter referred to as the "Sachs Report") was published in January 2005 and is the focus of much of the discussion in this chapter.[3]

The Millennium Campaign is designed to mobilize support for the MDGs among member states. This task entails coaching member states on how to comply with the commitments and convincing them that greater consistency across trade, finance, education and other ministries is crucial.

Millennium Development Goal Reports (MDGRs) are, in essence, individual country report cards. Country-level operations represent the fourth, and most important, component of the MDG strategy. MDGR country-level monitoring entails collecting and analyzing data on progress toward achieving individual MDGs. This task is facilitated by the UN Development Group, which has provided a model reporting format and is also responsible for operational country-level activities. UN Country Teams assist countries in designing and implementing policies necessary for successful progress.

The Five-Year Review

Although the MDGs are stated in general, global terms, the Sachs Report drives home the point that they are, essentially, country-level goals. As such, one must be careful in interpreting the seeming overall "progress" toward achieving any single goal. Since the intent of the MDG process is to raise the standard of living of the poorest peoples of the world and to eliminate extreme poverty and the conditions that coexist with it, "it is the poorest countries making the least progress that the *Millennium Declaration* and the Millennium Development Goals are meant to support, not the ones making the most progress even without the Goals."[4]

It is especially important to state this up front, given that much of the "global" progress made so far is the result of progress made in two countries with extremely large populations: China and India. In addition, operationalizing the goals and transforming them into policy initiatives must be done at the country-level and below. Poverty reduction is viewed as the primary responsibility of the developing countries themselves, and governments need to be held accountable to make serious efforts to attain them. This latter point emerged as a fundamental element of the *Monterrey Consensus*, which the Sachs Report calls the "fulcrum" of the MDGs. The consensus that was formalized at the 2002 International Conference on Financing for Development articulated the framework for a global development partnership between developed and developing countries for joint action to reduce poverty. Special emphasis was placed on responding to the needs of the least developed countries (LDCs), African countries, landlocked countries and small island developing states. It reaffirmed the call for rich donor countries to increase their international development assistance to the 0.7 percent gross national product (GNP) level—a target that for a long time had been little more than an elusive pipe dream. As the report puts it, no "well intended" impoverished country is to be left behind.[5]

Regional Progress

In global terms, some progress can be noted since 1990 in certain MDG indicators. Gross domestic product (GDP) per capita in the Global South, for example, rose by more than 21 percent. Headcount poverty decreased from 28 to 21 percent. Prevalence of undernourishment decreased from 20 to 17 percent. Under-age-five mortality declined from 103 per 1,000 live births to 88. Access to improved drinking water supplies and sanitation facilities rose from 71 to 79 percent and 34 to 49 percent, respectively. There also have been notable disappointments—in particular, the increased incidence of HIV infection.[6]

Any optimism provided by such statistics is tempered by tremendous differences both across and within regions. In certain parts of the developing world, conditions remain stagnant, if not worse. Many of the positive trends are taking place in eastern and southern Asia. Even there, much progress can be accounted for by strides made in China and India, as noted above. Yet other parts of Asia have also registered significant improvements.

In stark contrast, sub-Saharan Africa is not on track with regard to achieving any of the goals. Here, the poverty rate actually rose slightly since 1990 and HIV/AIDS rages on in pandemic proportions. Some progress can be noted with respect to universal primary schooling, reducing gender disparity in education, women's equal representation in national parliaments and improving access to safe drinking water in rural areas. However, even in these areas, the region is lagging far behind targets for attaining the goals by 2015. As in other regions, not only are there marked variations from country to country in Africa, but also within countries, especially between urban and rural populations.

The results in other regions can be succinctly summarized as follows with intra-regional variations discussed below. North Africa is largely on track with respect to reducing extreme poverty and child mortality, and ensuring environmental sustainability. It is moving in the right direction on most other goals, with the notable exception of youth unemployment, which remains high. In East Asia, significant improvements have been made in some goals—reduction of poverty, hunger, gender disparity in education and infant health, with lags in others—pockets of poverty, reducing hunger, access to safe drinking water, sanitation, high tuberculosis (TB) rates and improving the lives of slum dwellers. Southeast Asia has witnessed similar strides—improvement in some goals, such as poverty, hunger, gender parity in education, child mortality—and lagging in other goals, such as access to safe drinking water, universal primary education and sustainable development. With regard to youth unemployment, ground is being lost here as it is in almost every other region. South Asia is on track with regard to the eradication of poverty, provision of safe drinking water in both rural and urban areas and sanitation in urban areas. It is lagging in most other goals and losing ground on HIV/AIDS. Simply put, both West Asia and Oceania are off track for most goals. The Latin American and Caribbean region is on track for hunger, education, gender parity, child health and urban drinking water, but lagging in sustainable development (especially deforestation) and sanitation, and losing ground with regard to youth unemployment. Finally, both poverty and hunger continue as major problems in countries that are part of the Commonwealth of Independent States (CIS) in Europe and Central Asia. In other areas, there is some progress, but mostly lagging, with serious environmental concerns and a growing prevalence of HIV/AIDS and TB. With regard to universal primary education, Asian CIS countries are on track as a group, but European CIS country rates still remain below those of 1990. The high point in both parts of the CIS is gender equality, for which the targets have either been met or are on track.

Reasons for Failure

The Sachs Report identifies four reasons why the world is not on track for attaining the MDGs to date: governance failures, poverty traps, pockets of poverty and policy neglect. Good governance is seen as essential for development. Sustained economic growth can flounder if governments fail to uphold the rule of law, pursue sound economic policies that ensure a proper balance between public and private sectors, protect basic human rights and encourage and support the growth (e.g., capacity-building of health and education) of civil society. [7]

When a large portion of the population is mired in extreme poverty, it is difficult if not impossible to make investments needed to reach the goals. Such a situation is dubbed a "poverty trap"—where the economy is too poor to achieve robust and sustained economic growth or sometimes even to grow at all. Poverty traps are common in least developed countries. In this context, the Sachs Report stresses the importance for countries to develop long-term strategies tailored to local conditions to climb out of the trap, such as making appropriate investments in agriculture and human capital development. In the poorest countries, it will require a "big push" in order to meet the 2015 MDG target.[8]

Also problematic are entrenched pockets of poverty. Even when countries have been able to make significant economic development strides, the advances are highly uneven, leaving many people mired in poverty. The gaps may be geographic, ethnic, rural versus urban, or "haves" versus "have-nots" (slum dwellers). Regardless, they often place a substantial drag on overall economic growth and sustainable human development.[9]

Finally, in many cases, the MDGs are not being met because of specific policy neglect. At play may be poor public administration, inadequate public infrastructure, powerless ministries, lack of public investment capacity, or specific policy biases such as ethnic bias.[10] The Ugandan government's forced relocation of 1.6 million Acholi people into Internally Displaced Persons (IDP) camps is one of the most glaring examples of such policymaking.

How to Get on Course

The Sachs Report argues that even for the poorest countries, the MDGs are still achievable. Attaining the goals, of course, requires the political will to do so and intensive efforts by all parties. The report makes specific recommendations in several areas, each of which is discussed below.

MDG-based Poverty Reduction Strategies

A critical element for achieving the MDGs is to frame them as concrete policy objectives in the country context, not as abstract global goals. The Sachs Report proposes a major shift in development thinking and practice. Instead of thinking about how to accelerate progress to achieve the goals, the report calls for an integrated "MDG-plus" strategy focused on what it will take to achieve the goals. Specifically, the report argues that development planners need to think and work back from the 2015 targets and timelines. If the goals are to be attained, "what sequence of investments and policies is required and what constraints, financial and otherwise, need to be overcome?"[11]

This recommendation calls for UN member states to place the MDGs at the center of their overall poverty reduction strategy. It also entails the production of a detailed assessment of countries' public investment requirements.[12]

Public Investments

Poor developing countries are confronted with severe resource constraints. The Sachs Report recommends that MDG-based poverty reduction strategies be designed around seven public investment policy "clusters." Extreme poverty is often centered on the smallholder farm. Thus, major investments are needed to increase agricultural productivity of smallholder farmers, raise rural incomes and expand rural access to essential public services and infrastructure needed to get farm products to markets. In urban areas, new investments are needed to promote job creation in the manufacturing sector, increase security of tenure, expand city-wide infrastructure and upgrade living conditions of slum dwellers. Universal access to education and essential health services are key as well, and require substantial public investment, which is all too often lacking. New major investments are required to ensure universal primary education and to expand secondary and higher education. More aggressive public support and investment is needed to overcome pervasive gender bias and to promote gender equality and empowerment of women. Investment is needed in improved resource management for providing clean water, food, disease control and other conditions of a healthy environment. Lastly, science and technology as foundations are needed to build national capacities. Here, investments are required to expand science and technology education, promote business opportunities in science and technology, and promote related infrastructure development. Each of these public investment clusters are interdependent and need to be treated in integrated planning terms.[13]

Rapid Scale-Up

Given the broad range of policy interventions required and the need to reach large parts of the population in order to put countries on track for achieving the MDGs, national programs need to be rapidly scaled up. The Sachs Report outlines specific actions in this regard. First, concrete policy objectives and associated action plans, with effective political leadership, need to be established. Second, governments need to launch special initiatives targeted to build national and local capacity in public management, infrastructure and human resources. A main objective in this regard is to enhance direct service delivery. Reproducible and appropriate local delivery mechanisms that complement other policy interventions need to be utilized. Finally, effective monitoring systems are required that will enable those implementing the scale-up to make mid-course corrections. Making scale-up work requires both putting communities at the center of the process, and providing long-term funding commitments and technical support from the outside.[14]

Good Governance

As noted above, the Sachs Report boldly asserts that good governance is a crucial prerequisite for successful rapid scale-up. It is important to distinguish between bad volition (i.e., corruption) and weak governance (i.e., inadequate capacity). In the case of bad volition, there is little hope of attaining the MDGs through governmental means. In cases where capacity is the problem, investment in capacity-building, public administration and policy reforms may make a major difference. In either case, enhancing the role of civil society in the policy process and promoting sound economic policies in support of the private sector should help.[15]

Civil Society and Private Sector Contributions

Civil society, although often overlooked, is a key component to achieving the MDGs. Communities and nongovernmental organizations (NGOs), among others, can help to facilitate poverty reduction strategies in several ways. Not only can they serve as important advocates for the MDGs in local and national contexts, but they also can identify priority investments, mobilize resources, create implementation strategies and ensure that women, the poor and other often marginalized groups are included. Finally, civil society organizations can serve as valuable partners for monitoring and evaluating MDG-oriented programs.[16]

The private sector can contribute to poverty reduction as well. By increasing productivity, for example, private business can increase employment as well as wages. Public-private partnerships can assist in enhancing the delivery of critical services. Advocacy for MDGs is another important potential role for private business leaders, who often occupy influential roles in local communities.[17]

Africa's Special Needs

Not only is sub-Saharan Africa not on track for achieving any of the MDGs, conditions there are utterly intolerable from the perspective of most of the world's population. Depicted in the Sachs Report as being stuck in a poverty trap, the region has been especially vulnerable due to high transport costs and small markets, low agricultural productivity, a very high disease burden, a history of adverse geopolitics and very slow diffusion of technology from abroad. Since most of the population in sub-Saharan Africa is concentrated in interior areas, the cost of getting goods to and from ports is relatively much greater than in most other regions. Also, transportation infrastructures in the region do not facilitate long over-land transit. Most national markets in Africa are small and have limited access to global trade. Even though agriculture is a mainstay for most African economies, most African farmers are faced with severe constraints. Adequate water is a major concern, for example, as is poor soil nutrition. The fact that Africa is home to roughly three-quarters of the world's annual HIV/AIDS-related deaths does not help matters.[18]

Despite these conditions, the Sachs Report presents a hopeful perspective on the region's ability to attain the MDGs. The keys are good governance and adequate public investment in several priority areas: rural and urban development; health; education; human resources; gender equality; science, technology and innovation; regional integration; and public sector management.[19]

Investment Priorities

Development is not a "one-size-fits-all" proposition, the Sachs Report reminds the world. Development investment priorities in other regions are likely to be quite different than in sub-Saharan Africa, for example. While East Asia is home to 271 million poor people, it has been one of the fastest growing regions of the world in recent decades. Economic progress in the region has been marked by contrasts both across and within countries. China, where over one third of the region's poor reside, has led the way in economic growth with an average growth rate of 8.2 percent over the past two decades. Yet, even within China, stark contrasts persist between coastal provinces that have shown remarkable vibrancy and rural western and central provinces that lag behind. In countries in East Asia that remain seriously off track to meeting the goals, such as Cambodia, Indonesia, Lao People's Democratic Republic, and Myanmar, investments are needed in: healthcare, education and social service delivery; rural infrastructure and agriculture; environmental management, science and technology development; and public management.

In South Asia, priority investment areas include: basic education, nutrition and health services; rural infrastructure and poverty alleviation; slum upgrading; public management; environmental management; and conflict-resolution and peace-building. In this region, India has been the strong performer, but, again, sub-national variations are considerable.

To reverse declines in Central Asian countries, the report proposes ratcheting-up investment in a number of areas, including urban and rural infrastructure development, cross-border cooperation in critical capacity-building areas, public management, health service delivery systems and modernizing and improving education.

Although somewhat better situated with regard to achieving the MDGs than most other developing regions, Latin America's sluggish economic growth needs a boost. Here, the Sachs Report calls for: MDG-based investments; targeting marginalized regions and populations; upgrading slum, urban and rural infrastructure development; science and technology research and education; cross-border cooperation; environmental management and healthcare, especially toward HIV/AIDS.

In the Middle East and North Africa, both strong regional approaches and national action are called for, paying special attention to problems such as rapidly growing unemployment. The latter is the result of an exploding youth population and urban density pressures.

In many of the transition and CIS countries in eastern and Central Europe, there are critical investment deficits. A priority investment area is governance and public management. Other regional groupings that need special investment priority include LDCs, landlocked countries, small island developing states and countries vulnerable to natural hazards. In each case, the investment priorities differ. For landlocked developing countries, for example, investments in cross-border cooperation, trade facilitation and infrastructure development are crucial for assuring access to world markets and needed goods and services. Remote small island states, on the other hand, have very special investment needs in information and communication technology development, and environmental issues.[20]

Strategies for Countries Marred by Conflict

Unfortunately, more than half of the LDCs farthest away from achieving the MDGs are, or have recently been, involved in conflict. Others have experienced serious stress from nature, such as those countries plagued by natural disasters or persistent civil strife. In each, it is difficult to focus resources on reducing poverty, improving human well-being and promoting sustainable human development. Dubbed as "fragile states," MDG-based development strategies in these areas need to pay explicit attention to conflict prevention and risk management.

The Sachs Report calls for scaling up MDG-related conflict prevention programs and poverty reduction strategies that facilitate narrowing ethnic, racial and other divisions within communities. They should focus on the development of decentralized and participatory decision-making structures and processes that directly involve marginalized groups. Increased transparency, accountability and specific investments should be included.

For countries already engaged in conflict, the first priority is, of course, to reduce and stop the conflict. Here, good management is essential as is adequate and well-placed humanitarian assistance. The report argues that "donor agencies should aim to provide ongoing MDG-based financial and technical assistance to maintain or restore basic infrastructure and the provision of social services, delivered in a way that reaches refugees and people in conflict zones without worsening the conflict."[21] In cases where the government is no longer credible, external support for the government may worsen the situation. Support will therefore need to be channeled through multilateral agencies or NGOs. In post-conflict situations, large investments may need to be focused on war-torn areas, IDPs, the rebuilding of basic infrastructure and administrative capacity and service delivery capabilities.

Foreign Aid

The international development assistance support system lags far behind the requirements to make the MDG process successful. The Sachs Report identifies 10 central problems. First, little serious emphasis has been placed on improving the operational relationship between development donors and recipients. Second, the partnership between donors and recipients does not address country-level needs systematically; there is no coherent set of operational objectives. In this context, donors tend to stress the crucial importance of good governance in the development process, yet aid flows tend to concentrate on governments that are emerging from conflict and where governance is weak. Third, while development is a long-term process, most processes operate with a short-term perspective. Fourth, although most poor countries require technical support to scale up investments, those international agencies most capable of providing such knowledge have been asked to concentrate on sector-specific small pilot projects. Fifth, multilateral agencies have not been effectively coordinating their assistance activities. In fact, they often find themselves in competition for donor government funding. Sixth, development assistance is not framed or organized to respond effectively to recipient needs. Seventh, the targets for debt relief are often based on arbitrarily set indicators rather than on MDG-based needs. Also, the quality of bilateral aid is often a problem. It tends to be unpredictable, driven by donor desires—sometimes geopolitically determined—as opposed to recipient needs. Ninth, major MDG priorities are systematically overlooked. Finally, policy incoherence is pervasive.[22]

For each of these 10 "don'ts," the report offers a list of 10 "do's." For example, donor assistance needs to be coordinated effectively at the country level in the field and a much larger share of ODA should be provided in the form of budget support in countries that are well governed. In summary, development partnerships need to be MDG-based and recipient-need oriented.

Trade

The current global trading order represents an unbalanced playing field for poor developing countries. In the context of the MDG process, two important trade issues are at stake: improving market access and terms of trade vis-à-vis developed countries, and improving competitiveness for low-income countries' exports through investments in infrastructure and trade facilitation.

Unfortunately, the sense of euphoria that had emerged from the November 2001 launching of the Doha Round of World Trade Organization (WTO) negotiations has withered (see Chapter 6 for details). The Sachs Report recommends that the WTO move forward, before 2025, on the total elimination of barriers on all merchandise trade, on increased liberalization on trade in services, and on universal enforcement of the principles of reciprocity and nondiscrimination in a way that reinforces the attainment of the MDGs.

Furthermore, the report proposes specific actions on three persistent problem areas for developing countries: agriculture, nonagricultural market access and trade in services. Also, since developing countries tend to be in positions that do not enable them to benefit as fully as developed countries do from free trade, there is need for poorer countries to receive short-term adjustment assistance.[23]

Regional and Global Goods

The Sachs Report argues that country-level investment, ODA, trade reforms and debt relief will likely not be enough to achieve the MDGs in most countries. Increased investment in regional and global goods is therefore required and the regional context of national development is important. This is not only true for market expansion, economic growth and trade, but also for access to vital resources, and for a peaceful and ecologically sound environment. The report recommends that the international community support the development of four types of regional goods: infrastructure for transportation, energy and water management; coordination mechanisms needed for managing trans-boundary environmental issues; institutions to promote economic cooperation; and mechanisms for political cooperation to promote good governance.

Yet, the provision of regional goods remains grossly underfunded. This is the case even in respect to situations where regional infrastructure strategies exist, such as the New Partnership for Africa's Development. The report proposes reversing this trend by increasing direct international funding of regional organizations and making more development assistance funds available through regional institutions.

Increased investment of global goods is also critical for achieving the MDGs, especially with regard to mobilizing global science and technology, and fighting environmental degradation. In many cases, new technologies may unlock the doors to enhanced development opportunities.

MDG Summit +5

In September 2005, the General Assembly will convene a special high-level meeting of heads of state and governments in New York to discuss the issues surrounding the MDGs and their progress. In fact, General Assembly Resolution 145 called on the president of the Assembly to convene "informal interactive hearings" with representatives of NGOs, civil society and the private sector to provide input for the summit. These hearing were held June 23-24, 2005 at UN headquarters in New York. The Millennium Project report and its associated task force reports, along with the reports of the High-level Panel on Threats, Challenges and Change and the report of the Secretary-General, will serve as the major background papers for the summit.

In his report, Secretary-General Kofi Annan endorsed many of the recommendations of the Sachs Report. He called on governments to implement national development strategies that were bold enough to meet the MDGs and stressed the need for good governance, including the role of civil society in that regard. He called for dynamic growth-oriented policies aimed at promoting a vibrant private sector and endorsed the need for greatly increased public investment in the seven priority sectors as outlined by the Sachs Report.

SG Annan focused heavily on MDG 8 and reiterated proposals for enhancing trade and finance for development. Specifically, he stressed the need for the international donor community to establish concrete strategies for reaching the target ODA goal of 0.7 percent of GNP. As a means to this end, he called on member states to support the United Kingdom initiative to establish an International Financial Facility and to move forward on the Sachs Report's proposal for "Quick Wins," a set of actions that developed and developing nations can jointly launch to move forward the MDGs. He also reiterated the report's recommendations for debt relief, trade enhancement and ensuring environmental sustainability.[24]

Regarding global action, SG Annan focused on the need for an enhanced infectious disease surveillance and monitoring system, and revision of the International Health Regulations (*see Chapter 5*). Among other things, he reiterated the call for the establishment of a worldwide early warning system for natural hazards and reflected on the international community's responsibilities with regard to meeting the special needs of Africa.[25]

The MDG Targets—Where Are We Now?

The following section outlines in detail where the world stands in regard to meeting the Millennium Development Goals, according to target (*see* Table A). While each goal and the respective target(s) are reviewed, only those indicators for which reliable data exists are reviewed.

Goal 1: Eradicate Extreme Poverty and Hunger

Target 1: Halving, between 1990 and 2015, the number of people living on less than $1 a day

Eradication of extreme poverty lies at the heart of the MDG process. Yet, as we near the end of the First UN Decade for the Eradication of Poverty (1997-2006), the score card is mixed, if not outright disappointing. While the population of the Global South increased by more than one billion persons, the proportion of persons living in extreme poverty (that is on less than $1 a day) declined from 28 percent to 21 percent. In the same time period, the rate of undernourishment decreased 3 percent. Yet these are aggregated figures, camouflaging regional and sub-regional variations. Moreover, the tremendous strides made by the two most populous countries in the Global South, China and India, make such generalized observations misleading. As cautioned in the Sachs Report, "With more than 2.3 billion people in [China and India] alone, their major advances in poverty reduction drive developing world averages."[26] Advances in other East and South Asian countries have contributed to the substantial overall reduction in the region as well. Nonetheless, these two regions still contain the absolute largest number of poor people in the world.

At the other extreme is Africa, where just under half of the people live in extreme poverty. In North Africa, including portions of the Middle East, extreme poverty levels are very low and have remained so—at roughly 2 percent. In sub-Saharan Africa, however, over the last decade, the poverty rate rose from 45 percent to 46 percent, with almost 100 million more persons living on less than $1 a day. In 33 African countries, the average per capita GDP would not buy a half-a-cup of coffee in the United States—a mere 71 cents a day. In between is the Latin American and Caribbean region, where little change has occurred, and eastern Europe and Central Asia, where poverty is dramatically on the rise.[27]

One of the main indicators of Target 1 is the poverty-gap ratio, calculated by multiplying the percentage of people below the poverty line by the difference between the poverty line and their average consumption. The ratio for sub-Saharan Africa is almost three times greater than the next most impoverished region, southern Asia.[28]

Target 2: Halving, between 1990 and 2015, the proportion of people suffering from hunger

In the 1990s, the percent of the population in the developing world suffering from undernourishment—defined as food consumption insufficient to meet minimum levels of dietary energy requirements—fell slightly from 20 to 17 percent. In absolute terms, the number of undernourished people declined by only 19 million during the decade. Most of this gain, however, can be accounted for by improvements in large population countries in East and Southeast Asia. In the rest of the developing world and in most developing countries, undernourishment increased.[29]

According to the Sachs Report, only Latin America and the Caribbean, and parts of Asia have fewer undernourished people than a decade ago. In West Asia and Asian parts of CIS, the rate of undernourishment is increasing. Undernourishment remains very high in sub-Saharan Africa, South Asia and Oceania. The situation is most alarming in sub-Saharan Africa. Here, agricultural output per hectare is the lowest in the world and per capita food production has been declining. Among other factors, the loss of productive capacity resulting from the AIDS pandemic has taken a large toll.

The World Bank splits undernourishment into two categories: general prevalence of undernourishment and malnourished children, the latter of which is a major cause of child death. In this category, South and East Asia and the Pacific, Latin America and the Caribbean, and low and middle income economies on the whole have reduced child malnutrition by around 25 percent since 1990. Sub-Saharan Africa has seen a minimal reduction, while North Africa and the Middle East have witnessed an increase in child malnutrition.

In summary, the *Human Development Report 2002* (UNDP) found that the target of halving, between 1990 and 2015, the proportion of people suffering from hunger was being met in only 3 percent of countries, while 46 percent were on track. The other 51 percent were either lagging, slipping back or provided no data.

Goal 2: Achieve Universal Primary Education

Target 3: Ensure that, by 2015, children everywhere, boys and girls alike, will be able to complete a full course of primary schooling

Education is not only inextricably and dynamically linked to development, but it also can serve as an important gateway to poverty reduction and the attainment of other MDGs. Five years into the MDG process, several regions—North Africa, East Asia, Latin America and the Caribbean, and Asian CIS countries—are on track for achieving this goal. Overall, developing country primary school completion rates average 81 percent. Some progress is being made in South Asia and Oceania as well, but Southeast Asia and West Asia are lagging behind, and completion rates are actually declining in Eastern CIS countries. The region of greatest concern is, again, sub-Saharan Africa, where completion rates persistently hover around 50 percent. South Asia comes next at only around 70 percent.

In individual country terms, 86 nations are at risk for not achieving this MDG and, of these, 27 are seriously off track (i.e., they have a projected rate of completion of below 50 percent).[30]

Goal 3: Promote Gender Equality and Empower Women

Target 4: Eliminate gender disparity in primary and secondary education, preferably by 2005, and to all levels of education by 2015

Gender equality and the empowerment of women are viewed as essential components of sustainable human development. Thus, in addition to being targets in themselves, they are seen as requisites for attaining the other MDGs. The Millennium Project uses four indicators for this target: girls' equal enrollment in primary and secondary school, literacy parity between men and women, the share of employed women in the non-agricultural sector and women's equal representation in national parliaments. For the latter, all regions, with the exception of Latin America and the Caribbean—where significant increases were made between 1990 and 2004, have registered little progress. For the other indicators, progress has been limited and uneven.

In general, the situation with primary education has vastly improved since 1990. Yet this target is clearly not being met on the global scale. In the context of the 2015 target date, the situation looks better, but sub-Saharan Africa, South Asia and West Asia are lagging. Even in these regions, intra-regional differences provide some hope. Botswana, Lesotho, Namibia and Mauritius, for example, have already reached or surpassed the one-to-one ratio for primary school enrollment. Bangladesh has achieved a ratio of 1.02, and the Maldives of 0.99. In West Asia, excluding Iraq and Yemen, the other countries all have ratios above 0.90.[31]

Gender equality in secondary education, however, lags well behind primary education. While two regions have achieved parity, sub-Saharan Africa, South Asia and West Asia have registered no significant change and Oceania is showing only minimal progress. In South Asia, the parity ratio of girls to boys in secondary education stands at 0.79. It is only slightly higher in sub-Saharan Africa and western Asia at 0.79. In a few large countries, like India and Pakistan, fewer than 75 girls per 100 boys are enrolled in secondary education.[32]

Because literacy rates are closely associated with school enrollment levels, the figures in this particular target are not much different. Eastern Asia, south-eastern Asia, Latin America and the Caribbean, and the regions of the CIS have all achieved literacy parity. The other regions have made advancements but are lagging far behind. Southern Asia has the lowest overall regional rate at 72.5. Sub-Saharan Africa and North Africa also fall below 80, at 76.6 and 78.5, respectively. Oceania stands at 81.3 and western Asia at 85.6.[33]

The proportion of women in wage employment in the non-agricultural sector has increased in 93 of the 131 countries covered by the Millennium Project. However, women still generally find it difficult to enter the non-agricultural workforce. In only two regions—European CIS and Latin America and the Caribbean—do women make up more than 40 percent of the workforce outside this grouping. As of 2003, three regions were just at, or under, 20 percent: northern Africa (21.5 percent), western Asia (20 percent) and southern Asia (18 percent). Every region registered positive movement between 1990 and 2002.[34]

Goal 4: Reduce Child Mortality

Target 5: Reduce by two-thirds, between 1990 and 2015, the under-age-five mortality rate

Only a few regions are doing well with this target: North Africa, Southeast Asia, Latin America and the Caribbean, and European CIS countries. In sub-Saharan Africa, child mortality remains extremely high at 172 per 1,000 live births; the situation remains basically unchanged from 1990. According to the UNDP's *2002 Human Development Report*, only seven countries in the region were on track to achieving the goal. Twenty-four countries were far behind and 10 were slipping back. At the same time, 13 of the 25 countries in Central and eastern Europe and the CIS were far behind and two were slipping back. While registering progress, the child mortality rate in South Asia remains very high, second only to sub-Saharan Africa.

Goal 5: Improve Maternal Health

Target 6: Reduce by three-quarters, between 1990 and 2015, the maternal mortality ratio

The primary indicator used by the MDG project to gauge maternal health-care is maternal mortality. Sadly, not a single region is on track to meet Target 6. Maternal mortality rates—measured as the number of maternal deaths per 100,000 live births—remain alarmingly high in nearly every MDG region.

Sub-Saharan Africa has the most alarming ratio, which stands at 1,100 per 100,000. The lifetime risk for women in this region of dying during childbirth is one in 16. Sub-Saharan Africa is followed by northern Africa with a maternal mortality ratio of 450 and South Asia with a ratio of 410. Afghanistan, in particular, has the highest maternal mortality rate in the world. Iran falls at the other end with a rate of 76, while India and Pakistan are in between with rates of 540 and 500 respectively. Only in eastern Asia and in the regions of the CIS are maternal-mortality levels considered low. But even in eastern Asia, the ratio, which stands at 55, is two-and-a-half times that of the developed countries' average.[35] Clearly, the world has a long way to go to achieve MDG 5.[36]

Goal 6: Combat HIV/AIDS, Malaria and Other Diseases

Target 7: Have halted by 2015 and begun to reverse the spread of HIV/AIDS

As noted in Chapter 5, the global total of infected persons has reached its highest level ever, standing at around 40 million. Between 2002 and 2004, the number of persons living with HIV/AIDS increased nearly 50 percent in East Asia. Eastern Europe and Central Asia followed closely behind with a 40 percent increase. The Caribbean is home to the second-highest rate of HIV infection with a rate of 2.3 percent. Scarily, AIDS-related diseases are now the leading cause of death for persons aged 15 to 44 years in this region.[37]

Sub-Saharan Africa remains the most-affected region, with nearly two-thirds of all persons living with HIV and more than one-third of all AIDS-related deaths found here. Women and girls are increasingly affected, and sub-Saharan Africa is home to over three quarters of all women living with HIV. If there is any good news in the region, it is that HIV prevalence in sub-Saharan Africa appears to have stabilized at around 7.4 percent of the entire population. Also, it should be noted that there are many different AIDS epidemics in Africa, both across and within sub-regions and countries. West and Central Africa have relatively low infection rates compared to other sub-regions, for example. On the other hand, South Africa has the single largest number of infected persons: 5.3 million.

Target 8: Have halted by 2015 and begun to reverse the incidence of malaria and other major diseases

Malaria is the world's most common tropical disease, spread by mosquitoes and, as described in Chapter 5, endemic to large parts of the developing world. The vast majority of deaths (90 percent) are in sub-Saharan Africa and up to 90 percent of those victims are children under age five. Malaria-related deaths of young children in South and East Africa nearly doubled between 1990 and 1998 in comparison to the previous decade. Additionally, East Asia, southern Asia, and Latin America and the Caribbean are at moderate risk. While other regions are lower risk, no region is on track or achieving the target of halting or reversing the spread of malaria by 2015.[38]

With regard to tuberculosis (TB), once again, no region is on track or achieving this target. In fact, more than one third of the world's population is infected with TB. Low- and middle-income countries account for 90 percent of all cases. Luckily, most persons infected with the virus will never develop active TB. However, because HIV promotes the progression of latent TB, it is the leading cause of death of HIV-infected persons. It is also one of the leading causes of death of women of reproductive age. In sub-Saharan Africa, over three quarters of all persons with HIV/AIDS develop active TB. Twelve of the 15 countries in the world with TB infection rates over 400 per 100,000 are in the region, and most of these countries also are among the highest with regard to HIV prevalence. Swaziland has the highest number of both HIV and TB infections per capita. Its TB infection rate is a whopping 1,067 per 100,000. Although per capita rates are lower in the Southeast Asian region than in sub-Saharan Africa, 35 percent of all TB cases are found here. Added to this is the Western Pacific region, which includes Cambodia, China and Vietnam, with an estimated 22 percent of global cases. In western Asia, Latin America and the Caribbean, and northern Africa, TB incidence rates are low and declining.[39]

Goal 7: Ensure Environmental Sustainability

Gail Karlsson

The High-level Panel on Threats, Challenges and Change identified environmental degradation as one of the leading threats to world security. In its discussion of ways to prevent these threats from endangering international security, the panel observed that there is insufficient coherence in global environmental protection efforts at the global level, and that environmental concerns are rarely factored into security, development or humanitarian strategies. The panel recommended that ECOSOC provide greater leadership on the interconnections between different types of threats and focus on integrating the major themes of the MDGs.[40]

The recommendations put forward by the Sachs Report also highlighted the interconnections among the MDGs, stressing that poverty reduction strategies should include attention to environmental sustainability, access to water and sanitation needs.[41]

Target 9: Integrate principles of sustainable development into country policies and programs and reverse the loss of environmental resources

The Secretary-General's March 2005 *In Larger Freedom* report drew on the Millennium Project recommendations, advising countries to adopt time-bound environmental targets and to make new investments in resource management.[42] Then, in April 2005, the comprehensive Millennium Ecosystem Assessment, called for by SG Annan at the 2000 General Assembly, was released after years of work by nearly 1,400 experts from 95 countries. Two of its key messages were that "humans have made unprecedented changes to ecosystems in recent decades to meet growing demands for food, fresh water, fiber and energy," and that "the loss of services derived from ecosystems is a significant barrier to the achievement of the [MDGs]."[43]

The assessment's board members warned that human activity is putting such a strain on the earth's natural functions that its ability to support future generations cannot be taken for granted. They offered three recommendations: costs to natural ecosystems should be taken into account in all economic decisions so that nature's services are not treated as being free and limitless; local communities should be involved in conserving natural resources and receive a fairer share of their benefits; and protection of natural assets should be integrated into the central decision-making of governments and businesses, rather than being left to relatively weak environmental departments.

Indicators for measuring progress toward achieving Target 9 include protection of forests and biodiversity, reductions in climate change emissions, increased energy efficiency and expanded access to modern energy, and protection of the ozone layer. Progress in each is discussed below.

FORESTS

The Sachs Report indicated that, to date, only three regions are meeting the goal of reversing forest loss: East Asia and the European and Asian members of CIS. The Millennium Project's Task Force on Environmental Sustainability pointed out that forests contribute directly to the livelihoods of 90 percent of the world's 1.2 billion people living in extreme poverty by providing food, fuel, shelter, fresh water, fiber, bush meat and genetic resources. The primary causes of forest destruction are agricultural expansion, urbanization, and mining and energy production, aided by indiscriminate logging practices.[44]

Moreover, there is still no international treaty on protection of forests. That possibility is being considered by the UN Forum on Forests, which met again in May 2005 to review the effectiveness of international arrangements on forests and to discuss developing a comprehensive legal framework on all types of forests. Negotiations are also still ongoing regarding the financial structure and objectives for a successor to the 1994 International Tropical Timber Agreement on sustainable management of tropical forests.[45]

Closely linked to deforestation is the devastating impact of desertification, as a result of which hundreds of millions of people are at risk of becoming environmental refugees. The parties to the *Convention to Combat Desertification* last met between August 25 and September 5, 2003, with a seventh session scheduled to meet in Bonn, Germany, in October 2005. Effective action to implement the convention is particularly important in sub-Saharan Africa, where food supplies are decreasing and water is often "mined" from groundwater sources that are not replenished by rain or rivers.

BIODIVERSITY

In January 2005, UNESCO hosted an international conference with the theme, "Biodiversity 2005," to discuss global efforts to slow down the rate of species loss. The parties to the *Convention on Biological Diversity* have set out to: "achieve by 2010 a significant reduction of the current rate of biodiversity loss...as a contribution to poverty alleviation and to the benefit of all life on earth." In 2002, this objective was endorsed by the World Summit on Sustainable Development. Despite this international commitment, the Millennium Ecosystem Assessment reported that: "Human activities have taken the planet to the edge of a massive wave of species extinctions, further threatening our own well-being."[46] In his report, SG Annan observed that the unprecedented rate of biodiversity loss, which is worrying in its own right, also undermines people's health, livelihoods, food production, water supplies, and vulnerability to natural disasters and climate change.[47]

The 13th conference of the parties to the *Convention on International Trade in Endangered Species of Wild Fauna and Flora* met in Bangkok to review the status of particular species and consider improved implementation of the convention through economic incentives, guidelines for sustainable use and synergies with the Convention on Biological Diversity.

CLIMATE CHANGE AND ENERGY

The Secretary-General identified climate change as one of the greatest challenges of the 21st century.[48] Some of the anticipated negative effects of climate change on development goals include sea level rise and flooding, spread of tropical diseases, decreases in agricultural productivity, water scarcity and disturbance of ecosystems. Unless mitigated, climate change is likely to undermine efforts to achieve the MDGs.[49]

The entry into force of the *Kyoto Protocol* in February 2005, after ratification by Russia in October 2004, represented an important step forward in the international response to climate change threats, despite lack of support from the US. In December 2005, Canada will host the first Meeting of the Parties to the *Kyoto Protocol* in Montreal, in conjunction with the 11th session of the Conference of the Parties to the *UN Framework Convention on Climate Change* (the umbrella of the *Kyoto Protocol*). Even if fully implemented, however, the protocol will not be sufficient to prevent global warming caused by greenhouse gases that have already accumulated in the atmosphere and are still being emitted. The High-level Panel urged governments to "reflect on the gap between the promise of the *Kyoto Protocol*, re-engage on the problem of global warming and begin new negotiations to produce a new long-term strategy for reducing global warming beyond the period covered by the protocol (2012)." Those discussions began with a "seminar" for government experts in May 2005 in Bonn, Germany, to promote an informal exchange of views on effective mitigation and adaptation responses to climate change.

The UN Commission on Sustainable Development (CSD) will also be considering climate change and energy issues at its annual meetings in 2006 and 2007. Much of the focus will be on expanding access to modern energy sources in developing countries.

Both the High-level Panel and the Millennium Project Task Force on Environmental Sustainability emphasized the need for governments to promote low-emission, renewable energy sources and phase out subsidies for fossil fuels.[50]

OZONE LAYER

Recently, the Intergovernmental Panel on Climate Change, with SG Annan's praises, has been working in cooperation with the Technology and Economic Assessment Panel of the *Montreal Protocol on Substances that Deplete the Ozone Layer* to consider the effects of substances that both deplete the ozone layer and also contribute to greenhouse gas accumulation problems.[51] There are some chemical alternatives to ozone-depleting substances that are acceptable in terms of ozone layer impacts but have the drawback of being significant greenhouse gases.

Under the *Montreal Protocol*, developed countries agreed to eliminate by January 2005 their use of methyl bromide, a fumigant used to eliminate pests in crops such as tomatoes, strawberries, melons, peppers, cucumbers and flowers. In March 2004, the parties to the protocol granted "critical use exemptions" to 11 developed countries facing the January 2005 deadline for phasing out methyl bromide. UNEP Executive Director Klaus Toepfer warned that governments and the private sector need to work harder to speed up the development of ozone-friendly replacements and "send a powerful signal to both producers and users that methyl bromide does not have a future."[52]

Small Island Developing States: 10-Year Review of Action

In January 2005, Mauritius hosted an international meeting to review progress on implementing the Barbados Plan of Action, adopted in 1995 to address the special sustainable development issues affecting small island developing states. Because of their size and geographic isolation, small islands face serious economic challenges and limited trade options. Many small islands also face significant environmental vulnerabilities related to sea level rise and increased storm activity caused by global climate change. A devastating 2004 hurricane season in the Caribbean, and the recent Indian Ocean earthquake and tsunami, have raised additional fears about islands' vulnerability to natural disasters.

Climate change was one of the primary topics of the meeting in Mauritius, with Nauru, one of the low-lying islands in the Pacific Ocean, expressing concern that industrialized and oil-producing countries "continue to be in a state of denial" about human-induced climate impacts. No significant new initiatives on climate change were taken on, but the Mauritius Strategy adopted at the meeting placed new emphasis on developing effective adaptation strategies, as well as promoting energy efficiency, greater reliance on renewable energy sources and adoption of cleaner fossil fuel technologies.

With regard to natural disasters, the Mauritius Strategy called for stronger national and international frameworks for disaster management, and the UN Development Programme launched a new "resilience building facility" to help islands reduce their vulnerabilities.[53]

Target 10: Halve, by 2015, the proportion of people without access to safe drinking water and basic sanitation

The Millennium Project report breaks down the results in meeting this target between urban and rural areas. In urban areas, many regions have met the target for improved drinking water, but there has been no progress in sub-Saharan Africa and actually declining access in eastern Asia. Regarding urban sanitation services, most parts of Asia are on track except for eastern Asia, where progress is lagging, and again sub-Saharan Africa has made no progress. In rural areas, the only regions on track for meeting the drinking water goal are southern Asia and parts of northern Africa. Other developing country areas are progressing too slowly to be on track. Progress on expanding rural sanitation services has been very limited throughout all regions.[54]

According to the Millennium Project's Task Force on Environmental Sustainability, current per capita availability of water has declined by 50 percent over the past 40 years, and over half of the world's natural wetlands have disappeared. Furthermore, "irrigated agriculture accounts for 70 percent of water withdrawals worldwide, and about a third of water use depends on unsustainable withdrawals, mostly in Asia, the Middle East and Africa."[55]

Because of the importance of clean drinking water and sanitation to sustainable development, human health and poverty reduction efforts, the UN CSD spent two years concentrating on improving implementation strategies in these areas. At its April 2005 meeting (its 13th session), the CSD discussed rights-based versus needs-based approaches to water supplies, public versus private delivery systems and different financing methods. In the closing plenary, the spokesperson for the G77 and China stressed the constraints affecting developing countries in terms of both financial resources and institutional capacity to meet the MDG targets on water and sanitation, saying it was "deeply disturbing" that previously-agreed political commitments had not resulted in positive action due to some countries' "selfish agendas."[56]

The first point made in the resulting CSD 13 Decision was that a substantial increase in resources would be needed to meet the targets, including domestic resources as well as ODA. In addition, practical measures on water and sanitation should be integrated into countries' official poverty reduction strategies and development plans. Recognizing that the 2005 target for establishing ecosystem-based integrated water resource management (IWRM) programs will probably not be met by all countries, the CSD 13 Decision also called for accelerated technical and financial assistance to governments for preparation of national IWRM plans.

New investments in sanitation infrastructure are also needed to prevent pollution of community drinking water supplies and halt the spread of waterborne diseases. The CSD 13 Decision recommended targeted economic incentives and training programs to help public utilities, small-scale providers and community groups build and maintain new sanitation facilities, especially in high-impact places such as schools, work places and health centers.

Target 11: Achieve, by 2020, a significant improvement in the lives of 100 million slum dwellers

In its second *State of the World's Cities Report* for 2004/2005, the UN Human Settlements Program, known as UN-HABITAT, focused on globalization and urban culture, highlighting the challenges of multiculturalism and the need for inclusive societies to be able to deal with international migration trends. The report showed that poverty is actually increasing in many cities due to economic globalization, and that urban poverty is increasingly concentrated in neighborhoods of ethnic and racial minorities.

In the global world economy, foreign direct investment has been primarily concentrated in 10 countries, including China, Brazil, Mexico, Indonesia and Thailand. There is almost no foreign direct investment in the poorest countries, especially those in Africa. Consequently, in those countries, prospects are low for economic progress and there are few resources available for properly planned urban development. Meanwhile, the world's urban population is projected to grow from 2.86 billion in 2000 to 4.98 billion, with only a very small percentage of the 2.12 billion increase taking place in cities located in high-income countries.[57]

Privatization of water and power services in urban areas where consumers can afford to pay has left municipal authorities with the burden of trying to meet the needs of those too poor to pay the charges for basic services. Foreign companies tend to return their profits to shareholders in their own countries rather than extending services to unserved slums or squatter settlements. In cities where there is significant private investment by foreign companies, there also has been a weakening of public institutions as local governments have had to compete for investments by offering attractive terms and undermining environmental, zoning and labor regulations.[58]

The Millennium Project's special Task Force on Improving the Lives of Slum Dwellers suggested that governments recognize that poor people in cities are active agents, not passive recipients of development, and that governments should work with local communities to upgrade slum areas. Moreover, by acknowledging and supporting the "informal" economy that exists in these areas through policies that promote business development and skills training, governments should help people living in slums create more sustainable sources of livelihood.[59]

Natural Disaster Responses

On January 17, 2005, when the Millennium Project report was first released, the world was still shaken by horrifying reports about the many thousands of lives lost and the widespread damage caused by the tsunami in Southeast Asia. The outpouring of public and private aid showed how generous and sympathetic governments, businesses and citizens can be when confronted with human tragedy, even in distant lands.[60]

Coincidentally, January 2005 was also the time for the scheduled opening of the UN's World Conference on Disaster Reduction. One of the primary outcomes of the conference was an international commitment to establish an early warning system for earthquakes and tsunamis in the Indian Ocean. In addition, the conference launched a new UN initiative, the International Early Warning Programme, to improve countries' resilience to all types of natural hazards, coordinate regional cooperation on warning and support public education about disaster awareness.[61]

The adopted Hyogo Framework for Action 2005-2015 outlined policy recommendations for risk reduction measures, monitoring and warning systems, and effective preparedness activities to help countries cope more effectively with catastrophes.[62] Countries can reduce the number of lives lost and costs incurred due to natural disasters by preserving critical ecosystems, establishing warning systems, building stronger structures, and creating effective social and political response systems.

Even before the Asian tsunami hit, at the October 13, 2004, briefing on the International Day for Disaster Reduction, the Secretary-General of the World Meteorological Organization had stressed the importance of building a "culture of prevention" through improvements in risk assessments, forecasting for early warnings and public awareness programs. Between 1992 and 2001, natural disasters related to weather, climate and flooding killed 622,000 people and harmed another 2 billion, with economic losses estimated at $446 billion. At the same time, the Executive Director of the UN Environment Programme pointed out that environmental damage and poverty can be the factors that turn hurricanes and floods into disasters. He explained that preserving wetlands reduces flooding, maintaining forests on hillsides helps prevent landslides, and healthy mangroves and coral reefs break the impact of coastal storms and extreme tides.[63] Prior to the tsunami, Indonesia had lost about 1.65 million acres of mangroves due to development, thereby undermining essential coastal defenses.[64]

Goal 8: Develop a Global Partnership for Development

Roger Coate

Goal 8 is one of the most complex goals agreed to in the *Millennium Declaration*. It has seven targets that range from the special needs of least developed and landlocked countries to debt relief to the provision of essential drugs to those in need. Here, each target is examined in turn.

Target 12: Develop an open, rule-based, predictable, nondiscriminatory trading and financial system

With the collapse of negotiations at the Doha round of trade talks in Cancún in 2003, progress on this target seemed doubtful. By the end of July 2004, however, WTO members had agreed on a new negotiating framework and prospects seemed to have improved (*see Chapter 6 for details*). The most important breakthrough was in regard to the elimination of agricultural export subsidies by a specific date.[65]

Target 13: Address the special needs of least developed countries

The centerpiece for addressing the special needs of LDCs is a special debt relief program known as the Heavily Indebted Poor Countries (HIPC) initiative. Launched by the World Bank and IMF in 1996, HIPC aims to bring countries in debt into a position of debt sustainability via provided aid. The program has two stages: the decision point and the completion point. The first stage is a three-year period within which the debtor country must undertake sustained implementation of integrated poverty reduction and economic reform programs. At the end of that period, the World Bank and IMF determine whether the country has attained debt sustainability under traditional debt relief measures. If not, the country has reached the "decision point," and a special debt relief package is put together, involving further structural reforms and poverty reduction policies. Once these reforms and policies have been successfully implemented, the "completion point" is reached, entitling the country to full debt relief.

As of April 2004, 37 countries had qualified for debt relief under the HIPC initiative. Of these, 14 had reached the decision point and 13 had reached the completion point. For these 37 LDCs, the debt-to-gross national income ratio fell from 109 percent in 1997 to 86 percent in 2002.

Target 14: Address the special needs of landlocked countries and small island developing states

As reported under Target 15 below, ODA received in landlocked countries rose from 5.9 percent of recipient gross national income in 1990 to 7.5 percent in 2002. During the same period, ODA received by small island developing states dropped from 2.6 percent in 1990 to 1.0 percent in 2002.[66] No other comparative data has been provided for this target.

Target 15: Deal comprehensively with the debt problems of developing countries through national and international measures in order to make debt sustainable in the long term

As reviewed earlier, net ODA to all developing and least developed countries has been on the upswing in the last few years. In 2003, the ODA level to all developing countries was 0.25 percent of donor GNP. This was up from 0.23 in 2002 and 0.22 in 2001. Over the last decade, the proportion of total bilateral, sector-allocable ODA applied to basic social services has steadily increased. Similarly, the proportion of bilateral aid that is untied (i.e., aid that can go toward goods and services from all countries versus aid that must go toward goods and services from the donor country) rose from 67.6 percent in 1990 to 84.8 percent in 2002. ODA received in landlocked countries has also been on the rise—from 5.9 percent of recipient GNI in 1990 to 7.5 percent in 2002. The same was not the case in small island developing states where the percentage dropped from 2.6 percent in 1990 to 1.0 percent in 2002.[67]

MARKET ACCESS

The proportion of total developed country imports (excluding arms) from developing countries and LDCs admitted free of duty has been mixed over the past decade. For developing countries, the level increased substantially between 1996 and 2000 but since has fallen. For LDCs, there has been a rise from 68 percent in 1996 to 77 percent in 2000 to 81 percent in 2002. Average tariffs imposed by developed countries on agricultural products from developing countries and LDCs have declined marginally since 1996. In textiles the story is basically the same. The situation with regard to clothing has been a bit more mixed, although overall there has been a modest decline.

DEBT SUSTAINABILITY

There has been some significant progress with regard to the number of LDCs that have reached their HIPC completion points. The number has increased from one in 2000 to 14 in 2004. There also has been a marginal increase in the number of countries that have reached the decision point but not the completion point. Finally, debt service as a percentage of exports has declined dramatically in heavily indebted poor countries, from 20 percent in 1990 to 9 percent in 2002. The level for low- and middle-income countries remained about the same in this time period.

Target 16: In cooperation with developing countries, develop and implement strategies for decent and productive work for youth

Unemployment rates among individuals between the ages of 15 and 24 remains high throughout most of the developing world. In 2003, the rate was highest in northern Africa, where just under 30 percent of youth were unemployed. The next highest levels were found in sub-Saharan Africa and western Asia where the youth unemployment rates were 21.1 percent and 20.8 percent, respectively. The situation was only marginally better in Latin America and the Caribbean, and in Southeast Asia. Only in northern and sub-Saharan Africa where rates are so extremely high did they not increase over the decade. The share of youth unemployment in total unemployment is outrageously high, ranging from 29.6 percent in the CIS countries to over 62 percent for both South Asia and sub-Saharan Africa.[68]

Target 17: In cooperation with pharmaceutical companies, provide access to affordable, essential drugs in developing countries

Providing access to medicines to treat those afflicted with HIV/AIDS and other devastating diseases in poor countries has been especially difficult because it is bundled up with a variety of economic, politic, legal, and moral issues. Nearly all the drugs to treat such diseases are produced and controlled under license by pharmaceutical companies in the developed world.

In the context of the WTO's Agreement on Trade-Related Aspects of Intellectual Property Rights (TRIPS), negotiations have been underway in an attempt to find an acceptable balance between protecting the property rights of the pharmaceutical companies and providing access to the consumer. Under the TRIPS agreement, members are permitted to exercise "compulsory licensing" without the authorization of the property right holder under certain conditions. At the WTO Ministerial Conference in Doha in November 2001, a seeming compromise was struck. The *Doha Declaration* on the TRIPS Agreement and Public Health affirmed member states' rights to take whatever measures appropriate to protect public health and promote access to medicines for all. Accordingly, LDCs would be given until January 1, 2016, before being required to implement or enforce the TRIPS agreement with regard to pharmaceutical products. A number of technical issues still remain and no formal consensus has been reached.

Target 18: In cooperation with the private sector, make available the benefits of new technologies, especially information and communications

Whether in terms of telephone lines and cellular phone subscribers or personal computers and Internet users, access to information and communication technologies has improved markedly in all developing regions. At the same time, relative to developed regions, technologies' access remains very low.

The International Year of Microcredit (2005)

Andreea Florescu

One of the main objectives of the UN's International Year of Microcredit (2005) is to create inclusive financial sectors around the world.[69] An inclusive financial sector allows low-income individuals to access credit, insurance and other financial products[70] which are generally forbidden to the poor. The year's Programme of Action, adopted by the 59th General Assembly, also seeks to promote the rapid growth of microfinance programs, recognize the contribution of microcredit toward achieving the MDGs, raise public awareness about microcredit and the reliability of borrowers, and promote partnerships.[71]

One of the year's goals—encouraging partnerships for the promotion of microcredit—seems to have already been partially achieved. Private financial institutions such as Citigroup, ING and Visa have committed to expanding access to financial services to the world's "unbankable." And more than 80 countries have created national committees to organize activities such as high-level conferences and awareness campaigns to advance microcredit programs.[72]

The UNDP's Capital Development Fund (UNCDF) and the UN Department of Economic and Social Affairs are coordinating UN-specific activities for the special year. In addition, the Food and Agriculture Organization is promoting microfinance in support of agricultural and rural development; the UN Population Fund is concentrating on the contribution of microfinance to women's empowerment and health; the International Labour Organization is looking at the social aspects of microfinance (e.g., the risks of debt); and the World Bank is continuing its work with member states to promote inclusive financial services and to fund microfinance initiatives worldwide.[73]

This massive mustering of efforts attests to the success microfinance has already registered and to its potential for alleviating poverty. The mechanism by which small investments are transformed into sustainable economic activities is simple. A bank or microfinance institution

(MFI) gives a microloan, usually in the amount of a few hundred dollars, to a person or group of people deemed "unbankable" by traditional credit standards. As reported in an eight-year World Bank study, the returns can be tremendous. In Bangladesh, where the idea of microfinance began, 48 percent of the poorest households with access to microloans rose above the poverty line. And 93 percent of Brazil's estimated 16 million microentrepreneurs now run profitable businesses.[74]

But microcredit does not serve solely as an income generating mechanism—it transforms beneficiaries' lives profoundly. Clients are more likely to have access to healthcare and to send their children to school rather than to work. They are more aware of HIV/AIDS prevention strategies and family planning. Perhaps the most dramatic effect of microcredit is the empowerment of women, as female entrepreneurs.[75]

As stated by then-UNDP Administrator Mark Malloch Brown, "Microfinance...has become one of the key driving mechanisms towards meeting the Millennium Development Goals, specifically the overarching target of halving extreme poverty and hunger by 2015."[76]

Looking Forward

Despite the uncertainties involved in achieving the Millennium Development Goals, it is important to keep in mind that the assessments conducted to date are largely from a pre-MDG period when Official Development Assistance was in a constant slide to new low levels and commitments to the *Monterrey Consensus* had yet to materialize. Moreover, in some cases, such as maternal health, reliable comparative data are not available for the most recent years.

Regardless, the MDG process, including the pending MDG +5 Summit, is arguably the most important multilateral development breakthrough ever. It serves not only as a focusing mechanism, but also as a concrete action guide. It enables the world's nations to get a handle on capacity deficits and development investment priority needs. It serves to keep long-term development on both developing and developed country governments' agendas.

As noted in this chapter, achieving the MDGs by 2015 is still a possibility. The main question remains whether there is sufficient will within both developing and developed states to make and carry through the kinds of major commitments it will take to get the job done.

Commentary:
The Kyoto Protocol without the US
Gail Karlsson

The Secretary-General's High-level Panel on Threats, Challenges and Change recognized the entry into force of the *Kyoto Protocol* in February 2005 as a positive step toward preventing a significant threat to collective security. However, the United States, which accounts for about one quarter of the world's greenhouse gas emissions, has refused to ratify it. The Bush administration pronounced it "dead" in early 2001, arguing that it would harm the US economy, and that it was unfair because it did not curb emissions of large developing countries. Rather than taking regulatory steps to limit greenhouse gas emissions from the use of fossil fuels by industrial facilities, power plants and motor vehicles, the administration has endorsed only voluntary emission reduction actions (voluntary efforts under the *UN Framework Convention on Climate Change* proved to be ineffective). The US is also promoting investments in possible long-term technological solutions like fuel cells and hydrogen cars, placing little emphasis on fuel efficiency in today's vehicles or the adoption of already-available renewable energy technologies.

In the absence of US leadership, the EU has been primarily responsible for moving the *Kyoto Protocol* forward. UK Prime Minister Tony Blair has made it one of his personal missions to address global warming effectively and to involve the US in those efforts. In December 2004, at the 10th meeting of the parties to the *Convention on Climate Change*, the EU and other countries pressed for a meeting outside the contentious *Kyoto Protocol* processes to discuss climate change issues. In May 2005, the Secretariat organized a meeting with a specific proviso that it would not open any negotiations leading to new commitments.

In its submissions to the meeting, the US took a very long view, reaffirming its voluntary commitments under the convention, but asserting "the reality that addressing the issue of climate change will require the sustained effort by all nations over many generations." The EU, in turn, stressed the urgency of the situation, citing scientific research showing that the risks of climate change may be greater than previously reported.

These differences in perspective will not be resolved quickly. In the meantime, it is the world's poorest countries that are expected to suffer the most from climate change (e.g., droughts and floods). Those countries, where millions of people depend on subsistence agriculture for survival, also have the least resources for adapting to even more adverse climate conditions.

It is likely that, with rising oil prices and mounting evidence of disruptive environmental changes, the US will face increasing pressures both domestically and internationally to step up its response. The *Kyoto Protocol*'s emission credit trading system, originally suggested by US negotiators, is already placing a recognized economic price on carbon dioxide emissions, and can provide a viable, market-based approach to meeting current climate protection goals.

Endnotes

1. Thomas Weiss, David Forsythe and Roger Coate. The United Nations and Changing World Politics, Fourth Edition (Boulder: Westview Press, 2004).

2. UN Document A/RES/55/2 (2000).

3. *Investing in Development: A Practical Plan to Achieve the Millennium Development Goals* (Report of the Millennium Project to the Secretary-General), January 17, 2005. Hereafter referred to as the "Sachs Report."

4. Sachs Report, p. 3.

5. Sachs Report, pp. 3-4.

6. Sachs Report, pp. 13-14.

7. Sachs Report, pp. 28-52

8. Sachs Report, pp. 32-43, and 148.

9. Sachs Report, pp. 43-45.

10. Sachs Report, pp. 45-46.

11. Sachs Report, p. 56-57.

12. Sachs Report, pp. 55-62.

13. Sachs Report, pp. 63-94.

14. Sachs Report, pp. 96-105.

15. Sachs Report, pp. 110-121.

16. Sachs Report, pp. 126-136.

17. Sachs Report, pp. 138-145.

18. Sachs Report, pp. 148-153.

19. Sachs Report, pp. 154-157.

20. Sachs Report, 159-182.

21. Sachs Report, p. 186.

22. Sachs Report, pp. 193-199.

23. Sachs Report, p. 211, 213, 219.

24. *In Larger Freedom: Towards Development, Security and Human Rights for All*, (Report of the Secretary-General to the General Assembly), March 21, 2005. Hereafter referred to as "ILF."

25. Ibid.

26. Sachs Report, pp. 13-14.

27. "Millennium Indicators Database," *UN Statistics Division website*, 2005.

28. Ibid.

29. "Millennium Indicators Database (MID)," *UN Statistics Division website*, 2005.

30. Sachs Report, p 23. / Achieving Universal Primary Education by 2015: A Chance for Every Child, 4, 2003.

31. MID, 2005.

32. Ibid.

33. Institute for Statistics website, July 2004.

34. MID, 2005.

35. "Implementing the Millennium Declaration," *Millennium Development Goals website*, 2005.

36. "MI D, 2005" *UN Statistics Division website*.

37. *AIDS Epidemic Update 2004* (Report of UNAIDS), December 2004.

38. Global Fund website, 2005.

39. Ibid.

40. HLP, paras. 54, 287, 289.

41. *Environment and Human Well-Being: A Practical Strategy*, (Report of the UN Millennium Project), 2005.

42. ILF, para. 41.

43. *Living Beyond Our Means: Natural Assets and Human Well-Being*, Millennium Ecosystem Assessment.

44. *Environment and Human Well-Being: A Practical Strategy*, (Report of the UN Millennium Project), 2005.

45. International Tropical Timber Organization Press Release (April 2005).

46. MID, 2005.

47. ILF, para. 59.

48. ILF, para. 60.

49. Executive Summary, The Task Force on Environmental Sustainability.

50. UN Document A/59/565 (2004).

51. ILF, para. 57.

52. "11 Countries Receive Temporary Exemption to Toxic Substance Ban," *UN News Center*, March 28, 2004.

53. Earth Negotiations Bulletin, January 17, 2005.

54. "Major Trends in the Goals by Region," *Millennium Project website*.

55. *Environment and Human Well-Being: A Practical Strategy*, (Report of the UN Millennium Project), 2005.

56. *Earth Negotiations Bulletin*, April 25, 2005.

57. UN-HABITAT website.

58. Ibid.

59. "A Home in the City: Improving the Lives of Slum-Dwellers," *Millennium Project website*.

60. UN Press Briefing (2005).

61. ISDR Press Release (January 19, 2005).

62. *Earth Negotiations Bulletin,* January 24, 2005.
63. UN NGO Liaison Service, *Go Between,* 2004.
64. "Tsunami Environmental Damage Widespread, Experts Say," *PlanetArk,* January 19, 2005.
65. UN Document A/59/282 (2004).
66. Ibid.
67. Ibid.
68. Ibid.
69. International Year of Microcredit (IYM) 2005 website.
70. Ibid.
71. General Assembly Resolution 53/197.
72. IYM 2005 website.
73. Ibid.
74. World Business Council for SD.
75. IYM 2005 website. / UNCDF website.
76. UNCDF website.

Chapter 4

Human Rights & Humanitarian Assistance: Ensuring Individual Liberties, Delivering Necessary Relief

Lorna Davidson, Jacques Fomerand

Paradoxically, in an age of advanced human rights consciousness, we are also wit-nessing daily and on a massive scale the worst atrocities that human beings can perpetrate on one another—too often with the passive acceptance of others or under the benign gaze or even at the instigation of people in a position of power and influence.... Bold as we need to be in addressing these issues, we must be vigi-lant not to trigger a rollback in human rights.

—UN High Commissioner for Human Rights Louise Arbour
Press Briefing, July 22, 2004

Human Rights and the United Nations

Lorna Davidson

Two major crises, causing massive loss of life and widespread population displacement, have dominated the past year and a half. The earthquake and subsequent tsunami which struck off the coast of northern Sumatra on December 26, 2004 devastated homes and property, and killed or left miss-ing more than a quarter of a million people. Following initial shock and hor-ror at the scale of the tragedy, individuals and groups around the world reacted with unprecedented generosity, donating large sums of money for a huge relief operation. In contrast to this natural disaster, the ongoing crisis in the Darfur region of Sudan, an entirely man-made tragedy, has garnered significantly less attention or effective action to stem the violence and destruction that is affecting hundreds of thousands of people.

Beyond the fact that it is the result of deliberate human action, the situa-tion in Darfur is particularly horrifying for two reasons. First, there is signif-icant evidence that the government was involved in the violence committed by Arab militia groups, or Janjaweed, against civilians.[1] This means that these acts can be characterized not only as crimes but also as human rights violations. Second, despite evidence of these violations, which some have characterized as genocide, the UN's machinery failed to put a swift end to the crisis. It was not until May 2005 that the Security Council referred the situation, which had begun in early 2004, to the International Criminal Court.

While the shortcomings of the UN human rights system are starkly evident from the crisis in Sudan, the 60th anniversary of the organization is also an occasion to reflect upon the extent of what has been achieved in a relatively short period of time. This section therefore outlines the various developments in the field of human rights (i.e., basic rights and freedoms to which all humans are entitled, including the right to life and liberty, freedom of thought and expression, and equality before the law), which have been championed by the UN and that have resulted in the creation and functioning of a network of institutions to promote and protect human rights. Recent proposals to reform the UN system to enhance its human rights work are also discussed, along with some of the key challenges it has faced in 2004-2005 in individual states and at a thematic level. A discussion of humanitarian assistance (i.e., external aid provided in response to, as well as to prevent or mitigate, humanitarian emergencies) follows.

Looking Back

It is unlikely that the framers of the *UN Charter* ever envisaged the web of international instruments and agencies that now exist under the auspices of the UN to promote and protect human rights. The *Charter* states that one of the purposes of the UN is "to achieve international co-operation in...promoting and encouraging respect for human rights and for fundamental freedoms for all without distinction as to race, sex, languages or religion," but this language does not appear to contemplate vigorous action by the organization to ensure respect for human rights. Indeed, in 1945, when the *Charter* was adopted, the premise of the UN was that it was made up of independent sovereign states, and these states jealously guarded their sovereignty. It was many years before any UN body was empowered to criticize or condemn human rights violations.

In the *Charter*, the General Assembly and the Economic and Social Council (ECOSOC) were given responsibility for the human rights functions of the organization. ECOSOC, made up of 54 UN member states, was to set up functional commissions for, among other things, the promotion of human rights. Thus, in 1946, the Commission on Human Rights was created, with nine members elected by ECOSOC to represent their states. The task of the commission when it first convened in 1947 was to draft a *Universal Declaration of Human Rights*, which was completed and adopted on December 10, 1948. The declaration enunciated a range of rights, which it described as "a common standard of achievement for all peoples and all nations." It further stated the aspiration that "every individual and every organ of society...shall strive by teaching and education to promote respect for these rights and freedoms and by progressive measures, national and international, to secure their universal and effective recognition and observance." The declaration was not, however, legally binding on states; there was therefore no mechanism by which individuals or states could compel compliance with its provisions.

The Commission on Human Rights quickly began formulating the rights set out in the declaration as binding obligations on states. Unsurprisingly, this work generated a significant amount of controversy about what should be contained in a treaty on human rights. One of the most contested issues was whether economic, social and cultural rights should be included along with civil and political rights—a categorical division that appears nowhere in the declaration itself. Developed countries argued that only civil and political rights could be formulated as binding obligations on states and that economic, social and cultural rights were too vague and aspirational to merit such treatment. Developing countries accused developed countries of seeking to perpetuate structural inequalities, and pointed out that civil and political rights were meaningless without respect for economic, social and cultural rights. In the end, two instruments were drafted and finally adopted by the General Assembly in 1966: the *International Covenant on Civil and Political Rights* and the *International Covenant on Economic, Social and Cultural Rights*. It took another 10 years for them to gain sufficient state ratifications to come into force.

The two covenants, often referred to jointly as "the international bill of rights," form the basis of the international law of human rights that the UN strives to uphold. Other subsequent treaties—the *International Convention on the Elimination of all forms of Racial Discrimination*, the *Convention on the Elimination of all forms of Discrimination Against Women*, the *Convention Against Torture and other Cruel, Inhuman, or Degrading Treatment or Punishment*, and the *Convention on the Rights of the Child*—have built upon and strengthened the covenants. Numerous other human rights instruments have also been adopted under UN auspices, providing a strong network of international human rights standards and principles.

At its first session in 1947, the Commission on Human Rights concluded that it had no power to receive complaints of human rights violations, or to take action on such complaints.[2] However, individuals and organizations began to press for a stronger role for the commission with regard to such violations. In the early 1960s, growing outrage about colonialism and racist regimes in southern Africa led to a significant development in the role of the commission. In Resolution 8, adopted in 1967, the commission added an item to its agenda on the "question of violations" and directed its Sub-Commission on Prevention of Discrimination and Protection of Minorities to bring to its attention "any situation which it has reasonable cause to believe reveals a consistent pattern of violations." ECOSOC followed with Resolution 1235, authorizing the commission to "make a thorough study of situations which reveal a consistent pattern of violations of human rights." This mandate to examine violations within individual states was further developed in 1970, with the adoption of ECOSOC Resolution 1503, creating a confidential procedure for the receipt of complaints by the commission. These resolutions marked a turning point in the role of the Commission on Human Rights and opened the door for the development of future mechanisms to enforce human rights standards.

The political nature of the commission, made up of state representatives, ensured, however, that many serious human rights situations were never discussed or condemned. While this problem continues to plague the commission and reflects the fact that many states still insist that they should not be censured for their human rights record, developments at the commission in the 1970s and 1980s did make it increasingly difficult for states to avoid such international scrutiny. The body developed a system of working groups, special rapporteurs and independent experts—collectively known as the "special procedures"—to examine the human rights situation either in a particular country, or along particular thematic lines. In 2004-2005, there were 26 thematic mandates and 14 country-specific mandates, including special rapporteurs on torture, the right to food, the independence of judges and lawyers as well as independent experts on the situations in Haiti, Burundi and Sudan. The mandate-holders conduct country-visits and receive information from individuals and nongovernmental organizations (NGOs), and communicate with governments about individual cases. In addition to being able to directly pressure governments to prevent or cease human rights violations, they also provide a valuable voice at the UN for the victims of such violations.

Beyond ECOSOC and the General Assembly, the tremendous growth of the human rights movement over the past 60 years has resulted in the creation of further UN bodies and agencies with a human rights remit. Of these, the Office of the High Commissioner for Human Rights (OHCHR) has developed as the central organ of the UN human rights system. The creation of the OHCHR was the result of a gradual build-up of pressure, from early proposals for some kind of human rights champion who could take cases to the International Court of Justice, to the 1993 World Conference on Human Rights in Vienna. In December 1993, the General Assembly created the position of High Commissioner for Human Rights,[3] who would act as "the United Nations official with principal responsibility for United Nations human rights activities under the direction and authority of the Secretary-General."

The UN Human Rights System Today

In the 12 years since it was established, OHCHR has grown rapidly. The fourth High Commissioner to hold the post, Canadian Judge Louise Arbour, began working in July 2004, following the August 2003 death of the third High Commissioner, Sergio Vieira de Mello, in the bombing of the UN headquarters in Iraq. As part of the continual process of rationalization and reform within the UN, in 1997, the functions of the OHCHR were merged with the Center for Human Rights, which had previously operated as the UN secretariat for human rights. High Commissioner Arbour has begun a process of restructuring which will divide OHCHR into two divisions, one containing activities mandated by the treaty bodies (*see below*) and the commission, and the other focusing on activities mandated by the Security Council, General Assembly and Secretary-General.

Despite the breadth of its mandate and the increasing recognition that the promotion and protection of human rights are a central part of the work of the UN, the annual budget of the OHCHR that is allocated from the regular UN budget comprises less than two percent of the total UN budget.[4] Each year, the high commissioner must appeal to individual states for voluntary contributions to make up the shortfall between OHCHR's granted budget and its actual requirements to perform its tasks. In 2005, High Commissioner Arbour appealed for $59.8 million in voluntary contributions to supplement her office's regular budget of $30 million.

Treaty Bodies

Although not strictly UN creations, the "treaty bodies" that aim to address human rights issues are serviced by OHCHR and considered part of the UN. Made up of committees of independent experts, the treaty bodies monitor the implementation of each of the major international human rights treaties. One fundamental difference between the treaty bodies and the Commission on Human Rights is their independent and expert nature. They have authority to interpret the various provisions of the human rights treaties that they monitor in a manner that is broadly accepted. Some have the power to receive complaints of human rights violations from individuals or other state parties. However, none of the treaty bodies has the political power to enforce their pronouncements.

With regard to the *International Covenant on Civil and Political Rights*, only those states parties that have signed up to the complaints procedure contained in an *Optional Protocol* to the covenant can be subject to the quasi-judicial jurisdiction of the Human Rights Committee to determine whether violations have taken place in individual cases. During 2004, more than 5,000 complaints were directed to the Human Rights Committee under this procedure.[5] Other treaties with optional or compulsory complaints procedures are the *Convention Against Torture*, the *Convention on the Elimination of all forms of Racial Discrimination*, the *Convention on the Elimination of all forms of Discrimination against Women*, and the *International Convention on the Protection of the Rights of all Migrant Workers and Members of their Families*.

Another major disadvantage of the treaty bodies system is that it is slow. It can take several years for a complaint to be examined and a committee's views on its substance issued. Moreover, states often submit their reports to the committees years behind schedule, if at all, making achieving momentum for concrete action following the recommendations extremely difficult. After various discussions and proposals for reform, in 2004, OHCHR prepared draft guidelines for a streamlined system for state reporting.[6] At the time of this writing, these guidelines were expected to be discussed and revised by a meeting of chairpersons of the treaty bodies in June 2005.

Other Involved Bodies

It should first be noted that, while the Commission on Human Rights, the OHCHR and the treaty bodies are solely dedicated to human rights, there are other arms of the UN that play a significant role in the human rights field. Among these are the UN High Commissioner for Refugees (UNHCR), the UN Development Programme, the World Food Programme (WFP) and the UN Children's Fund (UNICEF), as well as the Security Council and the General Assembly. While their remit is the prosecution of serious violations of international humanitarian law, such as war crimes and crimes against humanity, the international criminal tribunals for the former Yugoslavia and for Rwanda, as well as the International Criminal Court, also have an important function in holding to account those responsible for acts of violence. Increasingly, the prosecution of international crimes that may also be categorized as serious human rights violations is seen as an essential element of ensuring that such violations do not recur. (*See Chapter 7 for further details.*)

The Commission on Human Rights: 61st Session

MEMBERSHIP

The 61st session of the Commission on Human Rights was held in Geneva from March 14 to April 22, 2005. Once again, the membership of the commission itself, now numbering 53 states, was the subject of significant criticism by NGOs and certain states. The fundamental problem is that among the members of the commission are some of the most serious abusers of human rights. Zimbabwe, Indonesia, China, Sudan, Russia, Saudi Arabia, Cuba and Nepal all currently hold seats on the body, and they consistently use their positions to stymie criticism of their own human rights records and those of their friends and allies. One of the procedures by which they are able to do this is the use of a no-action motion. A country such as Zimbabwe can put forward a motion calling for no-action on its human rights situation and will lobby hard among the rest of the members to ensure that the motion is passed. Unfortunately, it is not only the rights-abusing states that vote in favor of such no-action motions, but also others that take the view that the commission should not condemn or criticize particular states, but rather offer them technical assistance and support. These states argue that Item 9 of the commission's agenda (the question of the violation of human rights and fundamental freedoms in any part of the world) is used to put forward politically motivated resolutions, and that this agenda item should be scrapped. While there is no doubt that political considerations are prominent in the debates and voting at the commission, the removal of Item 9 would serve only to further emasculate it.

At the opening of the 61st session, US Under-Secretary of State for Global Affairs Paula Dobriansky stated that "we need to put a stop to the trend of the world's worst human rights abusers securing membership on the Commission to deflect criticism of their abuses at home."[7] However, the US also has succeeded in preventing the adoption of resolutions condemning its human rights record with regard to suspected terrorists held at Guantanamo Bay and elsewhere, and the abuse of detainees in Iraq.

The no-action procedure was used less at the 61st session than in previous years, primarily due to the fact that fewer resolutions were tabled under Item 9 of the agenda, seeking to condemn human rights abuses in individual countries. Only Russia attempted to use the procedure, to block a resolution on Belarus, but it was unsuccessful. Resolutions under Item 9 were passed regarding Cuba, Myanmar (Burma) and the Democratic People's Republic of Korea (DPRK), in addition to Belarus, but other countries with atrocious human rights records, such as Sudan and Nepal, were considered under Item 19 on advisory services and technical cooperation. The commission continued to consider the human rights situation in Uzbekistan under the confidential procedure established by Resolution 1503.

SPECIAL RAPPORTEUR REPORTS

At the commission's 60th session, resolutions were adopted to appoint new special rapporteurs for Belarus and the DPRK. These new special procedures reported to the 61st session. In his report, the special rapporteur on the situation of human rights in the DPRK stated that various critical challenges need to be addressed in the country; among them, the right to food, the right to life, the right to security of the person, the right to freedom of movement, the right to education and the right to freedom of expression. The special rapporteur on the situation of human rights in Belarus concluded that the continuous deterioration of the situation of human rights in Belarus was a matter of grave concern.[8] He said he regretted that he had been unable to visit Belarus and to exchange views with the Belarusian authorities due to a lack of cooperation. In his view, in order to improve the human rights situation, a deep reform of the political system and a dramatic restructuring of Belarusian society were needed.

Both countries' representatives challenged the special rapporteurs' reports, saying that they did not accept the role by which the special rapporteurs were established. The DPRK's representative even described the rapporteur's report as part of a propaganda plot fabricated by hostile forces seeking to overthrow the state system in the DPRK.

RIGHT OF VICTIMS

Among the thematic issues debated during its 61st session, the commission discussed the right of victims of human rights violations to a remedy, and approved a resolution creating a set of "Basic Principles and Guidelines on the Right to a Remedy and Reparation for Victims of Gross Violations of International Human Rights Law and Serious Violations of International Humanitarian Law."[9] On a similar theme, the commission adopted a resolution on impunity, and considered the updated set of principles for the protection and promotion of human rights through action to combat impunity. Once again, the commission failed to substantively debate the issue of human rights, to the regret of some states and NGOs. It did, however, request the appointment of a special representative on the issue of human rights and transnational corporations. This followed the preparation of a report by the High Commissioner for Human Rights on the responsibilities of transnational corporations and related business enterprises with regard to human rights. The report concluded that there are "gaps in understanding the human rights responsibilities of business" and that there is "a growing interest in discussing further the possibility of establishing a United Nations statement of universal human rights standards applicable to business." It noted that there are differing opinions about the draft "Norms on the Responsibilities of Transnational Corporations and Other Business Enterprises with regard to Human Rights" and recommended continued discussion and testing of these norms. In its resolution on the matter, the commission requested the appointed special representative, among other things, to identify and clarify standards of corporate responsibility and accountability, to elaborate on the role of states in regulating transnational corporations and other businesses with regard to human rights, and to compile a compendium of best practices.[10]

TERRORISM

One major subject of discussion at the Commission on Human Rights over the past several years, as well as across the whole UN system, has been the question of how to successfully combat terrorism while upholding basic human rights. Some governments and NGOs, as well as the UN Secretary-General, the High Commissioner for Human Rights and numerous UN human rights experts have expressed serious concerns about the manner in which the implementation of counter-terrorism measures in many states has impacted negatively on human rights. Numerous NGOs have campaigned for the appointment of a new special procedure by the commission to monitor and report upon the protection of human rights in the context of counter-terrorism measures; the idea has gained considerable support.

At its 60th session, the commission designated an independent expert, US Professor Robert Goldman, to assist the high commissioner in examining the issue and making recommendations.[11] High Commissioner Arbour presented a study on this topic to the 59th session of the General Assembly in October 2004. The study concluded that:

> "Owing to the wide range of rights coming under pressure from counter-terrorism measures, analysis by the special procedures has evolved in a dispersed and fragmentary way. Yet counter-terrorism measures are often implemented as a legal package, implicating a wide range of rights. The existing special procedures have thus been unable to provide a coherent and integrated analysis of the compatibility of national counter-terrorism measures with international human rights obligations."[12]

High Commissioner Arbour also found that the capacity of the treaty bodies to address such measures was limited. She concluded that "there are significant gaps in the consideration of national counter-terrorism measures by the United Nations human rights system" and "it may be necessary to consider taking steps that may affect mandates, processes and resources."[13]

Dr. Goldman also favored the creation of a new mechanism. His report emphasized the gaps in coverage of the human rights monitoring system with regard to counter-terrorism and recommended the creation of a special procedure with a "multidimensional mandate to monitor States' counter-terrorism measures." In its resolution on the issue, the commission requested that its chairman appoint an individual of recognized international standing and demonstrable expertise in human rights law as special rapporteur on the promotion and protection of human rights and fundamental freedoms while countering terrorism.[14]

Reform Proposals

As noted in Chapter 1, the report of the High-level Panel on Threats, Challenges and Change lays out a broad conception of collective security, emphasizing the interconnectedness of contemporary threats, including terrorism, poverty and armed conflicts. It notes that at its foundation, the UN was very much concerned with state security, but human security was quickly recognized as inextricably linked to the security of states. Central to all of the observations and recommendations put forward by the panel is its understanding that "any event or process that leads to large-scale death or lessening of life chances and undermines States as the basic unit of the international system is a threat to international security."[15]

Most significant to this discussion, the panel endorses the idea that there is a "responsibility to protect" incumbent upon every state. This responsibility is triggered in cases where there is large-scale human suffering in or across states, and the relevant governments are either unwilling or unable to bring it to an end. According to the panel, in such situations, the Security Council should authorize military intervention by third states, as a last resort. The panel's report does not specifically refer to serious human rights violations in relation to the responsibility to protect, but rather mentions situations involving genocide, ethnic cleansing and other large-scale killings.

Recognizing that human rights protection is now one of the key missions of the UN, the panel notes that the Commission on Human Rights "suffers from a legitimacy deficit that casts doubts on the overall reputation of the United Nations." It identifies membership as one of the most problematic factors inhibiting its work and recommends fundamental reform. In particular, the panel suggests that membership be expanded to all UN member states. It further recommends that states should designate prominent human rights figures as the heads of their delegations and that the commission should be supported by an advisory council or panel of 15 independent experts.

Reform of the commission along these lines would undoubtedly change the fundamental character of the body. However, it is questionable whether the inclusion of all UN member states on the commission would render it more efficient or effective. The problems experienced at the 59th General Assembly with regard to the use of the no-action motion demonstrate that a body with universal membership can be hijacked by rights-abusing countries. The panel's recommendations for greater Security Council consultation with the high commissioner on a regular basis, and with regard to the need to resolve the funding crisis faced by the OHCHR are, however, to be welcomed.

In his report, *In Larger Freedom: Towards Development, Security and Human Rights for All*, SG Annan picks up several of the themes enunciated by the High-level Panel. He too emphasizes the interconnectedness of human rights with both security and development, and highlights the role of the UN in realizing all three.[16] Among his concrete recommendations is an endorsement of the view that the High Commissioner on Human Rights should play a more active role in the deliberations of the Security Council, and that human rights must be incorporated into decision-making throughout the UN. He also agrees with the panel that OHCHR must be granted additional resources, and gives his support to the plan to introduce harmonized guidelines on state reporting to the human rights treaty bodies. With regard to the Commission on Human Rights, the Secretary-General proposes much more radical change than suggested by the panel. Noting the "credibility deficit" that has resulted from the presence of rights-abusing states among the members of the commission, he recommends the replacement of the commission by a smaller, standing Human Rights Council. He suggests that the members of the council be elected directly by a two-thirds majority in the General Assembly, and that those states elected should undertake to abide by human rights standards. In his view, such a Human Rights Council would be more accountable and representative.[17]

At its 61st session, the commission heard from the Secretary-General on his proposed reforms, and held an informal session to discuss the proposals. Several states voiced reservations about whether the suggested Human Rights Council would indeed resolve the problems plaguing the existing commission, whereas others declared their support for the idea. At the end of its session, the commission adopted a decision to establish an open-ended working group to reflect on the Secretary-General's recommendations with a view to contributing to the intergovernmental deliberations on the proposed reform in the General Assembly's 60th session.[18]

Country-Specific Human Rights Actions

The following section describes the situation in nine selected countries, where the UN human rights system faced particular challenges in 2004 and early 2005. Particular mention also must be made of the ongoing human rights crisis in Zimbabwe, where President Robert Mugabe and his Zanu-PF party maintain a tight grip on power. The ruling party, which took the majority of seats in Parliament after a March 2005 election that many consider to have been marred by serious irregularities and voter intimidation has destroyed the independent press, subverted the judiciary and sanctioned torture, killings and other serious acts of violence. There is also considerable evidence that the government is using food shortages as a tool against its political opponents.[19] Similarly, the military regime in power in Burma continued to ruthlessly suppress all forms of dissent in the country and to massively violate the rights of its people throughout 2004 and early 2005. There are thousands of political prisoners in Burma, and torture and mistreatment of detainees is common. Burma also is reported to have more child soldiers than any other country in the world.[20] Unlike some of the countries described below, the situation in both Zimbabwe and Burma is not the result of the inability of state institutions to protect the rights of the people, but rather illustrates the deliberate violation of basic human rights standards by government agents and officials who refuse to bow to international pressure to end their abusive practices.

Afghanistan

In December 2001, after the US-led intervention to overthrow the Taliban regime, the Bonn Agreement was signed, bringing an end to almost three decades of armed conflict in Afghanistan. These conflicts had generated an estimated 6 million refugees and 1.4 million internally displaced persons (IDPs),[21] and destroyed the country's infrastructure and economy. In addition, widespread, serious violations of basic human rights were committed. The Bonn Agreement set up an interim administration and significant progress was made in implementing the transition to a democratically elected government (*see Chapter 2 for details*). But many obstacles remain. Not least among these are the numerous past and ongoing human rights violations that must be addressed.

Discussion about ways to deal with past violations is now beginning within the country, driven by the Afghan Independent Human Rights Commission (AIHRC). In January 2005, during a visit to Afghanistan by the High Commissioner for Human Rights, the AIHRC launched a report entitled *A Call for Justice* based on consultations with approximately 6,000 Afghans. The report set out a series of recommendations to combat impunity and provide acknowledgement and reparation to victims.[22] The independent expert on the situation of human rights in Afghanistan has also stressed the importance of addressing past atrocities.[23]

Before ongoing violations of basic rights in Afghanistan can be brought to an end, the security situation needs to greatly improve. The reach of the government and nascent state institutions does not extend to all regions; regional warlords wield considerable power in many areas. Second, the opium industry needs to be curbed. With approximately 60 percent of the gross domestic product coming from opium cultivation and trade,[24] this industry has led to widespread corruption. Third, issues regarding the US-led coalition forces that remain in Afghanistan, ostensibly hunting down the remnants of the Taliban and Al Qaeda, need to be addressed. Coalition forces have detained an unknown number of individuals at American bases in Bagram, Kandahar and other undisclosed locations. Throughout 2004 and 2005, reports of the physical abuse of detainees, along with the perpetuation of inhuman conditions of detention have continued to emerge. However, UN and other human rights monitors have been denied access to detention centers, rendering it impossible to assess the scale of the problem or ensure an end to such abuse.

The Secretary-General's independent expert on the situation of human rights in Afghanistan detailed a catalogue of human rights abuses in his reports to the 59th General Assembly and the 61st session of the Commission on Human Rights.[25] Among these he gave particular emphasis to the inhuman conditions of detention in Afghanistan's prisons; extrajudicial killings, rape and torture committed by local commanders; weaknesses in the criminal justice system resulting in unlawful arrests and prolonged detention; trafficking of women and children; various forms of abuse and violence against women; and the lack of adequate housing, electricity, water and medical facilities. The independent expert acknowledged the efforts being made by the Afghan government to deal with these and other human rights issues, but noted that the current security situation and absence of state control over the entire country has rendered it impossible to ensure an end to many human rights problems. He therefore recommended, among other things, an increase in the deployment of foreign troops in Afghanistan to assist the government in tackling the immediate security problem, along with a package of urgent measures to restore confidence in the justice system, reform state security services and improve the protection of women. He also highlighted the allegations of abuse committed at US detention centers in Afghanistan and has demanded access to these locations. However, the mandate of the independent expert was not renewed at the 61st session of the Commission on Human Rights. The holder of the mandate, Professor Cherif Bassiouni, subsequently accused the US of being behind the decision not to renew the position, due to his criticism of its mistreatment of detainees and calls for access to detention centers.[26]

A range of other UN bodies and agencies are involved in efforts to improve the human rights situation within Afghanistan. Supported by OHCHR, human rights officers working at UNAMA, the UN peace mission there, investigate complaints of human rights abuses, make recommendations to the government, provide support and advice to the AIHRC and monitor developments. The UNHCR also has offices throughout the country, assisting in the return and reintegration of refugees and IDPs. Between March 2002 and September 2004, 3.5 million refugees returned to Afghanistan and there are numerous cases of disputes over title to land and property. UNHCR is also partnering with the AIHRC in a project to monitor the rights of returning refugees and IDPs.[27]

The presidential elections held on October 9, 2004 passed without serious incident, marking a milestone in Afghanistan's progress toward a peaceful and democratic future. It is to be hoped that the parliamentary elections scheduled for September 2005 will further entrench this progress, but much remains to be done to ensure that all Afghans, particularly women, can participate fully in the political and electoral process. In addition, as noted, there is an urgent need to improve security in all parts of the country and to demobilize and disarm militia groups. Without the continued commitment of the international community to support the nascent Afghan government, the country could easily slip backward into further rounds of violence and human rights abuse. The UN is playing a crucial role in this regard and must be provided with the resources to continue its work.

China

In March 2005, days before a visit to China by new Secretary of State Condoleezza Rice, the United States announced that it would not sponsor a resolution condemning China for its abysmal human rights record at the 61st session of the Commission on Human Rights. Describing the human rights situation in China as remaining poor overall, a senior State Department official told a Congressional committee that there were some "hopeful signs," particularly with regard to political prisoners.[28] The announcement came the same week that China released prominent political prisoner Rebiya Kadeer, who had been serving an eight-year sentence for leaking state secrets after she sent some newspaper clippings to her husband in the US. While human rights NGOs welcomed the release, they accused the Chinese government of playing "hostage politics" and expressed concern about the continuing use of laws and practices in China to detain and imprison individuals seeking to exercise their rights to freedom of expression and association.[29]

The Chinese government implements a harsh system of state control over all aspects of life in the country and has little tolerance for dissent. Individuals who attempt to speak out against the system are routinely detained and prosecuted on state security charges. Amnesty International has expressed serious concerns about the rise in 2004 and 2005 of cases of arbitrary detention of human rights defenders. In June 2004, several human rights activists were placed under effective house arrest in order to prevent them from marking the 15th anniversary of the Tiananmen Square crackdown. It was reported that their access to telephones and the Internet was also disrupted at that time.[30]

Among the other serious human rights issues that remain of concern in China are discrimination against individuals living with HIV/AIDS, forced evictions of families by local authorities and property developers, torture and mistreatment of detainees, and numerous abuses of individuals and groups considered to be advocating secession. The situation in the Xinjiang Uighur Autonomous Region is particularly serious, where the government fails to distinguish between the small minorities who advocate violent secessionist action from the rest of the Uighur population. Capitalizing on the post-September 11, 2001, fear of international terrorism, the Chinese government has cracked down on the Muslim Uighur community, which it has labeled as supporting terrorism. Reports indicate the routine use of arbitrary arrest and detention, physical mistreatment, prosecution behind closed doors, and execution of members of the community whom the state considers threatening. In addition, systematic repression of religion is practiced in Xinjiang.[31]

Despite holding a seat on the Commission on Human Rights, China has been hostile toward many UN human rights mechanisms. It still has not ratified the *International Covenant on Civil and Political Rights* and has not allowed several of the special procedures mandate-holders to visit the country. In 2004, China did invite the special rapporteur on torture to conduct a state visit, but at the last minute, requested that the rapporteur postpone his visit indefinitely. The Working Group on Arbitrary Detention was able to conduct a visit in September 2004, but complained that it was denied access to some prisoners.[32]

Côte d'Ivoire

A simmering crisis in Côte d'Ivoire erupted into serious violence in 2004, resulting in a further deterioration of the human rights situation in the West African country. Since September 2002, Côte d'Ivoire has been divided into two regions: the south controlled by the government, and the north controlled by rebel forces known as the "Nouvelles Forces." The split came after an attempted coup against President Laurent Gbagbo, who was declared winner of presidential elections held in 2000, despite serious irregularities and electoral violence.[33] The conflict between north and south has its roots in disputes over land and allegations by the northern population that the southern-dominated government is seeking to disenfranchise them.

In January 2003, the French government brokered the Linas-Marcoussis Accord, under which the political parties agreed to form a national reconciliation government, including rebel representatives. Agreement was also given to a program of disarmament, demobilization and reintegration (DDR) of forces. However, many of the terms of the accord were not fully implemented and the Nouvelles Forces suspended their participation in DDR discussions. In March 2004, government forces attacked a demonstration that was being held against its lack of implementation of the accord, killing at least 105 civilians and wounding 290. Twenty other individuals were reported to have "disappeared" after being taken into custody by security forces and pro-government militia.[34]

A second political deal was reached in July 2004 and a date was set for the DDR program to commence. However, in November 2004, the government broke its cease-fire and attacked rebel bases in the north of the country. Nine French peacekeepers and one foreign civilian were killed when government forces bombed a French military base in the northern town of Bouake and, in response, French forces destroyed most of the government's air force on the ground. Subsequently, mobs and pro-government militia groups went on the rampage in the capital, Abidjan, attacking UN personnel and foreign civilians, and looting and destroying property. The government used its control of the media to incite violence against French civilians and, as a consequence, foreign nationals were evacuated from the city. On November 15, 2004, the Security Council passed Resolution 1572, demanding an end to the broadcasting of messages inciting hatred and violence, and imposing an arms embargo on the country.[35]

The ongoing crisis in Côte d'Ivoire contributes to an extremely poor record of respect for basic human rights. Serious abuses are committed by both sides and the perpetrators of such abuses act with complete impunity. Both sides have killed, tortured, "disappeared" and arbitrarily detained their perceived opponents, and in the north there is no court system or judicial authority. In April 2004, a French-Canadian journalist, Guy-Andre Kieffer, who was writing about corruption in the cocoa industry, disappeared from Abidjan and is believed to be dead. Mass graves have also been uncovered, such as in Korhogo, where approximately 100 people were executed or suffocated.[36]

As described in Chapter 2, the UN peacekeeping mission in Côte d'Ivoire (UNOCI) was established in February 2004, and works alongside a French peacekeeping force. Among other tasks mandated to UNOCI, it accordingly deploys human rights officers around the country, who investigate and report on alleged violations. In addition, the UN sent two investigative commissions to Côte d'Ivoire in 2004; the first to look into the violence of March 25 and 26, when the security forces killed numerous demonstrators; the second to investigate serious violations of human rights and humanitarian law committed since the 2002 rebellion.

At the end of April 2005, a precarious peace existed in Côte d'Ivoire, following yet another peace deal signed by the various parties, brokered by South Africa under the auspices of the African Union (AU). However, with presidential elections scheduled for October 2005 and the northern rebels adamant that their candidates must be allowed to stand this time, the country could easily descend back into violence and further human rights abuse.

Democratic Republic of Congo

There was little improvement in the human rights situation in the Democratic Republic of Congo (DRC) in 2004-2005, and the UN suffered a severe blow to its credibility when allegations emerged that members of its peacekeeping force in the country were engaged in the sexual exploitation of women and girls. Following years of conflict that involved a range of armed groups and forces from at least seven foreign countries, in June 2003, a government of national unity was installed in the DRC. However, this government remains weak and divided between the various political parties; this has resulted in a failure to implement crucial aspects of the transition, such as security sector reform. In a report released in March 2005, the International Crisis Group (ICG) described the reality of the political situation as essentially unchanged from that which existed prior to the 2003 agreement and stated that "most of the 300,000 combatants in the country are deployed in the same positions and are controlled by the same military hierarchies as before the transition."[37]

A UN peacekeeping force (MONUC) has been in place in the DRC since 1999, but it has been unable to prevent or put a stop to fighting among the various factions, or avert attacks upon civilians. In the eastern part of the country, fighting between government forces and rebel groups continues and tensions mounted significantly in November 2004, with reports that the Rwandan government had sent forces into the DRC. In the Kivu region, thousands of civilians fled the fighting and homes and shops were looted by soldiers. Government and rebel forces committed serious human rights abuses, such as massacres, rapes and torture, and were not disciplined or held accountable. For example, in October 2004, rebels operating in the Ituri region were reported to have tortured 24 civilians and killed at least six of them. Other ongoing problems include the recruitment of child soldiers, attacks upon and threats against human rights defenders, and serious discrimination and violence against women. MONUC teams investigate allegations of human rights abuse, but they are hugely overstretched.[38]

In his report to the 61st session of the Commission on Human Rights, the independent expert on the human rights situation in the DRC reiterated his view that there is an urgent need for the creation of a fair and expeditious system of justice in the country to address ongoing abuses. He highlighted the precarious security situation in many areas and stated that the reasons for violence and insecurity could be found in the illegal exploitation of natural resources and related arms-trafficking. He further condemned the widespread commission of rape and sexual violence against women, including the sexual abuse allegations on members of MONUC. He referred to the beginning of investigations by the prosecutor of the International Criminal Court into crimes against humanity and other serious violations of international humanitarian law committed since 2002, and emphasized the need for such investigations and prosecutions to be conducted alongside domestic criminal proceedings. The commission continued to consider the situation in DRC under Item 19 of its agenda, and extended the mandate of the independent expert for another year.[39]

In March 2005, the Security Council renewed the mandate of MONUC until October 2005 and expressed its intention to renew it again for further periods,[40] but an array of measures is required to bring about improvement of the situation in the DRC and ensure an end to the widespread and serious abuse of human rights.

Iraq

The August 2003 bombing of the UN headquarters in Baghdad, along with the continuing insecurity that prevails throughout Iraq, has seriously inhibited the functioning of the UN and its human rights machinery in the country. With the UN Assistance Mission for Iraq (UNAMI) relocated to Jordan (*see Chapter 2 for details*), UN monitoring of and reporting on the human rights situation in Iraq has been extremely difficult. In addition, at its 60th session in 2004, the Commission on Human Rights failed to reappoint its Special Rapporteur on Iraq, removing an important source of information and advice on how greater respect for basic rights in Iraq might be achieved.

The prevailing climate of insecurity was of primary concern in the 2004-2005 period to the Iraq population. Unrelenting bomb and gun attacks on civilians have killed and wounded men, women and children and have been focused in particular on those considered to be cooperating with the US and other international forces, or with the interim Iraqi government. For example, on February 28, 2005, more than 120 civilians, police and National Guard volunteers were killed and more than 140 were injured in a car-bomb attack in Hillah, south of Baghdad. The car-bomb was detonated near a line of people applying for government jobs.[41] Such attacks have contributed to a generalized climate of fear, in which it is extremely difficult for rights to be realized. This fear of violence prevents many, particularly women and girls, from attending work or school, or going for necessary medical treatment.

Compounding and contributing to the ongoing attacks by insurgents, international forces in Iraq have been responsible for the serious abuse of members of the local population who have been arrested or detained in the course of their operations. As photographs and accounts of torture and inhuman and degrading treatment committed by US and UK soldiers emerged through 2004 and early 2005, outrage around the world turned to cynicism about the professed commitment of those countries to upholding human rights standards. In June 2004, a joint statement was issued by the participants attending an annual meeting of UN special procedures, requesting that the special rapporteurs on torture, the independence of judges and lawyers, and the right to health, along with the chairperson of the Working Group on Arbitrary Detention, be allowed to visit all persons detained by the US in Iraq, Afghanistan and at Guantanamo Bay. This request was denied by the US government.[42]

Reports also indicate that the new Iraqi security forces have been responsible for serious human rights abuses. Human Rights Watch has documented cases of arbitrary arrest, lengthy pre-trial detention and serious mistreatment of detainees, and has described such abuses as "routine and commonplace."[43] It has also reported that conditions of detention are extremely poor, with detainees being denied adequate food or water and held in severely overcrowded cells in unhygienic conditions.

There can be little doubt that there is an urgent need for change in Iraq to bring an end to attacks upon the population by insurgents and to drastically improve the human rights record of the new Iraqi state institutions. It is hoped that the new transitional government will garner the legitimacy that its predecessor did not, and that this will contribute to diminishing insurgent attacks.

Israeli-Occupied Territories

Continued violations of the right to life, the right to freedom of movement and breaches of international humanitarian law occurred in 2004 and early 2005 in the Israeli-Occupied Territories. At the 61st Commission of Human Rights session, the special rapporteur on the situation of human rights in the Palestinian territories occupied by Israel since 1967 specifically reported on military incursions by the Israeli Defense Forces (IDF) into the Gaza Strip, the demolition of houses and the effects of the construction of the so-called "separation barrier."[44]

Military incursions by the IDF during 2004 resulted in the deaths of hundreds of Palestinians, many as a consequence of reckless shooting and indiscriminate shelling from tanks in heavily populated areas. For example, in October 2004, the IDF entered the Jabaliya refugee camp and killed 114 people, including 34 children. This offensive was conducted in response to the killing of two Israeli children in Sderot by Qassam rockets fired by Palestinians. During the offensive, 91 homes were also demolished, 101 houses were damaged, and water, sewage and electricity networks were badly affected. The demolition of houses is a routine feature of military incursions by the IDF, rendering thousands of Palestinians homeless. In addition, house demolitions are carried out as part of "clearing operations" by the military, as a consequence of building without the required permits, and as a punishment inflicted upon the families and neighbors of Palestinians suspected of having carried out attacks against Israelis.[45]

In July 2004, the International Court of Justice rendered its Advisory Opinion on the legality of the "wall" being constructed by the Israeli government, ostensibly to protect the Israeli population from terrorist attacks. As described in Chapter 7, the court concluded that the construction of the wall was contrary to international human rights and humanitarian law, due to its effects on the lives of the Palestinian people, and advised that Israel was thus obliged to put an end to it. However, while construction has been halted in some areas due to an order of the Israeli High Court, the government continues construction of the wall in other areas. In his report to the Commission on Human Rights, the special rapporteur again emphasized the suffering generated by the wall, which has had the consequence of confiscating Palestinian land and seriously restricting freedom of movement among the Palestinian population. Restrictions upon the movement of those living near the wall, or within its closed zone, have resulted in the denial of access to education, employment and urgently needed healthcare.

The commission adopted four resolutions on Israel at its 61st session. First, the commission once again demanded that Israel rescind its decision to impose its laws, jurisdiction and administration on the occupied Syrian Golan. Second, the commission expressed grave concern about the continued construction of the wall inside the occupied Palestinian territory and about the expansion of Israeli settlements. Third, the commission condemned the use of force by Israel against Palestinian civilians, resulting in deaths, destruction of homes and damage to property and vital infrastructure. And fourth, the commission reaffirmed the right of the Palestinian people to self-determination.[46]

Nepal

As discussed in Chapter 2, when Nepal's King Gyanendra dismissed his government and declared a state of emergency in February 2005, he launched his country further into crisis. Among the widespread violations of human rights, forced "disappearances," arbitrary executions, torture and rape have been reported by the state's National Human Rights Commission and by national and international NGOs. Impunity for such abuses is pervasive, both among state military and security forces and the Maoist rebels. According to Human Rights Watch, no senior military or security force officer has been held accountable for "disappearances" in Nepal, and the government's failure to take steps to end the practice means that it should be characterized as government policy. The rebels commit fewer "disappearances," preferring to torture and publicly execute those accused of spying for or collaborating with the government. The rebels also routinely abduct students and young people to indoctrinate them and enlist them in the conflict, and extort money out of local communities to support their campaign.[47]

Among the repressive tools used by the state to conduct its counterinsurgency campaign is the Terrorist and Disruptive Activities Ordinance, which permits preventive detention of suspected terrorists for up to one year and the use of "necessary force" if any person or group hinders the work of the security forces. In addition, under the state of emergency, a number of rights were suspended, including freedom of expression, association and assembly, the right to privacy, the right to information, and the right to a constitutional remedy. While the Nepali king lifted the state of emergency at the end of April 2005, human rights groups expressed serious concern about ongoing restrictions and rights abuses. The media continues to operate under tight censorship and journalists are routinely threatened and intimidated, and sometimes killed. Human rights defenders have also been targeted by both sides in the conflict, with many being arrested and others forced to flee the country or go into hiding.[48]

At the 60th session of the Commission on Human Rights in 2004, a chairperson requested OHCHR submit a report on its activities in Nepal, including technical cooperation, to the commission's 61st session.[49] During the 2004-2005 period, several UN officials and experts have continued to voice their concern about the crisis in Nepal. In July 2004, a joint statement by a number of special rapporteurs, along with the special representative on human rights defenders and the Working Groups on Enforced or Involuntary Disappearances and on Arbitrary Detention, noted that since the beginning of the year, they had transmitted 146 urgent appeals to the

Nepalese government. The experts regretted that the government had failed to respond to many of these appeals.[50]

In its report to the commission's 61st session, OHCHR stated that the crisis in Nepal risked deteriorating further, and that no amount of UN technical support or advice could replace the government's responsibility to take action to end human rights abuses and combat impunity.[51]

In April 2005, the High Commissioner for Human Rights and the government of Nepal signed an agreement for the establishment of an OHCHR monitoring operation in Nepal, which will report on human rights violations, advise the government and provide support to local NGOs. The commission failed, however, to explicitly condemn the Nepalese government for its abuse of human rights.[52]

Russia (Chechnya)

Despite the fact that human rights abuses continued unabated throughout 2004 and early 2005, no resolution was tabled at the 61st session of the Commission on Human Rights on the human rights situation in Chechnya. At the 60th session, a resolution put forward by the European Union was defeated on a vote, and it appears that in 2005, there was a feeling that there was little point in seeking to introduce such a resolution a second time. This lack of action provides a depressing illustration of the manner in which powerful states can avoid censure by the UN's main human rights body.

The present conflict in the Chechen Republic of the Russian Federation has been ongoing for six years and, despite claims by the Russian government that the situation is "normalizing," combat between Russian and Chechen forces continues in some parts of the republic. Serious violations of human rights and humanitarian law are committed by both sides, including extrajudicial killings, forced "disappearances," torture and rape. In the vast majority of cases, the perpetrators of such abuses are never brought to account. Based on statistics provided by the Memorial Human Rights Center, Human Rights Watch has described Russia as the "world leader in enforced disappearances," with between 3,000 and 5,000 cases since 1999.[53]

Targeted assassinations have also killed numerous individuals suspected either of being rebels, or of being aligned with the Russian forces. In May 2004, the pro-Moscow Chechen president was himself assassinated by Chechen rebels, and elections were held in August 2004 to replace him with another president favored by the Russian government.

The conflict in Chechnya has spilled over into the nearby republics of Ingushetia and North Ossetia; abuses by Russian and Chechen rebel forces have been carried out there as well. In September 2004, an estimated 1,200 teachers, children and parents were held hostage in a school in Beslan, North Ossetia by a group of Chechen terrorists, later claimed to be led by Shamil Basayev.[54] The hostages were held for 58 hours, and at least 338 were killed when explosives rigged by the terrorists detonated, the school's gymnasium roof collapsed and the hostage-takers shot at those trying to flee. Following the tragedy in Beslan, Russian President Vladimir Putin announced further measures to centralize power in the Russian executive branch and the presidency.

Human rights defenders working in Chechnya or with the Chechen population also have been subjected to increasing threats, intimidation and attacks. Lawyers, representatives of NGOs, and the families of victims of human rights violations who lodge complaints have been arrested, tortured, "disappeared," threatened and even killed. Individuals who have complained to the European Court of Human Rights about the actions of Russian government forces have been subject to constant harassment and abuse. The UN's special representative on human rights defenders sent 14 communications to the Russian government in 2004, concerning 15 individual human rights defenders and three NGOs. In her report to the 61st session of the Commission on Human Rights, the special representative stated that "most of the reported violations occurred in the context of the ongoing conflict in Chechnya and were perpetrated against defenders working to expose the human rights situation in the region." She further reported that at least two human rights defenders working on minority rights and the violation of human rights in Chechnya were killed.[55]

As the time of this writing, new revelations about the existence of mass graves in Chechnya were emerging. Despite this and other evidence of the scale and seriousness of the human rights crisis in the republic, there seems little willingness among the international community to take on the Russian government on the issue. Without the support of powerful countries such as the US, the ability of the UN human rights system to address the situation in Chechnya is sadly limited.

Sudan (Darfur)

Since early 2003, the Sudanese government has used local Arab militia groups (Janjaweed) to conduct a scorched-earth campaign, intended to drive out rebels and their perceived supporters. By the end of 2004, this campaign had resulted in the destruction of hundreds of villages and the displacement of an estimated 1.8 million civilians. In addition, estimates indicated that at least 70,000 civilians may have been killed either directly by the government forces and their militia proxies or through conflict-related illness and malnutrition.[56]

Attacks are targeted at particular ethnic groups, namely the Fur, Masalit and Zaghawa, and are exacerbated by ongoing local conflicts over land between these "African" groups and Arab nomads. The first main government offensive in the region took place in late 2003, when militia forces were mobilized in response to rebel attacks in West Darfur. These militia were intended to supplement the small number of government troops in the region, and to carry out attacks alongside a campaign of aerial bombardment. From this time, villages and crops have been razed, homes looted and destroyed, men, women and children killed systematically, and thousands of women have been raped. These actions constitute serious human rights violations and crimes against humanity and, should it be proven that they were carried out with the intent to destroy a national, ethnic, racial or religious group, may also amount to genocide.[57]

For more than a year, the international community seemed paralyzed with regard to the situation in Darfur. Divisions within the UN Security Council prevented any action to address the crisis until June 2004, and despite the evidence of massive human rights abuses, a resolution condemning the Sudanese government was defeated at the 60th session of the Commission on Human Rights. On April 8, 2004, a cease-fire agreement was signed, with the government committed to "neutralize" the Janjaweed militias. Again, in July 2004, the Sudanese government promised to disarm the Janjaweed and ensure human rights. At the end of July, the Security Council passed Resolution 1556, which, among other things, asked the government to put in place international monitors and cooperate with observers sent by OHCHR. However, at the end of August, the Secretary-General reported to the Security Council that the government had done little to address human rights abuses or end the climate of impunity.[58]

In September 2004, the Security Council adopted Resolution 1564, threatening to impose sanctions on the Sudanese government if it did not comply with this and previous resolutions. It further authorized the establishment of an international commission of inquiry to investigate allegations of serious violations of international humanitarian law and human rights in Darfur and to determine whether acts of genocide had been committed. In August 2004, OHCHR sent eight human rights monitors to Darfur, and in September, the High Commissioner herself visited the region, accompanied by the UN Secretary-General's special adviser on the prevention of genocide, Juan Mendez. In November 2004, the Security Council carried out a visit to Nairobi, Kenya to discuss Darfur—a historic occasion for the body, meeting outside of New York. The Council adopted Resolution 1574 on November 19, but did not mention the government's obligation to disarm the Janjaweed, nor did it threaten sanctions.

On January 25, 2005, the International Commission of Inquiry on Darfur submitted its report to the Secretary-General, which was transmitted subsequently to the Security Council.[59] The members of the international commission concluded that the Sudanese government and the Janjaweed were responsible for serious violations of international human rights and humanitarian law, amounting to crimes under international law. In particular, government security forces and Janjaweed militia had carried out indiscriminate attacks, including killing of civilians, torture, enforced disappearances, destruction of villages, rape, pillaging and forced displacement throughout Darfur. The international commission also concluded that such attacks were carried out on a widespread and systematic basis and may amount to crimes against humanity. However, the group did not characterize the actions of the government as a policy of genocide. The perpetrators of abuses described in the report included a number of government officials. It further recommended that the Security Council refer the situation in Darfur to the International Criminal Court (ICC). Addressing the Security Council in February 2005, the High Commissioner for Human Rights repeated the commission's call for a referral to the ICC. On March 31, 2005, the Security Council adopted Resolution 1593, referring the situation in Darfur since July 1, 2002 to the prosecutor of the Court.[60] In early June 2005, an investigation was opened (*see Chapter 7 for further details*).

Among the other arms of the UN human rights system concerned with the level of the crisis in Darfur, the Human Rights Committee, which monitors the implementation of the *International Covenant on Civil and Political Rights*, requested in April 2005 that the Sudanese government submit a special report on its compliance with selected articles of the covenant.[61] While the Commission on Human Rights did not condemn the Sudanese government for its abuses of human rights in Darfur during its 60th session in 2004, it did appoint an independent expert to monitor the situation for a year. In July 2004, Emmanuel Akwei Addo was appointed to the position, and he reported to the 59th session of the General Assembly and the 61st session of the commission. Mr. Addo drew attention to close coordination between the Janjaweed and government forces in attacks upon civilian populations, despite denials by the government. He also highlighted systematic rape and sexual violence against women, and the looting of property. The special rapporteur on extrajudicial, summary or arbitrary executions also conducted a mission to Sudan in 2004, as did the special representative on IDPs and the special rapporteur on violence against women.

At the commission's 61st session, two draft resolutions on Sudan were put forward. The first, put forward by the European Union and others, condemned human rights violations in Darfur. The second, put forward by the African Group, condemned violations of international human rights and humanitarian law by all parties, and proposed the creation of a new special rapporteur on the situation of human rights in Sudan.[62] After intensive negotiation, the EU withdrew its resolution and the latter was adopted without a vote. However, human rights groups described the resolution as too weak and "disturbingly silent" regarding the responsibility of the Sudanese government for crimes under international law. Nonetheless, the Sudanese representative at the commission criticized the EU for its "inflexibility" in negotiating the resolution and objected that "the pre-determined attitude of condemning, shaming and naming unfortunately prevailed."[63]

While the gears of the UN human rights system appear to have shifted into operation with regard to the crisis in Darfur, and the Security Council has finally taken concrete measures to try to bring it to an end, it remains to be seen whether this will make a significant impact upon the situation on the ground. Sudan is a vast country which has gone through decades of conflict, and the scale of the crisis in Darfur, as well as in other parts of the country, requires an enormous amount of resources as well as continued international engagement.[64]

Looking Forward

Over the past 60 years, the UN has played an invaluable role in establishing respect for human rights as a central issue in international relations. Furthermore, a consensus has emerged that the promotion and protection of human rights is one of the paramount functions of the organization. However, there is also recognition of the fact that massive crises involving widespread violations of human rights continue to occur around the world, and the UN is often ill-equipped to deal with such crises promptly and effectively. The proposals for UN reform put forward by the Secretary-General and the High-level Panel, if implemented, will assist in building the UN's capacity to address serious rights abuses.

While much of the 60th General Assembly's attention will be focused on the debate over UN reform, including the creation of a new Human Rights Council, concerns about the capacity of the Assembly to address human rights issues will likely remain. At its 59th session, the Third Committee and plenary of the General Assembly demonstrated a disturbing trend toward paralysis, as illustrated by its inability to pass a resolution condemning the human rights situation in Darfur. Further use of the no-action motion might prevent other resolutions from being adopted in fall 2005.

It is crucial that the UN be granted the capacity by its member states, both in terms of material resources and through the prompt adoption of the necessary resolutions, to fulfill its human rights mandate. The implementation of Security Council resolutions on Darfur must be a priority for 2005, along with continued efforts to improve the security situation in Afghanistan and Iraq, where forthcoming elections could contribute to establishing the rule of law and ensuring a safer future. Much is at stake, and it is the responsibility of all individuals, peoples and states to make the realization of human rights a reality through a strong, effective and united community of nations.

Humanitarian Assistance and the United Nations

Jacques Fomerand

Since its fledgling and hesitant beginnings in the 1970s with the creation of the United Nations Disaster Relief Office (UNDRO), the UN appears to have acquired a firm foothold in the humanitarian business. Since 1991, the organization has issued no less than 220 Consolidated Appeals raising $27 billion in voluntary contributions. Last year alone, the UN Consolidated Appeals for more than 30 countries or regions, amounting to some $3 billion. From September 2003 to the end of August 2004, the UN assisted countries and regions affected by more than 50 natural disasters.[1]

The global reach of the UN humanitarian enterprise can be further underlined by its response to the December 2004 tsunami disaster. Demand for UN humanitarian relief indeed surged in the first two months of 2005 as UN assistance to the countries affected ranged from the provision of immediate shelter and food to urgent medical and preventive care.[2] Within four weeks after the disaster, the UN had raised $775 million or 79 percent of the Flash Appeal[3] to support ongoing reconstruction efforts. In the same timeframe, it had coordinated the distribution of food to 1.2 million people and supplied clean drinking water to 500,000 individuals.

With regard to the tsunami, the UN is credited to have satisfactorily performed its mobilizing and coordinating functions in what is considered the largest and most complex humanitarian effort it has even undertaken. Yet, while labeling it as an "overwhelming success," political observers also noted that the UN-led relief effort in the Pacific exposed the organization's "weaknesses in dealing with humanitarian crises elsewhere."[4] This apparent double standard touches on only one of the problems that have plagued the UN humanitarian system. The purpose of this section is to identify and discuss some of these "weaknesses" in light of the most salient humanitarian developments in 2004 and early 2005.

The UN Humanitarian System Today

Legitimacy

On November 11, 2004, the General Assembly held a day-long discussion on strengthening the coordination of UN humanitarian and disaster relief assistance. The debate, which covered much more than coordination, exposed once again the North-South fault lines that underpin the persisting tenuous atmosphere prevailing over the UN humanitarian enterprise. Developed (i.e., donor) countries were concerned about "effectiveness," "quality" and "accountability." In their view, greater attention to and improved coordination with governments, nongovernmental organizations (NGOs) and affected populations, as well as building local capacity, are key to ensuring sustainable results. They all emphasized the need to provide safe access for humanitarian and relief workers in order to ensure the requisite assistance for vulnerable populations, particularly women and children. But with the past few years' developments in Afghanistan and Iraq still fresh in many delegates' minds, only a few were prone to take public stands on Norway's admonition to separate humanitarian and development activities from political and military elements.

The norm of sovereignty, on the other hand, was of paramount importance to developing countries. As China put it most forcefully, the principles of "neutrality," "humanity" and "impartiality" should guide all humanitarian action by the UN. In addition, it was suggested that humanitarian assistance needed to be apolitical and offered only at the request of recipient governments. At the same time, southern countries argued that it was necessary to ensure a more equitable balance of humanitarian assistance across emergencies, including those of a protracted nature, and to bridge the gap between relief and development; this latter reform would achieve a "smooth transition" from humanitarian emergency assistance to post-conflict reconstruction and development. They also argued that the global level of financing for humanitarian operations should be increased and made more "predictable."[5]

Such debates were influenced by the observations and recommendations of the High-level Panel on Threats, Challenges and Change, which, as noted in previous sections of this book, pays considerable attention to humanitarian issues. In the context of its discussion of prevention and the legitimate use of force, the panel endorses "the emerging norm" that there is a collective international responsibility to protect.[6] Still, the mere idea that national governments might have responsibilities and be held accountable, both to their own people and to the wider international community, elicited icy reactions and terse admonitions.

The Non-Aligned Movement (NAM) reiterated its principled rejection of the so-called "right" of humanitarian intervention which has no basis in the *UN Charter* or in the general principles of international law. For example, in Indonesia, the responsibility to protect its citizens, and the right of the international community to intervene should states fail in discharging this "responsibility," undoubtedly had legitimate "moral and political justifications."

For southern countries participating in the discussion, development was the key priority to be addressed by a "revitalized" UN General Assembly and a "transformed," "democratic" Security Council. As Pakistan argued, because the High-level Panel's discussion of "state failure and the so-called responsibility to protect [was]…highly controversial it would be a mistake to prescribe interventionist approaches." Inaction in the face of genocide, ethnic cleansing or massive killings in the past stemmed from the lack of political will by the international community to act, not because of a legal vacuum. Under these conditions, Pakistan argued, "It is also pertinent to ask, when does this so-called 'responsibility to protect' arise? Does it arise at the verge of state collapse, on the eve of genocide? Or earlier, when conditions of poverty and underdevelopment make state collapse an inevitability? We believe that any presumed 'responsibility' to protect can become legitimate…when it is a continuation of sustained and visible international solidarity." This point was echoed by India, who asserted that poverty and internal conflicts were not simply the legacy of colonial rule or the result of current poor governance but of liberalization, globalization and the policies of international economic institutions.

Meanwhile, the Jamaican ambassador to the UN, speaking on behalf of the Group of 77, blasted the narrowness of the High-level Panel report's "conceptual underpinnings," specifically for its casting of development issues in the confines of security and prevention strategies. In his view, this approach would merely contribute to an undesirable increase of power in the hands of the Security Council and further undermine the authority of the Economic and Social Council (ECOSOC). For that very reason, there was widespread opposition to the idea of placing the Peace-building Commission proposed by the panel under the authority of the Security Council. Many felt that such a commission had to be integrated in a comprehensive under-standing of peace-building, take account of the full range of post-conflict development challenges, and be grounded in sustained commitment by the international community.[7]

Conceptual and Operational Uncertainties

Clearly, the UN humanitarian assistance system raises quasi-existential issues not only about the political legitimacy of humanitarian action but also about the governance of the UN and the substantive priorities of the organi-zation as a whole. The changing nature of humanitarianism since the demise of the Cold War has undoubtedly exacerbated that debate. One such development has been the increasing number of interventions described as "humanitarian" when, in fact, their objectives have been strategic, political or military-based. The issue is not new, but in the recent cases of Afghanistan and Iraq, the humanitarian principles of independence and neutrality have collided with the Manichean views of governments engaged in the zero-sum game of the war against global terrorism. In both countries, UN agencies have endeavored to adhere to these principles, but their access to populations in need has been constrained by lack of security.

The embedding of humanitarianism in peacekeeping operations initiat-ed since the 1990s has presented another scope of new challenges. Initial-ly developed in the course of the Cold War, the objective of UN peacekeep-ing operations was to help resolve interstate conflicts through the interpos-ing of lightly armed military personnel between the armed forces of the warring parties. In addition, their deployment hinged on the consent of the states concerned. Now, official UN documents define peacekeeping as an instrument designed to help conflict-torn countries and to create long-last-ing conditions for sustainable peace. UN peacekeepers not only monitor and observe peace processes today, but also assist in confidence-building meas-ures, power-sharing arrangements, electoral support, strengthening the rule of law, and economic and social development. Gone are the days when clearly identifiable armies fought during the day and rested at night while humanitarian crews picked up and attended the wounded.

One immediate consequence of this situation has been the increasingly tenuous safety of civilians and UN humanitarian personnel and is directly linked to accessing populations in need. In the eastern part of the Democ-ratic Republic of Congo, for instance, where violence hindered the delivery of humanitarian programs in food security, healthcare, water and educa-tion, some 3.3 million people were out of reach of aid groups.

In June 2004, the Security Council held a special meeting devoted to the protection of civilians in times of war. The head of the Office for the Coordi-nation of Humanitarian Affairs (OCHA), the entity responsible for the coor-dination of UN humanitarian actions, admonished that not enough progress has been achieved in the past decade in establishing what Secre-tary-General Kofi Annan previously labeled as a "culture of protection" toward civilians. At least 10 million civilians have been caught up in 20 separate wars around the world and are denied access to aid workers, warned OCHA head Jan Egeland, as he urged the Council to strengthen its efforts to protect civilians. Meanwhile, the wearing of a UN blue helmet or badge can no longer be deemed to offer protection from attack. Last year, at least eight UN staff were taken hostage in separate incidents and so far this year, at least 12 peacekeepers have been killed and at least 26 UN staff members remain under arrest, missing or detained.[8]

Forgotten Emergencies and the Funding Issue

The media is often blamed for the proliferation of "forgotten emergencies." Recent research commissioned by Alertnet, an online humanitarian news network run by Reuters, suggests that the Indian Ocean tsunami got more media attention in the first six weeks after it struck than all of the world's 10 worst emergencies combined in the past year. Identified by 100 humanitarian officials, academics and activists as "forgotten emergencies," these include: the Democratic Republic of Congo (DRC), Uganda, Sudan, West Africa, Colombia, Chechnya, Nepal and Haiti. The numbers are damning. The DRC, for example, is still smoldering in the wake of its civil war, which drew seven other African countries into the conflict and killed three to five million people. In Uganda, an 18-year-old insurgency led by a rebel group known as the Lord's Resistance Army (LRA) has killed up to 100,000 people and has been accompanied by the abduction of 30,000 children forced to serve as soldiers or sex slaves, as well as the displacement of 1.8 million people. And in Colombia, in four decades of internal strife involving guerrillas and right-wing paramilitary groups with ties to government armed forces, 35,000 have been killed and three million displaced.[9]

But the selectiveness of the media is only part of the story. Ultimately, it is governments that make the sovereign (and political) decision to intervene or to remain on the sidelines. A good indicator of their commitments is their actual funding of humanitarian crises.

Global levels of funding tend to fluctuate significantly from one year to the next. As indicated in Table A, governmental contributions reached a

Table A: Consolidated Appeals (as of April 30, 2005, in $US billions)

YEAR	ORIGINAL REQUIREMENTS	REVISED REQUIREMENTS	COMMITMENTS, CONTRIBUTIONS AND CARRYOVER	PERCENT (%) COVERED
2000	$2,093.	$1,922.	$1,139.	59%
2001	$2,485.	$2,559.	$1,416.	55%
2002	$4,668.	$4,375.	$2,952.	67%
2003	$5,182.	$5,220.	$3,958.	76%
2004	$3,004.	$3,412.	$2,174.	64%
2005	$4,165.	$4,405.	$1,827.	37%

Source: OCHA Consolidated Appeals Charts, 2000-2005.

peak of $4 billion in 2003 and plummeted to a low of $1.1 billion in 2000. In 2002 and 2001, they were $3 billion and $1.4 billion, respectively. As of April 2005, the figure was $1.8 billion and was expected to increase.

In addition, the idea that the humanitarian enterprise is primarily a Western undertaking linked to its political, economic and cultural agenda is not altogether farfetched. The same Western governments provide the bulk of humanitarian funding. In 2004, 10 countries (Canada, Denmark, Germany, Japan, The Netherlands, Norway, Sweden, Switzerland, the United Kingdom and United States) provided 58.1 percent of all humanitarian contributions. If the 15.5 percent share of the European Union is factored in, that number reaches nearly three quarters of the total. In contrast, the United Arab Emirates gave 2.1 percent, Saudi Arabia, 0.8 percent and the Russian Federation, 0.4 percent.[10]

There is a perennial pattern of unmet financial requirements ranging, overall, from a high of 45 percent in 2001 to a low of 24 percent in 2003. The World Food Programme recently lamented the fact that it had received only 10 percent of the $155 million it needed this year to feed more than 1.5 million people affected by past and current conflicts in Sierra Leone, Guinea, Liberia and Côte d'Ivoire.[11] Likewise, OCHA deplored that, in response to a more than $39 million international appeal for Côte d'Ivoire, The Netherlands alone had pledged $181,000, "or about 0.05 percent." These are only two recent examples. On the occasion of a mid-term review of the UN Flash Appeal for victims of the Indian Ocean, Mr. Egeland praised lavishly the international community for its "extraordinarily effective emergency relief effort" in response to the tsunami. At the same time, he underlined once again the "unmet needs elsewhere," and the dramatic condition of 30 million people affected by "forgotten" crises in Africa, Europe, the Middle East and Latin America. For those regions, by April 2005, the UN had received only $168 million, an amount representing less than 10 percent of the $1.7 billion the organization requested for 2005 and a mere "one-fifth of what Europe spends on ice cream per year."[12]

Within this overall framework, data suggests that the African continent remains underfunded. This point was forcefully brought to the attention of the Security Council in late January 2005 by Mr. Egeland who stated that "nearly four-fifths of the recent United Nations humanitarian appeals have addressed African problems, but the response has been slow to nearly nonexistent." Indeed, in 2004, the response to Consolidated Appeals for Africa from UN agencies and NGOs ranged from 10 percent for Zimbabwe to less than 40 percent for the Central African Republic and Côte d'Ivoire to around 75 percent for Sudan, Chad and Uganda.[13] Out of the 14 fund appeals that the UN has made for Africa in 2005, eight had attracted less than 20 percent of the requested amounts. In addition, there are significant differentials in per capita levels of assistance received by individual countries. The cost of assisting a tsunami survivor is estimated at $1.07 per person per day under the joint UN appeal compared with just $0.16 per person for assistance in Africa. As recent UNICEF Executive Director Carol Bellamy pointed out, Zimbabwe, one of the few countries with a National Plan of Action for Orphans and Vulnerable Children (OVC), received $4 per year in donor spending per HIV-infected person while Eritrea received $802, Uganda $319, Zambia $187 and Namibia, $101.[14]

"High profile crises" indeed get more attention and resources than other emergencies. East Timor and Kosovo have dropped out of the humanitarian radar screen and been replaced by Afghanistan and Iraq. In this regard, and bearing in mind the overall levels of humanitarian assistance for 2005, it is opportune to recall here that pledges of $8.3 billion covering two to three years were made at last year's pledging conference for Afghanistan. In addition, the US hopes to double this year's assistance to Afghanistan to more than $5 billion. Washington also spends $10 billion on military operations in Afghanistan. In 2003, the Iraq crisis drew almost half of the Consolidated Appeal for the year (slightly more than $2 billion). The tsunami may have had the same effect to draw resources from needy countries. Thus, the head of the WFP recently pointed out that donations in January 2005 to WFP's operations in Africa had dropped by 21 percent to $24 million compared to $29 million in January 2004. Donations for Africa amounted to just 5 percent of the $1.9 billion needed by WFP to reach the most vulnerable and hungry people so far in 2005, in spite of the fact that overall food needs in Africa represented two-thirds of WFP's global requirements. [15]

Long-Term Development

The funding issue is further heightened by the growing trend toward "integrated" UN missions which combine nation- and state-building activities with disarmament and other security measures (e.g., demining, police training), human rights, gender equality projects and longer-term rehabilitation. The rationale behind this trend is the recognition that poverty is a major cause in triggering humanitarian crises, and that development policies linking economic, social and political factors can potentially prevent such crises.

By and large, prevailing development policies and practices at the national and international level offer little grounds for comfort. The market-oriented policies put in place over the past two to three decades have heightened inequalities both within and among nations, as documented by various issues of the UN Development Programme's (UNDP) Human Development Report. Related concerns have been expressed by a number of UN organizations. At the February 2005 meeting of the Governing Council of the International Fund for Agricultural Development, increasing social inequality in parts of Asia and the lack of beneficial policies and institutions in West and Central Africa were cited as creating major challenges to poverty eradication efforts.[16] Moreover, according to another UNDP study, the world's 50 least developed countries spent an estimated $5.1 billion in 2002 just on servicing their debts.[17]

Against this backdrop, it will come as no surprise that, in a February

2005 debate of the Security Council on the regional aspects of peacekeeping, the Secretary-General warned that reforming the security sectors and reintegrating former militia members into their communities in West Africa (there are some 200,000 ex-combatants in the region) needed funds that had not been forthcoming.[18]

Reform Proposals

In a recent study, two humanitarian enterprise experts noted that the humanitarian system today was not the driving force of donor behavior, and that the policy framework of the system was both inconsistent and contradictory. One of the authors later compared the system to a poorly patched-up assembly line, stating: "The upshot of our system is not badly made cars. It is a badly made emergency response system, with funding for Zambia but not Zimbabwe; funding for water but not vaccinations...funding for food, but not seeds; support for children, not adults; for women, not men." Perhaps, the worst upshot of today's humanitarian assistance regime is the world's "forgotten emergencies," as noted above.[19]

On the positive side, there is room for improvement. The problems, both operational and conceptual, are known and proposals for change are on the table. An important source of ideas has been the so-called Good Humanitarian Donorship initiative which originated from a 2003 conference in Sweden with 16 donor governments, representatives of UN agencies, international NGOs and academics. Last December, UK Minister for International Development Hillary Benn put forward a six-point program that would replace the current *ad hoc* system of fundraising which often fails to get sufficient relief supplies to where they are needed quickly enough with a new UN humanitarian fund; the fund would be set at $1 billion a year and UN humanitarian coordinators could draw from it.[20] The statement was accompanied by an offer to put about $180 million into the fund (roughly 15 percent of the annual total and a quarter of the UK's humanitarian assistance) for quick release to UN coordinators on the ground when crises erupt. The fund would be placed under the control of the Secretary-General and administered by the head of OCHA. At the time of this writing, the G8 was considering the proposal. In the meantime, the AU has begun drawing up plans to establish a 15,000-strong African stand-by force by June 2006. The entire contingent would ideally be able to be deployed within 30 days should an order from the AU's Peace and Security Council come forward. In addition, a "robust" rapid-reaction force, able to be deployed in 14 days, would be set up by 2010 to prevent genocide if the international community failed to step in.[21]

Before closing this section, it is important to note that the UN's humanitarian agencies are only part of a much broader network encompassing both individuals and organizations, many of which are far less constrained by politics. Whatever the imperfections of the overall system, the "anarchy of altruism," coupled with the normative appeals of the UN, have kept humanitarian issues on the international community's agenda.

Country-Specific Humanitarian Assistance

Tsunami-Impacted Region

In all likelihood, the full human toll of the tsunami will probably never be known. New figures are still coming in requiring upward estimates. Indonesia bore the brunt of the disaster as the number of people killed in the Aceh province exceeded 125,000 and more than 650,000 were displaced. In Sri Lanka, more than 30,000 people died in the tragedy and over 500,000 were displaced. In India, 16,300 people perished and 650,000 were left homeless. One third of the Maldives Islands' entire population, some 100,000 people, was directly affected as the waves severely damaged 53 of the country's 199 inhabited islands.

Raw data only partially convey the devastating fury of the disaster. The tsunami inflicted a loss of more than half a billion dollars on the fishing sector of the seven worst-affected countries, with over 111,000 vessels destroyed or damaged, 36,000 engines lost and 1.7 million units of fishing gear ruined. According to UNDP, in the Seychelles, the tsunami destroyed roads, bridges, public utilities and houses in coastal areas, and flooded commercial and fishing piers. In Thailand, where tourism contributes 5 to 6 percent to total GDP, the impact on the national economy has lead to a drop in forecast of GDP growth for 2005 from 6.3 percent to 5.6 percent. The damage caused to Indonesia's environment is pegged at $675 million and the country faces a massive loss of livelihood with the destruction of about 40,000 hectares of rice paddies and 70 percent of its fishing industry. [22]

Whatever the exact figures may be, the very scale of the catastrophe sparked an unprecedented outpouring of global relief aid. Within two weeks of the tsunami, donor countries had pledged $717 million to a UN appeal for emergency relief and reconstruction of 10 Asian countries. [23]

By the end of February 2005, overall aid pledged from or through governments, NGOs, businesses and private sources totaled $6.28 billion. According to OHCA, Germany was the largest contributor with $683 million, followed by the Asian Development Bank ($600 million), private donations ($576 million), Japan (about $500 million), the European Commission ($494 million), France ($443 million), Australia ($431 million), the United States ($354 million) and Canada ($351 million). By mid-March, 90 percent of the UN's Flash Appeal of $979 million (for the period January to June 2005) had already been covered. While UNHCR and UNDP remained underfunded, the WFP had received all it had sought in the appeal and was then feeding 455,000 people in the Aceh region of Indonesia. [24] Likewise, UNICEF had received its full requested amount.

The initial response was slowed down by "logistical constraints" ranging from lack of familiarity with the terrain, torrential rains, overloaded airports, and lack of communications facilities, fuel storage, water treatment units and more. But as scores of humanitarian and relief NGOs and governmental organizations poured in[25] and as several countries deployed military assets, including an American aircraft carrier, the 1.8 billion people impacted did begin to see relief. Fortunately, political issues remained muted and, by and large, did not disrupt the humanitarian effort. In spite of a shaky cease-fire in their fragile three-year-old truce, the Sri Lankan president promised to work with the Tamil Tigers to bring aid to rebel-controlled areas. In the Indonesian province of Aceh, torn by a more than two-decade-long merciless civil war, a cease-fire was called and the government of Indonesia, setting aside its prickliness about foreigners, lifted a ban on international aid agencies entering the province.

On the ground, the ever-familiar squabbling and rivalries between various UN agencies yielded to cooperation and compromise. OCHA head Jan Egeland was firmly in charge of the overall UN and international effort.[26] Stung and tarnished by its handling of the Oil-for -Food Programme in Iraq (*see below*), the UN instituted new financial tracking of its tsunami procedures to ensure public accountability of how money was spent.[27] One month after the catastrophe, it was said that Mr. Egeland could legitimately draw a positive balance sheet of a "remarkably, singularly effective, swift and muscular" international response that had saved tens of thousands of lives against tremendous odds.[28]

By late January, in Sri Lanka, UNHCR had provided plastic sheeting, mats, mosquito nets, kitchen sets and clothing for more than 150,000 survivors. Children were beginning to go back to school. There were also signs the UN agencies and volunteers involved in aid were speedily moving into the next phase of recovery and rebuilding.[29] For example, UNHCR provided shelter to some 100,000 people in Aceh and WFP was running food-for-work projects to help hundreds of thousands of survivors return to a productive and independent way of life.

After summer 2005, it was expected that the immediate relief efforts would be followed by a longer-term rehabilitation program. The Food and Agriculture Organization (FAO), for example, would help rehabilitate the region's fishing industry with nets, gear and repaired boats. Initial steps were taken by the UN Educational, Scientific and Educational Organization (UNESCO) to build a tsunami early warning system knitting together existing national systems. And UN-HABITAT was beginning to enter into agreements with authorities to help rebuild homes and ensure disaster-resilient shelters.[30]

Overall, the international and political will to help and receive assistance remained present. Political and military conflicts which might have hindered access of humanitarian workers and supplies were held in abeyance. And when the March 28, 2005 undersea earthquake struck, hitting the already devastated region a second time, some 1,000 international staff and 250 international organizations were on the ground to help within hours.[31] If anything went (or is going) wrong in the Asian tsunami disaster relief effort, it might rather be found in the persistent reports of large piles of international donations which, for a variety of reasons, have yet to reach their intended targets.[32]

Afghanistan

The security environment in Afghanistan improved in 2004 and the country has undoubtedly made some progress since the demise of the Taliban government in late 2001. Contributing factors include an increase in strength of the Afghan army and police, and an expanded presence of the International Security Assistance Force (ISAF). The inauguration of President Hamid Karzai on December 2004 and the constitution of a Cabinet three weeks later have helped as well (*see Chapter 2 for details*). As a result, more than 3.5 million Afghan refugees have come home from Pakistan and Iran under the aegis of UNHCR. And 54.4 percent of primary age children were in school by the end of 2004.[33]

Yet, the country is still quite fragile. There were outbursts of violence in the first several months of 2005, one of which killed three persons, including a UN worker. According to a UNDP report, one in two Afghans can still be classified as poor, more than half the population is severely impacted by drought and adult literacy rates stand at just 28.7 percent of the population. A "massive skills deficit" continues to plague such sectors as police, teachers and engineers. Illicit narcotics trade still dominates Afghanistan's economy. UNHCR estimates that there are around 1.2 million Afghans in camps and an unknown number living in cities and villages. (Some 400,000 Afghan refugees may return home during this year's repatriation season.) And while some 1.2 million girls have enrolled in Afghanistan's primary schools since 2002, more than 1 million primary-school-age girls are still not attending classes. Finally, donors still fund more than 93 percent of Afghanistan's national budget.[34]

Within this context, the UN is playing a relatively modest role. The UN peace mission there (UNAMA) and UNDP are assisting in preparations for fall elections. With an overall operational budget of $341 million from April 2003 to September 2005, WFP is providing food to nearly six million people. After the harshest winter and heaviest snowfalls in years cut off tens of thousands of Afghans from food supplies, WFP also has provided food to more than 100,000 snowbound Afghans (in some cases by means of airdrops) and taken preventive measures to alleviate the impact of possible subsequent flooding. UNHCR distributed more than 1,000 tents to 7,300 Afghan refugees made homeless by flooding in Pakistan's Balochistan region. UNICEF has been helping the Ministry of Education to provide basic classroom stationery and materials to schools nationwide.[35] And in cooperation with the Afghan government, UNICEF launched a three-day national polio vaccination campaign targeted at an estimated 5.3 million Afghan children under age five in an effort to finally eradicate the virus from the country.

Côte d'Ivoire

A French brokered agreement, known as the Linas-Marcoussis Agreement, ended the conflict between Côte d'Ivoire's government-run south and a rebel-held north in January 2003. It even briefly brought in a government of national reconciliation. But in mid-2004, despite a UN peacekeeping presence, the fragile cease-fire was dramatically broken. Mediation efforts, prodded by France and South Africa, have made some progress. The security situation, however, has remained tense.

As a result, the humanitarian predicament of Côte d'Ivoire has further deteriorated, especially in the education, health, water and sanitation sectors. Some 3.5 million persons are in need of humanitarian assistance. Access to those in need is, however, severely constrained in the West.[36] According to UNICEF, the *de facto* partition of the country and continuing civil war has meant no school, no vaccinations and a fresh threat of polio for some 700,000 children in the north.[37] The World Health Organization (WHO) and UNICEF jointly organized vaccination campaigns in 2004 to contain and eradicate cholera, yellow fever, meningitis and poliomyelitis. But the vulnerable persons in the north and west are still lacking access to medicines, medical equipment and professional health workers. Humanitarian actors have increasingly been concerned with the growing needs of 500,000 IDPs who are becoming more and more dependent on humanitarian assistance.

SG Annan has made several appeals for "maximum restraint" as political tensions increase. The timing of the elections scheduled for October 2005 appears increasingly unrealistic. The Security Council, after imposing sanctions last November, may be running out of options to settle the situation. Meanwhile, the socio-economic predicament of the country is hardly a source of optimism. The Ivoirien deficit continued to increase in 2004 and the November 2004 violence forced 125 out of 500 foreign-owned businesses to close down, leaving 30,000 people unemployed.

Democratic Republic of Congo and the Great Lakes Region

In the wake of the events of early 2005, whatever optimism characterized the humanitarian outlook for the Great Lakes Region at the beginning of 2004 has evaporated. In Burundi, the massacre of Congolese refugees in Gatumba and rebel attacks in Bujumbura Rurale put a damper on encouraging developments. In Uganda, attacks by the Lord's Resistance Army (LRA) continued to subject civilian populations in the northern and northeastern parts of the country to terror and hardship. And in the Democratic Republic of Congo, where the UN peacekeeping mission has just over 16,000 troops in place, the situation has been far more disquieting.

In brief, inter-ethnic violence fed by external intervention and internal state failures is slowly sinking large portions of the DRC back into anarchy. Rwanda and Uganda maintain security arrangements with leaders of armed groups along their borders with Congo. Militias are on the rampage, with no exception to who might be a target. And aid agencies are being harassed. In fact, intensified fighting between ethnic militias has forced aid organizations to suspend their food and medical assistance.[38]

Despite a formal end to DRC's five-year war, the country is suffering the world's worst humanitarian crisis, outstripping, according to the UN, that of Sudan's Darfur region (*see below*). According to aid agencies, malnutrition and preventable diseases kill 1,000 people every day. Many schools and hospitals have been destroyed. Cases of pneumonic plague have been identified, compounded by the constant threat of drought and the rapid spread of HIV/AIDS.[39] Since 1999, over 60,000 people have died in Ituri, where clashes between militias are often as much over the control of tax and mining revenues as ethnic rivalries. The number of people displaced by conflict in the DRC is now estimated at 3 million, 2.5 million in the east alone. That number has swelled in recent months.

The humanitarian activities of UN organizations in the field, including those of OCHA, UNFPA, UNESCO and WHO, have primarily focused on direct life-saving and life-sustaining assistance, including advocacy activities highlighting the needs of children and IDPs, the provision of essential food and non-food items, agricultural inputs and training for IDPs and vulnerable households, and HIV testing and counseling to refugees and migrants.[40] UNHCR is also planning to repatriate thousands of individuals into Equateur. In the eastern part of the DRC, more than 88,000 IDPs are receiving humanitarian aid.[41]

Haiti

Much of the work of the UN Stabilization Mission in Haiti (MINUSTAH) over the past year has been devoted to bringing a semblance of law and order to the country where armed gangs and former soldiers have been involved in repeated violent incidents, mainly in the capital. As noted in Chapter 2, in mid-March 2005, the demobilization process began with a group of 325 former members of the country's armed forces laying down their arms.[42] And after extensive consultations, a timetable for local, parliamentary and presidential elections was drawn up for fall 2005. The human toll of the tropical storms which severely hit the island in fall 2004 was mitigated by the relief operations mounted by the UN with the support of MINUSTAH. General food distribution by WFP has since been replaced by more targeted programs.

Whether these improvements will be sustainable and cumulative remains to be seen. Humanitarian assistance, particularly for vulnerable groups and communities, is still required. In this respect, the Secretary-General noted in his latest report to the Security Council that only $13.7 million had been pledged out of the $37.3 million requested from the international community in an October 2004 Flash Appeal (approximately 37 percent of the amount requested) and that the transitional government still had "to develop concrete projects that could effectively utilize the assistance provided."[43]

In mid-April 2005, two separate fact-finding missions of the Security Council and ECOSOC converged on Haiti to assess the progress made so far by the transitional government in disarmament, national dialogue and the organization of elections. They also intended to help Haiti devise and implement long-term, sustainable development strategies, including issues such as unemployment, the use of aid and coping with natural disasters.[44]

Iraq

The role devolved to the UN in Iraq was spelled out in Security Council Resolution 1483 of May 2003, in which the Council entrusted the UN with coordination functions. Under the authority of a special representative of the Secretary-General reporting to the Council, the UN was thus expected to coordinate humanitarian and reconstruction assistance by UN agencies and NGOs, promote the safe and voluntary return of refugees, help efforts aimed at restoring national and local institutions for representative governance, and promote human rights and economic reconstruction of the country. The work of the special representative was supposed to take place within the framework of guidelines developed by the Secretariat shortly before the outbreak of the US-led war in spring 2003. The guidelines emphasized that all UN agencies "retain full control of UN humanitarian operations inside and outside Iraq...[and] must ensure that their operational indepedence is guaranteed at all times." This meant maintaining their ability to obtain and sustain access to all vulnerable populations in all parts of Iraq and to provide them with aid "in an equitable, neutral and impartial manner and without any political conditions attached."[45]

The August 2003 bombing of UN headquarters in Baghdad and the subsequent withdrawal of most international UN staff from Iraq reduced to rubble this re-statement of good humanitarian intentions. Under the umbrella of the UN Assistance Mission in Iraq (UNAMI), some 23 UN agencies now "coordinate" international aid to Iraq and offer assistance in the rebuilding of the country in 11 sectoral "clusters": education and culture; health; water and sanitation; infrastructure and housing; agriculture, water resources and environment; food security; mine action; refugees and internally displaced persons; governance and civil society; poverty reduction and human development; and electoral support. On the political side, the role of the UN has focused on the provision of advisory and technical electoral assistance to Iraq's Independent Electoral Commission.[46]

As a result of the continued insecurity, coalition forces have, in effect, assumed responsibility for humanitarian conditions in the country and placed restrictions on access to areas of Iraq where people were in dire need. For instance, the attack on Fallujah at the end of 2004 created a humanitarian disaster as medical help could not reach wounded civilians.[47] By the same token, concerns that collaboration with the military could compromise the neutrality of humanitarian organizations have been ignored, a most unwelcome development at a time when the dependence of the Iraqi population on humanitarian assistance was becoming more acute. (In late 2004, the WFP reported that 6.5 million Iraqis were dependent on food rations.)

Aside from food aid, rising unemployment and persistent health, water and sanitation problems have compounded Iraq's humanitarian crisis brought about by the 1991 Gulf War and nearly 13 years of comprehensive economic sanctions that were, in part, mitigated by the Oil-for-Food Programme. Many maintain that psychological disorders have increased with the general climate of fear and the soaring of sectarian crime. Years of neglect, war and looting have crippled the response capacity of Iraq's health system to contain soaring rates of deadly infections. At the same time, according to the UN Human Rights Commission's Special Rapporteur on the Right to Food, malnutrition among the youngest Iraqis has almost doubled since the US-led invasion toppled Saddam. A recent UNDP survey of nearly 22,000 households confirms these scattered findings and also brought to the forefront that there is more illiteracy now than in past generations. In addition, the survey results show that youth with a high school education or better are suffering from 37 percent unemployment.[48]

The fall of Baghdad, the capture of Saddam Hussein, the transfer of authority to the interim government and this year's elections have all been hailed as major turning points for Iraq. Yet, the country's infrastructure and humanitarian situation remains in shambles. Clearly, reconstruction and aid efforts in this country will be needed for years to come.

Oil-for-Food*

The Oil-for-Food Programme was established by the Security Council on April 14, 1995 as a temporary measure to alleviate and mitigate the unintended consequences of the UN's sanctions regime, which was imposed on Iraq in the wake of its 1990 invasion of Kuwait. The program was designed to allow Iraq, under UN control, to export oil and import food and humanitarian supplies. Operations under the program started in December 1996. From that date until March 2003, Iraq sold more that $65 billion in oil through the program and issued $38 billion in letters of credit to purchase humanitarian goods and equipment. The $27 billion balance was used to cover Gulf War reparations, UN administrative and operational costs for the program, and the expenditures incurred for the IAEA and UNMOVIC weapons inspection programs.

In Security Council Resolution 1483 of May 2003, civilian sanctions on Iraq were lifted and the program was closed (it formally terminated in November 2003). The program's ongoing humanitarian projects, assets and contracts with suppliers were transferred to the Coalition Provisional Authority (CPA). The balance of unencumbered funds was handed over to the Development Fund for Iraq, which is under the direction of the CPA.

In financial terms, the Oil-for-Food Programme was the largest program ever administered by the UN. Nine UN agencies were involved in its implementation and before the US-led invasion some 893 international staff and 3,600 Iraqis worked for the program.

Almost immediately after its closing, the program became the target of allegations of improprieties in its management and administration, casting a long shadow over the UN and specifically the Secretary-General. A dozen or so probes into the program have been set in motion, most of them in the US. On April 21, 2004, SG Annan announced the formation of an independent panel to conduct an inquiry into the management of the program. Chaired by Paul Volcker, former chairman of the board of governors of the US Federal Reserve System, the panel (formally known as the Independent Inquiry Committee or IIC) was given authority to investigate possible violations of UN accounting, administrative and management procedures and potential illicit activities by UN officials, personnel, agents and contractors.

A January 2005 IIC report accompanied the release of 58 audits conducted by the UN's Internal Audit Division during the existence of the program. A lengthier interim report issued on February 3, 2005 made it clear that the most serious violations of the sanctions had occurred outside the program and involved oil smuggling with Iraq's neighbors. On this point, the data cited by the IIC vary widely from one investigation to another. The total sum siphoned off from illegal oil smuggling by the Hussein regime reaches some $13.6 billion, while funds extorted from the program range from $1.7 billion to $7.5 billion. The IIC also established that the administrative expenses of the program (funded from 2.2 percent of oil sales under the program) had been disposed of properly. Finally, the IIC concluded that three contractors had not been selected in 1996 in conformity with established UN financial and competitive bidding rules. It also found that the program's head had had an "irreconcilable conflict of interest," for using his position to solicit and receive oil allocations from Iraq.

Concurrently, the IIC has been conducting a separate line of investigation into the procurement of a contractor that employed the Secretary-General's son, Kojo Annan, with a particular focus on two sets of questions: Did the Secretary-General use improper influence to get the contract for the company (Cotecna, a Swiss company)? And, did his son trade on his family name to get his job and lobby UN officials to award the contract to his employer? In a further interim report issued in March 2005, the IIC found no evidence that the Secretary-General had used any influence in the awarding of the lucrative humanitarian goods contract to the Swiss company but, in its view, he should have more aggressively investigated a possible conflict of interest after a British newspaper reported the link in January 1999.

On the strength of these findings, the Secretary-General feels that he has been vindicated. The IIC has not produced any "smoking gun" of personal impropriety. Prompt disciplinary action has been taken against presumed delinquent UN staffers and SG Annan has thoroughly reorganized his inner office. Furthermore, the Volcker group has yet to provide an answer to the key question as to how much blame should be laid at the doorsteps of the Security Council and its member states, where the ultimate power over the Oil-for-Food Programme rests. A final report is due out over summer 2005.

The fracas over the UN's and the Secretary-General's leadership, as well as the legality of the US-led war in Iraq, should not distract anyone from the fact that, by and large, the Oil-for-Food Programme did succeed in its humanitarian objectives. According to official figures, the program enabled the import of enough food to feed 27 million Iraqis. All Iraqi residents were entitled to receive a monthly oil-for-food basket and 60 percent of the population is believed to have been totally dependent on it. The nutritional value of the food basket almost doubled between 1996 and 2002. The prevalence of underweight children decreased from 23.4 percent in 1996 to 10 percent. Chronic malnutrition decreased from 32 percent in 1996 to 24 percent in 2002. Healthcare delivery services in Iraq also improved significantly. In the central and south regions of the country, surgical and laboratory capacity expanded by 40 percent and 25 percent, respectively, between 1997 and early 2003. The rate of transmission of communicable diseases, such as cholera, malaria, measles, mumps, meningitis and tuberculosis was significantly reduced. In the northern part of the country, cholera was eradicated and the incidence of malaria was reduced to 1991 levels. Finally, the incidence of measles declined to levels ranging from 4 percent to 8 percent and, like the rest of the country, the north remained polio-free for almost three years.

Israeli-Occupied Territories

The February 2005 summit between Israeli Prime Minister Ariel Sharon and Palestinian President Mahmoud Abbas has generated a guarded sense of optimism in the Occupied Palestinian Territories. The Palestinians vowed to stop acts of violence and Israel pledged to cease military activities. But more than four years of open conflict and political stalemate have taken a heavy humanitarian toll.

Israeli security measures continue to restrict the Palestinians' access to work, education and health services. According to FAO, food security has declined both in quantity and quality for nearly three quarters of the West Bank and Gaza populations, with four out of 10 households identified as "chronically insecure." Segments of the Palestinian population living in isolated areas depend entirely on the delivery of critical health, sanitation and education supplies by UN humanitarian agencies.[49] Four years ago, 22 percent of the entire population in the Occupied Territories was believed to live below the poverty line of $2.10 per day. This figure stands now at almost 50 percent and, according to the World Bank, could further increase under current conditions.[50]

On the basis of a vulnerability analysis and mapping conducted in April 2004, the WFP determined that 480,000 non-refugee Palestinians were in immediate need of food assistance and projected to distribute over 76,400 metric tons of various commodities for a total of $41.6 million between September 2004 and August 2005. In addition, UNICEF manages a $17 million program on the West Bank and Gaza covering health, protection and education. The agency expanded its support for the training of healthcare providers and continues to provide assistance to children and families during military incursions in the form of basic clothing items and teaching kits.[51]

Democratic People's Republic of Korea

Self-imposed political isolation, catastrophic droughts, floods and soil erosion in the 1990s and a long-lasting economic downturn have combined to turn the Democratic Peoples' Republic of Korea (DPRK) into a food-deficit country. Domestic cereals production is forecast to improve through the 2004-2005 marketing year (from November to October) but not sufficiently enough to meet the population's food requirements. Some 6.5 million people, a quarter of the total population, live at subsistence level and are dependent on assistance provided by WFP. The UN agency's 2005 emergency operation sought 500,000 tons of food, valued at $200 million. As of late March, only 215,000 tons worth $70 million had been secured, almost all of it committed last year and prompting the agency's officials to warn about possible cuts in its assistance. One noteworthy development is the government's recent efforts to expand upon a FAO-sponsored pilot project of watershed management initiated in 2001; the project aims to reverse diminishing forest quality and increase the country's agricultural output.[52]

Liberia

Under the close watch of the UN Mission in Liberia (UNMIL), 15,000 troops and 1,060 civilian police, the security situation in Liberia has remained relatively calm over the past year. As called forth in the 2003 Comprehensive Peace Agreement, which put an end to the 14-year-long civil wars, preparations are being made for elections to be held in October 2005. With more than 100,000 former combatants disarmed, numerous UN agencies are making a dent in humanitarian aid here.

An estimated 100,000 refugees from Ghana, Guinea, Côte d'Ivoire, Nigeria and Sierra Leone have voluntarily returned and over 8,000 have come back assisted by UNHCR. WFP is providing food assistance to over 250,000 IDPs and returnees. FAO is handling agricultural support and training programs. WHO has supported the re-establishment of county health teams. UNESCO has provided assistance in the development of school curricula. And UNICEF has constructed water points and latrines in schools.[53]

Still, the Secretary-General has warned that these accomplishments remain "fragile." The authority of the National Transitional Government dominated by representatives of the three armed groups left standing when Liberia's civil war ended has not been restored. The disarmament and demobilization of militia fighters and rebel factions was completed by UN peacekeepers in October 2004, but the recruitment and training of a new broad-based national army set to begin in spring 2005 has been delayed due to a lack of funds.[54]

In addition, international donors have complained repeatedly about endemic corruption at high levels within the Liberian government. Observers draw attention to the fact that close associates of former President Charles Taylor, who remains in exile in Nigeria, maintain regular contacts with former Liberian military commanders and business associates. A World Bank mission visiting Liberia in February 2005 warned that donor funding hinged on the determination of the government to crack down on corruption and show greater transparency in its finances.[55]

Clearly, the process of state-building has hardly started and threatens the country's path to recovery and rebuilding. Students and government workers are displeased with the inability of the government to deliver basic services. Property disputes among ex-combatants and returnees over the illegal occupation of plantations have flared up with ominous ethnic and religious undercurrents. Close links between Nouvelles Forces and the pro-government in Côte d'Ivoire appear to have developed with former Liberian factions. The World Bank has been at the heart of international efforts to rebuild Liberia's shattered infrastructure and coordinate inflows of foreign aid. A donor conference in New York in spring 2004 had pledged $520 million in aid for the reconstruction of the country, but according to the UN Humanitarian Coordinator in Liberia, only 69 percent of those pledges have been honored.[56] The tsunami effect also seems to have impacted WFP's plan to help feed 940,000 refugees and IDPs in Liberia this year: "The amount of food distributed by WFP to most beneficiaries in Liberia has been cut in stages since August to just 1,350 calories per day...due to a shortfall in funding from the international community," WFP Chief of Staff Michael Stayton told reporters in March 2005. "We are trying to look at the possibility of diverting some funding from the Indian Ocean to address the food aid needs in West Africa."[57]

Russia (Chechnya)

Estimates of the human death toll in Chechnya vary. At least 13,000 Russian soldiers and approximately 200,000 Chechens have been killed, and hundreds of thousands of people been displaced in two wars since the break-up of the Soviet Union in 1991, when Chechnya claimed independence. Chechnya has become an increasingly lawless place, dangerous for aid workers, reporters and civilians. Calls by the EU, the Commission on Human Rights and NGOs to safeguard human rights have fallen on deaf ears as the conflict has been subsumed by Russian President Vladimir Putin under the rubric of the war against global terrorism (local human rights groups estimate that between 3,000 and 5,000 people have "disappeared" since the beginning of the conflict). Judging from the large number of unfunded and stillborn projects entertained by the UN and other organizations, neither reconstruction nor relief seems to be on the radar screen for this region. As of March 2005, only slightly over 1 percent the $60 million worth of projects proposed by relief organizations had received funding.[58]

Sierra Leone

All early warning signals appear to have been turned off in Sierra Leone. The overall security situation is calm and stable, enabling the progressive downsizing of the UN peace mission there (UNAMSIL). The final report of the government's Truth and Reconciliation Commission was presented to the president in early October 2004 and subsequently released to the public. With the assistance of UNAMSIL and UNICEF, a child-friendly version of the report has been prepared for incorporation into the national school curriculum. Since the voluntary repatriation program started in late September 2000, more than 270,000 Sierra Leonian refugees have been repatriated, a large number of them with the assistance of UNHCR. The repatriation of Liberian refugees from Sierra Leone has begun as well and, according to UNHCR, is expected to be completed in 2006. There are still 66,000 Liberian refugees living in camps in the southern and eastern parts of the country.

The real concern is the longer-term transition from recovery and reconstruction to sustained development. GDP growth is expected to exceed 7 percent, but it is unclear whether the country can sustain such a rate. Postconflict aid has been scaled down by the donor community. The macroeconomic stability of the country is being threatened by rising oil prices and increases in the prices of commodities, notably rice. Adverse developments in the region, such as the continuing instability in nearby Côte d'Ivoire and the newly emerging conflict in Togo might also imperil the fragile progress achieved by Sierra Leone. As the Secretary-General put it, "much remains to be done to address the underlying causes of the conflict in the country, in order to attain durable stability and long-term national recovery."[59]

Sudan

THE SOUTHERN INSURGENCY

On January 9, 2005, the Islamic government of Sudan signed a peace agreement with the Sudan People's Liberation Movement/Army (SPLM/A), a Christian rebel group, bringing to an end a civil war that had raged since 1983 and taken two million lives through disease, starvation and violence. The peace agreement, achieved with considerable prodding by the Bush administration, made provisions for power-sharing arrangements, a merging of military forces, a degree of autonomy for the south and more equitable distribution of economic resources, including oil. The accords also stipulate that, in six years, the people of southern Sudan will have the opportunity to vote on whether they want to secede.

Months before the agreement was negotiated, the UN Secretariat had begun looking into the logistics of a possible peacekeeping operation. In early February 2005, warning that the civil war there could not "quickly or easily be dispatched to history," SG Annan formally recommended that the Security Council establish a peace support mission in southern Sudan and called on member states to contribute more than 10,000 troops and 700 civilian police to the operation. On March 24, the Council unanimously endorsed the proposals.

The new mission will monitor and verify the cease-fire agreement, help to set up a disarmament, demobilization and reintegration program for ex-combatants, and promote national reconciliation and human rights. As the report of the Secretary-General to the Council emphasized, the mission faces "daunting logistical challenges." Access to the region is difficult and hampered by annual rains. Landmines and unexploded ordnances pose another major threat. After more than two decades of warfare, there is no infrastructure and basic services are lacking. In 2002, the entire region had only about 1,500 hospital beds and some estimates put the number of doctors in the region at just over 100. According to UNICEF, most of southern Sudan is, in fact, served today by some 66 odd humanitarian organizations primarily involved in emergency healthcare.

THE DARFUR REGION

The vote to extend a mission to southern Sudan followed a year of delays and inaction amidst rising complaints that world powers were failing to respond to what the UN had called the world's worst humanitarian crisis in Sudan's northwestern province of Darfur.[60] The violence there started in early 2003 when two rebel movements took up arms against the Sudan government. As in the south, the conflict flared up as a result of protests over the distribution of economic resources. While the causes of the conflict are complex, its roots lie in a long-running dispute between settled farming tribes, which in Darfur tend to be African, and predominantly Arab nomadic herders over control of an ever scarcer supply of arable land. By the end of 2004, it was reported that about 70,000 people have died, another 1.8 million were internally displaced and 200,000 more had fled over the border into Chad.

The Security Council repeatedly condemned the attacks on civilians and humanitarian workers and cease-fire violations "vowing" "no impunity" for war crimes in Darfur. While lauding the AU's decision to deploy up to 4,000 troops in Darfur, with a limited mandate (so far only half that number have arrived), the Council has also threatened on several occasions to impose sanctions against the government if it failed to stem the violence. The Sudanese government, however, continues to deny any wrongdoing and claims that the Darfur crisis is an internal matter of no concern to the international community, erecting obstacles to humanitarian workers and taking no action to improve the security condition.

In September 2004, under Resolution 1564, the Secretary-General established an independent commission to "investigate reports of violations of international humanitarian law and human rights law in Darfur by all parties, to determine...whether or not acts of genocide have occurred, and to identify the perpetrators of such violations with a view to ensuring that those responsible are held accountable." Four months later, the commission issued a report which found that, while the Sudanese government had not conducted a policy of genocide, both its forces and allied Janjaweed militias had carried out "indiscriminate attacks, including killing of civilians, torture, enforced disappearances, destruction of villages, rape and other forms of sexual violence, pillaging and forced displacement." The commission also concluded that rebel forces in Darfur were responsible for possible war crimes and recommended that the Council refer its dossier on the crimes to the International Criminal Court.[61] The report was immediately criticized by the main rebel group fighting the Sudanese government in Darfur for having found no sufficient evidence of genocide. The Sudanese government blasted it for being "emotional."

All through that period, the Secretary-General and his senior aides, Special Representative Jan Pronk and OCHA head Jan Egeland, spent much of their time trying to broaden the access of humanitarian agencies to people in need in Darfur and to galvanize the world to take action. In his reports to the Council, the Secretary-General has been blunt both in tone and substance, blaming both the Khartoum government and the rebels for failing to seek a negotiated solution to the conflict: "The Janjaweed's boldness, be it in regard to theft, attacks on civilians or armed movements, is a direct consequence of inaction by the Government to rein in, let alone disarm or arrest, these groups." Meanwhile, he added, rebel forces continue to harass relief workers, refuse to reveal their positions to the AU cease-fire monitoring force in place, and fire on helicopters belonging to the AU and WFP.[62]

The Secretary-General also called for a strengthening of the AU force on the ground. Mr. Egeland, briefing journalists in Geneva on a meeting of the UN's humanitarian coordinators in crisis areas, warned that as many as three million Sudanese people could become internally displaced within the Darfur region by the end of this year unless the warring parties reached a peace agreement and aid agencies were granted full access. Pressure has also come from UN human rights bodies, as noted in the first section of this chapter.[63]

Acting under Chapter VII of the *Charter*, the Council adopted two resolutions in quick succession that broke new ground in the long-standing political impasse over what to do about Darfur. On March 29, 2005, a US-sponsored resolution adopted by a 12 to 0 vote with three abstentions (Algeria, China and the Russian Federation) majority, the Council imposed sanctions on individuals suspected of having committed atrocities or broken cease-fire agreements. In a subsequent resolution, adopted by a 11 to 0 vote with four abstentions (Algeria, Brazil, China and the United States), the Council officially referred the Darfur situation to the prosecutor of the ICC. [64]

How promptly and smoothly these resolutions will be implemented remains to be seen. The Secretary-General has transmitted to the ICC a sealed list of 51 names of people suspected of war crimes and crimes under international law which had been drawn up by the commission.[65] But the Sudanese government remains defiant. Three days before the Council's adoption of its resolution referring the Darfur question to the ICC, the Sudanese government announced that it had made its first arrests of police, military and security forces accused of war crimes and crimes against humanity and that they would be tried by Sudanese courts. In other acts of defiance, the government has challenged the UN to produce evidence to support its assessments of the death toll in the Darfur region over the past 19 months and accused humanitarian agencies of using only a portion of donors' funds while retaining much of it for their own activities.[66]

Meanwhile, the situation on the ground remains volatile and insecure. Clashes between the government and rebels, attacks against international and national aid workers, rape, abuse of children, and torture by security forces continue unabated. More than 1.5 million people have been driven from their homes and are totally dependent upon relief agencies for food, shelter, clothing and medical treatment. Of those who were not displaced, three and a half million lack sufficient food, 22 percent of children are malnourished and the incidence of fatal illnesses has risen dramatically. In spite of some improvements in IDP and refugee camps, the humanitarian effort largely remains hostage to the willingness of the Sudanese government and local authorities to play by the rules of the humanitarian game. UNICEF complains that it has access only to five to 10 percent of the territories and to one third of the six million inhabitants in Darfur. It took some doing for Mr. Pronk to obtain "three days of tranquility" from the government to enable WHO, UNICEF, NGOs and the Sudanese Health Ministry, with the help of some 40,000 volunteers, to vaccinate 5.9 million children under age five against polio.[67]

FINANCIAL AID

Another issue has been donor support. In Darfur, the massive humanitarian effort unfolded in the absence of a political solution to the conflict. In contrast, southern Sudan, where a peace accord ended the civil war, was neglected by donors and the humanitarian/reconstruction response was virtually absent. As of March 2005, donors had contributed only $380 million out of nearly $1.5 billion in total funds requested through the 2005 UN Work Plan for Sudan. The lion's share of the donations to Sudan went toward food assistance while other sectors, such as health, education, shelter and water, received 3 percent or less. On average, Darfur received about 75 percent of the donated funds while southern Sudan received slightly more than 14 percent. National programs including mine action, infrastructure and the rule of law got an 8 percent allocation, while the rest of the Sudan, including the east and the transitional areas, got no more than 1 percent.[68]

Financial circumstances have significantly evolved after an April 2005 donors' conference sponsored by the Norwegian government. Reacting to an impassioned plea by the Secretary-General, participants pledged $4.5 billion for the recovery and reconstruction of Sudan's pacified southern and northern areas over the next two and a half years. This was nearly $2 billion more than the $2.6 billion the Secretary-General had requested. Among those countries making pledges, the EU announced that it would contribute $765 million, the UK $545 million, Norway $250 million and Denmark $90 million. The US is planning to give between $1 and $2 billion. Indications are that some of this money may not be released in the absence of progress toward a political settlement in the Darfur region. Under the agreement reached between the Sudanese government and the SPLM/A, southern leaders won 28 percent of government positions, a separate southern administration and 50 percent of southern wealth. Now the Darfur insurgents want their share of government positions and wealth, and they have made clear their intent to fight until their demands are met.[69]

Be that as it may, the UN finds itself in the unenviable position of having to take care of the millions of people displaced or affected by the ongoin conflict in Darfur and to make preparations for the repatriation of 550,000 refugees in neighboring countries as well as an estimated 4.1 million IDPs in the south. Under the circumstances, it is doubtful that Sudan will disappear from the headlines.

Western Sahara

More than 13 years after they agreed to a cease-fire, the parties in Western Sahara remain deadlocked. In his interim report to the Security Council on the work of the UN Mission for the Referendum in Western Sahara (MINURSO), the Secretary-General told the Security Council that he was still prepared to help the Moroccan government and the Frente POLISARIO (Popular Front for the Liberation of the Saguia el-Hamra and Rio de Oro) find a solution to their dispute as neither side appeared to have any plan to resume hostilities since the operation began in 1991. In fact, family visits programs allowing refugees living in camps in southwestern Algeria and residents of towns in Western Sahara to see each other had been successfully implemented. But there were no signs of breakthrough in the stalled peace process.[70] While extending the mandate of MINURSO, the Security Council also asked the Secretary-General to examine the possibility of reducing the size of the mission, a sign that the Council may lose patience with the continuing stalemate. In the meantime, by and large forgotten by the international community, 165,000 Western Sahara refugees are still living in camps in neighboring Algeria, while some 300,000 people remain in the disputed territory, all of them depending for their survival on assistance provided, among others, by UNHCR and WFP.

Looking Forward

Darfur and the Indian Ocean tsunami stand as the two polar symbolic opposites of a humanitarian scale where most cases actually fall in between these extremes. Indeed, there is much "greyness" in the 2004-2005 humanitarian landscape that is neither novel nor especially surprising. For decades now, the humanitarian community has had to learn how to operate within the framework of a "system" fraught with conceptual, operational and political uncertainties.

Yet, however "sloppy" the UN humanitarian enterprise may be, at the end of the day, it saves lives. Six months after the tsunami, WFP had provided food aid to 1.2 million survivors in Indonesia, Maldives, Myanmar, Somalia and Sri Lanka. UNICEF had immunized 1.2 million children against measles and provided nearly 850,000 with Vitamin A supplements. These statistics offer the incontrovertible proof of the viability and continuing rationale of the United Nations' humanitarian work.

Commentary:
Human Rights Values and the World's Power States

Lorna Davidson

Addressing an International Summit on Democracy, Terrorism and Security, on the first anniversary of the Madrid train bombing, United Nations Secretary-General Kofi Annan made yet another plea for states to ensure respect for human rights in implementing measures to combat terrorism. Ever since the September 11, 2001 attacks, the Secretary-General and a chorus of UN human rights officials have emphasized that respect for human rights must be central to any effective counter-terrorism strategy. However, in his speech on March 10, 2005, SG Annan noted with regret that "many measures which States are currently adopting to counter terrorism infringe on human rights and fundamental freedoms."

One of the most worrying developments since September 11th has been the extent to which the United States, along with close allies such as the United Kingdom, has contributed to the erosion of human rights principles in the name of counter-terrorism. First, rights-abusing governments and regimes have been given, or perceive themselves to have been given, tacit approval to arbitrarily detain, torture and otherwise mistreat particular individuals or groups when this is done in the name of the "war on terror." Second, international human rights standards have been directly challenged by the actions of the US and its attempts to justify them. In particular, following revelations of torture and other forms of mistreatment meted out to detainees held in Guantanamo Bay, Afghanistan and other undisclosed locations, endeavors by US officials to redefine torture or argue that it might be justified in some circumstances, have struck a serious blow to the human rights movement. Those who have been involved in human rights advocacy over previous decades find themselves having discussions and arguments with state officials about issues that they had thought were long-since settled. The prevalence of impunity for senior US officials implicated in the abuse of detainees has also been noted around the world, at a time when efforts to combat impunity appeared to have reached a critical mass. Third, the power of the US, and indeed the UK, to exert their influence for positive human rights change in a range of countries has been greatly diminished.

All 191 UN member states must reaffirm their commitment to upholding the human rights standards that have been so painstakingly developed over the past 60 years, particularly when faced with the threat of terrorism. Those states which have failed to respect basic rights under guise of counter-terrorism should be named and shamed at the 60th session of the General Assembly, as well as assisted by the new special rapporteur to bring their practices back into line with international standards.

As SG Annan stated in March 2005, "Compromising human rights cannot serve the struggle against terrorism."

Endnotes

Human Rights

1. Report of the International Commission of Inquiry (IIC) on Darfur to the UNSG, January 25, 2005.
2. Report of the Commission on Human Rights to ECOSOC, February 11, 1947.
3. General Assembly Resolution 48/141.
4. OHCHR Annual Appeal 2005.
5. Ibid.
6. UN Document HRI/MC/2004/3 (2004).
7. US Department of State (DOS) Press Release (March 17, 2005).
8. UN Documents E/CN.4/2005/34 and 35 (2005).
9. UN Document E/CN.4/2005/L.48 (2005).
10. UN Documents E/CN.4/2005/ L.93 (2005), E/CN.4/2005/102 and Add.1 (2005), E/CN.4/2005/91 (2005) and E/CN.4/2005/L.87 (2005).
11. UN Document E/CN.4/RES/2004/87 (2004).
12. UN Document A/59/428 (2004).
13. Ibid.
14. UN Document E/CN. /4/2005/103 (2005). / UN Document E/CN.4/2005/L.88 (2005).
15. *A More Secure World: Our Shared Responsibility* (Report of the High-level Panel on Threats, Challenges and Change), December 1, 2004.
16. *In Larger Freedom: Towards Development, Security and Human Rights for All*, (Report of the Secretary-General to the General Assembly), March 21, 2005. Hereafter referred to as "ILF."
17. ILF, para. 183.
18. UN Document E/CN.4/2005/L.101 (2005).
19. "Zimbabwe: An assessment of human rights violations in run-up to March 2005 parliamentary elections," *Amnesty International (AI)*, March 15, 2005.
20. World Report 2005, *Human Rights Watch (HRW)*, 2005. / Country Report on Human Rights Practices (Burma), February 28, 2005.
21. UN Document A/59/370 (2004).
22. A Call for Justice: A National Consultation on Past Human Rights Violations in Afghanistan, 4, January 2005
23. UN Document E/CN.4/2005/122 (2005).
24. Ibid.
25. UN Document A/59/370 (2004). / UN Document E/CN.4/2005/122 (2005).
26. "Ex-UN envoy: US feared discovery of prison abuse," *Chicago Tribune*, April 29, 2005.
27. *Global Appeal 2005* (Afghanistan), UNHCR. / UN Document A/59/744-S/2005/183 (2004).
28. Testimony of Michael G. Kozak, *Committee on International Relations*, March 17, 2005.
29. AI Press Release (March 17, 2005).
30. "People's Republic of China: Human Rights Defenders at Risk – Update," *AI*, March 1, 2005. / UN Document E/CN.4/2005/64/Add.1 (2005).
31. "Devastating Blows: Religious Repression of Uighurs in Xinjiang," *HRW*, April 12, 2005.
32. UN Document E/CN.4/2005/6/Add.4 (2004).
33. Country Reports on Human Rights Practices (Côte d'Ivoire), *DOS*, 2004.
34. World Report 2005 (Côte d'Ivoire), *HRW*, 2005.
35. Security Council Resolution 1572 (2004).
36. World Report 2005 (Côte d'Ivoire), *HRW*. / UN Document S/2004/697 (2004).
37. "The Congo's Transition is Failing: Crisis in the Kivus," *ICG*, March 30, 2005.
38. "D.R. Congo: Fleeing Civilians Face Grave Risks," *HRW*, December 21, 2004. / "D.R. Congo: Executions, Torture by Armed Groups in Ituri," *HRW*, October 22, 2004. / "Democratic Republic of Congo: Mass rape–time for remedies," *AI*, October 26, 2004.
39. UN Document E/CN.4/2005/120 (2005)./ UN Document E/CN.4/2005/L.38/Rev.1 (2005).
40. Security Council Resolution 1592 (2005).
41. UN Document S/2005/141 2005). / "Iraq Car Bombing Causes Carnage," *BBC News*, February 28, 2005.
42. UN Document E/CN.4/2005/51/Add.1 (2005).
43. "The New Iraq?," *HRW*, January 2005.
44. UN Document E/CN.4/2005/29 (2005).

45. "2005 UN Commission on Human Rights: the UN's chief guardian of human rights?," *HRW*, 2005. / Report of the Special Rapporteur, 2005.

46. UN Documents E/CN.4/2005/L.15 (2005), E/CN.4/2005/L.2/Rev.1 (2005), E/CN.4/2005/L.4 (2005) and E/CN.4/2005/L.5 (2005.)

47. "Clear Culpability: 'Disappearances' by Security Forces in Nepal," *HRW*, February 1, 2005. / UN Documents E/CN.4/2005/65/Add.1 (2005) and E/CN.4/2005/114 (2005).

48. "Nepal: A long ignored human rights crisis is now on the brink of catastrophe," *AI*, February 2005. / AI News Release (May 3, 2005).

49. UN Document E/CN.4/2004/127 (2004).

50. UN Press Release (July 14, 2004).

51. UN Document E/CN.4/2005/114 (2005).

52. UN Press Release (April 11, 2005). / AI News Release (April 12, 2005). / FIDH, Position Paper, 4. / UN Document E/CN.4/2005/L.90 (2005).

53. "Worse than War: Disappearances in Chechnya–A Crime against Humanity," *HRW*, March 2005.

54. Country Reports on Human Rights Practices (Russia), *DOS*, 2004.

55. UN Document E/CN.4/2005/101 (2004).

56. UN Document E/CN.4/2005/8 (2004).

57. *See Convention on the Prevention and Punishment of the Crime of Genocide,* 1948, Article 2.

58. UN Document S/2004/703 (2004).

59. Report of the IIC on Darfur to the UNSG, January 25, 2005.

60. UN Document S/RES/1593 (2005).

61. "Committee on UN Treaty Requesting Account of Human Rights Compliance from Sudan," *UN News Service,* April 1, 2005.

62. UN Document E/CN.4/2005/L.33/Rev.1 (2005). / UN Document E/CN.4/2005/L. 36/Rev.3 (2005).

63. Human Rights First Media Alert (April 21, 2005). / Commission on Human Rights Press Release (April 21, 2005).

64. Kofi Annan, "Billions of Promises to Keep," *New York Times,* April 13, 2005.

Humanitarian Assistance

1. *OCHA in 2005: Activities and Extra-budgetary Funding Requirements,* OCHA, 2005. / OHCA Financial Tracking Service (FTS) website. / UN Document A/59/374 (2004).

2. UN Press Release (January 24, 2005).

3. Mandated by the GA, the UN uses Consolidated Appeals to plan, implement and monitor humanitarian activities. The outcome is a Common Humanitarian Action Plan and an "appeal" or plan outlining the strategies of aid donors and their funding requirements in response to an emergency. "Flash Appeals" are similar, issued in response to impending or developing catastrophes. Separate appeals may be issued by UN agencies.

4. "Tsunami Relief Success Spurs Calls for Change," *Financial Times,* February 15, 2005.

5. "General Assembly Discusses UN Humanitarian and Disaster Relief Assistance," *UN News Center,* November 11, 2004.

6. HLP Report.

7. *See* for example: Statement, Ambassador Kumalo of South Africa, Fourth Informal Meeting of the Plenary on the HLP Report, January 27, 2005. / Statement, Ambassador Asmady of Indonesia, Informal Consultations of the GA, February 22, 2005.

8. UN Press Release (March 28, 2005).

9. AlertNet website, *Reuters.*

10. OHCA Financial Tracking Service (FTS) website.

11. IRIN News website, March 4, 2005.

12. UN Press Releases (April 6, 2005 and April 8, 2005).

13. UN Press Release (January 27, 2005.)

14. UN Press Release (February 15, 2005). / UN Press Release (March 18, 2005).

15. UN Press Release (February 14, 2005).

16. UN Press Release (February 18, 2005).

17. "Hope: Building Capacity: Least Developed Countries Meet the HIV/AIDS Challenge," *UNDP website.*

18. UN Press Release (February 25, 2005).

19. Ian Smillie and Larry Minear. The Charity of Nations: Humanitarian Action in a Calculating World. (Bloomfield, CT.: Kumari-

an Press, 2004). / Tufts University Project.

20. *The Guardian*, December 30, 2004.

21. UN Integrated Regional Informational Networks Report, March 23, 2005.

22. UN Press Releases (January 21, 2005, January 25, 2005, February 17, 2005).

23. Victor Mallet, "IMF and World Bank Support Debt Relief for Tsunami-ravaged Nations," *Financial Times*, January 7, 2005.

24. OCHA and WFP websites. / UN News Center.

25. ReliefWeb website.

26. Frances William, "UN Disaster Response 'Proves a Point': Supporters argue the organization alone has expertise to oversee response to catastrophe," *Financial Times*, January 12, 2005.

27. Judith Miller, "UN Moves to Devise System for Tracking Relief Money," *New York Times*, January 10, 2005.

28. UN Press Release (January 26, 2005).

29. Ibid.

30. UN Press Releases (January 31, 2005, February 3, 2004 and May 5, 2005).

31. UN Press Release (March 29, 2005)./ UN Press Release (April 1, 2005).

32. Shawn Donnan, Taufan Hidayat and Ray Marcelo, "Frustration for Donors as Aid Piles up on Docks: Red tape and corruption hinder delivery," *Financial Times*, May 12, 2005.

33. UN Press Releases (February 17, 2005, April 7, 2005 and May 8, 2005). / UNDP Press Release (February 21, 2005).

34. UN Document A/59/744-S/2005/183 (2005). / UN Press Releases (February 21, 2005, March 8, 2005, March 18, 2005 and April 4, 2005).

35. UN Press Releases (February 24, 2005, March 8, 2005, March 10, 2005 and March 18, 2005).

36. UN Document S/2005/186 (2005).

37. *The State of the World's Children 2005* (Report of UNICEF), 2005.

38. UN Press Release (March 9, 2005).

39. UN Press Releases (December 17, 2004, March 9, 2005, February 25, 2005 and February 18, 2005).

40. Humanitarian Appeal 2005 for Great Lakes, *OCHA*.

41. UN Press Release (April 5, 2005).

42. UN Press Release (March 14, 2005).

43. UN Document S/2005/124 (2005).

44. UN Press Release (April 6, 2005). / UN Press Release (April 13, 2005).

45. OHCA website.

46. UN Press Releases (March 2, 2005, March 18, 2005, March 28, 2005, March 30, 2005 and April 25, 2005).

47. Global Policy Forum website.

48. Ibid. / UNDP Press Release (May 12, 2005). / "UNDP in Iraq," *UNDP*.

49. UN Press Release (February 15, 2005). / UN Press Release (April 1, 2005).

50. OCHA in 2005. / UN Press Release (April 6, 2005).

51. WFP and UNICEF websites.

52. UN Press Releases (January 27, 2005, March 30, 2005 and April 21, 2005).

53. UN Document S/2005/177 (2005).

54. UN Press Release (March 29, 2005).

55. Ibid.

56. "Liberia: World Bank says tougher action needed to tackle corruption," *IRIN News website*, February 21, 2005.

57. *IRIN News website*.

58. ReliefWeb website.

59. UN Document S/2004/965 (2004). / UN Press Release (May 5, 2005).

60. UN Press Release (February 8, 2005).

61. UN Press Release (February 1, 2005). / Lydia Polgreen, "Both Sides of Conflict in Darfur Dispute Findings in UN Report," *New York Times*, February 2, 2005.

62. UN Press Release (March 11, 2005).

63. UN Press Releases (March 7, 2005, March 16, 2005, February 14, 2004 and April 1, 2005).

64. UN Press Release (March 29, 2005). / UN Press Release (March 31, 2005).

65. UN Press Release (April 4, 2005).

66. "Sudan Arrests 15 Accused in Darfur Crimes," *Reuters*, March 29, 2005. / "Sudan Tells UN to Back up its Darfur Death Toll," *Reuters*, March 15, 2005.

67. UN Press Release (January 7, 2005).

68. UN Press Release (March 21, 2005).

69. Andrew England, "Darfur Peace Hopes Dim as Rebels Demand Power," *Financial Times*, March 17, 2005.

70. UN Press Release (January 28, 2005).

*The facts and analysis in the Oil-for-Food Programme section are drawn from the official site of the UN Oil-for-Food Programme, UN News Center, UN Press Releases, Volcker Panel reports and briefings, Fox News website, The Guardian, and AP and Reuters articles between January and June 2005.

Chapter 5

Health: Preventing Infectious Diseases, Securing Well-Being

Yanzhong Huang

> *In the 20th century, science gave us the power to prevent or cure most of the infections that kill children and young adults. It was an extraordinary achievement. Our concern now in the 21st century is to make sure we can keep and increase this wonderful new capacity. That can only be done by realizing its potential to promote well-being in all parts of the world, for all people, not just some of them.*
> —World Health Organization Director-General Lee Jong-Wook
> *Remarks at Bio Vision, The World Life Sciences Forum, April 2005*

As the United Nations approaches its 60th anniversary, it will certainly be credited for its crucial contributions to mitigating traditional threats to international security. Meanwhile, it faces extraordinary challenges in a transformed international system. The growing non-traditional threats of infectious disease are increasingly testing the relevance and effectiveness of this international organization. With leadership and partnership, advocacy and action, the UN can fulfill equally the high ideals enshrined in the opening words of its *Charter*, namely, "to promote social progress and better standards of life in larger freedom." But to move forward, it is important to examine where the UN has been on the global health security front.

Looking Back

The 1970s marked the peak of a golden era in public health. With the widespread use of antibiotics, vaccines, pesticides and other powerful antimicrobials, many formerly formidable infectious diseases became easier to prevent or cure. This progress, in conjunction with a vigorous worldwide public health campaign against infectious diseases as well as striking improvements in water treatment and food preparation techniques, led to dramatic improvement in the quality of human life. In fact, in 1980, the World Health Organization (WHO) declared smallpox eradicated. For the first time in history, a major disease had been completely vanquished thanks to the UN, its specialized agencies and member states. This success nurtured a strong belief in the world's ability to leave the age of infectious disease permanently behind, echoed by WHO's "Health for All, 2000" accord, which envisioned that most of the world's population would live long lives ended only by the chronic diseases of the millennium.

This expectation of human triumph unfortunately failed to materialize.[1] According to the 2004 WHO World Health Report, infectious diseases remain the leading cause of mortality on the planet. Of 57 million deaths in 2002, about 11 million, or 19 percent were due to infectious or parasitic diseases. Over the past three decades, the world has seen the emergence of at least 30 new infectious diseases, including HIV/AIDS, Ebola and Severe Acute Respiratory Syndrome (SARS). Meanwhile, the new century witnessed the re-emergence of malaria and tuberculosis in new and more potent forms. The challenge of managing new and re-emerging infectious diseases is compounded by growing concerns about people developing resistances to treatment and by the lack of drugs available to those in need.[2] All this highlights the potential danger of a global epidemic of a new infection, such as pandemic influenza.

The magnitude of threats and their impact on all facets of society call for an approach that both supports and maintains prevention and control on one hand, and effectively responds to public health emergencies on the other. To that end, it is imperative for national governments to beef up their state capacities, but leadership and partnership at the international level are also critical. This is especially vital for developing countries, where purely endogenous solutions are unlikely to be successful. These challenges require the UN to go beyond the traditional military conflicts to map out a new and broader strategy of collective security, one that tackles threats from state and non-state actors, and threats to national security and human security like disease.

Fortunately, in September 2000, the UN did just that, setting forth a new development framework enshrined in the Millennium Development Goals (MDGs), three of which are directly related to health in general and one of these to infectious disease in particular. These include: reducing child mortality; improving maternal health; and combating HIV/AIDS, malaria and other diseases. In addition, Secretary-General Kofi Annan's High-level Panel on Threats, Challenges and Change, and Jeffrey Sachs' *Investing in Development: A Practical Plan to Achieve the Millennium Development Goals* report pay special attention to the deterioration of the global health system and its vulnerability to new infectious disease (*see box on reform*).

These calls to action are vital to moving the UN and the world forward and clear of one of today's major security threats, namely, infectious disease. This chapter looks at each of the challenges ahead.

HIV/AIDS as the Century's Challenge

HIV/AIDS Demography

Since its emergence, the HIV/AIDS pandemic has infected nearly 70 million people. It is estimated that the total number of individuals currently living with HIV is around 40 million. In 2004, just under five million became newly infected, a number greater than in any previous year. Also in 2004, approximately three million people died from AIDS, more than ever before and more than from any other infectious disease. (*See Table A.*)

The impact of AIDS on children is equally staggering. Of the nearly five million new infections in 2004, 13 percent are children under 15 years old. According to a UN report, AIDS now accounts for 3 percent of deaths in children under five years old, but in hard-hit countries, this figure may be as high as 50 percent. Worldwide, 15 million children have been orphaned by AIDS and the number is expected to increase sharply in coming years. In addition, millions of other youth are living in households in which an adult is sick due to HIV/AIDS.[3] According to UNAIDS, fewer than 3 percent of orphans and vulnerable children are receiving public support for most services (except in Eastern Europe).[4]

Sub-Saharan Africa remains by far the region worst hit by the epidemic. With just over 10 percent of the world's population, the region is home to nearly two thirds (64 percent) of all people living with the disease. In 2004 alone, 3.1 million people in the region were estimated to be newly infected, while 2.3 million died of AIDS. According to a 2005 UNAIDS report, in the worst case scenario, over the next 20 years, an additional 89 million people in Africa could be infected, and there could be a four-fold increase in deaths from AIDS.[5]

Outside Africa, HIV prevalence is highest in the Caribbean at 2.3 percent. The most dramatic increase in infection rates, however, is taking place in East and Central Asia, and in Eastern Europe. Between 2002 and 2004, the number of people living with HIV in East Asia rose by 50 percent. In Eastern Europe and Central Asia, there are nine times more people living with HIV than 10 years ago. As of December 2004, an estimated 7 million people in South and Southeast Asia were living with HIV, including 890,000 who became infected in that year. Meanwhile, more than 1.7 million people were living with HIV in Latin America. In fact, the epidemic expanded in every region in 2004, including North America and Western Europe, where early prevention successes have given way in recent years to increases in risky sex-

Table A: Global Summary of the AIDS Pandemic (estimates as of December 2004)

Number of people living with HIV in 2004	Total	**39.4** million
	Adults	37.2 million
	Women	17.6 million
	Children under 15	2.2 million
People newly infected with HIV in 2004	Total	**4.9 million**
	Adults	4.3 million
	Children under 15	640,000
AIDS deaths in 2004	Total	**3.1 million**
	Adults	2.6 million
	Children under 15	510,000

Source: UNAIDS, AIDS Epidemic Update 2004.

ual behavior. In all regions, the epidemic disproportionately targets the most vulnerable and marginalized segments of the population, such as commercial sex workers, injecting drug users (IDU), street youth and prisoners.

Prevention and Control

With the inclusion of HIV/AIDS in the Millennium Development Goals, specifically calling on all 191 member states of the UN to take efforts to halt and reverse the spread of HIV/AIDS by 2015, the fight against AIDS is now firmly placed among the world's top development priorities. In 2004, the UN Millennium Project Task Force 5 Working Group on HIV/AIDS proposed two concrete targets:

- Reduce prevalence among young people to 5 percent in the most affected countries and by 50 percent elsewhere by 2015.
- Ensure that affordable and effective antiretroviral therapy is available to all who need it by 2015.

A growing number of international actors—UN agencies, international nongovernmental organizations, foundations, bilateral donors and their contractors—are involved in delivering, funding or overseeing AIDS-related services. Through UNAIDS and its cosponsors, the UN not only has placed the epidemic at the top of the global agenda and built international consensus around basic elements of a comprehensive response, but also has played a crucial role in translating the political commitment and consensus into concrete action. For example, WHO's 3 by 5 Initiative, which seeks to provide antiretroviral treatment to three million people living with AIDS in developing and transitional countries, has helped galvanize action in the broader international community to scale up access to AIDS treatment and care. By the end of 2004, about 700,000 people were receiving antiretroviral therapy. Initial data demonstrate that adherence and treatment success rates in developing countries are similar to if not higher than those obtained in wealthy, industrialized countries.[6]

New initiatives have been launched at the regional level as well. The International Congress on AIDS in Asia and the Pacific (ICAAP) is holding its seventh session in July 2005 in Kobe, Japan under the theme of "Bridging Science and Community" to allow all affected communities to participate in the development of AIDS prevention, treatment and care strategies.[7] This gap between science and education about the disease will also be addressed as one of the six topics in the 14th International Conference on HIV/AIDS and Sexually Transmitted Infections in Africa, to be held in December 2005 in Abuja, Nigeria.[8]

In the Caribbean, the Caribbean Community and the Pan-Caribbean Partnership against HIV/AIDS, for example, have been successful in negotiating for reduced prices for antiretroviral drugs and mobilizing resources for HIV/AIDS activities. And in October 2004, the Pan-Caribbean Partnership held is fourth annual general meeting in Bridgetown, Guyana under the theme "Leadership through Partnership," to focus on an accelerated agenda for care and treatment, and the increasing availability of antiretrovirals for people living with HIV/AIDS.[9] Regional initiatives and cooperation have been growing in Central and Eastern Europe as well. In response to the virtual absence prior to 2003 of antiretroviral treatment training programs in this region, a regional HIV knowledge hub was launched in Ukraine in 2004, which trained 66 caregivers in its first year.[10]

At the national level, political commitment has increased in the hardest-hit countries and those threatened by growing epidemics. More leaders in sub-Saharan Africa, Asia and the Caribbean have taken personal responsibility for implementing national AIDS programs. In an effort to break the stigma that discourages testing in Lesotho, for example, Prime Minster Pakalitha Mosisili and more than 80 senior civil servants were publicly tested for HIV in March 2004.[11] This more direct involvement by a growing number of national leaders has led to an increase in the number of countries with comprehensive, multi-sectoral national AIDS strategies and government-led national AIDS coordinating bodies. In China, for example, discourse and action surrounding HIV/AIDS have changed dramatically in recent years, with national leaders facing the epidemic with a greater sense of awareness, openness and responsibility. In 2003, the country introduced a new national prevention, treatment and care program. This was followed by the establishment of a more powerful coordination body to help guide national HIV/AIDS policy in February 2004;[12] most recently, the government urged domestic and international businesses to join in the fight against AIDS.[13]

In September 2005, the UN General Assembly is anticipated to discuss the international progress in the aforementioned initiatives as well as the implementation of the 2001 *Declaration of Commitment on HIV/AIDS*, in which member states pledged to coordinate to reverse the pandemic via efforts at the regional and global level. The assembly will receive a report on the declaration's progress with special reference to the targets set for 2005 (e.g., reducing the proportion of infants infected with HIV by 20 percent, reducing HIV prevalence among young men and women aged 15 to 24 in the most affected countries by 25 percent). This should motivate national leaders in affected countries to redouble their efforts in fighting HIV/AIDS.

Women and HIV/AIDS

Many may not know that HIV/AIDS has a disproportionate impact on women in terms of access to prevention, diagnosis and treatment, even infection rates. While just under half of all people living with HIV globally are female, women and girls make up almost 57 percent of those living with HIV in sub-Saharan Africa, constituting three quarters of all women with HIV worldwide. In other regions, particularly Eastern Europe, Asia and Latin America, the proportion of women and girls living with HIV continues to grow.

Around the world, female vulnerability to HIV/AIDS is primarily due to inadequate knowledge about AIDS, insufficient access to HIV prevention services, inability to negotiate safer sex and a lack of female-controlled prevention methods such as female condoms and microbicides. All this reflects profound gender, class and other inequalities. For example, even though maintaining multiple partner relationships is a high risk behavior, it is considered a key survival strategy in some regions of the world for poor women who have difficulties in meeting basic needs. Furthermore, research has confirmed a strong correlation between violence against women, including intimate partner violence, and women's likelihood of HIV infection.[14]

As a result, women bear the brunt of the epidemic's impact. According to UNAIDS, in comparison to men, women are more likely to take care of sick people, to lose jobs, income and schooling as a result of illness, and to face stigma and discrimination. In hopes of reversing this trend, in early 2004, UNAIDS launched the Global Coalition on Women and AIDS to promote effective action to reduce the impact of AIDS on women and girls. The coalition is a movement of networks and organizations supported by activists, leaders, government representatives, community workers and celebrities. It is dedicated to, among others things, promoting access to new prevention options, ensuring equal access by women and girls to care and treatment, protecting the property and inheritance rights of women and girls, reducing violence against women and supporting ongoing efforts toward universal education for girls.

The subject was given further attention by the 2004 World AIDS Campaign, which sought to raise awareness about, and help address, the many issues affecting women and girls with regard to HIV/AIDS. The campaign culminated on World AIDS Day (December 1), which explored how gender inequality contributes to the AIDS epidemic and encouraged people to address female vulnerability to HIV.[15]

Vaccine Collaboration

Despite the progress the scientific establishment has made on extending the survival of people with HIV, the development of effective HIV vaccines for clinical application has not been very successful. Recent progress in the HIV vaccine area includes the completion of several phase I and phase II trials of candidate vaccines. But scientific hurdles and logistical problems remain. For example, it is difficult and costly to conduct vaccine efficacy trials at multiple sites against different globally prevalent HIV strains with different transmission patterns. It is worth noting that of the more than 70 phase I trials that have taken place since 1978, by 2003, only four phase I/II trials had been conducted in sub-Saharan Africa, even though this region accounts for about two thirds of all infections worldwide.[16]

Overcoming these challenges will require a degree of collaborative scientific activity and commitment well beyond the existing global effort.[17] In June 2003, an international group of scientists proposed the creation of an international alliance called Global HIV Vaccine Enterprise, which would seek to accelerate HIV vaccine development by enhancing coordination, information sharing and collaboration globally.[18] The plan to coordinate global HIV vaccine research was endorsed by leaders of the G8 summit in June 2004. In November of that year, the US National Institute of Allergy and Infectious Diseases unveiled its plan to build a Center for HIV/AIDS Vaccine Immunology. As the first tangible outgrowth of the Global HIV Vaccine Enterprise, the center will set priorities for AIDS vaccine research and development and address problems already identified as key obstacles to the AIDS vaccine development.[19] In early February 2005, about 50 experts from developing and industrialized countries presented and discussed their HIV vaccine research and development efforts at the first WHO-UNAIDS Meeting of Global Partners Promoting HIV Vaccine Research and Development in Switzerland. The goals of the Global HIV Vaccine Enterprise received a strong boost when the Bill & Melinda Gates Foundation later pledged up to $360 million to support an array of innovations aimed at advancing the development of an HIV vaccine.[20]

The Global Fund

Supported by but not formally part of the UN system, The Global Fund to Fight AIDS, Tuberculosis and Malaria represents a unique global public-private partnership between governments, civil society, the private sector and affected communities for attracting and distributing additional resources for HIV/AIDS prevention and treatment. The Global Fund was established, with a push from SG Annan, in 2002 to collect donations and distribute grants to those countries severely affected by these diseases. In 2004, the Global Fund established performance measurement systems for its own operations as well as for grant progress in recipient countries; this completed a major proportion of a four-level measurement framework including operational performance, grant performance, system effects and impact. Analysis of the first 27 grants from the Global Fund shows that 70 percent of them are "progressing satisfactorily," 22 percent are "underperforming but demonstrate potential" and 8 percent have "inadequate performance."[21]

To date, the Global Fund has committed $3 billion in 128 countries to finance aggressive interventions against HIV/AIDS, tuberculosis and malaria.[22] At the end of 2004, financing had made it possible for 130,000 people to receive antiretroviral treatment and more than one million to receive voluntary HIV testing. Through a wide-range of prevention programs, the Global Fund has also enabled grant-funded recipients to reach tens of millions of people. By enabling the training of over 350,000 people to fight HIV, tuberculosis and malaria in 2004, the Global Fund is laying the foundations to scale up treatment to hundreds of thousands in 2005.[23] As of January 2005, the Global Fund had approved funding to ultimately support the provision of antiretroviral therapy to an estimated 1.6 million people in resource-deficient settings.[24]

Funding and Recommendations

Despite advances in medicine and funding, the world's response to the epidemic remains profoundly inadequate. Not only does the epidemic continue to spread in much of the world, but most effective prevention and treatment initiatives remain at the project stage, rarely reaching national scale. According to a report by the Futures Group, an organization headquartered in Washington, DC, few at-risk people in developing countries receive key prevention services: only 3.6 percent of injecting drug users had access to harm-reduction strategies, such as needle exchange, and only 3 percent of HIV-infected pregnant women were offered drugs to prevent mother-to-child transmission.[25]

In addition, donations are still well short of the amount needed to comprehensively address the global epidemic. By 2007, UNAIDS estimates a 50 percent shortfall in the resources needed to provide treatment and prevention worldwide. Lack of coordination between different funding resources further impedes the global efforts to scale up AIDS prevention and treatment. Under United States President George W. Bush's Emergency Plan for AIDS Relief, significant new resources are provided to national AIDS programs, including access to treatment. However, anti-HIV drugs purchased with the emergency plan's money must be approved by the US Food and Drug Administration (FDA), and none of the cheap, generic drugs that meet WHO's standards have received FDA approval to date. Critics therefore charge that funding will be wasted on brand-name drugs.[26]

Given these challenges, it is clear that committed leadership, in conjunction with coherent strategy, enhanced health system capacities, optimized coordination and reduction of duplication in efforts is necessary. Such strategies have been successful, arresting the epidemic at an early stage in countries such as Brazil and Senegal or reversing its growth after it has taken stronger hold in countries such as Uganda and Thailand.[27] To further this success, in a high-level meeting co-hosted by UNAIDS in April 2004, the United Kingdom and United States endorsed the "Three Ones" principles to achieve the most effective and efficient use of resources. The "Three Ones" principles promote: *one* agreed AIDS action framework that provides the basis for coordinating the work of all partners; *one* national AIDS coordinating authority with a broad-based multi-sector mandate; and *one* agreed country-level monitoring and evaluation system. A major challenge in the near term will be to promote the adherence of all stakeholders to this approach. And in March 2005, leaders from donor and developing country governments, civil society, UN agencies and other multilateral and international institutions agreed to form two groups: a Global Task Team on improving coordination among multilateral institutions and international donors, and a working group to review and revise the assumptions for the development of a clear understanding of the financial resource needs for AIDS. The groups are to be facilitated by the UNAIDS Secretariat and are meant to be representative of all stakeholders.[28]

New Infectious Diseases and Governing the Global Health System

Analyses of emerging and re-emerging infectious diseases have made clear that today's societies are confronting growing infectious disease threats. As SARS demonstrated, an infectious disease outbreak, be it naturally occurring or deliberately caused, can have tremendous implications for social-political stability, economic development and national security. In March 2004, WHO launched a three-year performance improvement program to strengthen its capacity to support member states and others in preparing for and responding to health-related crises such as SARS. The program deals with problems triggered by sudden catastrophic events (e.g., earthquakes and hurricanes), complex and continuing emergencies, as well as "slow-onset process" such as the gradual breakdown of a country's social-political institutions due to "economic downturn, populations affected by chemical poisoning or the impact of a fatal disease."[29]

The following section examines specific efforts made by WHO and other UN agencies around the world to control emerging and re-emerging infectious diseases using, in part, this model.

The Marburg Virus

The outbreak of Marburg hemorrhagic fever in October 2004 in Angola has constituted an extreme test of national and international capacity in addressing a disease-caused health emergency. To scientists, both the outbreak's location and its manifestation are unusual. This was the first time Marburg was identified in southwestern Africa; previously, the disease was known to occur only in Eastern and Central Africa. Unlike the typical hemorrhagic fever virus, about 75 percent of cases occurred in young children.[30] Perhaps more important, the disease has a case fatality rate higher than 90 percent, making the outbreak the largest and most lethal on record for this rare disease.[31] As of May 3, 2005, the Ministry of Health in Angola had reported 308 cases, of which 277 were fatal. In Uige Province, the epicenter of the outbreak, 297 cases, which led to the death of 266 people, were reported.

At the request of the Angolan government, international response to the outbreak began on March 22, 2005. Because of the extreme rarity of this disease and its similarity to other infectious diseases, rapid detection of Marburg in patients has been difficult. In the meantime, affected populations, watching their neighbors, colleagues and family members develop sudden, dramatic symptoms with no effective treatment in sight, have developed great anxiety. This, in turn, has led to a crisis of confidence in the system—communities have hid cases and bodies because they are untrusting of public health authorities and the international teams fighting the disease.[32] Another challenge in stopping the outbreak is to overcome logistical hurdles in a poor, war-ruined country like Angola. Weakened by almost three decades of civil war, the country lacks healthcare facilities and has weak infrastructures for water supply, electricity, communication and transportation.

At the time of this writing, new cases continued to be identified in Uige. Experts from WHO's Global Outbreak Alert and Response Network (GOARN) are in the province working to contain the outbreak through infection control, surveillance of new cases, and tracing and management of people in contact with the patients. The agency has also been focusing on training health workers and raising the awareness of the disease among locals. To date, the risk of international spread has remained low.[33]

Avian Influenza

Avian influenza, better known as "bird flu," is an infectious disease of birds caused by type A strains of the influenza virus. Avian influenza viruses do not normally infect species other than birds and pigs. The first documented infection of humans with an avian influenza virus occurred in Hong Kong in 1997, when a particular strain infected 18 humans, of which six died.[34] The Hong Kong outbreak is not the first time a virus jumped from birds to humans. Recent studies found that the virus behind the 1918 "Spanish Flu," regarded as the most deadly disease event in human history, retained many of the same characteristics of its avian ancestors.[35] The disease was so severe and its clinical course so unfamiliar that existing health institutions were completely unprepared to deal with it. In less than a year, an estimated 25 to 30 percent of the world population fell ill and more than 40 million people died.[36]

Most infectious disease experts agree that the world now stands on the verge of another influenza pandemic.[37] In January 2004, Thailand and Vietnam reported their first human cases of avian influenza. These cases were directly linked to the historically unprecedented outbreaks of avian influenza in poultry that since 2003 have rapidly affected eight Asian nations (Cambodia, China, Indonesia, Japan, Laos, South Korea, Thailand and Vietnam). According to WHO, "all prerequisites for the start of a pandemic were met save one: efficient human-to-human transmission."[38]

Mass culling of infected and exposed birds initially appeared to work well in containing the outbreak. After a brief lull, however, new lethal outbreaks among poultry were reported by five Asian countries in July 2004. In August, Malaysia reported its first outbreak. Cases were detected later in the Democratic People's Republic of Korea. Evidence indicates that the virus is now endemic in parts of Asia, having become firmly entrenched in poultry.[39]

As of April 15, 2005, there have been 88 human cases of avian influenza in Vietnam (68), Thailand (17) and Cambodia (3), resulting in 51 deaths.[40] Studies show that the H5N1 strain of avian flu has become progressively more pathogenic for poultry and can survive several days longer in the environment than in the past. Evidence further suggests that H5N1 virus is expanding its mammalian host range. It has recently been shown to cause severe disease and deaths in captive tigers and experimentally infected domestic cats, which were not previously considered susceptible.[41]

Although the timing of a future pandemic cannot be predicted, efforts have been made to estimate its consequences. Modeled on a mild pandemic of 1968, the best case scenarios predict two to seven million people would die and tens of millions would require medical attention. If the next pandemic virus is a very virulent strain, deaths could be much higher.[42] If the pandemic resembles that of 1918, some scientists have pointed out that, given today's world population, it could kill at least 72 million.[43]

In addition to human suffering, the pandemic can rapidly take on significant political, economic and social dimensions. Already, recent avian influenza outbreaks have devastated many local economies, particularly those that rely on poultry for their subsistence. So far, close to 140 million domestic birds have died or been culled in Southeast Asia, and loss of their flocks has left many farmers in deep debt.[44]

Clearly, endemic influenza represents one of the most significant global public health emergencies of today. Yet despite the legacy of the previous pandemics, there is a general lack of preparedness for an upcoming one. This is so in part because much remains to be understood about the molecular basis of influenza pathogenesis, and the virulence and transmissibility of influenza. The uncertainty over the risk posed by avian influenza to human health has placed policymakers in a dilemma: how can governments justify committing already scarce public health funds to an unpredictable but potentially catastrophic event?[45]

Perhaps more important, many countries affected by the avian influenza do not have effective diagnostic tools and surveillance systems essential for early warning and timely response. They also lack effective communication and coordination between related governmental agencies (e.g., ministry of health, ministry of agriculture, ministry of trade and animal husbandry).

In order to avert an influenza pandemic, or, if that has failed, to mitigate the consequences of a pandemic, national governments are advised to increase their surveillance of affected poultry stocks and strengthen surveillance of human beings. They must also raise public awareness of disease risks. Governments in Asia, in particular, must make the fight against the influenza virus a top priority, and to commit more financial resources to national and regional anti-bird flu efforts. Meanwhile, international communities need to help finance the projects that would strengthen animal health services and laboratories to improve virus detection and ultimate eradication. SG Annan has urged that greater resources be given by the World Health Assembly (WHO's supreme governing body, or WHA) to the WHO's GOARN network so that it can "coordinate the response of a broad international partnership in support of national health surveillance and response systems." He also has indicated his willingness to use his powers under Article 99 of the *UN Charter* to call to the attention of the Security Council "any overwhelming outbreak of infectious disease that threatens international peace and security."[46]

As pointed out by the Secretary-General and the UN High-level Panel report, it is "triply imperative" to build global disease response capabilities as a means to fight new emerging infectious disease, defend against the threat of biological terrorism and build effective, responsible states.[47]

Health Efforts after the Indian Ocean Tsunami

Dana Butunoi

The international community is still recovering from the Indian Ocean tsunami that struck 12 nations on December 26, 2004. It will take years if not decades, experts predict, for the region to rebuild and resume its normal capacities. According to the World Health Organization, more than 290,000 people have been killed or are missing, with children comprising more than one third of all deaths.

The UN Children's Fund (UNICEF) and WHO played a primary coordinating response regarding health issues, dispatching immediately to the damaged areas to evaluate the potential health threats faced by survivors and to provide crucial support to national health authorities. (Many other UN agencies were involved in humanitarian relief efforts.) WHO teamed up with Ministry of Health officials and other actors to avoid overlap and to draw up an action plan. It was not long before more than 200 leading specialists in communicable disease from around the world arrived to assist in water quality control, rapid health assessment and management of infectious diseases. They also helped to deal with health information systems and to launch public information campaigns on hygiene, as WHO's Health Action in Crisis unit had issued strong warnings of salmonellosis, typhoid, cholera, hepatitis and other injury–related health problems.

Thanks to the quick work and support of the UN agencies, member states, NGOs and others, as of June 2005, there were no major disease outbreaks in the region. WHO's Global Outbreak Alert and Response Network, along with surveillance and outbreak early warning systems, certainly helped control the situation. To date, thousands of children have been vaccinated against measles. Water supplies have been chlorinated and leakages in distribution pipes have been repaired. Proper access to health facilities and services, including immunization, are being addressed on a continuing basis.

Looking ahead, a clear disaster preparedness agenda has to be established, concentrating more on health and psychological trauma—which affected many victims—and on streamlining tasks. WHO has to launch harmonized techniques and standards for future use, and setting up a pool of forensic pathologists for mass fatalities and dead bodies is essential. These issues were discussed at the WHO-sponsored conference on tsunami relief in May 2005 in Thailand and are included in the major directives of a WHA resolution adopted on May 20, 2005.

"By applying what we have learned, we can be better prepared," said WHO Special Representative David Nabarro at the conference.

Addressing Ongoing Infectious Diseases

Malaria

Malaria is a life-threatening parasitic disease transmitted by mosquitoes. As of 2004, 107 countries and territories had reported areas at risk of malaria transmission. Although this number is significantly lower than in the 1950s, 3.2 billion people, or half of the world's population, are still at risk. According to a recent WHO-UNICEF report, around 350 to 500 million clinical disease episodes occur annually. Around 60 percent of the cases of clinical malaria and over 80 percent of the deaths occur in sub-Saharan Africa. In endemic African countries, malaria was reported to account for 25 to 35 percent of all outpatient visits, 20 to 45 percent of hospital admissions and 15 to 35 percent of hospital deaths. This inflicts a great burden on already fragile healthcare systems in these countries.[48]

In addition to acute disease episodes and deaths in Africa, malaria contributes significantly to overall child mortality by causing anemia in children and pregnant women, as well as adverse birth outcomes, including miscarriage, stillbirth, premature delivery and low birth weight. The disease is also responsible for an annual GDP reduction of up to 1.3 percent in some African countries and for hindering children's schooling and social development through both absenteeism and disease-associated illness.[49]

In 2005, Africa and the world commemorated Africa Malaria Day on April 25, with a new theme, "Unite against Malaria," to highlight the crucial element of a successful fight against malaria: partnership. In 1998, WHO, UNDP, UNICEF and the World Bank founded Roll Back Malaria (RBM), a global partnership that includes malaria-endemic countries, their bilateral and multilateral development partners, the private sector, academia and international organizations. This global partnership has been expanded with the establishment of the Global Fund to Fight AIDS, Malaria and Tuberculosis. At the end of 2004, Global Fund financing had provided more than 300,000 people with highly effective artemisinin combination treatments (ACTs) for malaria and more than 1.35 million families with insecticide-treated mosquito nets.[50]

Thanks to the combined efforts of different actors under the RBM umbrella, a number of countries, including those with limited resources, are now moving forward with their own malaria control programs. According to the current World Malaria Report, since 2001, 42 malaria-endemic countries have adopted ACTs and more people are receiving long-lasting insecticide-treated mosquito nets through innovative new programs.

In view of the key role malaria control has played in poverty reduction and development in high burden countries, MDG Goal 6 set the target of halting and reversing the incidence of malaria by 2015. A more immediate goal has been set by the RBM partnership, to halve malaria-associated mortality by 2010. However, much like the HIV/AIDS crisis, a lack of funds is a major obstacle to achieving both these goals. According to the World Malaria Report 2005, $3.2 billion per year is needed to effectively combat malaria in the 82 most impacted countries. In 2005, only $600 million was received.[51]

Tuberculosis

For centuries, tuberculosis (TB) has been known as a major scourge of the human species. Globally, there are two billion people infected with TB. Each year, more than eight million people become sick with infectious TB. Of these new cases, nearly one million are due to TB/HIV co-infection, and a further 300,000 cases are resistant to major TB drugs. TB is a leading cause of death among women with nearly three-quarters of a million of women dying of TB every year, and over three million contracting the disease. Children are vulnerable to TB infection as well because of frequent household contact: over 250,000 children die every year of TB.[52]

Lack of basic health services, poor nutrition and inadequate living conditions contribute to the spread of TB. But TB is not just a disease of poverty: it is also a cause of poverty. As TB infects people mainly in their economically and reproductively active years, the impact of illness on communities and households is very high. Every year in India alone, more than 300,000 children leave school due to their parents' TB. Moreover, the costs to households are higher for TB than most other diseases due to the length of the treatment period (six to eight months). It is estimated that TB depletes the incomes of the world's poorest communities by a total of $12 billion a year.[53] In short, TB threatens the poorest and most marginalized groups, disrupts the social fabric of society and slows or undermines gains in economic development.

Given the huge costs TB imposes on households and communities, particularly those in developing countries, TB control is also included in the MDGs just as malaria and HIV/AIDS are included. The globally agreed targets for TB are: by 2005, to diagnose 70 percent of new smear-positive cases and cure 85 percent of these cases; by 2015, to have halted and begun to reverse TB incidence. In 2001, the Stop TB Partnership launched a $9 billion, five-year Global Plan to Stop TB. The focus of the plan was to control TB in the 22 highly-impacted countries that account for 80 percent of global TB cases.[54]

Based on case reports and WHO estimates, 22 countries had reached the targets for case detection and treatment success by the end of 2003. Since 2000, the number of TB cases reported by DOTS (Directly Observed Treatment Short-Course) appears to have been accelerating. The 1.8 million smear-positive cases notified by DOTS programs in 2003 represent a case detection rate of 45 percent. If the improvement in case-finding between 2002 and 2003 can be sustained, the case detection rate will be 60 percent in 2005. The rate of treatment success in the 2002 DOTS cohort was 82 percent on average, unchanged since 2000.[55]

Financing of the global efforts to stop TB has been facilitated by the Global Fund, which at the end of 2004 had financed DOTS-based treatment for

385,000 patients. While the number is not high relative to global need, it reveals the increasing acceleration of Global Fund interventions.[56]

In a recent global TB report, WHO identified major hurdles of DOTS expansion: shortage of trained staff, lack of political commitment, weak laboratory services, and inadequate management of multi-drug-resistant TB and of TB/HIV co-infection. In order to reach the 70 percent case detection target, WHO recommends the recruitment of TB patients from non-participating clinics and hospitals, especially in the private sector in Asia, and from beyond the present limits of public health systems in Africa. In order to reach the target of 85 percent treatment success, it recommends that a special effort be made to improve cure rates in Africa and Eastern Europe.[57]

Fortunately, all high-burden countries are known to have set a strategic plan for DOTS expansion and, except Russia and Thailand, have fully integrated TB control functions with essential national health services. Since 2002, there has been a big increase in budgets of national TB control programs and a big improvement in the funding available for TB control in high-burden countries, despite a funding gap of $119 million in 2005. Whether the world will meet the MDGs by 2015, particularly those targets on TB, depends on the rapidity of implementing DOTS programs and the effectiveness the programs can be adapted to meet the challenges posed by TB/HIV co-infection, especially in Africa, and drug resistance, especially in Eastern Europe.[58]

Polio

Throughout the 1940s and 1950s, polio was one of the most feared diseases in the world. Today, it is confined mainly to parts of Africa and South Asia. Over the course of 2004, the Global Polio Eradication Initiative, launched by WHA in 1988, continued to make progress in Asia while geographic distribution of wild-type poliovirus was reduced in Afghanistan, India and Pakistan, with a total of just 194 cases reported compared with 336 for the same period in 2003. In Egypt, polio transmission fell to its lowest level ever. In contrast, the campaign suffered a setback in sub-Saharan Africa. Because of the suspension of immunization against the disease in Nigeria, and low routine immunization coverage in some neighboring countries, reported cases of polio in Niger and Nigeria increased to 814 by March 2005 compared with 395 for the same time in 2003. In addition, 254 cases occurred in 12 previously polio-free countries.[59]

In response to the polio epidemic in sub-Saharan Africa, heads of state and representatives from the Organization of the Islamic Conference adopted in October 2003 a landmark resolution to wipe out polio. This was followed by a second resolution on polio eradication, adopted by the Islamic Conference of Foreign Ministers at its 31st Session in June 2004. In October, the African Union launched the Synchronized Pan-African Immunization Campaign against Poliomyelitis in 23 countries of central and western Africa. African leaders attending the Fourth African Union Summit in January 2005 adopted a decision "to ensure that every child receives polio immunization in 2005." Despite these ample initiatives, lack of funding remains the greatest hurdle facing the Global Polio Eradication Initiative. Even though G8 leaders renewed their pledge to finance eradication activities in June 2004, the funding gap for activities in the second half of 2005 was $75 million and the gap for activities in 2006 was $200 million.[60]

With sufficient financial and political commitment from governments, polio transmission can be stopped globally by the end of 2005. Success depends on reaching all children in the remaining endemic districts. All countries are urged to maintain and strengthen polio surveillance and high population immunity.

Other Health Issues

Maternal and Child Health

In all cultures, families and communities acknowledge the need to care for mothers and children. In the 20th century, this purely domestic concern was transformed into a public health priority. The priority status of helping mothers and children, however, has failed to translate into similar gains in their health. Attending to all of the 136 million annual births is one of the major challenges facing the world's health systems. It is estimated that, each year, at least 3.3 million babies are stillborn, more than 4 million die within 28 days of birth, and a further 6.6 million children die before reaching their fifth birthday. Maternal deaths also continue unabated. Each year, 529,000 women die during pregnancy, childbirth or shortly after the baby has been born. They leave behind devastated families, many of which are pushed into poverty.[61]

As discussed in Chapter 3, Millennium Development Goals 3 and 4 aim to reduce by two thirds the under-age-five mortality rate and to reduce by three quarters the maternal-mortality ratio. In line with these and other goals, in May 2004, the 57th World Health Assembly adopted WHO's first strategy on reproductive health, intended to help countries stem the serious repercussions of reproductive and sexual ill-health. The strategy targets five priority aspects of reproductive and sexual health, including combating sexually transmitted infections such as HIV and reproductive tract infections. A recent WHO report believes that maternal and child mortality could be sharply reduced through wider use of key interventions and a "continuum of care" approach that begins before pregnancy and extends through childbirth and into the baby's childhood. The success of this approach requires greatly strengthened health systems with maternal and child healthcare at the core of their development strategies. This includes capacity-building at a national level and, within health districts, rehabilitating the health workforce's remuneration, ensuring universal access to healthcare, and sustaining political commitment to mobilize and redirect the considerable resources required.[62]

World Health Day 2005:
Maternal and Child Health in India

Hosted by the government of India, the World Health Organization's global commemoration of World Health Day 2005 took place in New Delhi on April 7. This year's theme was "Make Every Mother and Child Count." Focusing on maternal and child health, the day presented a unique opportunity to highlight an invisible health crisis and to bring all stakeholders together to apply solutions that work.

The event was launched in India to draw the government's attention toward maternal and child healthcare specifically. The country is on the list of 51 "slow progressing" countries in terms of infant, child and maternal mortality. Despite the decline in infant mortality and neonatal mortality rates, the overall downward trend started to falter in India in the 1990s. Among the 27 million infants born in the country annually, 10 percent do not survive their first five years. In absolute terms, India contributes to a quarter of the annual under-age-five mortality rate worldwide. In addition, one third of the world's malnourished children live in India and about 50 percent of all childhood mortality cases in India are attributable to malnutrition.[63]

As Secretary-General Kofi Annan said in a World Health Day message, the point is to "highlight the problem, but above all, to stimulate action." Following the ceremony, a three-day forum focusing on maternal, newborn and child health was held in India, which attracted health officials, medical professionals and advocates from around the world. Before the meeting ended, the *Delhi Declaration* was adopted, committing participants to maternal and child healthcare and setting the stage for decisive action in India.[64]

The Elderly and Disabled

Aging and disability are both public health challenges. In 2000, there were 600 million people aged 60 and older. Over the first half of the 21st century, the global elderly population is projected to expand more than three times to reach 2 billion in 2050. At the same time, since the likelihood of disability increases with age, it is hardly surprising that about 600 million people in the world today experience disabilities of various types. The global disabled population is increasing, as a consequence of general population growth, medical advances that preserve and prolong life, war injuries, landmines, HIV/AIDS, malnutrition, chronic conditions, substance abuse, accidents and environmental damage.[65]

Aging and disability are particular problems for the developing world. According to WHO, about two thirds of all older people and 80 percent of the world's disabled population reside in developing countries. For this segment of the population, the primary struggle is not just finding access to basic services such as healthcare and rehabilitation facilities, but also to survive and meet basic needs, such as food and shelter.

Moreover, an aging population leads to an increase in cardiovascular diseases, cancers, pulmonary and other chronic diseases worldwide. This "epidemiological transition," in turn, will generate greater needs for healthcare and put considerable strains on systems in all societies in the future. Meanwhile, the effectiveness of overall anti-poverty efforts is undermined because disabled people are generally excluded from development activities. In Uganda, for example, disabled people are nearly 40 percent more likely to be poor. In Honduras, disabled people have an illiteracy rate of 51 percent as opposed to 19 percent for the general population. Further, a new study jointly published by the World Bank and Yale University notes that disabled people are also at increased risk of contracting HIV/AIDS due to physical abuse, the lack of intervention and appropriate preventive outreach.[66]

These problems are certainly not unique to the developing world. Even in the developed world, the high life expectancy at birth means that the very old (age 80 and over) is the fastest growing population group. The "graying" societies and the rising disease burden are certain to significantly increase the cost of healthcare. It will also lead to the rise of aged dependency ratio–the ratio of the elderly compared to those of working age, affecting negatively on future labor force and productivity.

In April 2002, the UN Second World Assembly on Aging unanimously adopted the *Madrid Political Declaration and International Plan of Action on Aging.* The plan of action prioritizes access to primary healthcare to provide older people with "regular, continuing contacts and care" to prevent or delay the onset of chronic, often disabling diseases and to enable them to be important resources to their families and societies. Since then, a series of international conferences on aging have adopted what is called the active aging conceptual approach to help tackle the public health implications of aging.[67] In September 2004, WHO launched *Towards Age-Friendly Primary Health Care.* The Age-Friendly principles will serve as a tool for awareness-raising among older people and their healthcare practitioners, ultimately leading to the establishment of minimum standards to determine the age-friendliness of primary healthcare centers.[68]

In November 2004, the World Bank and its partners kicked off the second Disability and Development International Conference. The conference reflected a growing consensus that addressing problems like disability is part of the integral fight against poverty, and that it is crucial countries adopt development policies that include the concerns and needs of disabled people.[69]

UN Reform Recommendations Related to Health

Both the High-level Panel and the Secretary-General's reports focus on health reform, in the following areas:

On HIV/AIDS

• The international community, along with leaders of affected countries, needs to mobilize resources, commit funds and engage civil society and the private sector in disease-control efforts, especially in responding to HIV/AIDS and in rebuilding local and national public health systems throughout the developing world.

• The Security Council, working with UNAIDS, should host a second special session on HIV/AIDS to explore future effects of HIV/AIDS and to identify a long-term strategy for diminishing the threat.

On public health emergencies

• Members of the WHA should provide greater resources to GOARN to increase its capacity to cope with disease outbreaks.

• The Security Council should consult with the WHO Director-General to establish the necessary procedures for working together in the event of a suspicious or overwhelming outbreak of infectious disease.

On biological weapons

• States parties should commit themselves to further measures to strengthen and accede to the *Biological and Toxin Weapons Convention* and to negotiate for a credible verification protocol.

Looking Forward

In the 60th General Assembly meeting, member states will surely follow up on the outcomes of the Millennium Summit and discuss the reports regarding suggested reforms of the global health security system. Specific agenda items include the implementation of the *Declaration of Commitment on HIV/AIDS* and an update on the Roll Back Malaria efforts in developing countries, particularly in Africa. Since maternal and child health is the focus of 2005 World Health Day, delegates are also expected to discuss the advancement of women and the promotion and protection of the rights of children. There will be an update on the implementation of the outcome of the Fourth World Conference on Women and of the 23rd special session of the General Assembly, which focused on gender equality and development. In addition, delegates are expected to discuss social development, including questions relating to the world social situation and to youth, aging, disabled persons and the family. Finally, against the background of the recent tsunami disaster, delegates will discuss international strategies for disaster reduction efforts aimed at strengthening the coordination of emergency humanitarian and disaster relief assistance of the UN, including special economic assistance.

Commentary:
International Health Regulations—the SARS Example
Yanzhong Huang

International Health Regulations (IHR) provide the only legally binding international instrument to govern international health regimes in today's world. They standardize the procedures to be followed by all countries in controlling infectious diseases of international importance. Prior to the emergence of SARS (Severe Acute Respiratory Syndrome), IHR—set in 1969 by the World Health Assembly—were seriously dated. For example, they required the reporting of only three infectious diseases: cholera, plague and yellow fever. In addition, under IHR, the reporting of pathogen-induced morbidity and mortality was exclusively the domain of sovereign states. Historically, nations have sought to suppress the flow of information regarding endogenous epidemics to avoid significant negative effects upon their economy and society, such as the collapse of tourism or decline in foreign investment. In this sense, China's early attempts to suppress the flow of information to the World Health Organization regarding SARS, and Canadian officials' insistence that WHO travel advisories were erroneous, both reflect this historical pattern of tension between sovereign states and the UN.

Despite these problems, some important changes have taken place in the international health governance regime since the 1970s. According to David Fidler, a leading expert on international law and public health, beginning in the 1990s, there has been a merging of "horizontal germ governance," in which sovereign states are the dominant actors in regulating international microbial traffic, and "vertical germ governance," in which states, intergovernmental actors and non-state actors work in coordination to reduce disease prevalence inside states. In 2003, the SARS epidemic had a profound impact on international health governance. To the extent that the Bubonic Plague of the 14th century was a progenitor of the existing international system in which sovereign states are the principal actors, the SARS epidemic appeared to confirm the transition to new forms of health governance, described by Mr. Fidler as "the post-Westphalian era," in which non-state actors have increasing influence on global governance. During the WHA meetings of May 2003, member states stipulated that WHO should redouble its efforts to garner and analyze data from non-state actors. Specifically, the assembly requested that the WHO Director-General "take into account reports from sources other than official notifications." The SARS epidemic has dramatically increased the power and authority of WHO, which employed its new-found freedom to issue global alerts and travel advisories when it deemed appropriate, and not subject to the consent of affected member states.

The approval by member states at the May 2003 assembly meeting of these radical acts appears to confirm the existence of an entirely new governance context for infectious disease control. Under this new configuration of global health governance, non-state actors would provide WHO with information for analysis and subsequent dissemination to global civil society without the consent or even the consultation of targeted countries.

It is important to note that while revising the IHR, along with the ensuing change in international health governance, might provide strong disincentives for member states to cover up disease outbreaks, they may also lead to misapplications and excessive responses that disrupt international travel and trade. As David Heymann of WHO has pointed out, Peru in 1991 and India in 1994 both suffered severe economic consequences of reporting an IHR-mandated disease when neighboring countries and trading partners imposed measures in excess of those permitted by the IHR. In the Indian case, the appearance of pneumonic plague resulted in mass exodus, risking spread of the disease to new areas. IHR alone cannot control the spread of infectious disease. Strengthening health system capacities at the national level is equally important for an effective global health governance structure.

In May 2005, the 58th World Health Assembly took these concerns into account. It approved a new set of IHR to manage public health emergencies of international concern. The new rules seek to ensure maximum protection of people against the international spread of disease, while minimizing interference with world travel and trade. Both the UN High-level Panel report and Secretary-General Kofi Annan's *In Larger Freedom* report support strengthened IHR as well. The issue is therefore now on the 60th General Assembly's plate.

Endnotes

1. Laurie Garrett, "The Return of Infectious Disease," *Foreign Affairs*, January/February 1996.
2. *Ending the War Metaphor: The Future Agenda for Unraveling the Host-Microbe Relationship* (Report of the Institute of Medicine), March 2005.
3. UN Document A59/765 (2005).
4. *AIDS Epidemic Update 2004* (Report of UNAIDS), December 2004.
5. *AIDS in Africa: Three Scenarios to 2025* (Report of UNAIDS), 2005.
6. *3 by 5 Progress Report* (Report of WHO), December 2004.
7. Seventh International Congress on AIDS in Asia and the Pacific website.
8. CDC website.
9. *BBC Monitoring International Reports,* Caribbean Media Corporation News Agency, October 16, 2004.
10. UN Document A59/765 (2005).
11. *AIDS Epidemic Update 2004* (Report of UNAIDS), December 2004.
12. Bates Gill, J. Stephen Morrison and Drew Thompson. *Defusing China's Time Bomb: Sustaining the Momentum of China's HIV/AIDS Response* (Report of the CSIS HIV/AIDS Delegation to China), April 13-18, 2004.
13. Joseph Kahn, "China's Vice Premier Urges Businesses to Help With AIDS Fight," *New York Times,* March 18, 2005.
14. *AIDS Epidemic Update 2004* (Report of UNAIDS), December 20044.
15. UNAIDS website.
16. WHO Press Release (2005).
17. Emilio A. Emini and Wayne C. Koff, "Developing an AIDS Vaccine: Need, Uncertainty, Hope," *Science,* June 25, 2004.
18. Richard D. Klausner *et al,* "The Need for a Global HIV Vaccine," *Science,* June 27, 2003.

19. Jon Cohen, "The First Shot in a Highly Targeted Strategy," *Science*, November 19, 2004,

20. Jon Cohen, "Huge HIV Vaccine Gift from Gates," *Science*, February 25, 2005.

21. *Investing in the Future: The Global Fund at Three Years* (Report of The Global Fund to Fight AIDS, Tuberculosis and Malaria), 2004/2005.

22. Global Fund website.

23. *Investing in the Future: The Global Fund at Three Years* (Report of The Global Fund), 2004/2005.

24. UN Document A59/765 (2004).

25. Jon Cohen, "International AIDS Meeting Finds Global Commitment Lacking," *Science*, July 23, 2004.

26. Ibid.

27. *Combating HIV/AIDS in the Developing World* (Report of the UN Millennium Project Task Force 5 Working Group on HIV/AIDS), February 2004.

28. UNAIDS website.

29. WHO website.

30. Martin Enserink, "A Puzzling Outbreak of Marburg Disease," *Science*, April 1, 2005.

31. "Marburg Hemorrhagic Fever in Angola," *WHO website*, April 22, 2005.

32. Martin Enserink, "Crisis of Confidence Hampers Marburg Control in Angola," *Science*, April 22, 2005.

33. WHO website on Marburg.

34. WHO website on Avian Flu.

35. Edward C. Holmes, "1918 and All That," *Science*, March 19, 2004.

36. WHO website on Avian Flu.

37. *The Threat of Pandemic Influenza: Are We Ready?: A Workshop Summary* (Report of the Institute of Medicine), 2005.

38. *Strengthening Pandemic Influenza Preparedness and Response* (Report by WHO to the 58th WHA), April 7, 2005.

39. Ibid.

40. "Recent Avian Influenza Outbreaks in Asia," *CDC website*, April 26, 2005.

41. *Strengthening Pandemic Influenza Preparedness and Response* (Report by WHO to the 58th WHA), April 7, 2005.

42. Martin Enserink, "WHO Adds More '1918' to Pandemic Predictions," *Science*, December 17, 2004. / *See* also WHO website.

43. Martin Enserink, "WHO Adds More '1918' to Pandemic Predictions," *Science*, December 17, 2004.

44. UN Press Release SAG/334 (2005).

45. WHO, "Governments in a dilemma over bird flu," May 1, 2005.

46. *In Larger Freedom: Towards Development, Security and Human Rights for All* (Report of Secretary-General Kofi Annan), March 21, 2005.

47. UN Document A/59/565 (2004).

48. *World Malaria Report* (WHO, 2005).

49. "Roll Back Malaria: Malaria in Africa," *WHO website*.

50. Global Fund, "Investing in the Future: The Global Fund at Three Years," 2005.

51. WHO Press Release (May 3, 2005).

52. Global Fund and WHO websites.

53. Global Fund website.

54. Ibid.

55. *Global Tuberculosis Control—Surveillance, Planning, Financing* (Report of WHO), 2005.

56. *Investing in the Future: The Global Fund at Three Years* (Report of The Global Fund), 2004/2005.

57. *Global Tuberculosis Control—Surveillance, Planning, Financing* (Report of WHO), 2005.

58. Ibid.

59. UN Document A58/11 (2005).

60. Ibid.

61. *World Health Report 2005* (Report of WHO), 2005.

62. Ibid.

63. *The Times of Hindu*, April 8, 2005

64. WHO website.

65. Ibid.

66. "Partners Kick off International Conference on Disability and Development," *World Bank website*.

67. "International Plan of Action on Aging: Report on Implementation," *WHO website*, April 2005.

68. WHO Press Release (2004).

69. World Bank website.

Chapter 6

Trade: Negotiating Between and Across Borders

David Lynch

More than one billion people still live below the extreme poverty line of $1 per day and, according to the UN Secretary-General, 20,000 people die from poverty each day. Trade is not the answer to all the world's problems, but it can make a powerful contribution to international efforts for development. We must ensure this contribution is realized and that the enormous potential of globalization is harnessed for the benefit of people the world over.
— World Trade Organization Director-General Supachai Panitchpakdi
World Trade Organization Public Symposium, April 2005

With fewer barriers to trade and more goods and services crossing borders, the world trading system is more open than ever before. To proponents of the world trading system, this is good news, but numerous barriers to trade remain, distorting efficiency, slowing global economic growth and ultimately, sustaining poverty. Proponents want remaining barriers removed and view the current World Trade Organization (WTO) negotiations—called the Doha Development Agenda (DDA)—as the best way to further reduce such barriers.

Critics of the world trading system are more varied in their criticism. Some think that reduced barriers to trade encourage corporations to seek out economic efficiency at the expense of other values; corporations promote a "race to the bottom" in search of low taxes, low wages and lax environmental regulations. Other critics, including many of the poorer WTO members, argue that reduced barriers to trade mean that global economic efficiency is valued over equality; the poorest are forced to compete with the wealthy.

It is precisely the higher level of economic openness that leads to these cross pressures for more, fewer or different trade regulations. To fully understand these pressures, it is important to understand how the world trading system was established and how much it has evolved.

Looking Back

The United Nations' interest in trade began with the belief that the global economic disasters in the 1920s and 1930s provided fertile ground for the seeds of political extremism to take root. Lack of international economic cooperation and coordination gave way to economic conflict—competitive currency devaluations and higher tariffs—which deepened the economic crisis. According to the architects of the post-World War II economic order, this crisis contributed to political extremism, and therefore to World War II itself. Infused with this belief, political and economic leaders were determined to create institutions that would foster economic cooperation, liberalization and peace.

Meeting in Bretton Woods, New Hampshire in 1944, delegates from 45 countries agreed to construct three institutions: the International Monetary Fund (IMF), the International Bank for Reconstruction and Development (IBRD), more popularly known as the World Bank, and the International Trade Organization (ITO).[1] The ITO's draft charter called for an ambitious ITO that would attempt to manage matters such as employment rules and trade in services. The charter, however, never made it through the United States Congress. Instead, the less sweeping General Agreement on Tariffs and Trade (GATT), originally intended to be a provisional agreement that would begin the process of lowering tariffs until the ITO was in place, became the world's primary trade institution.[2] Entering into force in 1948, GATT proved to be a long-lasting institution that, over time, significantly lowered barriers to trade and thus contributed to the post-World War II economic expansion. GATT principles of reciprocity (that trade barriers should be mutually reduced in negotiations) and non-discrimination among GATT members ensured that lower tariffs to one member extended to all members, with exceptions for granting poor countries even lower barriers and for forming free trade areas like the European Union.[3]

GATT members successfully lowered barriers to trade by negotiating in "rounds" to jointly lower tariffs. By the end of the Kennedy Round in 1967, the sixth round of GATT negotiations, industrial tariffs had dropped dramatically. Further liberalization would require dismantling trade barriers that were more complex and controversial than tariffs. Thus the seventh round, the 1979 Tokyo Round, signified a shift in the GATT negotiations' focus and complexity toward "behind the border" issues. These topics, such as subsidies to industry and government procurement, had once been considered matters of domestic concern, but since they had clear trade repercussions, they increasingly became a focus of GATT negotiations. This trend continued in the Uruguay Round negotiations, which created the UN's World Trade Organization and expanded multilateral trade rules into more economic sectors, and continues in today's round of WTO negotiations, referred to as the Doha Development Agenda. The Uruguay Round did not end GATT but rather made it evolve into the WTO. (Technically, the GATT, now called GATT 1994, is one portion of the rules that make up the WTO. GATT 1994 has no independent legal status.)

The WTO today is a member-driven organization; members make the rules that govern all aspects of the WTO. The members are most typically countries, but some other entities are also members, such as the EU. There is a director-general—currently Dr. Supachai Panitchpakdi of Thailand—and a Secretariat, both housed in Geneva, Switzerland.

Multilateral trade negotiations have become more complex over time for another reason: the number of GATT and WTO members has risen dramatically. When the GATT went into effect in 1948, there were only 23 signatories. There were 84 by the end of the Tokyo Round in 1979, 110 by the signing of the 23,000 page Uruguay Round in 1994, and 148 members and observers are participating in the ongoing Doha Development Agenda.[4]

The World Trade Organization Today

Management

The WTO celebrated its 10th anniversary on January 1, 2005. To some, the anniversary was a reminder of how remarkable it was that the Uruguay Round participants were able to find consensus over so many issues. The round, which culminated in the Marrakesh Agreement in April 1994, lasted more than seven years and signaled a number of departures from previous GATT agreements. In addition to establishing the WTO, it led to the inclusion of agriculture, textiles and apparel in the GATT's trade liberalization process. These economic sectors are by far the most important to developing nations for both employment and exports; thus, exclusion from GATT, along with the 10-year-phase in period for textiles and apparel, and the continued agriculture subsidies in developed nations, had long served as evidence for critics that the multilateral trading system's rules favored developed nations. Second, the Uruguay Round included trade in services (General Agreement on Trade in Services, or GATS) and the provisions governing the treatment of intellectual property (Trade Related Aspects of Intellectual Property Rights, or TRIPS), both of which are of particular importance to developed nations. Third, the Uruguay Round further increased focus on behind-the-border issues such as subsidies to industries. Fourth, the Uruguay Round required that the agreement be a "single undertaking," meaning that members had to accept or reject the agreement in its entirety, with only a few optional clauses. Fifth, the Uruguay Round included the Dispute Settlement Understanding (DSU), which governs the resolution of trade disputes at the WTO and created a more rigorous dispute resolution process than existed under GATT.

WTO's dispute resolution system has been highly controversial because it has been much-used and because it can authorize WTO members to raise barriers to trade against WTO members that fail to follow WTO rules. From its inception on January 1, 1995 to October 22, 2004, there had been 317 cases filed with the DSB. That is as many as the old GATT dispute resolution process handled in nearly 50 years.[5] Many cases are resolved before moving to the panel stage. Of the 317 cases filed over this period, 159 cases have been adjudicated through 129 panels.[6]

Membership

The WTO Secretariat has been stretched much further than initially anticipated because of the high level of interest in matters ranging from DSB rulings to the agency's own governance. Much concern has been focused on the degree of participation by developing nations in the organization's negotiations and proceedings. There has been concern, however, over the lack of representation in WTO proceedings by developing countries, especially least developed countries (LDCs),[7] as well as by nongovernmental organizations' (NGOs) who need greater institutional channels to influence WTO negotiations. To address this problem, WTO staff has given seminars for developing nations' officials to educate them about the WTO system, and WTO members have donated expertise and funding for representation at the DSB proceedings. There also have been some positive changes such as public symposia and other outreach efforts, leading to greater access to information about the WTO and its proceedings for NGOs. Still, even some WTO members feel excluded from unofficial gatherings held just before, or on the sidelines of, official meetings.

Despite concerns over representation, the WTO continues to grow: Cambodia became the 148th member in October 2004; it is the second LDC to join the organization using the "working party" negotiation process. To accede to the WTO, applicants must have their economy examined by WTO members, negotiate agreements with WTO members, be voted in by WTO members and accept the terms of entry. Specifically, it is necessary to establish a working party consisting of any interested WTO members and the applicant to examine the applicant's economy and create terms of accession.

Other notable recent WTO accession developments include the December 2004 authorization to establish working parties for Afghanistan and Iraq. Libya, which had first applied to join in 2001, finally reached this step in July 2004.[8] For Libya, this demonstrates its growing acceptance by Western countries despite its alleged procurement of weapons of mass destruction.

On April 20, 2005, there were 31 applicants authorized to negotiate WTO entry. In addition to the three countries recently authorized to develop working parties—Afghanistan, Iraq and Libya—these applicants include Algeria, Andorra, Azerbaijan, Bahamas, Belarus, Bhutan, Bosnia and Herzegovina, Cape Verde, Ethiopia, Kazakhstan, Laos, Lebanon, Montenegro,[9] Russia, Samoa, Saudi Arabia, Serbia, Seychelles, Sudan, Tajikistan, Tonga, Ukraine, Uzbekistan, Vanuatu, Vietnam and Yemen.[10]

Two of these WTO applicants stand out in terms of trade stature and political power: Russia and Saudi Arabia. Both have recently made strides toward WTO membership and are hopeful that WTO membership will come in the upcoming year or so. For Saudi Arabia, a significant step would be agreement with the US over Saudi accession terms. In May 2005, a US-Saudi agreement was close,[11] but Russia still has to achieve bilateral agreements with a number of its trading partners and then, like other entrants, must sign a multilateral agreement with all WTO members.[12]

Vietnam has increased the pace of its accession negotiations in an attempt to enter the WTO as well. This country is aiming to do so as soon as possible to compete with China, as China has better access to developed nations' textiles and apparel markets, given the end of quotas for these products on January 1, 2005. As of May 2005, US trade officials estimated that Vietnam still needed to create or change approximately 30 laws to further liberalize its economy for WTO entry. On May 20, 2005, Vietnam announced that it had reached bilateral agreements with eight out of 20 WTO members that have asked for talks. These bilateral agreements have not yet been notified to the WTO and some members of Vietnam's working party have said that Vietnam must further speed up its bilateral negotiations and domestic reforms if they are to join the WTO by the Hong Kong Ministerial Conference in December 2005.[13]

Iran is another WTO hopeful although its membership application, started in 2001, had been held up by the US. It was not until March 2005 that US Secretary of State Condoleezza Rice reported that the US had finally dropped its long-held objection to Iranian WTO membership as part of negotiations with Iran about its nuclear program. France, Germany and the United Kingdom had a hand in this change of course by helping to convince the US to allow Iran to join WTO in exchange for Iran fully opening its nuclear program to UN inspections.[14] At the time of this writing, Iran had just officially gained approval for a working party.[15]

Improvements and Reform

In 2003, WTO DG Supachai commissioned a report to make recommendations about how the WTO might be more effective. His Consultative Board issued its report, *The Future of the WTO: Addressing Institutional Challenges in the New Millennium*, in January 2005. The eight-member board, which includes academics and practitioners on trade policy, calls for many steps to be taken by the WTO and its members in the years to come. They note that cooperation with other intergovernmental organizations is beneficial, but express concern that "the creation and interpretation of WTO rules is for WTO members alone and should be preserved from undue external interference." Observer status should be granted to other intergovernmental organizations, they argue, "solely on the basis of potential contribution to the WTO's role as a forum for trade negotiations."[16]

Similarly, the board applauds the increases in external transparency in recent years, but calls for guidelines for WTO relations with civil society and for some limits in those relationships: "the Secretariat is under no obligation to engage seriously with groups whose express objective is to undermine...the WTO." The report goes on to say that WTO should make a special effort to assist local civil society organizations in LDCs, especially those in Africa.

The board supports trade liberalization, but also recognizes that developing nations struggle to adjust to such change, and thus proposes that international development agencies develop or improve adjustment assistance programs. With regard to the DSU, the board argues that WTO should reject any proposed reforms that would include any sort of "diplomatic veto" over dispute panel decisions. They make a number of other DSU recommendations including opening some hearings to the public.[17]

The members caution that WTO's core principle of "Most Favored Nation" (MFN) status has been severely endangered by preferential trade agreements (PTAs) which include partial or comprehensive free trade agreements (FTAs), customs unions and common markets between two or more countries (e.g., the EU), or asymmetrical preferential trade access programs (e.g., the ACP-EC Partnership Agreement which gives most African, Caribbean and Pacific states favored access to the EU's market). A clarification of the rules to forming PTAs—found in Article XXIV of GATT 1994 and currently being negotiated in the DDA—is required, according to the board's report. It also calls for the significant reduction of tariff barriers and non-tariff barriers in the DDA round to minimize the market distortions and confusion created by PTAs.[18]

Finally, the board suggests the WTO scale back the goal of total consensus in decision-making. They suggest instead that WTO members consider increasing the "variable geometry" approach to trade negotiations in which WTO members would not have to adhere to all aspects of a WTO negotiation round. Given the difficulty WTO members have had in recent negotiations (i.e., in Cancún), this might allow members who are more committed to liberalization on a given trade issue to forge ahead.[19]

There is some contradiction between the Consultative Board's proposals on reduced consensus and its proposals on PTAs. On PTAs, the board calls for more clarity and consistency to simplify trade, yet it also considers the greater use of plurilateralism, or similar arrangements in which some WTO members move toward deeper levels of liberalization and others opt out.

Overall, the board report aims to strengthen the roles of the director-general and secretariat. The director-general's role should be clarified, they say, based upon the advice of past directors-general. The director-general and secretariat should have the capacity and standing to be at the center of negotiations during ministerial meetings. A chief executive officer to strengthen management in the secretariat is recommended as is greater policy analysis from the secretariat in order to bolster its role as "guardian of the WTO system." Finally, the board asks for a larger WTO budget.[20]

The Secretary-General's High-level Panel on Threats, Challenges and Change added its two cents to trade reform negotiations as well, primarily calling on nations to finish DDA at the latest in 2006. It also notes that increased trade opportunities are important for sustainable development in poor countries, and thus, developed countries should reduce trade barriers.

Starting on September 1, 2005, Pascal Lamy, a former EU trade commissioner, will take over as WTO Director-General and will therefore be responsible for facilitating consideration of the Consultative Board recommendations and other proposed trade reforms. (Current DG Supachai will become Director-General of the UN Conference on Trade and Development or UNC-TAD). Given the central importance of developed nation reductions in agricultural supports for completing the DDA, Mr. Lamy may prove to be an asset for DDA supporters. His native France is the most vociferous defender of rich country agricultural subsidies and many WTO members feel he might ease French farmers' resistance more than a non-French director-general.[21]

Doha Development Agenda

The Doha Development Agenda, or DDA, is the most complex negotiating round in international trade relations to date. Simply launching the DDA was itself an achievement as lingering concerns over the Uruguay Round made the subsequent negotiations difficult to launch as symbolized by the protests and riots at the Seattle Ministerial meeting in November 1999. The protestors were concerned with the environment, health, human rights and jobs, but the main difficulty in launching the talks centered upon whether developed nations were willing to address issues of the greatest interest to developing nations, such as reduced agriculture subsidies in wealthy nations, cheaper access to patented medicines and less stringent adherence to trade rules for poorer nations (so-called "special and different" status and "implementation" issues). The DDA was finally launched in Doha, Qatar in 2001 with the signing of the *Doha Declaration*, which set broad outcomes and serves as a roadmap to completing the DDA.

The DDA's ambitious agenda has already led to numerous missed deadlines, but this is to be expected in trade negotiations. One significant step was supposed to have been the Cancún Ministerial Conference in September 2003, but WTO members failed to reach consensus. Developing nations banded together more assertively and effectively than in many previous WTO negotiations while developed nations were not yet prepared to move on a number of issues, most importantly, significant reductions in their agricultural support, such as subsidies to produce or subsidies to export.

Agricultural supports in wealthy countries have been widely blamed for depressed farm prices in poor countries. According to the Organization for Economic Cooperation and Development (OECD), total farm supports to OECD countries (mostly developed countries) reached $349 billion in 2003. This is nearly $1 billion per day and is approximately the same amount as the combined annual GDP of all of sub-Saharan Africa. OECD farmers can, on average, attribute 32 cents of every dollar they earn to agricultural supports.[22] Because of the levels of these supports, developing nations put this highest on their DDA agenda, but developed countries did not find sufficient consensus at Cancún about how to reduce these supports.

The official end date goal for the DDA was to have been January 1, 2005. Now, the widely-stated consensus is that a broad deal on the DDA must be reached by the sixth WTO Ministerial Conference in Hong Kong in December 2005 in order to give negotiators sufficient time to wrap up the details of a broad agreement before US President George W. Bush's authority to negotiate trade agreements expires in July 2007.[23] This "fast-track" authority, officially called Trade Promotion Authority (TPA), is due to run out at that time, but the Bush administration has asked for, and will likely get, a two-year extension. Without fast track, any trade agreement brought to Congress can be amended beyond recognition and would require the renegotiation of the DDA. Thus, it is not considered an exaggeration to equate the end of fast track authority with the real end of the DDA.

Moving Past Cancún

On August 1, 2004, there was some redemption for Cancún's failings. In July of that year, WTO members negotiated the "July Package," as it is informally known, and made significant headway on some of the most vexing issues that led to Cancún's lack of consensus.[24] Most significantly, developed WTO members agreed to reduce agricultural subsidies and to end export subsidies. They also agreed to recognize cotton trade as highly important—but not to create a separate cotton-only branch of the DDA negotiations, as some developing country cotton producers had hoped. Also, WTO members agreed to consider one of the four so-called Singapore issues—trade facilitation—in the DDA and to leave the other three issues—investment, competition policy and transparency in government procurement—out of the DDA.[25]

The exclusion of three Singapore issues was seen as a victory for developing countries who viewed these issues as potentially adding administrative difficulties to trade. The July Package's coverage of trade facilitation includes recognition that any new trade facilitation requirements should be linked with the ability of countries to afford it. WTO members hope that trade facilitation negotiations could lead to reductions in so-called "at the border" barriers to trade, such as customs fees and inspections.[26]

There are, however, still significant arguments about the degree to which the various types of domestic support serve as export subsidies and what date the export subsidies—the most damaging to developing nations' farmers—will end. The EU's traditional use of export subsidies to assist its farmers is fairly straightforward, but other domestic support policies for agricultural are more complex. US food aid, for instance, is seen by critics as a clever way to disguise US export subsidies. Food surpluses in the US are shipped to countries facing famine, alleviating hunger crises, but also helping US farmers and harming farmers in the recipient country and in countries that might otherwise be able to sell to the recipient country. Most of the concern about these domestic supports is with the disruption of farming in developing nations. Still, others fear deep cuts in agricultural supports will increase the price of imports and decrease the level of food aid given.

Next Steps

Despite the success of the July Package, there are numerous agricultural trade issues that remain problematic. For instance, one reason for failure at Cancún was a dispute over cotton. Four poor cotton producers—Benin, Burkina Faso, Mali and Chad—had launched the Cotton Initiative in June 2003, shortly before the September 2003 Cancún Ministerial Conference, seeking cotton specific negotiations in the WTO and immediate relief from developed country subsidies. They did not get this at Cancún, but in the July Package, they were able to officially heighten the status of cotton in the negotiations. The July Package called for a subcommittee on cotton to examine all facets of the agricultural sector negotiations as they apply to cotton.[27] The results of this are yet to be seen.

Also in the July Package, WTO members committed to the principle that agriculture product areas with higher tariffs would face the deepest cuts, but did not confirm how much deeper and what exceptions would be allowed.[28]

In fact, the momentum gained from the July Package had been lost on a highly technical but critical matter: how to accurately calculate existing agricultural tariffs to serve as a baseline from which tariff negotiations could progress. To explain, some countries have tariffs by volume, such as a $1 tariff per ton of a given product's import. More typically, tariffs are per import value, such as 1 percent of the value of a given import. Thus, DDA negotiators have been trying to convert tariffs by volume into tariffs by value. This technical point was contentious because higher tariffs will likely be subjected to deeper cuts in the negotiations and because there are some discrepancies between world prices and actual import prices for some products in some countries. Now that the agricultural tariff conversion issue has been settled—a joint WTO-OECD meeting in May 2004 agreed on how to do the conversions, the hard bargaining of actual tariff reductions can begin.[29]

Other stalled agricultural negotiations of the DDA had to do with the fact that a number of developing nations are less than eager to make significant concessions until they see tangible movement in the agricultural talks from developed countries. Free trade proponents hope that greater movement in agriculture will allow other contentious issues to move forward. For instance, the DDA negotiations are far behind schedule in tackling trade in services. In May 2005, DG Supachai described services negotiations as having "fallen into a sense of torpor that seems difficult to escape from." Developed nations, especially the US, tend to want more open trade in services and developing nations tend to be more hesitant, except in one area of trade in services—mode 4, the movement of natural persons. It is a small portion of trade in services, but has been contentious.[30]

In addition to the issues listed here, there are many other outstanding issues to be resolved before the DDA negotiations can be finished. These includes tariffs on non-agricultural products, intellectual property rights (e.g., patents and copyrights) and rules about various trade remedies such as anti-dumping procedures (i.e., retaliating against unfairly "dumped" imports).

Regional Agreements

Ardent free traders have sometimes been accused of being evangelical in their devotion to the religion of free trade. "Fundamentalist" free traders have always viewed regional trade agreements (RTAs) as sins because they divert trade from its most efficient or "godly" path to less natural paths established by governments through politics or "pagan worship." Yet, some free trade proponents have dissented from this fundamentalist free trade line, largely on pragmatic grounds. The pragmatist free traders argue that one can never be sure if global trade barriers will continue to fall, so increasing free trade within a regional grouping promotes free trade overall. Indeed, many pragmatic free traders argue that free trade within regional groupings can help build support for multilateral free trade.

The discord over Cancún seems to have made countries more interested in RTAs. For example, Australian Prime Minister John Howard cited the "glacial pace" of liberalization in the WTO as one rationale for Australia pursuing bilateral free trade agreements.[31] Australia is not alone. Between January and August 2004, 21 RTAs were notified to WTO, bringing the total number of agreements in force to 206. Approximately 30 more agreements were signed between 2003 and 2004 and await entry into force while some 60 more have been proposed or are being negotiated.[32] In addition to RTA growth, the agreements themselves are becoming more varied. Some, but not all members of a regional group, for instance, might form bilateral or regional FTAs with countries outside their group. The result is that there are different trade rules for different countries.

DG Supachai's Consultative Board, in its report *The Future of the WTO* report, lamented that, "MFN is no longer the rule; it is almost the exception." The report blamed the "spaghetti bowl" of customs unions, common markets, regional and bilateral free trade areas, preferences and an endless assortment of miscellaneous trade deals. For instance, the EU's array of trade agreements is so extensive that its MFN tariffs are fully applicable to only nine countries.[33] Despite this, interest in RTAs of all sorts shows no signs of slowing.

The following section describes recent negotiations over regional and free trade agreements according to region.

Africa

African free trade agreements or FTAs are notoriously complex and confusing. There are numerous sub-regional groupings in Africa, usually with cross-cutting membership, making the spaghetti bowl reference seem too simplistic. Africa is, however, making efforts at continent-wide free trade through the African Economic Union. The continent's leaders hope to unite the many regional groupings and establish an African Economic and Monetary Union by 2028. Most African countries are linked to the US through the African Growth and Opportunity Act, which grants member countries preferential access to US imports and exports. The US is also negotiating an FTA with the South African Customs Union.

The EU currently grants preferential treatment for African exports through the Africa, Caribbean and Pacific-European Community Partnership Agreement and intends for these preferential trade agreements to be supplanted by more reciprocal FTAs. Toward that end, the EU began negotiating with the Southern African Development Community in 2004.[34]

Americas

There has been much movement on regionalism in the Americas in recent years. However, most of that movement has *not* been in the Free Trade Area of the Americas (FTAA), the broadest RTA in the region. FTAA negotiations began in 1994 and were supposed to lead to a single comprehensive trade agreement by January 1, 2005, covering the Americas from the tundra of Canada all the way to the Tierra del Fuego in Argentina with one glaring exception: Cuba. Instead, in November 2003, FTAA members agreed to disagree and established two tracks: the less ambitious Common Set of provisions for all FTAA members—called "FTA lite" by some—and a plurilateral negotiations track for those members that seek deeper integration. A single vigorous version of the FTAA is the regional agreement in the Americas that the US wants the most, but Brazil (most importantly) and Venezuela (most vocally) are hesitant. Brazil is not eager to negotiate an RTA in which it will be easily overshadowed by the giant US economy. It would prefer to deepen integration in South America and then negotiate with the US from a stronger position. Indeed, even for the US, deeper integration in the FTAA might politically require more integration in the DDA; because the US sugar industry will fight any opening of its protected market in the FTAA negotiations, the US argues that any opening in US sugar markets must come in global trade negotiations. The FTAA missed its January 1, 2005 goal for a comprehensive agreement and the negotiations continue to be stalled.

Aside from the FTAA, South American integration took a significant step in December 2004 with the founding of the South American Community of Nations. It hopes to form an EU-like organization eventually, but until then, represents a uniting of Mercosur, the Common Market of the South, with the Andean Community trade grouping. Because Brazil is the dominant economy in South America, some view this as an extension of Mercosur, which has been expanding in recent years. Today, it encompasses all of South America, although at varying levels of integration. Argentina, Brazil, Paraguay and Uruguay have long been full members, meaning they are in a customs union; Bolivia, Chile and Peru are associate members; Mexico now seeks associate membership in Mercosur; and Andean Community members Bolivia and Peru, already associate Mercosur members, will soon be joined by Colombia, Ecuador and Venezuela.[35]

The EU and Mercosur's efforts to create a cross-regional trade agreement remain stalled on the EU's hesitation to open its agricultural markets, an issue of central importance to rising agricultural power in Brazil. For its part, the US has said it will follow a policy of "competitive liberalization" in South America whereby US bilateral and multilateral trade agreements will encourage other countries to liberalize with the US so as not to be shut out of the American market.

The US has been very active negotiating RTAs in recent years; trade agreements with Singapore, Chile and Australia have entered into force. The US is considering or negotiating FTAs with Andean Community members Colombia, Ecuador and Peru, as well as Panama, Thailand and the South African Customs Union members Botswana, Lesotho, Namibia, South Africa and Swaziland.[36] It also has recently negotiated FTAs with Bahrain, Morocco and many Central American countries through the Central American Free Trade Agreement (CAFTA) signed in May 2004. CAFTA initially included Costa Rica, El Salvador, Guatemala, Honduras and Nicaragua—in August 2004, the Dominican Republic joined. CAFTA is hotly controversial in US Congress. The US sugar industry is dead-set against the agreement.

It is important to note that US bilateral and regional trade agreements have pushed a hard line on intellectual property rights. Critics argue poorer countries have less negotiating leverage relative to the US in bilateral or regional negotiations than they do in the WTO's multilateral setting. Because the WTO allows a variety of intellectual property standards to be accepted, regional and bilateral trade agreements are venues for vigorous intellectual property rights supporters such as the US to press their case.

Asia and the Pacific

Regional agreements of numerous types are flowering within the Asia-Pacific region, and between the region and outside partners. Since China entered into RTA competition, other large Asian traders are accelerating their efforts to establish trade agreements. Japan and South Korea are particularly interested in forming RTAs in the region; Singapore has been aggressive at forming RTAs; and now India has shown interest in FTAs in Asia outside its already-established agreements in South Asia.

China is negotiating an FTA with the Association of Southeast Asian Nations (ASEAN) countries and is considering FTAs with Australia, New Zealand, Chile and the Gulf Cooperation Council countries. China, Japan, South Korea and the ASEAN countries are considering establishing an East Asian Community (EAC) that would be a regional FTA, but it remains unclear how much integration its potential members want. Continued political tension between China and Japan suggest the prospects for deep integration are limited. There are different views about which countries should be included in such an organization. In December 2005, the East Asian Summit will be held in Malaysia, a country that has made it known it does not want Australia and New Zealand included in such a body if one is formed. This might be difficult as Australia and New Zealand are scheduled to begin an FTA with ASEAN and are pressing for inclusion in the EAC.[37]

In the meantime, ASEAN integration is growing, but faces some controversy over Myanmar's upcoming turn as chair of the association. Myanmar has a poor human rights record and its government is best known for jailing Nobel Peace Prize winner Aung San Suu Kyi.

United States-China Trade Relations

The growing acrimony between the US and China over trade is similar to the US-Japan trade relationship of the 1980s and 1990s. In both cases, the US ran enormous bilateral trade deficits and the financial relationship became increasingly important. Japan held, as China currently holds, significant US government debt. And in both instances, the US was concerned with job losses from massive increases in imports, and thus accused the other of unfair trade practices.

There are important differences as well: Japan was feared because it seemed to be overtaking US companies' market share and technological edge while the US feared its top economic position was being eroded. These fears subsided in the 1990s when Japan struggled economically and the US enjoyed a long run of growth and low inflation. In the case of China, however, US fears are not about its economic leadership, at least not yet, but more about jobs. This strain was made worse with the end of textile and apparel quotas on January 1, 2005. Chinese clothing exports to the US did increase dramatically for some categories of goods, leading the US to seek safeguards (temporary barriers against import surges) against Chinese imports. Such safeguards are legal for the US to impose under the provisions of the US-Chinese agreement on China's WTO accession, but certainly go against the spirit of the WTO, as China has pointed out. China has placed an export tariff on some textile and apparel items in order to reduce some of the political pressure from the US, but US pressure remains high because of another issue: the low value of its currency, the yuan, relative to the US dollar.

Cheap Chinese wages are difficult enough to compete against, but an artificially low exchange rate helps keep Chinese exports cheap in the US. This has led many in the US to call for China to revalue its currency from its peg of approximately 8.28 per dollar—a rate that has held since 1994. Two members of US Congress introduced legislation that would punish China if it does not revalue the yuan. The Bush administration has spoken more gruffly about Chinese foreign exchange policies, but resisted branding China as a "currency manipulator," an action that would require the US to open negotiations on the matter. Much of this shouting is for a domestic audience. It is unclear whether China's revaluing the yuan would make much difference for US import levels. A more highly valued yuan would, however, make imported inputs cheaper for Chinese manufacturers. A higher valued yuan might also encourage US exports to China, assuming it did not slow down the Chinese economy substantially. Those US exports, however, would likely be in agriculture or sectors other than the hard-hit US apparel industry.

At the time of publication, China seemed to be moving toward increasing the value of the yuan, but on its own timetable.[38]

Europe

The European Union's "big bang" expansion of May 2004 increased membership by 10 to 25. As a result, the European Economic Area, an FTA between the EU and three of the European Free Trade Agreement (EFTA) countries—Iceland, Liechtenstein and Norway (EFTA member Switzerland opted out)—encompasses 28 countries, roughly 450 million people and nearly 20 percent of world trade.[39] Then, in June 2004, the EU reached agreement on the long-sought *EU Charter*. The EU was on the move both wider and deeper, or so it seemed. The deeper integration of the *Charter* needed approval in all 25 EU countries to come into force. After approval in 10 countries, the *Charter* lost in public referenda in France and The Netherlands in May and June 2005, respectively. At the time of this writing, it was clear that the EU had quite a mess on it hands. It has to either renegotiate the document so that there are varying degrees of integration or conduct a re-vote in France and The Netherlands—the *Charter* cannot go into full effect without full approval.

As it stands, the 300-page document calls for a more united Europe with a foreign minister to represent the EU, a Bill of Rights and a stronger EU Parliament, among other things. The *Charter* is highly symbolic of the EU's commitment to integration and thus the *Charter's* failure in two founding countries demonstrates the EU's contentious and confusing relationship.[40]

Four countries have official candidate status with the EU: Croatia, Bulgaria, Romania and Turkey. Croatia, however, was put on hold because the country is not fully cooperating with the International Criminal Tribunal for the former Yugoslavia. Specifically, Croatia has been asked to arrest General Ante Gotovina, suspected of war crimes against Serbs.[41] Entry into the EU requires applicant nations to have a good human rights record.

Middle East and North Africa

The regionalism that has spread so rapidly around the world has been noticeably less pronounced in the Middle East and North Africa. Certainly countries in this region are less open economically and also have had some significant political differences. Still, there has been some heightened interest in RTAs in recent years. The Gulf Cooperation Council (GCC) members—Bahrain, Kuwait, Oman, Qatar, Saudi Arabia and the UAE—will start FTA negotiations with China[42] and there are other RTA plans for both within the region, and between the region and outside countries and groups.

Inside the region, 18 of 22 Arab League members seek to establish an Arab Free Trade Area by 2008. Such an FTA may not be set up so quickly, however, given that the Arab League's annual meeting is often characterized by discord. At the March 2005 Arab League event, some leaders did not attend and some that did refused to be photographed together.[43] An Arab FTA may get some outside help, however. The Euro-Mediterranean Partnership Agreements have nudged Jordan, Egypt, Morocco and Tunisia toward an FTA by 2006. And not to be outdone in regionalism, the US is promoting bilateral FTAs in the region with the goal of establishing the Middle East Free Trade Area by 2013. It already has formed bilateral FTAs with Israel, Jordan and Morocco, signed a free trade agreement with Bahrain in 2004 and is currently negotiating bilateral FTAs with the UAE and Oman.[44]

Other Trade Agreements and Amendments

Multi-Fibre Arrangement

One of the tangible advantages developing countries got out of the Uruguay Round negotiations was the end of the Multi-Fibre Arrangement (MFA) and the establishment of the agreement that governed its 10-year phase-out: the Agreement on Textiles and Clothes (ACT). The MFA ensured that textiles and apparel remained outside GATT's trade liberalizing rules by applying quotas to them. For developing nations, this was particularly galling given their low wages and therefore comparative advantage found in the labor-intensive character of the textile and apparel sector. It served as proof of the developed nations' dominance in GATT. It was no surprise then that the Uruguay Round's elimination of the MFA quotas through the ACT initially drew complaints from developing countries, primarily about its slow phase-out of quotas.

Since the MFA phase-out began in 1995, developing nations that export apparel have become increasingly concerned that large low-cost producers—especially China and potentially India—will reap the benefits of the end of quotas at their expense. China was not in the WTO when the quota reductions began in 1995 and had many dramatic and painful economic reforms to undertake before it could join. India, long a significant textile and apparel producer, has gradually opened to foreign investment and seemed to be a bigger threat as the textile and apparel quotas ended. Eager anticipation for the end of quotas in developing nations turned to hesitation and even dread because many countries' textile and apparel industries owe much of their origin to other producers' quotas being full. That purpose is now gone.

In the first few months without quotas in 2005, imports from China surged higher in both the US and EU, prompting both to begin investigations into imposing tariffs to safeguard against import surges. The US, Turkey and Argentina have already placed safeguards on some Chinese imports, which are allowed under China's terms of entry into the WTO, but will not be allowed after 2008. China has taken some steps to slow the increase in exports by imposing a small export tax on some apparel, but this seems primarily symbolic.[45]

The question remains whether industries in developing countries with smaller or less efficient textile and apparel production will survive. With quotas gone, suddenly, developing nations' producers feel they must beat China's low wages, low transportation costs (compared to some developing nations) and vast scale. Moreover, it is expected that those developing nations that can do more than just apparel assembly will have an advantage. For instance, if a country can efficiently produce textiles locally to supply its low wage apparel assembly, it might be able to compete with China. But efficient textile production is capital-intensive and, therefore, massive investment in China bodes well for producers there while also further intimidating many developing nations. Other potentially large developing country producers, such as India, seem poised to gain from these trends, but most developing countries are deeply concerned.

Some have taken steps to make their production more efficient, or to distinguish themselves from Chinese and Indian production in other ways. Central American producers, for instance, signed CAFTA with the US to eliminate all tariffs on textiles and apparel shipped to the US if it includes US cloth or yarn. Many developing nations might find such arrangements geographically more difficult while others are concerned that such arrangements would help their apparel industry at the expense of their textile industry. Also, the advantages of favored access through bilateral or regional trade agreements will be diminished if the DDA brings down textiles and apparel tariffs, which remain higher than other industrial goods in most countries.[46]

Byrd Amendment

The Byrd Amendment, a law passed in 2000 by the US Congress to prevent dumping, was seen as a violation of WTO rules even before the WTO ruled against it. Nevertheless, any company exporting to the US has to follow it. Under the law, officially known as the Continued Dumping and Subsidy Offset Act of 2000, companies accused of exporting to the US at unfairly low prices pay a penalty. What is unique and especially contentious about the Byrd Amendment is that the penalty money goes to the US companies harmed by the dumping. To US anti-dumping supporters, this is a much needed boost for beleaguered US manufacturers and it puts real teeth in US anti-dumping laws. To detractors, it creates a powerful incentive for companies to file frivolous anti-dumping complaints. Frivolous or not, since the amendment's passage, US anti-dumping cases have shot up and other countries are now using their own anti-dumping provisions at much higher rates.[47]

A WTO dispute panel ruled that the Byrd Amendment violated trade rules in September 2002. In November 2004, with the US having not removed it from the books, another WTO panel authorized Brazil, Canada, the EU, India, Japan, Mexico and South Korea to place penalty tariffs on imports from the US.

Most of these countries have held off in doing so, but in May 2005, Canada and the EU began placing 15 percent tariffs on a number of imports from the US. The EU estimates its tariffs are likely to total $150 million in 2005 and expect them to reach more than $1 billion in the following US fiscal year. Despite the Canadian and EU tariffs and President Bush's disapproval, the Byrd Amendment remains popular in Congress and is not expected to end anytime soon.[48]

Airbus-Boeing Dispute

Airplane producers Airbus and Boeing are giants and when giants battle, they make a lot of noise. They certainly have been making quite a racket and now, much of it will be heard within the WTO's dispute resolution process. In May 2005, the US officially reactivated its case against the EU for its support of Airbus and the EU reactivated its complaint against the US for its support of Boeing. Boeing used to dominate large airplane production, but Airbus is now the world's largest producer. The US argues that EU launch aid—which guarantees Airbus the repayment of launch costs if a new line of airplanes does not sell—is not compatible with WTO rules. The EU has long argued that Boeing also gets subsidized by military contracts and that aid from Washington State is not compatible with WTO rules. Many expect that the WTO will rule against both the US and the EU over this issue. This is potentially the largest dispute to come before the WTO's dispute resolution panel and, oddly, comes at a time when airplane production is increasingly global, not national in scope.[49]

Looking Forward

As described in this chapter, the immediate challenge for the world trading system is to agree on a draft of the Doha Development Agenda by the December 2005 Hong Kong Ministerial Conference before President Bush's authorization to negotiate runs out. There are also numerous ongoing regional negotiations and many trade disputes to work out: the Byrd Amendment and the ongoing battle between the EU and US over subsidies given to Airbus and Boeing are but two of these disputes. But the most significant challenge to the trading system is how to pull the poor out of poverty in a way that is economically, environmentally, socially and politically sustainable. The most significant step would require developed nations to open the agricultural sector and reduce those agricultural supports that harm developing nation producers. Developed countries must realize that social issues—such as establishing labor standards and environmental regulations in trade regulations—will never be agreed to by poor countries until a greater level of trust is established and until economic conditions in developing countries improve. For their part, developing countries need to open their economies to each other. The stakes at the DDA are high—to avoid another Cancún situation, both developed and developing nations need to make not only compromises but also some sacrifices.

Commentary:
Turkey and the European Union
David Lynch

In May 2004, the European Union took a dramatic step by enlarging to 25 members. The new entrants, primarily former communist countries, signified not just a larger EU, but a more diverse EU in terms of language, culture and level of economic development. The Union's diversity could increase again if accession negotiations with Turkey are successful. If acceded, Turkey would be the first country in the EU whose territory is not primarily European; Turkey has one foot in Europe and the other across the Bosporus Strait in Asia. Furthermore, many question whether Turkey is "sufficiently" European, as it would be the first Islamic country in the EU and amplifies the symbolism associated with this enlargement. This is especially true given heightened tensions found in many EU countries between the majority populations and Muslim citizens and immigrants over such controversial incidents as the March 11, 2004, bombings in Madrid and the French ban on wearing religious symbols in public schools.

As a result, both Turkey and the EU have been doing some soul-searching. Modern Turkey was founded on Mustafa Kemal Ataturk's militant secularism, but the country is an overwhelmingly Islamic nation with Islamic political parties. To some Turks, EU membership is too western. EU countries, meanwhile, view their societies as open and tolerant, but find this claim increasingly difficult to maintain when their fellow non-Muslim citizens, or they themselves, express hesitation at integrating with an Islamic country.

There are also more tangible difficulties to Turkish entry in the EU. Turkey would be a significant increase to the EU in terms of population and area and, like many of the new EU entrants, it struggles economically. What sets Turkey apart from these countries is its combination of size and poverty. Moreover, critics argue that it has been slow to liberalize its political system, especially its human rights record on the treatment of Kurds.

Turkey's potential inclusion in the EU is influencing the ratification of the *EU Charter* in some countries as well. In France, for instance, where the *EU Charter* was rejected, some 450,000 French-Armenians urged a no-vote to pressure Turkey to publicly accept responsibility for the Turkish massacre against Armenians from 1915-1917. Tension over whether to call this episode genocide, as the Armenian government and the Armenian diaspora have called for, or to call it a massacre, as EU governments describe it, or to call it a civil war, as the Turkish government insists, has been heightened with the 90th anniversary of the start of the mass killings.

It is possible that if Turkey apologizes for the mass killings—and does so with gravity and tact—it would be a step toward exorcising this ghost of its history. At the same time, the EU's self-image and its reputation, especially in the Islamic world, will certainly be influenced by its handling of Turkey's potential EU entry.

Endnotes

1. "Key Economic Events 1944 Bretton Woods Agreement," *Government of Canada website*. / Walter Goode. Dictionary of Trade Policy Terms. Fourth edition. (Cambridge University Press/ WTO, 2003).

2. "The GATT Years: from Havana to Marrakesh" and "GATT: A brief history," *WTO website.*

3. Michael J. Trebilcock and Robert Howse. The Regulation of International Trade. Second edition. (Routledge, 2002).

4. Jeffrey Schott and Jayashree Watal. "Decision Making in the WTO," The WTO After Seattle. (Institute for International Economics, 2000).

5. WTO Press Release 353 (2003).

6. UN Document WT/TPR/OV/10 (2004).

7. Ibid.

8. *WTO News*, WTO website, July 28, 2004, October 13, 2004 and December 13, 2004.

9. Note: Serbia and Montenegro have separate applications despite that they are currently one country.

10. UN Document WTO/ACC/11/Rev.5 (2005). / "Accessions," *WTO website.* / "Cambodia Raises WTO membership to 148," WTO News, October 13, 2004.

11. "Saudi Arabia Seeks WTO Deal with US within Weeks," *Reuters*, May 2, 2005.

12. "Russia Has Chance to Join WTO in 2006—EU," *Reuters*, May 9, 2005.

13. "Chair Says Viet Nam Must Complete Bilaterals Quickly to Meet Ambition," *WTO News*, May 20, 2005. / Ho Binh Minh, "US Urges Vietnam to Press on with Economic Reform," *Reuters*, May 6, 2005. / James Hookaway and Murray Hiebert, "Prickly Issues on Tap for US-Vietnam Visit," *Wall Street Journal*, May 10, 2005. / Michelle Nichols, "Vietnam backs Australia's Bid for East Asia Summit," *Reuters*, May 5, 2005.

14. "Bush: US, Europeans Speaking with 'One Voice' on Iran," *CNN website*, March 11, 2005.

15. "Accession Working Parties Established for Iran, Sao Taome and Principe,"

WTO News, May 26, 2005.

16. *The Future of the WTO, Addressing Institutional Challenges in the New Millennium* (Report of the Consultative Board to WTO Director-General Supachai Panitchpakdi), January 2005. Paras 6-7, conclusions. Hereafter referred to as Consultative Board report.

17. Consultative Board report, paras 8, 16, 21, conclusions.

18. Consultative Board report, Chapter II, paras 60, 105.

19. Consultative Board report, paras 25-26.

20. Consultative Board report, paras 30-37.

21. WTO Press Releases (January 4, 2005, April 29, 2005). / "Update 6: Cuttarre Pulls Out of Race to be WTO Chief," *Associated Press*, April 29, 2005.

22. "OECD Agricultural Policies 2004: At a Glance," OECD, 2004. / UN Document WT/TPR/OV/10 (2004).

23. WTO Sixth Ministerial Conference website. / "Time to Rev the Engine," *Economist*, April 28, 2005.

24. UN Document WT/L/579 (2004).

25. "A Step Forward," *Economist*, July 7, 2004.

26. "Trade Facilitation, Doha Round Briefing Series," The *International Centre for Trade and Sustainable Development (ICTSD)*, December 2004.

27. "Overview of the July Package, Doha Round Briefing Series," *ICTSD*, December 2004.

28. "Farm Accord Spurs WTO Trade Talks," *Wall Street Journal*, August 12, 2004. / "Agriculture: Doha Round Briefing Series," *ICTSD*, December 2004. / UN Document WT/L/579 (2004).

29. "Progress at Last," *Economist*, May 5, 2005.

30. "OECD Council at Ministerial Level, Remarks by the Director-General," *WTO website*, May 4, 2005. / "Trade in Services: Doha Round Briefing Series," *ICTSD*, December 2004.

31. Steve Lewis and Kimina Lyall, "PM's Parting Shot at WTO," *The Australian*, December 2, 2004.

32. UN Document WT/TPR/OV/10 (2004).

33. Consultative Board report, paras 60, 74.

34. Jo-Ann Crawford and Roberto V. Fiorentino, "The Changing Landscape of Regional Trade Agreements," *WTO Discussion Paper 8*, 2005.

35. UN Document WT/TPR/OV/10 (2004).

36. Ibid. / "US Free Trade Agreements," US International Trade Administration website.

37. Jo-Ann Crawford and Roberto V. Fiorentino, "The Changing Landscape of Regional Trade Agreements," *WTO Discussion Paper 8*, 2005. / "Vietnam Backs Australia's bid for East Asia Summit," *Reuters*, May 4, 2005. / Steve Lewis and Kimina Lyall, "PM's parting shot at WTO," *The Australian*, December 2, 2004.

38. Michael M. Phillips, "White House Intensifies Pressure on China to Let Yuan Appreciate," *Wall Street Journal*, May 18, 2005.

39. UN Document WT/TPR/OV/10 (2004).

40. "What the Charter Means for the EU," *Wall Street Journal*, April 22, 2005. / Dan Bilefsky, "Dutch Lean Toward Sinking EU Charter," *Wall Street Journal*, May 19, 2005. / "Germany Approves EU Constitution," *Deutsche Welle*, May 5, 2005.

41. "EU postpones Croatia entry talks," *BBC News*, March 16, 2005.

42. "China, GCC Agree to Start FTA Talks," *People's Daily Online*, July 7, 2004. / Jo-Ann Crawford and Roberto V. Fiorentino, "The Changing Landscape of Regional Trade Agreements," *WTO Discussion Paper 8*, 2005.

43. Hassan M. Fattah, "Conference of Arab Leaders Yields Little of Significance," *New York Times*, March 24, 2005.

44. USTR Press Release ("United States to Begin Free Trade Negotiations this Week with the United Arab Emirates and Oman," March 8, 2005).

45. Fong Mei Fong, "Backlash Is Likely as Chinese Exports of Apparel Surge," *Wall Street Journal*, March 28, 2005.

46. "A New World Map in Textiles and Clothing," *OECD Policy Brief*, October 2004. / Paul Magnusson, "Who'll Survive the Textile Trade Shakeout?" *Business Week*, December 20, 2004.

47. Martin Crutsinger, "Trade War Promises to Hurt US Jobs," *Associated Press*, April 29, 2005. / Scott Miller, "EU, Canada Plan Extra 15% Tariff on US Exports," *Wall Street Journal*, April 1, 2005.

48. Ibid. / "Byrd Amendment Retaliatory List," *US International Trade Administration website.*

49. Elizabeth Becker, "Europe Revives Its Trade Case Against Boeing Subsidies," *New York Times*, May 31, 2005. / "US Reopens WTO Case over Airbus Support," *Reuters*, May 30, 2005.

Chapter 7

International Law: Treaty-Making, Governance and the Advancement of Justice

Lawrence C. Moss

> *The main engine of international law-making has become the treaty. Today, thou-sands of treaties not only govern or endeavor to govern the great issues of war and peace—the United Nations Charter, the North Atlantic Treaty, the Hague and Geneva Conventions, and so on—but also unending aspects of the economic and social life of the peoples of the world. But for international law, aircraft would not fly across national boundaries...epidemics would spread unhindered by cooperative medical action...limits of jurisdiction in the seas would be anarchical; copyrights and trademarks would not be recognized abroad; and arbitral awards would be deprived of foreign recognition and enforcement.*
>
> —International Court of Justice Judge Stephen M. Schwebel
> *American Society of International Law, 2005*

The functions of international law and justice continue to grow in scope and importance in three major spheres. First, the United Nations General Assembly continues to lead the codification and advancement of international law through its treaty-making processes. Second, the debate over the legality of the Iraq war, and the threats posed by terrorism and weapons of mass destruc-tion, have provoked re-examination of the *UN Charter*; specifically those rules governing the use of military force in self-defense and the Council's use of its inherent law-making powers. Third, as the international war crimes tribunals established by the Security Council for Rwanda and the former Yugoslavia move toward completion of their work, hybrid national/international tribunals for Sierra Leone and Cambodia get underway, and the permanent Internation-al Criminal Court investigates its first referrals, the prosecution of individuals for war crimes, genocide and crimes against humanity is now firmly estab-lished as a central purpose of international law.

Looking Back

The UN's 1945 *Charter* is the cornerstone of modern international law, and its central provisions prohibit the use of military force except in limited self-defense circumstances and when authorized by the Security Council to maintain international peace and security. These rules were widely disregarded during the Cold War, although even then, states using military force without Council authorization often sought to justify themselves with expansive claims of self-defense. The centrality of the *Charter's* collective security scheme was revived by the Security Council's role in authorizing the 1991 Gulf War, and by numerous peacekeeping missions authorized by the Council over the past 15 years. Since the 2003 Iraq war, the rules governing the use of force have again became a divisive issue, as has the Council's use of Chapter VII powers to legislate measures against terrorism.

A world court to adjudicate disputes between states actually antedates the UN. The Permanent Court of International Justice was established in 1921 under the League of Nations. The *UN Charter* replaced that court with a similar International Court of Justice (World Court). Other tribunals have since been created to determine certain interstate disputes and claims of private parties against states. Two *ad hoc* international criminal tribunals are operating in the former Yugoslavia and Rwanda; there is also a special court in Sierra Leone and a fourth beginning in Cambodia. The decisions of these courts are shaping a new and growing body of international criminal law while the International Criminal Court (ICC) is expected to become the central institution in administering such law.

The development and codification of international law through the General Assembly and its subsidiary organs, such as the Sixth Committee and the International Law Commission, has been one of the great successes of the UN, far exceeding the expectations of its founders. A substantial number of proposed treaties are under development at any given time, and in most years, one or more emerge and are adopted by the Assembly, and then opened for signature and ratification by states. A particular triumph of the Assembly's law-making processes was the adoption in 1998 of the *Rome Statute* establishing the ICC. Most recently, the 59th General Assembly adopted two new treaties—on nuclear terrorism and on jurisdictional immunity of states and their property.

Moving forward, the 60th session of the General Assembly will be extraordinary, in that provisions of the *UN Charter* itself, including the application of the basic rules for the use of force, the composition of the Security Council, the continued existence of bodies established by the *Charter*, and the possible creation of a new Council on Human Rights, will all be before member states for consideration. Fundamental issues concerning the organization and the *Charter* have been raised by the challenge of meeting terrorist threats, the worldwide debate over the legality of the Iraq war, and widespread criticism of the current Commission on Human Rights. Many of these concerns have been considered by the Secretary-General's High-level Panel on Threats, Challenges and Change, and by the Secretary-General himself in his report *In Larger Freedom: Towards Development, Security and Human Rights for All*; they are addressed in a legal context in this chapter.

Law-Making at the United Nations

Although the preamble to the *UN Charter* states that one of the goals of the organization is "to establish conditions under which justice and the respect for the obligations arising from treaties and other sources of international law can be maintained," the development of new international law was not originally one of the central purposes set for the UN. In fact, it has turned out be an area where the UN has been enormously successful. This section focuses on the work of the UN's law-making bodies, the international legal issues before the 60th General Assembly, and the established treaties that are or will be open for signature and ratification in 2005 and 2006.

The General Assembly and Subsidiary Bodies

Article 13 of the *UN Charter* empowers the General Assembly to "initiate studies and make recommendations for the purpose of...encouraging the progressive development of international law and its codifications." The Assembly is the ideal body to forge political consensus on proposed treaties as it is the main representative body for all 191 member states. It is important to note that the Assembly is not, however, a legislative body and has no power to require or force nations to accede or adhere to any treaty. Treaties can, of course, be negotiated on a bilateral or multilateral basis outside the UN processes, but it is a striking success of the UN system that it has been responsible for such a large proportion of universal multilateral treaties.

While proposals for new treaties commonly originate in the General Assembly, they are generally referred to subsidiary bodies for further study and negotiation before returning to a plenary session of the Assembly for approval. In addition to various special conferences, *ad hoc* committees and working groups, the General Assembly has established three such bodies on a permanent basis: the Sixth Committee, the International Law Commission (ILC) and the UN Commission on International Trade Law (UNCITRAL). The ILC and UNCITRAL are expert bodies and report to the Assembly through the Sixth Committee.

The ILC, established in 1947, primarily focuses on public international law and consists of 34 legal experts elected to five-year terms as individuals, not as representatives of their governments. (The next election of ILC members will be held during the Assembly's 61st session in 2006.) The ILC meets annually in Geneva, and consults widely with governments, outside legal experts and regional legal bodies to draft treaties.

UNCITRAL, which focuses on private international law, was established in 1966 to further the progressive harmonization and unification of the law of international trade. UNCITRAL is comprised of 60 member states elected by the General Assembly, allocated amongst different geographic regions. Members of the commission are elected to six-year terms with the terms of half the members expiring every three years.[1]

The Sixth Committee balances the academic expertise of the ILC and

UNCITRAL with political experience and direction. The committee is one of six Assembly "Committees of the Whole," with each of the UN member states having one vote in each one of these committees. The Assembly often establishes working groups, *ad hoc* or special committees under the Sixth Committee umbrella to study legal issues and negotiate the language of proposed treaties. These groups operate only by consensus; their work is then considered by the Sixth Committee, which also strives for consensus, but may take votes. The full General Assembly generally adopts the recommendations of the committee. Following is a select number of recent committee recommendations.

Sixth Committee Actions

The 59th General Assembly session placed 19 items on the agenda of the Sixth Committee. These items may remain under study and consideration for years, moving back and forth between the ILC or UNCITRAL, one or more *ad hoc* committees or working groups, and the Sixth Committee and plenary sessions of the Assembly before an international conference is convened to discuss the issue or before final action is taken.

Terrorism

Terrorism, in one form or another, has been on the Assembly's agenda since its 27th session in 1972, when the Ad Hoc Committee on International Terrorism was established.[2] Since then, four conventions, including the *International Convention for the Suppression of Terrorist Bombings* (1997) and the *International Convention for the Suppression of the Financing of Terrorism* (1999), have emerged from the General Assembly, in addition to eight others developed by specialized multilateral bodies that deal with aircraft, nuclear materials and maritime navigation.

The 59th session witnessed the adoption of a 13th convention against terrorism, the *International Convention for the Suppression of Acts of Nuclear Terrorism*. This convention was the first international legal instrument on terrorism to be adopted by the General Assembly since the terrorist attacks of September 11, 2001. It requires states to criminalize the use, threat to use or possession with intent to use radioactive or nuclear materials or devices, and requires states to cooperate in the investigation, prosecution and extradition of persons who commit terrorist acts using such materials or devices.[3] The convention, which requires ratification by 22 states to go into effect, will be open for signature in fall 2005.

Despite this progress, the present *ad hoc* committee on terrorism and the Sixth Committee have failed to develop a comprehensive legal framework on terrorism, stymied by the inability of member states to agree on a definition of "terrorism." The two major stumbling blocks are whether the definition should include the use of force by states against civilians, and whether peoples under foreign occupation have a right to resistance. Issues arising out of the Israeli-Palestinian conflict, in particular, have inflamed this debate.

As described in Chapter 1, the definition issue was considered in detail in the UN High-level Panel's December 2004 report, *A More Secure World: Our Shared Responsibility*. The panel concluded that legal norms against state violations are already in place and that the preamble to a definition of terrorism should simply recognize the *Geneva Conventions* and other instruments which regulate state use of force against civilians. The panel further concluded that whether or not there is a right of resistance to occupation is not relevant, as "there is nothing in the fact of occupation that justifies the targeting and killing of civilians."

Secretary-General Kofi Annan has fully embraced the High-level Panel's definition of terrorism, a proposal he described as "having clear moral force." He urged that a comprehensive convention against terrorism utilizing that definition be adopted by the 60th General Assembly.[4]

The terms of a comprehensive convention which would include a definition of terrorism are likely be a central legal topic at the 60th Assembly session, with extensive discussion possible at the plenary level and within the Sixth Committee and working group. Many countries of the Organization of the Islamic Conference may continue to oppose defining terrorism to bar terrorist acts committed in the course of resistance to occupation, while some western states may aim to extend the prohibition against harm to noncombatants to police and off-duty military personnel. At the same time, several human rights nongovernmental organizations (NGOs) will likely argue that governmental conduct should not be excluded from the definition as suggested by SG Annan and the panel,[5] while others would like the definition of terrorism to specifically exclude acts of military personnel in their official capacity.

Cloning

A proposed international convention against the reproductive cloning of human beings was placed on the Assembly's 56th session agenda in 2001. Initiated by France and Germany, it sought to prohibit the reproductive cloning of human beings but would allow medical research using therapeutic cloning (i.e., the cloning of stem cells found within human embryos for scientific and medical research toward finding cures for diseases and treatment for defective tissues) to continue. An *ad hoc* committee was created to draft a convention.[6] Since then, annual discussions have revealed near universal support for a ban on the cloning of human embryos, but have demonstrated sharp division over whether therapeutic cloning is ethical or should remain lawful. Countries including Costa Rica, the Philippines and the United States, together with the Holy See, have fought for a complete ban, while Belgium, China, Singapore, France and the United Kingdom oppose an international ban on therapeutic cloning and would prefer to leave its regulation to individual states. At its November 19, 2004 meeting, the Sixth Committee gave up attempting to achieve an international convention and instead adopted a proposal by Italy to establish a working group aimed at producing a declaration on the issue.[7]

That working group was unable to achieve consensus on the terms of a declaration, and on February 18, 2005, passed the issue unresolved to the Sixth Committee. A draft resolution by Costa Rica calling on states to "prohibit all forms of human cloning inasmuch as they are incompatible with human dignity and the protection of human life,"[8] was taken up first after a procedural vote. Three amendments offered by Belgium that would allow therapeutic cloning as long as it was not "incompatible with human dignity" were then rejected in close votes. (One Belgian proposal failed by the cliffhanger vote of 55 to 52 with 42 abstentions.) The Sixth Committee then recommended a draft declaration intended to call for a complete ban on cloning, whether reproductive or therapeutic, to the General Assembly by a vote of 71 to 35 with 43 abstentions.[9] In March 2005, an Assembly plenary session adopted the *United Nations Declaration on Human Cloning*[10] by a vote of 84 to 34, with 37 abstentions.[11] The declaration has no binding legal effect, but does express the moral and political views of a plurality of states, thereby setting a norm that, ironically, remains controversial.

The declaration does not impede cloning by any nation that wishes to pursue or allow it. In fact, just two months after the declaration was adopted, scientists in South Korea, which had voted against the declaration, announced a major breakthrough in producing human embryos through cloning and then extracting stem cells that are exact genetic matches of individuals, and thus, less likely to be rejected by a patient's immune system.[12]

Strengthening the Organization

In 2004, the Assembly asked the Special Committee on the Charter of the United Nations and on the Strengthening of the Role of the Organization to consider implementation of the provisions of the *Charter* related to assistance to "third" states affected by the application of sanctions (i.e., countries that were not the intended target of sanctions). Delegations within the special committee variously reaffirmed the usefulness of sanctions as a tool in the maintenance of international peace and security, expressed concern regarding the implication of sanctions for third states and the civilian population of targeted states, welcomed the recourse to targeted sanctions by the Security Council to minimize their negative effects and called for the Security Council to undertake an assessment of the humanitarian implications of sanctions prior to their imposition. They also asked for assistance to third states and civilian populations affected by sanctions, possibly through establishment of a trust fund.[13]

The 2005 session of the special committee is expected to continue its discussion of sanctions, but also to consider all proposals for strengthening the role of the UN in the maintenance of international peace and security.[14] It will also consider the proposals regarding the Trusteeship Council in the Secretary-General's 1995 report *Renewing the United Nations: A Program for Reform*. The major proposals regarding changes to the Security Council contained in the High-level Panel report and in *In Larger Freedom*[15] will go to the high-level General Assembly plenary session on UN reform, but the drafting of proposed *Charter* provisions may well be assigned to this long-established special committee, before going back to the full Assembly.

Immunity

The *Convention on Jurisdictional Immunities of States and Their Property* was adopted by the General Assembly in 2004,[16] completing a process begun in 1991 when the ILC completed draft articles defining the scope of immunity of a state and its property from the jurisdiction of the courts of another state. The convention "reflects an emerging global consensus...that states and state enterprises can no longer claim absolute immunity from the proper jurisdiction of foreign courts and agencies, especially for their commercial activities."[17] While it reaffirms the immunity of states and their property from the jurisdiction of the courts of another state, unless a state has expressly consented to jurisdiction or participated on the merits in a court proceeding in a court of the other state, it provides significant exceptions as to certain commercial transactions, employment contracts, personal injury or property damage and other exceptions defined in the convention.

Some states have domestic legislation in this area, but most do not. Sixth Committee discussion in 2004 and 2005 expressed hope that the convention would lead to a harmonization of the practice of states as to jurisdictional immunities, particularly for those states that rely on customary international law to shape their practice. The convention constituted a compromise text which reflected a balance between the interests of developing and developed states designed to achieve consensus. The Assembly resolution adopting the convention reaffirmed the understanding that it does not cover criminal proceedings.[18]

Nationality and State Succession

The nationality of natural persons in relation to the succession of states is another matter that has long been on the General Assembly's agenda. The ILC completed draft articles on the subject in 1999 and governments have been invited to submit comments.[19] The Assembly's aim is to prevent persons from losing their nationality and becoming "stateless" when their former nation is succeeded by another. As there has been division between nations over whether or not the draft articles should be made into a convention or a declaration, the topic was referred to the 63rd session (2008) pending further comments by governments. In the meantime, the Assembly has recommended that states consider the draft articles in the context of their own nationality issues.[20]

Safety of Personnel

The scope of legal protection under the *Convention on the Safety of United Nations and Associated Personnel* has been on the agenda since 2001, when the General Assembly established an *ad hoc* committee to consider recommendations made by the Secretary-General to strengthen and enhance the protective legal regime for UN staff and associated personnel.[21] The 1994 convention protects UN peacekeepers including their associated personnel (e.g., NGO workers on contract with the UN), but does not generally cover personnel in other UN operations, including humanitarian aid workers and election inspectors. Negotiations over a protocol to the convention that would extend its coverage to such personnel have not yet reached a consensus. Potential host countries fear that the obligation to "take all appropriate measures to ensure the safety and security" of such workers, and to immunize them from interrogation and custody for even ordinary crimes, might be burdensome and, in some situations, unreasonable. This item will remain under active consideration at the 60th General Assembly.

Host Country Relations

The 2004 report of the Committee on Relations with the Host Country raised important legal questions under the *Convention on the Privileges and Immunities of the United Nations*, and the Headquarters Agreement between the UN and the United States. The committee discussed the policies and programs of the US and of New York City, as host to the UN's headquarters, as they affect the normal functioning of the UN missions and efforts to continue to ensure the security of those missions and the safety of their personnel. Complaints by some member states regarding the implementation of the New York City Parking Program for Diplomatic Vehicles adopted in 2002[22] were assessed at length by the committee, as the UN Legal Counsel had advised that the program was consistent with international law so long as it was properly implemented.[23] Delegations also referred to instances of travel restrictions, delays in the issuance of entry visas and custom delays, and urged the US to resolve existing problems in accordance with the Headquarters Agreement.[24]

Wrongful Acts

The ILC also completed work on draft articles regarding responsibility of states for internationally wrongful acts in 2001 and recommended that the General Assembly call for an international conference to work toward adoption of a convention. The proposed articles have broad application in international law, establishing remedies (e.g., countermeasures, restitution, compensation) that can be applied to states that commit a "breach of an international obligation," and more substantial remedies for states that commit "the most serious breaches of obligations under norms of preemptory general international law."[25] Sixth Committee discussion noted recent examples of international courts and tribunals, citing certain provisions of the draft articles as the authoritative statement of the law in this area, but some speakers objected to various provisions of them. Debate over transforming the articles into a declaration versus a convention again arose, forcing the topic to be handed over to the 63rd session. It is hoped that by then, all governments will have submitted comments and the Secretariat will have submitted a compilation of decisions by international courts and tribunals referring to the draft articles.[26]

The International Law Commission

The most recent International Law Commission report summarizes the work of its 56th session held in 2004. The General Assembly has called for member states to provide the ILC with comments on the draft articles regarding diplomatic protection and the draft principles on allocation of loss in the case of trans-boundary harm arising out of hazardous activities.[27] The former gives rules as to when states may exercise such protection and to whom, while the latter covers both damage to specific persons and property, and impairment of the environment.

The 2004 ILC session also continued work on creating guidelines for reservations, interpretative declarations and other unilateral statements by states party to treaties. Progress on the responsibility of international organizations, the unilateral acts of states, shared natural resources and the fragmentation of international law (i.e., difficulties arising from the diversification and expansion of international law), remain at an earlier stage of discussion.[28]

UNCITRAL

In considering the report of the UN Commission on International Trade Law on its 37th session held in June 2004,[29] the Sixth Committee noted the body's most significant achievement of the year: adoption of the Legislative Guide on Insolvency Law. The guide is intended to aid in the development and adoption of effective national insolvency regimes (e.g., compromises, liquidation).

The UNCITRAL Model Arbitration Law, designed to assist states in reforming and modernizing their laws on commercial arbitration procedures, was adopted by the commission in 1985, and has been enacted into law by many countries. UNCITRAL is actively considering a new Article 17 regarding the power of an arbitral tribunal to grant interim measures of protection, and the duty of courts to recognize and enforce such interim measures.[30] UNCITRAL also has working groups underway considering issues of law regarding procurement, transportation, electronic commerce and secured transactions.

Geneva Conventions

The Sixth Committee spent some time in 2004 and 2005 discussing the status of the 1977 *Additional Protocols* to the *Geneva Conventions of 1949* and the protection of victims of armed conflicts. Protocol I strengthened the protection for victims of international conflicts, and Protocol II did the same for victims of non-international conflicts. Based on its report, the General Assembly called upon member states that have not yet done so to ratify the two *Additional Protocols* and urged further measures to develop international humanitarian law with regard to protecting victims of armed conflict.[31] The agenda item was then put off until the 61st Assembly (2006).

The Push for Signatures and Ratifications

Each fall, the Treaty Section of the UN Office of Legal Affairs presents a special annual "treaty event" to facilitate the signature and ratification of states to important treaties that have yet to be ratified by a number of member states. The September 2005 event highlights 32 multilateral treaties that are open for ratification, approval, accession or *still open for signature.

HUMAN RIGHTS

1. International Covenant on Economic, Social and Cultural Rights (December 1966)*
2. International Covenant on Civil and Political Rights (December 1966)*
3. Optional Protocol to the International Covenant on Civil and Political Rights (December 1966)*
4. Convention on the Prevention and Punishment of the Crime of Genocide (December 1948)
5. Convention against Torture and Other Cruel, Inhuman or Degrading Treatment or Punishment (December 1984)*
6. Optional Protocol to the Convention against Torture and Other Cruel, Inhuman or Degrading Treatment or Punishment (December 2002)*
7. International Convention on the Protection of the Rights of All Migrant Workers and Members of their Families (December 1990)*
8. Optional Protocol to the Convention on the Rights of the Child on the involvement of children in armed conflict (May 2000)*
9. Optional Protocol to the Convention on the Rights of the Child on the sale of children, child prostitution and child pornography (May 2000)*

REFUGEES

10. Convention Relating to the Status of Refugees (July 1951)
11. Protocol Relating to the Status of Refugees (January 1967)

PENAL MATTERS

12. Rome Statute of the International Criminal Court (July 1998)
13. Agreement on the Privileges and Immunities of the International Criminal Court (September 2002)
14. Convention on the Safety of United Nations and Associated Personnel (December 1994)

TERRORISM

15. International Convention for the Suppression of Terrorist Bombings (December 1997)
16. International Convention for the Suppression of the Financing of Terrorism (December 1999)
17. International Convention for the Suppression of Acts of Nuclear Terrorism (April 2005)

ORGANIZED CRIME AND CORRUPTION

18. United Nations Convention against Transnational Organized Crime (November 2000)
19. Protocol to Prevent, Suppress and Punish Trafficking in Persons, Especially Women and Children, supplementing the United Nations Convention against Transnational Organized Crime (November 2000)
20. Protocol against the Smuggling of Migrants by Land, Sea and Air, supplement-

ing the United Nations Convention against Transnational Organized Crime (November 2000)

21. Protocol against the Illicit Manufacturing of and Trafficking in Firearms, Their Parts and Components and Ammunition, supplementing the United Nations Convention against Transnational Organized Crime (May 2001)

22. United Nations Convention against Corruption (October 2003)*

ENVIRONMENT

23. Kyoto Protocol to the United Nations Framework Convention on Climate Change (December 1997)

24. Rotterdam Convention on the Prior Informed Consent Procedure for Certain Hazardous Chemicals and Pesticides in International Trade (September 1998)

25. Stockholm Convention on Persistent Organic Pollutants (May 2001)

26. Cartagena Protocol on Biosafety to the Convention on Biological Diversity (January 2000)

LAW OF THE SEA

27. United Nations Convention on the Law of the Sea (December 1982); Agreement relating to the implementation of Part XI of the United Nations Convention on the Law of the Sea of December 10 1982 (July 1994)

28. Agreement for the Implementation of the Provisions of the United Nations Convention on the Law of the Sea of December 10 1982 relating to the Conservation and Management of Straddling Fish Stocks and Highly Migratory Fish Stocks (August 1995)

DISARMAMENT

29. Comprehensive Nuclear-Test-Ban Treaty (September 1996)*

30. Convention on the Prohibition of the Use, Stockpiling, Production and Transfer of Anti-Personnel Mines and on their Destruction (September 1997)

HEALTH

31. WHO Framework Convention on Tobacco Control (May 2003)

LAW OF TREATIES

32. Vienna Convention on the Law of Treaties (May 1969)

Source: Treaty Section, UN Office of Legal Affairs.

The Security Council and Global Governance

As discussed above, the General Assembly is not a legislature, but develops international law through a process of building consensus around proposed treaties. Even after those treaties are adopted by the Assembly, UN member states are only bound by their provisions when they voluntarily sign and ratify the treaties. There has always existed the possibility, however, for the Security Council to create international law that is binding on member states, and in response to the September 11, 2001 terrorist attacks, this has now occurred.

Under the *UN Charter*, once the Security Council determines "the existence of any threat to the peace, breach of the peace or act of aggression," it has, in general, the power to order non-military measures, or if these are inadequate, the use of armed force, "to maintain or restore international peace and security."[32] By far the most commonly applied non-military measures mandated by the Council are sanctions, described by Article 41 as "complete or partial interruption of economic relations and of rail, sea, air, postal, telegraphic, radio and other means of communications." The UN body is not limited to sanctions however; it may broadly "decide what measures not involving the use of armed force are to be employed to give effect to its decision, and it may call upon the Members of the United Nations to apply such measures."

The Security Council has taken extraordinary measures in response to the 2001 terrorist attacks. Resolution 1373, unanimously adopted on September 28, 2001, in broad terms, required all member states to "prevent and suppress the financing of terrorist acts," criminalize the collection of funds intended to be used by terrorists, and freeze the funds of terrorists and related persons and entities. Borrowing language from the *International Convention for the Suppression of Terrorist Financing* that was adopted by the General Assembly in December 1999 but had not yet gone into effect, Resolution 1373 essentially made those provisions, along with some new anti-terrorist-financing provisions, binding on all member states regardless of whether they had signed or ratified the convention. The resolution also required states to warn others of potential terrorist attacks, deny safe havens to terrorists, assist criminal prosecutions of terrorists by other states and institute border controls to prevent the movement of terrorists.[33] Furthermore, it established a Counter-Terrorism Committee (CTC) under the Security Council umbrella to monitor implementation of the resolution via reports from nations and other means. This resolution was a remarkable departure from the traditional lengthy processes of consensual law-making whose products, even once adopted by the General Assembly, only become binding on member states if they voluntarily ratify them.

Another resolution, 1540, unanimously adopted by the Council in 2004, requires all states to forebear from supporting any attempts by non-state actors to acquire, use or transfer nuclear, chemical or biological weapons. It also mandated that all states institute domestic controls and adopt national legislation to prevent the proliferation of such weapons, especially for terrorist purposes. Furthermore, it established a committee under the Security Council to monitor implementation of the resolution, and required all states to submit reports to this "1540 Committee."

The Council as a Legislative Body

The two resolutions noted above demonstrate the will of the Council to use its latent powers to respond aggressively to the threat posed by international terrorism. There are important questions remaining, however, about the Council's suitability to act as a supranational legislative body. For starters, it lacks the resources to do the extensive fact-finding which would normally precede the adoption of legislation. Second, its membership is not particularly representative of the world community and does not afford a right for states which are not members of the Council to negotiate, or to be consulted, as to the terms of proposed "legislation." While such a legislative role might seem most legitimate to deal with emergencies, the universal obligations thus imposed will not necessarily expire or be replaced by a negotiated multilateral treaty. Third, the Council is ill-equipped to implement or enforce its legislation; it has no administrative or managerial staff.[34] Overall, many view these circumstances as reasons why the Security Council should refrain from creating international law.

Neither the High-level Panel report nor the Secretary-General's report directly discusses this emerging legislative role of the Security Council or how it might be utilized, or limited, in the future. The potential for the Council to continue to act as a legislative body may be one subtext, however, behind the discussion of Council reform. Both reports call for bringing "into the decision-making process countries more representative of the broader membership, especially of the developing world," and increasing "the democratic and accountable nature of the body."[35]

The Use of Force

The *UN Charter* principles governing the use of military force may be stated quite simply, but their application, and whether member states may use force in other circumstances to preempt emerging threats or alleviate humanitarian crises, has greatly divided the world community. As referred to in Chapter 1, Article 2(4) of the *Charter* requires that "all States refrain in their international relations from the threat or use of force against the territorial integrity or political independence of any state." Article 51 preserves "the inherent right of individual or collective self-defense if an armed attack occurs against a Member of the United Nations, until the Security Council has taken measures necessary to maintain international peace and security." As noted, only where the Security Council has determined a threat, breach of peace or act of aggression where non-military means of redress are inadequate, may it authorize military action.

Effective regulation of the use of force by the Security Council to date is certainly not one of the UN's success stories. The UN body was paralyzed by the Cold War soon after the creation of the UN, rendered ineffective by the vetoes held by the US and the then-Soviet Union. A significant exception was the authorization for member states to use force under the UN flag to rebuff North Korea's aggression against South Korea,[36] made possible only by the absence of the Soviet delegate. Article 2(4) was substantially undermined by expansive claims that military action was taken for self-defense or in collective self-defense by "regional" alliances, including the claims of self-defense by the USSR in Hungary in 1956 and in Afghanistan in 1979, and those by the US in the Dominican Republic in 1965, in Vietnam in 1966, in Grenada in 1983, in Libya in 1986 and in Panama in 1989.[37]

In fact, there have been perhaps hundreds of incidents of member states using military force in disregard of the *Charter* rules, but the end of the Cold War brought the hope that the Security Council could begin to effectively govern the use of force to maintain or restore international peace and security. A major precedent was established when the war to repel the Iraqi invasion of Kuwait was authorized in advance by the Council in Resolution 678.

The second Iraq War severely tested Security Council governance of the use of force. While the public debate alluded to issues of preemptive self-defense against a "rogue state" developing weapons of mass destruction (WMD), international lawyers debated the narrower question of whether the alleged breach by Iraq of certain Council resolutions permitted the US-led coalition to use force. The US and the UK claimed Resolution 678's authorization to use force against Iraq was revived by Iraq's alleged "material breach" of cease-fire and Resolution 678's requirement that it disarm itself of all WMD. They also argued that Iraq failed to heed the final demand to disarm contained in Resolution 1441, and the threat of "serious consequences" in that resolution therefore authorized them to use military force.[38] Opponents argued that the terms of both Resolution 678 and 1441 required that any new use of force against Iraq first receive explicit Council authorization, which the US and the UK were unable to obtain.[39]

The *Charter* scheme governing the use of force is more directly challenged by the new US National Security Strategy released by the White House in September 2002. The strategy statement claims that the very large-scale dangers posed by terrorists with WMD justify the US acting militarily to eliminate and preempt such threats, without any requirement that an actual attack has occurred or is imminent.

As noted in Chapter 1, the High-level Panel clearly rejects the argument that such preemptive self-defense can be employed without prior Security Council authorization. The panel does allow for collective military action to deal proactively and preventively with dangerous combinations of terrorists, WMD and irresponsible states, but only with the authorization of the Council. It calls for improving the quality and objectivity of the Council's decision-making so states will feel more confident when submitting to its judgments. With somewhat less discussion, the Secretary-General's report concurs, retaining for the Security Council a monopoly over decisions to use force against threats that are latent but not imminent, and calling for the Council to more clearly enunciate, and then follow, the principles it will use in deciding whether to authorize the use of force.[40]

Humanitarian crises have also posed a challenge to the *Charter* rules governing the use of force. A number of major instances of intervention justified on humanitarian grounds were undertaken during the Cold War years without Security Council authorization, including Tanzania's intervention in Uganda in 1979 to topple Idi Amin, and France's intervention the same year in the Central African Republic to remove Emperor Bokassa. The Council became more active in reviewing proposed humanitarian interventions after the end of the Cold War, and authorized substantial military interventions in Somalia in 1992, in Bosnia and Herzegovina in 1993 and in Rwanda in 1994. These were widely-accepted applications of the Council's powers, but did perhaps enlarge the concept of threats to the peace under Chapter VII to encompass humanitarian crises.

The Responsibility to Protect, an influential report issued in 2001 by the International Commission on Intervention and State Sovereignty, organized by Canada, argued that "sovereign states have a responsibility to protect their own citizens from avoidable catastrophe—from mass murder and rape, and from starvation—but that when they are unable or unwilling to do so, that responsibility must be borne by the broader community of states."[41] The report observed however that the *UN Charter* does not contain any "humanitarian exception" to the Article 2(4) and Article 2(7) prohibitions, and prior Security Council approval must still be sought to legitimate the use of force. "The task is not finding alternatives to the Security Council as a source of authority, but to make the Security Council function far better than it has."[42]

The High-level Panel report embraced "the emerging norm that there is a collective international responsibility to protect, exercisable by the Security Council authorizing military intervention as a last resort, in the event of genocide and other large-scale killing, ethnic cleansing or serious violations of international humanitarian law which sovereign Governments have proved powerless or unwilling to prevent."[43] It also called for better policies to facilitate military intervention to protect endangered people, but did not go on to consider legitimating such interventions with prior Council approval. The Secretary-General agreed but noted there remain "sensitivities involved in this issue."[44] The instances where the use of force might arguably be justifiable as necessary and proportionate to meet a humanitarian crisis, but a P-5 veto blocks action, may be rare, but they are significant as they involve a conflict between the international community's "responsibility to protect" and the fundamental *Charter* restrictions on the use of force. The stage is thus set for continued discussion of the legal principles as to the use of force so central to the purpose of the UN.

Determining Disputes between States

Since the UN's founding, there has been much progress toward establishing accountability and meting out justice for crimes committed against humanity thanks to international criminal tribunals and, most recently, the International Criminal Court. There have been some 43 international judicial bodies, of which 16 are presently functioning, and at least 82 other international quasi-judicial entities and mechanisms. The private sector has also been active in establishing bodies for the arbitration of commercial disputes, notably the International Court of Arbitration established by the International Chamber of Commerce, and the London Court of International Arbitration. The following section reviews a number of judicial bodies and their recent application of international public law and international criminal law in transnational disputes.

World Court

As one of the central purposes of the UN, Article 2(3) of the *Charter* directs that "[a]ll members shall settle their international disputes by peaceful means." The International Court of Justice (ICJ, better known as the World Court) is the primary judicial body for carrying out this role. Sitting in The Hague, The Netherlands, the ICJ hears only disputes between states, but may also render advisory opinions at the request of the General Assembly or other UN organs.[45] All UN member states are *ipso facto* parties to the Statute of the ICJ, but they are only subject to ICJ jurisdiction insofar as they have agreed to submit a particular dispute to the Court, or recognized compulsory jurisdiction *vis a vis* other states which have also accepted compulsory jurisdiction. The 15 ICJ judges are elected for a term of nine years and may be re-elected.

The 60th General Assembly will, with the Security Council, elect five ICJ judges to begin terms in February 2006. Candidates, nominated initially by national groups chosen by their governments, must receive an absolute majority of votes in both the General Assembly and the Security Council to be elected; P-5 members have no veto power over these votes. In 2004 and early 2005, ICJ judges acted on the following cases.

The Wall in the Occupied Palestinian Territory

The most significant ICJ decision of the past year originated with a request by the General Assembly to the court for an advisory opinion as to "the legal consequences arising from the construction of the wall being built by Israel, the occupying Power, in the Occupied Palestinian Territory."[46] In its decision in *Legal Consequences of the Construction of a Wall in the Occupied Palestinian Territory, Advisory Opinion* 43 ILM 1009 (2004), the ICJ first rejected claims that it had no jurisdiction because the question presented was not properly referred by the Assembly, or that it was not a "legal question." It further rejected arguments that it should decline jurisdiction because Israel had not agreed to submit the dispute, because the question was only part of the larger Israel-Palestinian political dispute, because an ICJ opinion might impede the Middle East peace process, or because there was insufficient evidence presented as to the underlying factual questions.[47] By a vote of 14 to 1, the Court then held:

- The construction of the wall by Israel, as the occupying power in the occupied Palestinian territory, violated international law.
- Israel is under an obligation to cease construction of the wall, to dismantle the parts already built, and to repeal related statutes and legislation.
- Israel is under an obligation to make reparation for all damage caused by the construction of the wall.
- The General Assembly and Security Council should consider what further action is required, taking into account these opinions.[48]

The Court overruled a claim that Israel acted within its right of self-defense against terrorist attacks under Article 51 of the *Charter* and Security Council Resolutions 1368 and 1373, holding that terrorist attacks against Israel were not imputable to a foreign state.

There was a dissent issued by American Judge Thomas Buergenthal who said that "the Court did not have before it the requisite factual bases for its sweeping findings; it should therefore have declined to hear the case." Judge Buergenthal agreed with the applicability of both international humanitarian and international human rights law, but argued that the terrorist attacks from the occupied territory into Israel proper might invoke Israel's rights of self-defense, and the Court did not have sufficient facts to evaluate Israel's significant self-defense claims.[49]

By a vote of 13 to 2, with Dutch Judge Pieter Kooijmans joining Judge Buergenthal in dissent, the Court also directed:

> "All states are under an obligation not to recognize the illegal situation resulting from the construction of the wall and not to render aid or assistance in maintaining the situation created by such construction; all states party to the *Fourth Geneva Convention* relative to the Protection of Civilian Persons in Time of War of August 12, 1949, have in addition the obligation, while respecting the *United Nations Charter* and international law, to ensure compliance by Israel with international humanitarian law as embodied in that convention."

Subsequent to the 2005 decision, the General Assembly called on Israel to adhere to the ICJ decision by a vote of 150 to 6, with 10 abstentions.[50]

NATO's Kosovo Campaign

Another 2004 ICJ decision was notable for what the Court determined it could *not* decide. In eight separate *Case[s] concerning Legality of Use of Force*, Serbia and Montenegro brought claims against eight NATO states for the 1999 air strikes against Serbia launched in response to Serbia's gross violations of human rights in Kosovo. As noted, the Kosovo campaign raises troubling questions under the *UN Charter*, as no prior Security Council authority was obtained for the bombing of Serbia. Serbia further brought claims under international humanitarian law and international human rights law. The ICJ dismissed the case however, unanimously holding that it had no jurisdiction as the former Yugoslavia was not an official UN member, and therefore not a party to the ICJ Statute, at the time it initiated the cases in April 1999.

Liechtenstein v. Germany

In its 2005 decision in *Liechtenstein v. Germany*, a claim for property of Liechtenstein confiscated by Germany in Czechoslovakia in 1945, the ICJ also decided it had no jurisdiction, due to provisions of the *European Convention for the Peaceful Settlement of Disputes* to which Germany and Liechtenstein are parties. The ICJ found that the dispute relates to facts or situations prior to February18, 1980, the date when the European Convention entered into force between the parties, depriving the ICJ of jurisdiction.

Mexico v. United States of America

In *Avena and other Mexican Nationals (Mexico v. United States of America)* (2004), the ICJ held by a vote of 14 to 1 that the US had violated the rights under the *Vienna Convention on Consular Relations* and *Optional Protocols* of

1961 of 51 Mexican nationals charged with capital crimes, by not adequately informing them of their right to seek assistance from Mexican consular officials. This was the third consecutive ICJ ruling against the US for violating this convention. On February 28, 2005, President Bush and the US Attorney General directed state courts in the US to comply with the ICJ ruling to grant "review and reconsideration" to claims that the Mexican inmates' cases had been harmed by their not having been allowed to contact consular officials.

On March 9, 2005 however, the US withdrew from the *Optional Protocol* to the Vienna Convention under which it was subject to compulsory ICJ jurisdiction for claims it had violated the convention, although remaining party to the terms of the convention itself.[51]

It is important to note that while an increasing number of states have accepted compulsory ICJ jurisdiction under Article 36 of its statute,[52] less major powers now do so.

In other ICJ updates, two cases have been fully briefed and argued at the ICJ and are awaiting decision: *Armed Activities on the Territory of the Congo (Democratic Republic of Congo v. Uganda)* and *Frontier Dispute (Benin/Niger)*. Ten further cases remain pending before the court.

International Tribunal for the Law of the Sea

The International Tribunal for the Law of the Sea (ITLOS), established in 1996, hears disputes between states under the *UN Convention on the Law of the Sea*, which entered into force in 1994. ITLOS is composed of 21 independent members elected to nine-year terms, with one-third of the tribunal elected every three years by secret ballot by states party to the convention. In June 2005, an Assembly of the current 148 states parties to the convention was scheduled to elect seven ITLOS judges for terms beginning September 30, 2005.

The convention, negotiated over many years, established a comprehensive legal framework for regulation of the world's oceans and their resources, including fisheries, mineral resources, maritime research and environmental protection, and rights on the high-seas. Submission to dispute-resolution procedures is compulsory, either under the ICJ, an arbitral panel, or ITLOS.

The Juno Trader Cases

ITLOS rendered only one decision in the past year. In *The "Juno Trader" Case (Saint Vincent and the Grenadines v. Guinea-Bissau)*, the flag state of the reefer vessel *Juno Trader* sued Guinea-Bissau under the convention for detaining the ship and its crew for having allegedly infringed on Guinea-Bissau's exclusive fisheries zone. The tribunal unanimously ordered the prompt release of the ship upon the posting of a 300,000 Euro bond, finding that Guinea-Bissau had violated the provisions of the convention for the prompt release of an arrested vessel and its crew.[53]

One other case is pending before ITLOS but dormant: a joint application by Chile and the European Community to assess their mutual compliance with the convention regarding swordfish stocks within Chile's exclusive economic zone. ITLOS has abstained from further proceedings based on a provisional settlement between the parties; the special chamber established by the tribunal to hear the case will expire on January 1, 2006.[54]

Administering International Criminal Law

The Treaty of Versailles contemplated an international tribunal to try then-German Emperor Wilhelm II following World War I for crimes "against international morality and the sanctity of treaties," but the effort collapsed when The Netherlands, where Wilhelm II had taken refuge, refused to expedite him.[55] World War II Allies considered summary execution of major war criminals, but at the insistence of the US, in the London Agreement they instead established the International Military Tribunal (IMT), commonly known as the Nuremberg Tribunal. The IMT *Charter* contained a provision allowing the tribunal to try persons guilty of a new offense of "crimes against humanity," defined as "murder, extermination, enslavement, deportation and other inhuman acts committed against any civilian population, before or during the war, or persecutions on political, racial or religious grounds in execution of or in connection with any crimes within the jurisdiction of the tribunal, whether or not in violation of the domestic law of the country where perpetrated."

The first session of the UN General Assembly unanimously affirmed the "principles of international law" recognized in the *UN Charter* and the Judgments of the Nuremberg Tribunal, and directed its codification committee to begin formulation of an International Criminal Code containing those principles. The Assembly further defined a crime of genocide in 1946[56] and adopted the UN *Genocide Convention* in 1948.[57] Today, the special criminal tribunals for the former Yugoslavia and for Rwanda, and the ICC, have come about as part of the renewal of the UN's original purposes following the end of the Cold War.

International Criminal Tribunal for the former Yugoslavia

The International Criminal Tribunal for the former Yugoslavia (ICTY) is the first truly international criminal court to judge individuals for the most serious international crimes. Acting under Chapter VII, the Security Council established the ICTY in 1993 in The Hague to bring to justice those responsible for committing genocide, crimes against humanity and war crimes in the territory of the former Yugoslavia since 1991.[58] The Tribunal's jurisdiction is limited to crimes committed on the territory of the former Yugoslavia (including Bosnia and Herzegovina, Serbia and Montenegro, Croatia, Kosovo, Macedonia and Slovenia), and is concurrent but primary over other courts in the former Yugoslavia and around the world.[59] Jurisdiction runs from January 1, 1991 until a date to be determined by the Security Council.

As of May 13, 2005, 162 individuals had been indicted by the ICTY, of whom 128 had appeared in proceedings. Of these, 55 received judgment (37 with final sentence, and 13 remaining in the appeal stage), five were acquitted (three at trial, and two on appeal), five had their charges withdrawn and five died before trial. Nine defendants are currently on trial, including former Yugoslav President Slobodan Milosevic, whose trial commenced in February 2002, with the prosecution closing its case on February 2, 2004, and the defense case opening on August 31, 2004. Fifty-three defendants remain in a pre-trial stage.

While the ICTY long suffered from a difficulty in securing the arrest of indictees, the capture or surrender of over 20 in the past year has produced a substantial backlog of cases awaiting trial. Sixty accused are currently in detention and 18 have been provisionally released while awaiting trial. Two important recent arrests were those of Momcilo Perisic, the Yugoslav Army chief of staff during the wars in Croatia and Bosnia, and Kosovo Prime Minister Ramush Haradinaj, indicted for his wartime role as commander of the Kosovo Liberation Army.[60] Radovan Karadzic and Ratko Mladic, two important Bosnian Serb wartime leaders indicted for genocide, are still fugitives.

The most important long-term contribution of the ICTY may be to substantially develop the body of international criminal law through its indictments, judgments and appeal decisions. Significant judgments have elaborated upon the application of the *Geneva Conventions*, for example, and have defined sexual violence (especially rape) as a war crime and a crime against humanity; identified a non-derogable general prohibition of torture in international law; defined the elements of the crimes of genocide, enslavement and persecution; applied international humanitarian law to internal armed conflicts as well as international conflicts; clarified the nature of individual criminal responsibility; and shaped procedural law issues.

The Security Council enunciated a "Completion Strategy" for the ICTY and the parallel Rwanda Tribunal (*discussed below*) that called for completing investigations by the end of 2004, all initial trials by the end of 2008, and all work (including appeals) by the end of 2010.[61] These are "target dates" and not yet binding on the tribunals. The looming target dates, and eventual final deadlines, will require the ICTY to determine which cases to try, and which to send back for trial in national courts. Concerns have been expressed about the effect of this process on due process rights and prosecutorial independence, as well as the quality of the national courts that may try the transferred cases.[62] In the first instance of referring a case back to a national court for trial, on May 17, 2005, the ICTY referred the case of Radovan Stankovic, a Bosnian Serb charged with crimes against humanity and war crimes involving enslavement and rape, to the War Crimes Chamber of the State Court of Bosnia and Herzegovina.[63]

International Criminal Tribunal for Rwanda

The International Criminal Tribunal for Rwanda (ICTR), located in

Arusha, Tanzania, prosecutes individuals charged with genocide, crimes against humanity and serious violations of international humanitarian law committed in Rwanda during the year 1994. Acting under Chapter VII, the Security Council established the ICTR in 1994 with a very similar statute to that of the ICTY.

The ICTR's jurisdiction extends to individuals charged with crimes and violations specifically common to Article 3 of the *Geneva Conventions* and of *Additional Protocol II*. It is limited to crimes committed in the territory of Rwanda, by nationals of any state, between January 1, 1994 and December 31, 1994, except that Rwandan nationals may be prosecuted for crimes committed in the territory of neighboring states. The ICTR has concurrent but primary jurisdiction over other courts. Once an accused individual has been tried by the tribunal, that person cannot be tried again on the same charges by national courts, but if tried first in national courts, they may in some circumstances be re-tried by the ICTR.

Like the ICTY, the ICTR has made a lasting contribution to the development of international criminal law. Especially notable was the "Media Case," in which three defendants were convicted of using magazine and radio media to incite and coordinate Hutu violence against the Tutsis. These cases were affirmed on appeal, although motions for reconsideration are still pending.[64] The *Akayesu* case, decided by the ICTR in 1998, was the first in which an international tribunal was called upon to interpret the definition of genocide as defined in the *Convention for the Prevention and Punishment of the Crime of Genocide* (1948).[65] The guilty plea and subsequent conviction of Jean Kambanda, former Prime Minister of Rwanda, represented the first time that an accused person acknowledged his guilt for the crime of genocide before an international criminal tribunal, and the first conviction of a head of government for the crime of genocide. Although Kambanda later challenged his guilty plea and conviction on appeal, both were affirmed.[66]

Like the ICTY, the ICTR once lagged seriously behind its arrests. By October 2002, fewer than 70 suspects had been arrested and only 11 trials had been completed. The ICTR had particular problems securing cooperation from states as to the arrest of suspects, including from Rwanda due to concern there that the tribunal lacked authority to render death sentences over the possibile current government figures who might be investigated. There were also significant allegations of corruption involving ICTR staff and defense lawyers.[67]

The tribunal has since increased its efficiency. As of July 2004, 17 judgments involving 23 accused had been rendered, of whom 20 were convicted and three were acquitted.[68] There are now 26 cases in progress, 16 awaiting trial and nine accused still at large. There is concern, however, that the prosecutor has not completed many investigations of alleged crimes by Rwandan Patriotic Front soldiers, so those individuals may not be prosecuted at all.[69]

There is particular concern as to the application of the Security Council's "Completion Strategy" (*discussed above*). A UN Board of Auditors concluded that it does not seem possible for the ICTR to complete its work by 2010.[70] Transfer of ICTR cases to the Rwandan courts is problematic, as they may be unable to handle the load. Over 120,000 people are in custody awaiting trial in Rwanda, and by some estimates, it could take well over 100 years to process them all. The decision as to the final deadlines to be imposed on the work of the ICTR is in the hands of the Security Council.

Special Court for Sierra Leone

The Special Court for Sierra Leone (SCSL) differs from the ICTY and ICTR, as it was not mandated by the Security Council under Chapter VII, but was established by a treaty negotiated between the UN and the government of Sierra Leone in 2002. Based in Freetown, the Court hears charges against those most responsible for mass killings, mutilations, sex crimes and other grave human rights violations carried out in Sierra Leone during the conflict over control of the country's diamond fields since 1996 (although the conflict actually began in 1991).

The SCSL has jurisdiction to prosecute crimes against humanity, in particular, war crimes applicable in non-international armed conflict in violation of Article 3 common to *Geneva Conventions* and of *Additional Protocol II*, and other grave violations of international humanitarian law relating to civilians, civilian objects and child soldiers. The statute also allows prosecution of criminal offences under Sierra Leonean law, including particular sexual offences against girls and the wanton destruction of property, but does not automatically override domestic jurisdiction.

At the time of writing, according to the court, the SCLC had indicted 13 persons associated with all three of the country's former warring factions for charges including murder, rape, extermination, acts of terror, enslavement, looting and burning, sexual slavery, conscription of children into an armed force, and attacks on UN peacekeepers and humanitarian workers. The trial of three other Revolutionary United Front (RUF) leaders began on July 5, 2004; the trial of three Civil Defence Force leaders began on June 3, 2004; and the trial of the three Armed Forces Revolutionary Council accused is scheduled to begin before the end of 2005.

The SCSL's most high-profile target, former Liberian President Charles Taylor, is a fugitive in Nigeria, which has granted him asylum and so far refused to extradite him to stand trial. He is accused of supporting, training and arming RUF rebels and perpetuating the civil war to gain access to and smuggle out Sierra Leone's diamonds, and supporting the RUF's campaign against Sierra Leone civilians.[71] The whereabouts and fate of the last accused, Johnny Paul Koroma (former military head of state), are unknown.

It is important to note that the court does not recognize the blanket amnesty given to all parties by the 1999 Lomé Peace Accords, as Security Council Resolution 1315 determined that immunities cannot bar prosecution for international crimes. The court has since determined that the amnesties also should not apply to domestic crimes.

Khmer Rouge Tribunal

Approximately two million people died by execution or from starvation between 1975 and 1979 in Cambodia under the Khmer Rouge government led by Pol Pot, but the tribunal established by treaty between the UN and Cambodia is only now nearing operation. After the UN withdrew from negotiations in February 2002, General Assembly Resolution 57/225 of December 2002 prompted its renewal, and the agreement between the UN and the Royal Government of Cambodia concerning the Prosecution under Cambodian Law of Crimes Committed during the Period of Democratic Kampuchea (UN-Cambodia Agreement) was signed in March 2003. The Cambodian government tried to back out of the deal at the last minute, but on October 4, 2004, the Cambodian Legislature ratified the agreement to create a Khmer Rouge Tribunal (KRT).

The KRT will be a mixed national-international court. A majority of the judges will be Cambodian, but decisions will require a super-majority so that at least one international judge will have to vote in favor of each decision. While Cambodian procedural law will apply, with additional due process guarantees negotiated by the UN, the substantive law is largely international. The KRT will have jurisdiction to prosecute senior Khmer Rouge leaders for: genocide, as defined in the UN *Convention on Genocide*; crimes against humanity, as defined in the *Rome Statute* of the International Criminal Court; war crimes, as defined by the *Geneva Conventions*; and homicide, torture and religious persecution, as defined by Cambodian law.

International Criminal Court

Jurisdiction and Management

The relatively quick establishment of the permanent International Criminal Court was a huge achievement for the UN's law-making processes and for the involvement of nongovernmental organizations in those processes. The court was suggested by the president of Trinidad and Tobago in a speech to the General Assembly in 1989, and referred to the International Law Commission for study by the Assembly in 1990. In 1994, the ILC presented a draft statute for the ICC. From 1996 to 1998, six sessions of a UN Preparatory Committee which included member states and NGO representatives, were held at UN headquarters in New York to discuss and refine the terms of draft statute and work toward a consensus. By July 1998, after five weeks of intense deliberations among 140 government and 200 NGO delegates who had gathered in Rome, Italy, the *Rome Statute* of the International Criminal Court was adopted by a vote of 120 to 7, with 21 abstentions.

Jurisdiction under the *Rome Statute* is "automatic": a state party to the treaty accepts the court's jurisdiction over all crimes within its scope. The ICC may only act where the state on whose territory the crimes were committed or the state of nationality of the accused have ratified the treaty or accepted the court's jurisdiction over the crime (except as to referrals by the

Security Council). The ICC is not a substitute for national systems, but may only act where national systems do not themselves investigate or prosecute, or where they are "unable" or "unwilling" to do so adequately, as defined in the statute.

There are three possible "triggers" for investigation by the ICC Prosecutor: (1) referral by states parties or countries accepting its jurisdiction; (2) information from victims, NGOs, or any other reliable source; and (3) referral by the Security Council such as that which occurred over Darfur, Sudan. Referral is of "situations," not individuals; it is for the prosecutor to decide which, if any, individuals should be prosecuted.

The ICC only has jurisdiction to prosecute the "most serious crimes of concern to the international community" such as genocide, but the *Rome Statute* does contain some notable elaborations on existing international law. Crimes against humanity must be committed pursuant to a widespread or systematic attack. There is a high threshold for crimes against humanity, both that there be the "multiple commission of acts," and that they be carried out "pursuant to a state or organizational policy." In fact, the full list of crimes that constitute war crimes under the statue is exhaustive, including 34 crimes committed in international conflicts and 26 in non-international conflicts.

Another major unique item about the *Rome Statute* is that it explicitly refuses to recognize the traditional immunity of heads of states. In addition, military and civilian leaders who knew that soldiers under their command were about to commit a crime but did not try to prevent it may be held responsible.

The *Rome Statute* entered into force on July 1, 2002, and the ICC today is located in The Hague. Presiding Judge Philippe Kirsch and UN Secretary-General Kofi Annan signed an agreement providing a framework for the relationship between the two institutions on October 4, 2004. The agreement, among other things, includes the exchange of representatives, the participation of the ICC in the UN General Assembly as an observer, administrative cooperation, the provision of conference services on a reimbursable basis, and the use of the UN "laissez-passer" as a valid travel document by some ICC officials. The agreement also defines the mechanisms of cooperation between the Security Council and the court concerning a referral by the Council of a situation in which crimes under the jurisdiction of the court appears to have been committed. One such referral took place over the past year, as discussed below, along with four other ongoing ICC investigations.

Democratic Republic of Congo

In 2003, various governments, NGOs and individuals submitted information to ICC Prosecutor Luis Moreno Ocampo regarding massive atrocities in the Democratic Republic of Congo (DRC), an ICC member, and the prosecutor began a preliminary evaluation. The conflict in the DRC is the deadliest documented conflict in African history. Nearly four million people have lost their lives since 1998, the majority of them women and children.

While the dossiers submitted by NGOs were still under preliminary evaluation, on April 19, 2004, DRC President Lawrence Kabila formally requested that the ICC investigate and prosecute those responsible. On June 23, 2004, the prosecutor announced the court's formal investigation into the alleged atrocities, indeed the first-ever formal investigation of any situation by the ICC. On March 15, 2005, the ICC's Pre-Trial Chamber held its first-ever status conference to review the progress of the investigation. The prosecutor objected to this hearing, arguing that there were none of the specific circumstances under which such a conference is contemplated by the rules of procedure, but was overruled by the Appellate Chamber. Further judicial action approved the prosecutor's request for forensic examinations. The DRC situation remains under active investigation, but no indictments have yet been made.

Uganda

In December 2003, Ugandan President Yoweri Museveni referred the 18-year-old conflict between The Lords' Resistance Army (LRA) and the Ugandan army to the ICC, the first formal referral by a government to the ICC. Both sides have been accused of human rights violations, with the LRA accused of abducting more than 30,000 children and forcing them to fight, carry out hard labor and serve as sex slaves to commanders. The ICC has jurisdiction over crimes committed on Ugandan territory after July 1, 2002.

On July 29, 2004, ICC Prosecutor Moreno Ocampo announced the launch of a full investigation into the ongoing human rights violations in Uganda. In April 2005, the prosecutor met for three days with leaders of the Acholi, Lango, Iteso and Madi communities to discuss his investigation, responding to local Ugandan concern that its investigation and indictment of key rebel leaders would undermine peace efforts.[72] In a subsequent joint statement, they "agreed to work together as part of a common effort to achieve justice and reconciliation" in Uganda.[73] The prosecutor further said he would consider suspending prosecutions against the LRA if the prosecutions were not "serving the interests of justice." However, he stressed that while prosecutions could be suspended if they were interfering with the peace process, they could not be closed. The Uganda situation remains under active investigation, with no indictments yet made.

Central African Republic

On January 7, 2005, the ICC announced that it had opened an investigation into the situation in the Central African Republic (CAR) where human rights concerns between October 2002 and March 2003 involved atrocities against civilians such as extrajudicial executions, rape and torture by both government and opposing forces. The case was referred to the ICC by the CAR government, which may have had a political aim of discrediting the opposition by asking the ICC to investigate. However, an ICC investigation can, in fact, extend to both sides in the conflict. The prosecutor has yet to decide whether to advance to a formal investigation as has been done in the Congo and Uganda. Another concern is that the CAR has not yet signed the ICC's Agreement on Privileges and Immunities, which expands upon the *Rome Statute* and safeguards ICC investigations.

Côte d'Ivoire

It is interesting to note here that the first three ICC investigations have all originated with formal referrals by governments of human rights situations on their own national territories, rather than initiated by the prosecutor as a result of information supplied by NGOs, or referred by the Security Council. There is a fourth possible investigation under consideration based upon a declaration by Côte d'Ivoire accepting ICC jurisdiction over crimes on its territory after September 19, 2002.[74] Côte d'Ivoire has signed but not ratified the *Rome Statute* so the prosecutor is sending a mission to the country to determine whether there is sufficient evidence to open a formal investigation into alleged war crimes that occurred during the civil war that erupted there in September 2002. While the government may have sought the ICC's help in bringing to justice rebel forces in that war, the prosecutor has pointed out he will consider the conduct of all individuals involved in the situation as required by the statute.

The Darfur Region of Sudan

Perhaps the biggest milestone for the ICC this past year has been the Security Council referral of the situation in Darfur, Sudan, to the court. This was the first referral of a case to the ICC by the Council. As pointed out in previous chapters, more than 2.2 million people have been affected by the civil war in Darfur, with half the region's villages destroyed, and more than one million people displaced since early 2003.[75] A UN Commission of Inquiry established by the Security Council reported on January 25, 2005, that Sudanese government and Janjaweed militia had committed war crimes and crimes against humanity, and recommended referring the evidence to the ICC for investigation and prosecution. A few months later, the Security Council had officially referred the case to the ICC, setting an important precedent for the court. But it was not without difficulty that the referral occurred—in fact, many criticize the length of time it took for the world to react to what many have called genocide.

The humanitarian crisis in the Darfur region provided a major test of will between the US and countries which support the ICC. After the Commission of Inquiry report came out, the US urged alternatives to the ICC, particularly a new hybrid tribunal such as the Special Court for Sierra Leone or an *ad hoc* tribunal such as the ICTR, to prosecute crimes committed in Darfur. Other states were determined that using the existing permanent court—the ICC—would be far more efficient than creating a new one. In the end, this along with the urgency of the humanitarian crisis in Darfur, helped to persuade the US not to block referral to the ICC.

There was one exception: nonparties to the ICC had to retain "exclusive jurisdiction" over their own nationals for crimes committed in the Sudan, rather than the concurrent, primary jurisdiction accorded under the "complimentarily" provisions of the *Rome Statute*. With 11 votes in favor and four abstentions (including the US), the Security Council adopted Resolution 1593 on March 31, 2005, officially referring the situation in Darfur since July 1, 2002, to the ICC Prosecutor. The prosecutor received a sealed list of 51 suspects, many of whom are at the top levels of the Sudanese government, from the UN Commission of Inquiry on April 5, 2005, and has begun his investigation.[76]

The determined opposition of the US to the ICC has been a major factor in the ICC's initial three years. The US actively participated in the treaty negotiations prior to and during the Rome conference, was influential on important provisions, including the definitions of crimes and coverage of internal as well as international conflicts, but was unable to secure a requirement that prosecutions be approved by vote of the Security Council (where the US has a veto). The US was one of only seven countries to vote against the statute in Rome, but the Clinton Administration later signed the treaty on December 31, 2000, the last possible day to do so without fully acceding to the treaty.

The Bush administration initially participated in preparatory committee sessions of the court, in which it sought complete exemption from ICC jurisdiction for the US and other nonparties to the treaty. In May 2002, however, as the treaty was about to enter in effect following the 60th ratification, the administration announced it would not cooperate in any way with the ICC and declared that the US never intended to ratify the treaty. The US then took several very aggressive steps to insulate itself from the possibility of ICC jurisdiction.

First, the US vetoed the extension of the Bosnian peacekeeping mission in the Security Council on June 30, 2002, until the other members relented to US demands and passed Resolution 1422 on July 12, 2002, which exempts personnel and officials from non-parties to the *Rome Statute* from ICC jurisdiction related to UN authorized missions. Second, the US has secured bilateral immunity agreements (so-called "Article 98" agreements) prohibiting the surrender of all US nationals and current and former employees of the US government and military (including non-nationals) to the ICC. As of May 3, 2005, 100 countries had signed such agreements, most under pressure of loss of all US military and financial aid. Third, the US campaign of opposition to the ICC was codified in the American Servicemembers' Protection Act (ASPA), signed into law on August 2, 2002. Subject to waivers at the discretion of the US President, ASPA prohibits US cooperation with the ICC and US military assistance to ICC parties, and pre-authorizes military action to free US military and certain other personnel detained by the ICC.

Despite this fervent opposition, at least 45 countries have refused to sign bilateral immunity agreements, countries continue to ratify and accede to the *Rome Statute* and the ICC has progressed in its initial investigations. Sponsors of General Assembly resolutions relevant to the ICC frequently include strong endorsements of the court. The US continually calls for votes on amendments to remove these endorsements. The ensuing debates are often contentious and the votes so far have always defeated the amendments by very large margins. At the 59th session, the Assembly adopted Resolution 59/43 by consensus, calling on all states to consider ratification or accession to the *Rome Statute*, but the US again rose to disassociate itself from the resolution.[77] It is not likely the determined US campaign against the ICC will end anytime soon, but the US abstention on the Darfur referral raises hope of a somewhat more pragmatic attitude in selected circumstances.

Looking Forward

The General Assembly this year will be called upon to address the *UN Charter* itself, if the composition of the Security Council is to be changed as recommended by the High-level Panel. Also spurred by reform proposals, vigorous debate may be expected in the General Assembly and Sixth Committee as to the proposed definition of terrorism.

Consideration of the panel's recommendations for improving the quality and objectivity of Security Council decision-making as to the use of force, whether for anticipatory self-defense or to address humanitarian crises, will fall to the Council itself. Council discussion of these issues in the abstract may well gloss over substantial differences. The real crunch would come were there to be a move to authorize sanctions or military force to address proliferation of WMD, perhaps in Iran or North Korea. If certain states were to use force or impose sanctions in the absence of Council authorization, it would once again plunge the UN and the collective security scheme of the *Charter* into crisis.

The coming year will also witness the international criminal tribunals working feverishly to resolve their caseloads and move toward completion of their work; more cases are likely to be referred back to national courts in Rwanda and states of the former Yugoslavia. The Special Court for Sierra Leone should be in the midst of trials of leaders of all three groups involved in the civil war in that country, while the Khmer Rouge Tribunal will just be getting underway in Cambodia. Of course, all eyes will be on the International Criminal Court as it investigates the five referrals now before it, all involving countries in Africa.

Commentary
The Legality of Anticipatory Self-Defense
Lawrence C. Moss

In the 1941 Atlantic Charter, Franklin Delano Roosevelt and Winston Churchill called for the "abandonment of the use of force" by nations, envisioning "a permanent system of general security." In 1945, the United States, then the world's sole nuclear power, led the drafting of the *UN Charter*, establishing legal rules prohibiting the use of force except in self-defense or when explicitly authorized by the Security Council. While the rules regarding the use of force were widely disregarded during the Cold War, it was again the victorious superpower that revived them—and the role of the Security Council in legitimizing the use of force, by seeking Council authorization to eject Iraq from Kuwait.

The failure to win clear Security Council approval for the launch of the second US-led Iraq war in 2003 has had serious consequences for the efforts of the countries that went to war, and for the UN. The reports by the High-level Panel on Threats, Challenges and Change and by the Secretary-General call for maintaining the current *Charter* rules, and expanding the Security Council to better represent today's powers and the broader UN membership. Most importantly, they call upon the Council to apply the *Charter* provisions on a consistent, objective, principled basis, so all states may have confidence in its determinations.

Looking ahead, will the preeminent military power again throw its weight behind the principle of rules-based collective security, as it did in 1945 and 1991? Will it set an example, and help set guidelines which will apply to other great powers that might one day equal the US in economic and even military power? Initial responses from the US praised the two reports but glossed over some differences, welcoming, for example, the assertion that the self-defense provisions of Article 51 of the *UN Charter* not be changed, but attempting to carve out an expanded "anticipatory right of self-defense," especially applied to "new threats posed by terrorism and weapons of mass destruction." Yet both the High-level Panel and Secretary-General's reports state that anticipatory self-defense rights extend only to imminent threats, and that preventive military action may be taken against threats that are not imminent only with the Council's authority.

Ambiguity as to these rules will not do. Indeed, the failure over Iraq was in part due to the lack of clarity in Resolution 1441, leaving the nations of the world room to argue as to whether the use of force had or had not been authorized. The Security Council should speak clearly in the future as to whether it has authorized force, and its members should reaffirm now that preventive military action to eliminate non-imminent threats may be taken only with Council authorization. Failure to do so leaves the door open to unrestrained "preventive" military actions by numerous countries against neighbors they fear might one day do them harm.

Endnotes

1. UN Document A/Res/174 (1947). / UN Document A/Res/2205 (1966).
2. UN Document A/Res/3034 (1972).
3. UN Document A/Res/59/290 (2005). / Estanislao Oziewicz, "UN Passes New Treaty on Nuclear Terrorism," *Toronto Globe and Mail*, April 14, 2005.
4. *In Larger Freedom: Towards Development, Security and Human Rights for All* (Report of Secretary-General Kofi Annan), March 21, 2005. Hereafter referred to is "ILF."
5. Statement, *Human Rights Watch*, May 18, 2005.
6. UN Document A/56/192 (2001).
7. UN Document A/59/516 (2004).
8. UN Document A/C.6/59/L.27/ADD.1.
9. UN Document A/L/3271 (2005).
10. UN Document A/Res/59/280 (2005).
11. UN Document A/59/PV.82 (2005).
12. Gina Kolata, "Koreans Report Ease in Cloning for Stem Cells," *New York Times*, May 20, 2005. / "Stem Cells: The dogs bark, but the caravan still moves on," *Economist*, May 21, 2005.
13. UN Document A/59/33 (2004).
14. UN Document A/Res/59/44 (2004).
15. UN Document A/59/2005 (2005).
16. UN Document A/59/38 (2004).
17. D. Stewart, "The UN Convention on Jurisdictional Immunities of States and their Property," *American Journal of International Law (AJIL)*, 2005.
18. UN Document A/Res/59/38 (2004).
19. UN Document A/Res/54/112 (1999). / UN Document A/Res/55/153 (2000).
20. UN Document A/59/504 (2004). / UN Document A/Res/59/34 (2004).
21. UN Documents A/Res/55/175 (2001), A/55/637 (2000), A/Res/56/89 (2002) and A/Res/57/28 (2003).
22. UN Document A/AC.154/355/annex (2002).
23. UN Document A/AC.154/358/annex (2002).
24. UN Document A/59/26 (2004). / UN Document A/59/511 (2004).
25. UN Document A/56/10 (2001).
26. UN Document A/59/505 (2004). / UN Document A/Res/59/35 (2004).
27. UN Document A/Res/59/41 (2004).
28. M. Matheson, "The Fifty-Sixth Session of the International Law Commission," *AJIL*, 2005.
29. UN Document A/59/17 (2004).
30. UN Document A/CN.9/54.
31. UN Document A/59/506 (2004). / UN Document A/Res/59/36 (2004).
32. *UN Charter*, Articles 25, 48-49.
33. E. Rosand, "Security Council Resolution 1373, the Counter-Terrorism Committee, the Fight Against Terrorism," *AJIL*, 2003.
34. *See* for example: S. Talmon, "The Security Council as World Legislature," *American Journal of International Law*, 2005.
35. ILF, para 169.
36. Security Council Resolutions 82, 83, and 84 (1950).
37. A. Cassese. International Law. (Oxford University Press, 2001). / T. Franck, "Who Killed Article 2(4)? Or Changing Norms Governing the Use of Force by States," *AJIL*, 1970.
38. W.H. Taft IV and T.F. Buchwald, "Preemption, Iraq and International Law," *AJIL*, 2003. / N. Rostow, "Determining the Lawfulness of the 2003 Campaign Against Iraq," *Israel Yearbook on Human Rights*, 2004.
39. T. Franck, "What Happens Now? The United Nations After Iraq," *AJIL*, 2003. / Letter, The Association of the Bar of the City of New York to President Bush (October 15, 2002).
40. ILF, paras 122-126.
41. *The Responsibility to Protect* (Report of the International Commission on Intervention and State Sovereignty, International Development Research Centre, Ottawa, 2001).
42. Ibid.
43. *A More Secure World: Our Shared Responsibility*, Report of the High-level Panel on Threats, Challenges and Change, December 2004, para 203.

44. ILF, para 135.
45. *UN Charter*, Article 96.
46. UN Document A/Res/ES-10/14 (2003).
47. Advisory Opinion, "Legal Consequences of the Construction of a Wall in the Occupied Palestinian Territory," *ICJ*, 2004.
48. Ibid.
49. Ibid.
50. UN Document A/Res/ES-10/15 (2004). / P. Reynolds, "Israel's Barrier and the World Court," *BBC*, February 23, 2004. / M. Pomerance, "The ICJ's Advisory Jurisdiction and the Crumbling Wall Between the Political and the Judicial," *AJIL*, 2005, among others.
51. A. Liptak, "US Says it Has Withdrawn from World Judicial Body," *New York Times*, March 10, 2005.
52. ICJ website.
53. Judgement, "The 'Juno Trader' Case (Saint Vincent and The Grenadines v. Guinea-Bissau), Application For Prompt Release," *ITLOS*, December 18, 2004.
54. Order, "Case Concerning the Conservation and Sustainable Exploitation of Swordfish Stocks in the South-Eastern Pacific Ocean (Chile/European Community), *ITLOS*, December 16, 2003.
55. A. Cassese, *International Law*, 266.
56. UN Document A/Res/96 (I) (1946).
57. UN Document A/Res/260 (III) (1948).
58. UN Document S/Res/827 (1993).
59. Statute of the International Criminal Tribunal for the former Yugoslavia, 1993.
60. "Gotcha: A rush of defendants go to The Hague, but the biggest fish still swim free," *Economist*, March 12, 2005. / M. Simons, "Court on Crimes in Former Yugoslavia Hits Its Stride," *New York Times*, May 15, 2005.
61. UN Document S/Res/1503 (2003).
62. D.A. Mundis, "The Judicial Effects of the 'Completion Strategies' on the Ad Hoc International Criminal Tribunals," *AJIL*, January, 2005. / L.D. Johnson, "Closing an International Tribunal While Maintaining International Human Rights Standards and Excluding Impunity," *AJIL*, January, 2005. / "Justice at Risk: War Crimes Trials in Croatia, Bosnia and Herzegovina, and Serbia and Montenegro," *Human Rights Watch*, October, 2004.
63. Decision on Referral Of Case Under Rule 11, "Prosecutor v. Radovan Stankovic, Bis, Case No. IT-96-23/2-PT," *ICTY*, May 17,2005.
64. Ferdinand Nahimana, Jean-Bosco Baraygwiza and Hassan Ngeze (Appellants) v. The Prosecutor (Respondent), Case No. ICTR-99-52-A.
65. The Prosecutor (Respondent) v. Jean-Paul Akayesu, Case No. ICTR 96 4-T.
66. Jean Kambanda v. The Prosecutor, Case No. ICTR 97-23-A.
67. ICTR website.
68. UN DOCUMENT A/59/183 (Ninth Annual Report of the ICTR, July 2004).
69. R. Dicker and J. Wechsler, "Letter to the Security Council," *Human Rights Watch*, June 24, 2004.
70. UN Document A/59/5/Add. 11 and 12 (2004).
71. "Africa's Most Wanted Man: Global law v. local warlord," *Economist*, May 12, 2005.
72. "Justice versus reconciliation: Hunting Uganda's child-killers," *Economist*, May 5, 2005.
73. ICC Press Release (April 16, 2005).
74. CC Press Release (February 15, 2005).
75. "Darfur Deadline: A New International Action Plan," *ICG Africa Report No. 83*, August 2004.
76. "Lengthening the Arm of Global Law," *Economist*, April 9, 2005.
77. UN Document A/59/PV.65 (2004).

Essays

The year 2005, the United Nation's 60th anniversary, has been called the "year of reform." In March 2005, Secretary-General Kofi Annan released a 62-page document titled In Larger Freedom: Towards Development, Security and Human Rights for All. It comprises SG Annan's package of proposals for improving and strengthening the world body. All 191 heads of state will convene in September 2005 for a special summit to discuss this package, in the context of the Millennium Declaration's five-year review, before the full General Assembly's 60th session begins.

The ideas presented in the report are drawn significantly but not exclusively from the reviews SG Annan commissioned on security (the High-level Panel report on Threats, Challenges and Change discussed in Chapter 1) and development (Jeffrey Sachs' Millennium Project covered in Chapter 3). The reviews were issued in late 2004 and early 2005, respectively. The report outlines recommendations in four areas: freedom from want, covering development; freedom from fear, covering peace and security; freedom to live in dignity, covering rule of law, human rights and democracy; and strengthening the United Nations, covering institutional reforms.

In the following pages, a group of prominent individuals—including ambassadors to the UN who will be directly involved in the fall 2005 summit—present their views on the package of proposals, and suggest some ideas of their own.

A More Vibrant General Assembly

Anders Lidén, *Permanent Representative of Sweden to the United Nations*

The United Nations turns 60 this year. It should be the year of reform. Globalization and rapid changes in the threats and challenges that the world community faces require a world organization that is legitimate and up to the task.

We—the member states—should be ready to agree on certain principles, such as the link between development, security and human rights; the rule of law; and collective responsibility for human security.

We also have to agree on how to make the UN more effective, legitimate and relevant. Institutional reform will be necessary, affecting the Security Council, the Economic and Social Council, the Secretariat and the General Assembly.

But why reform now? Did we not have the same debate 10 years ago when the UN turned 50? Some improvements have occurred since then, but on the whole, member states failed to look beyond limited national interests and thus prevented real change from happening.

This year, the chances should be better. Through his High-level Panel on Threats, Challenges and Change, Secretary-General Kofi Annan has made a commendable effort to introduce real change in the organization and to develop common ground among member states. He has given a push to the reform efforts and laid his own prestige on the line to see them through. There is also a sense of urgency because of the heavy criticism that the UN has faced lately for many of its shortcomings, when trying to cope with rising expectations and an expanded role. Even in Sweden, a longstanding supporter of the UN, many people have started to question the world organization.

Some have suggested that the UN be replaced by an organization for democracies only. This is indeed a bad idea. We need an organization that is truly global to provide a basis for legality and legitimacy in international affairs. It would be a disaster to go back to the past anarchy that was fertile ground for so many wars between states. Sweden believes in global multilateralism. For us, even the European Union, as important as it is, cannot replace the UN. To work only with those who share one's perspectives and ideas would be a recipe for narrow-mindedness and conflict.

Sweden's ambition is to help SG Annan in his efforts to make the UN the global peace organization for the future. We plan to be helpful and constructive in the negotiations to form a new consensus and to reform the organization. As Jan Eliasson, former UN Under-Secretary-General for Humanitarian Affairs and Swedish Ambassador to the United States, presides over the 60th session of the General Assembly, his role will be crucial in moving the negotiating processes forward. It will not be an easy task, as most countries still cling to their narrow national agendas. One example of the challenge of reform is the General Assembly, where a revitalization process has been going on for several years, but so far with only meager, mostly cosmetic results.

Most of my colleagues would like to see the Assembly become the vital organ it was intended to be, an organ for broad international understanding and agreement on current issues, not a forum for repetitive debates and obsolete agenda items. Today, the interesting thematic debates tend to take place in the Security Council even when their topics, such as legal questions, clearly belong in the Assembly. One reason is the prestige of the Security Council and the impression of an irrelevant General Assembly. There is rather a widespread suspicion that the permanent members of the Security Council wish to exclude others; that they wish to make decisions and lay down principles of international law based on their own national agendas and without any accountability.

It is not advisable to undermine the authority of the Security Council. The role of the General Assembly in relation to the Council, however, is an important subject for the future. It should be addressed, for instance, in the context of Security Council reform and the establishment of a peace-building commission, as proposed by the High-level Panel. But, without delay, the General Assembly should be the forum for major thematic and action-oriented debates on current issues, such as international terrorism, HIV/AIDS, poverty, environmental threats, the rule of law, the responsibility to protect, gender equality and international migration.

The working methods have to change to give time for the relevant debates. The role of the president of the Assembly has to be strengthened. A new culture of relevance should make it possible to delete obsolete agenda items and repetitive resolutions. The aim should be to introduce resolutions in the General Assembly with new operative and substantial elements.

Voting methods have to be improved. Last year, the election of 14 judges to the International Criminal Tribunal for the former Yugoslavia took two days and seven rounds of voting to accomplish, and required the full-time presence of the ambassadors of the countries involved. The introduction of optical scanners to expedite the counting of votes has now been proposed.

Overlap and duplication of work could be minimized through an overhaul of the Committee structure in the Assembly. Time limitations for interventions could be more effectively enforced. A beautiful idea—perhaps too much to hope for—is the introduction of music which increases in volume the longer a speaker has exceeded his time. The practice of interactive debates and a more disciplined request for documents from the Secretariat would also help make the Assembly a more interesting and relevant place.

Our hope in Sweden is that we will have a successful year of reform. We hope to see a more vibrant and focused General Assembly already during its 60th anniversary session.

A Stronger Prescription for Security: Dialogue

Dr. M. Javad Zarif,
Permanent Representative of the Islamic Republic of Iran to the United Nations

Sixty years after its founding, the United Nations remains the central and irreplaceable international organization responsible for maintaining world peace and security. The international order has evolved considerably since the end of World War II and the turbulent era of East-West rivalry. We now need a corresponding evolution of the UN to address the needs and challenges of today's increasingly interdependent world.

To advance a refashioned UN, the aspirations and concerns of its member states and the demands of the global populace—the true peoples of the UN—should be effectively addressed in a comprehensive, unbiased and transparent manner. This way, an overwhelming majority can claim and feel ownership over the process.

The Secretary-General's *In Larger Freedom: Towards Development, Security and Human Rights for All* report is an important step in this regard, having diagnosed some of the diverse and interconnected threats afflicting the world community. However, by taking at face-value the predominantly publicized interpretations of the threats emanating from one dominant global perspective, the report has lost sight of a fundamental threat—namely, the propensity to resort to coercion and violence by state and non-state actors. It is not clear whether the prescriptions presented by the report are likely to enhance the capacity of the international community to address the very threats that have been identified.

The failure of diagnosis is nowhere more apparent than in the report's ambivalence toward the twin dangers of mutually-reinforcing phobias: growing animosity and conflict between cultures and civilizations; and the propensity to resort to violence by state and non-state actors. Ironically, while these were at the heart of the debate for UN reform after the invasion of Iraq, the report has misdiagnosed this dual threat by ignoring the clash of cultures on one hand and broadening the license to resort to force under Article 51 of the *UN Charter* on the other.

The increasing prospects of a clash of civilizations and cultures, spreading hatred and serving as a breeding ground for extremism and terrorism, have been widely recognized. Yet the report neglects this major and emerging security threat, overlooking the paradigm of "dialogue among civilizations," which has already been agreed upon by the UN General Assembly as the most efficient means to tackle the growing threat of clash.

At the same time, while there is unanimity that Article 51 should not be rewritten or reinterpreted, the report does just that, broadening the scope of self-defense to permit preemption. Such a reinterpretation fails the test of legality and prudence; providing a pseudo-legal excuse for unilateral preemptive action can only exacerbate the atmosphere of tension and crisis that has beleaguered the international community.

The report argues that "lawyers have long recognized that [Article 51] covers an imminent attack as well as one that has already happened." It is evident that from a purely legal perspective, nothing can be further from the letter or the spirit of the *Charter* or the opinion of independent jurists. The judgments of the International Court of Justice in various cases emphasize that measures in self-defense are legitimate only after an armed attack occurs. Article 51, in no way, covers imminent threats, and international law does not confer any legitimacy to the dangerous doctrine of preemption.

If this dangerous license is infused into UN principles, it will lead to greater resort to violence in the international arena by opening the way for major powers as well as regional bullies to wage wars against others under the pretext of self-defense. There already have been too many cases that resort to the justification of imminent threat as an excuse for aggression.

An attempt to broaden this license indicates a failure to recognize the root causes of the current international crisis—that is, as noted above, militarism and the propensity to resort to exclusion, coercion and violence. A more objective assessment of the present-day threats would have led the report to recognize that the lofty objectives of "larger freedom" would be better served through promotion of dialogue.

In the same vein, combating terrorism as a multifaceted global menace requires a global, inclusive and comprehensive approach. Terrorism can and must be destroyed first and foremost by reversing the logic of violence and coercion, and by changing the mentalities and perceptions that "might makes right."

These threats are further exacerbated by the continued existence of stockpiled weapons of mass destruction of the nuclear-weapons states, not to mention new types of nuclear weapons, as well as articulation of new doctrines for their use against non-nuclear threats. The report partially recognizes this threat but fails to prescribe any meaningful remedy. Instead, it suggests new discriminatory restrictions on access to peaceful nuclear technology. This neglects the fact that any greater reward for non-membership or further disruption of the balance between rights and obligations of Nonproliferation Treaty (NPT) members under the non-proliferation regime will lead to its disintegration rather than the intended strengthening.

The current international political climate coupled with the deficiencies in *In Larger Freedom* regarding security threats make it imperative to question the feasibility and practicality (let alone legality or rationality) of the dominant interventionist paradigm. Doing so would make the UN truly responsive to the repeatedly articulated demand of the overwhelming majority of people across the globe, who have time and again shown their desire for compassion, dialogue and understanding instead of war, intervention and imposition.

A Time to Give Change a Chance

Diego Arria, *former Permanent Representative of Venezuela to the United Nations and Visiting Scholar at Columbia University*

In the 1990s, many delegates and officials discouraged discussion of changes in the UN system by using the excuse that it would "open a Pandora box." Not even the modest initiative of creating a military contingent that would be available for deployment in emergencies by the Security Council commanded the will of major member states. Today, however, such closed minds and international public opinion should not obscure the great opportunity presented in Secretary-General Kofi Annan's report, *In Larger Freedom: Towards Development, Human Rights and Security for All*. With his proposed package of reforms, based on weaknesses in the UN body, Pandora's box is now open for all to see just how much major changes are required—and how urgently they are needed.

Sixty years after the *UN Charter* was signed in San Francisco, cracks and metal fatigue in the UN are plain to see and this is precisely the time when a credible and forceful organization is needed more than ever. It has taken an insider to articulate the most ambitious overhaul to reconfigure and energize the world body. SG Annan has thrown his *In Larger Freedom* report like a gauntlet to the General Assembly, challenging its members to find "the glue of common interest...to perfect the triangle of development, freedom (human rights) and peace."

In Larger Freedom in its full context should translate into greater accountability, mainly by the privileged permanent members of the Security Council whose anachronistic power structure no longer represents the international community at large. This is a well-established fact. What is not clear is to what extent the addition of nine more members, with or without veto, permanent or not, will make a real difference. In my view, the enlargement of the Security Council is the least urgent element in the reform proposals on the table. Accountability and transparency, extremely scarce commodities in the dealings of the most important body of international policy, will not be ensured by increasing its size. Already the proposal is diving regions instead of uniting them.

It should not be ignored that there are countries which are icons of civility, human rights defenders, large peacekeeping contributors and true and mature democracies which lack the size of bigger countries (e.g., Sweden, Canada and The Netherlands). Size, population and GNP alone might not be sufficient to fit the bill in the present times. Except for Brazil—the only non-Spanish speaking South American country—and Mexico, and to some extent Argentina, the enlargement of the Security Council to bring on a Latin American state as a permanent member is a non-issue in the region. As one diplomat put it, the proposal "was strangled in its crib," and the opposition and divisiveness that it has generated worldwide guarantees that the Council's composition will remain unaltered.

At the 1944 Dumbarton Oaks Conference, Latin America had a chance to join as permanent member of the UN Security Council when then US Secretary of State Edward Stettinius proposed the inclusion of Brazil as the sixth member. But both the United Kingdom and Soviet delegate objected. Sixty years later, Brazil on its own is strongly campaigning for a place in the Council.

Aside from structural expansion, there are several more plausible reforms proposed in the Secretary-General's report—three of which I will address here. First, the idea of a Democracy Fund is a very significant initiative that should include the support of civil society organizations. These groups are often are the only ones interested in preserving and defending democracy in their countries. The *UN Charter* states, "we the people," not "we the governments." Global interdependence demands and needs a more legitimate and credible organization that can be achieved only by increasingly opening up the organization to civil society—a group that already plays an extremely valuable role in support of UN activities.

Second is the means to achieve the Millennium Development Goals by 2015. If done, 500 million people would come out of extreme poverty, 300 million would no longer go hungry and the lives 30 million children below five years old would be saved. If the goals are not met, however, according to Oxfam International, 45 million more children would die, 247 million people in sub-Saharan Africa would live on less than $1 a day and 97 million children would not have access to schools. These statistics speak volumes of the gravity of the situation and demonstrate that the world is gambling with its future. SG Annan was quite clear: "We will not enjoy security without development, we will not enjoy development without security, and we will not enjoy either without respect for human rights."

Third, the human rights council proposed by SG Annan would end the travesty of the present Human Rights Commission, which includes as its members some of the more infamous violators of human rights. Such spectacle has severely damaged the UN's image, despite the fact that the majority of operational human rights work is carried out by the staff of the Office of the UN High Commissioner of Human Rights. The commission, rather, is a political body representing the world's governments where positions are fought by many as a means to defend their rights "not to respect human rights."

It is important to point out that none of these changes can occur unless the Secretary-General is given the authority and the resources to pursue a one-time staff buyout to refresh and reorganize the UN to meet current needs. The specter of the Cold War is still very visible in the composition of its personnel as well as in its management. The UN cannot in any way be hostage to personnel limitations and labor union practices should not have a role in an entity entrusted by 191 countries with the maintenance of peace and international stability

It is not clear whether the 60th General Assembly will pick up the Secretary-General's gauntlet in fall 2005. The world may very well hear, once again, about the risks of opening up Pandora's box. But unless the Assembly develops the conscience and conviction that prompted SG Annan to present his report, "we the people" will suffer the consequences.

A Multidimensional Call to Member States

Gunter Pleuger, *Permanent Representative of Germany to the United Nations*

When it comes to the United Nations, I am always ready to take up the battle. I believe in the institution, the only universal forum in which all nation states meet to tackle the problems of an interdependent world. I believe in the values and principles of the UN as enshrined in its *Charter*: respect for human rights and the dignity of the human person, the rule of law, democracy and freedom, and the promotion of social progress and better standards of life.

As we celebrate the 60th anniversary of the founding of the UN, I cherish the achievements of this noble institution. It has played a key role in decolonization, saved the lives of thousands of refugees and internally displaced persons, supplied vital relief in natural disasters and catastrophes, and deployed more than one million military and civilian police personal in more than 60 peacekeeping missions in an effort to stabilize regions and maintain peace and security around the globe.

Sixty years after its founding, the values and principles of the UN remain just as important. Yet, we must realize that the world has changed. As Secretary-General Kofi Annan noted in his speech before the General Assembly in September 2003, the UN "has come to a fork in the road," a moment "no less decisive than in 1945 itself." The world faces new threats and challenges to peace and security, and thus, the UN must adopt new means of efficiently and effectively addressing these.

SG Annan's comprehensive report, *In Larger Freedom: Towards Development, Security and Human Rights for All*, points out the main areas in which reform and progress are needed: development, security, and the rule of law, as well as institutional and administrative matters.

Development and security are inextricably linked. But while it is obvious that there cannot be security without development, we also need to focus on the importance of development itself. Poverty and disease threaten the lives of more people than do weapons of mass destruction or terrorism. For the majority of the people in the world, therefore, development remains their primary concern. The Millennium Development Goals as contained in the *Millennium Declaration* must be implemented and the means to achieve these goals, such as debt relief and innovative financial mechanisms, must be carefully considered.

Security today is increasingly threatened by terrorism, weapons of mass destruction, and failing states, which, taken together, form a truly deadly triangle. Therefore, as the Secretary-General has recommended, it is of utmost importance that the international treaty regime be strengthened by adhering to and implementing the relevant conventions. And while we must acknowledge that there might be a need to preempt deadly attacks by resorting to the use of force, it will be important to agree on criteria or principles to guide the Security Council in its decisions to authorize such actions. We have to prevent the erosion of the international system based on the *UN Charter* that is without precedent in the history of international relations.

In its recent decision on Sudan, the Security Council has, for the first time, referred a situation to the International Criminal Court. The establishment of the court is a milestone in the fight against impunity as a vital element of the rule of law. The UN can play an important role in the promotion of the rule of law worldwide–in setting standards, but also in incorporating the rule of law–"transitional justice"–into its peacekeeping efforts. Today, peacekeeping missions are multidimensional. In many cases, the task at hand is nothing less than nation-building in all its aspects. With respect to developing the ability to re-establish the rule of law in conflict and post-conflict societies, I welcome the Secretary-General's proposal to create a dedicated Rule of Law Assistance Unit within the Secretariat.

The UN has been sharply criticized because of the so-called "oil-for-food scandal." While it is true that certain administrative procedures must be made more transparent, the campaign against the UN and the Secretary-General is otherwise largely unfounded. I, for one, have not forgotten the fact that, with this program, the UN saved millions of Iraqi people from starvation. Ninety percent of the Iraqi "food basket" was provided by the Oil-for-Food Programme, and 60 percent of the Iraqi population relied entirely upon it. This was one of the most challenging endeavors the UN has ever undertaken, one to be regarded as a proud achievement.

If we want the UN to continue to perform its unique role in the world, we have to reform its constituent parts. These simply do not reflect today's realities. At present, there are 191 member states, 140 more than at the time the UN was founded. Therefore, we must adjust the constituent bodies accordingly, increasing their effectiveness and representativeness. This is especially vital for the Security Council, which bears primary responsibility for the maintenance of international peace and security. The Council should be expanded in both the permanent and non-permanent categories and include developing as well as developed countries.

I am optimistic that the UN member states will take up this task and make the adjustments needed to meet the challenges of today's world. I am enthusiastic about the likelihood that the September Summit will produce the agreement necessary to do so. There might be "cassandras" among politicians, diplomats and UN bureaucrats, but in the end, all will come to realize that there is no alternative to the UN.

A Commitment to Globalization

Bakï Ilkïn, *Permanent Representative of Turkey to the United Nations*

The international order as we knew it is undergoing historical transformation. Common values are becoming the norm as we increasingly witness democracy, respect for human rights, the rule of law, free market dynamics and good governance spread wings across the globe. The forces of globalization are bridging wide divides. It is a time replete, more than ever before, with the opportunity to build a better future and advance the cause of the common good of humanity.

Secretary-General Kofi Annan has set the stage with *In Larger Freedom: Towards Development, Security and Human Rights for All*. It is now up to us to translate his vision into reality and deliver on reform. In Turkey's view, structural reform, terrorism and sanctions are among the most important of the SG's proposals.

His agenda calls for structural reform of the UN's intergovernmental organs, including invigorating the General Assembly, enlarging the Security Council, strengthening the Economic and Social Council, transforming the Commission on Human Rights and putting the overall UN house in order. Restructuring the Security Council is one of the most important and certainly most controversial aspects of UN reform.

In this connection, Turkey fully concurs with the general view that the Security Council must be rendered more democratic and representative of the organization's membership. With the same token, enlargement of the Council has to strike an optimum balance between the increase in seats and efficiency in its dealings. Enlargement of the Council should not undermine the role and effectiveness of the General Assembly, nor should it erode the delicate balance between the two.

Enlargement should enable all member states to participate at greater frequency in the Council on a rotational basis, rather than the present system in which a country like Turkey, with the record and capacity to contribute to the maintenance of peace and security, has not been able to serve on the Council in 40 years.

Turkey also opines that an equitable system of rotation should be based on the existing regional groups. Setting certain criteria for eligibility to membership on the Security Council could serve useful. However, if the bar is set too high and the criteria become too restrictive or exclusive, the principles of fair representation and rotation would be eroded.

As such, the two options proposed for Security Council enlargement fall short of meeting the expectations of the general UN membership. At best, they provide a basis for further deliberation to find a model which comprises the elements of a compromise acceptable to all.

The criteria related to participation in peacekeeping operations need to be reconsidered. Contributions of member states to the maintenance of international peace and security, as referred to in Article 23 of the *Charter*, cannot and should not be limited to their contributions to UN-led peacekeeping operations. Peace and security are indivisible as are the contributions of individual countries. In the case of Turkey, its commitment to peacekeeping across the globe continues through its participation in and support for not only UN, but also through various NATO- and European Union-led missions, including commanding the NATO-led International Security Assistance Force in Afghanistan.

Moreover, Turkey is the organization's fifth largest contributor of civilian police to UN-led missions. A restrictive interpretation of the criteria proposed in the SG's report, however, would make Turkey appear to be making no substantive contribution to UN peacekeeping or to international peace and security in general. If regional organizations are not encouraged to make contributions to peacekeeping operations under the UN mandate, then the UN would be required to shoulder this responsibility alone.

The question of reform is not limited to the expansion of the Security Council. The UN cannot be renovated in a selective manner, modifying the composition of some organs, while leaving others intact. Reform must be across the board.

In addition to structural reform, measures to combat and prevent terrorism need to be addressed. Turkey, who for many years endured immense human casualties and material loss at the hands of terrorists, was among the first to join the global coalition mobilized against terrorism. Turkey welcomes the suggestions put forth by SG Annan for the prevention of terrorism, as well as for a comprehensive strategy to eradicate this universal threat. The recent adoption of the *International Convention on the Suppression of Acts of Nuclear Terrorism* is an important contribution to this effort.

Finally, sanctions warrant particular attention in the course of UN reform. Although the sanctions regime is far from perfect, it remains an indispensable means to give effect to the decisions of the Security Council. Enhancing and ensuring the effectiveness of the sanctions regime should be a priority. The sanctions regime should be provided with a sound and structured framework. Past experiences have clearly demonstrated that preventive and enforcement measures be "smart." The best way to achieve this goal is to start off with measures that are flexible and can be implemented in the most focused manner that the conditions permit. In this context, the option of "soft sanctions," such as imposing visa bans or freezing assets, should be given much attention.

At the same time, since the implementation of sanctions creates, in one way or other, negative impacts on third states, the object should be to minimize all possible fallouts from the outset. Turkey's own experience in the aftermath of the Gulf War is a case in point.

Overall, we need not look much further than from where we started for an effective and credible UN in a world of larger freedom. The challenge is to restructure and integrate the core functions of the UN without creating the differentiation that characterized the Cold War era. The objective should be to recapture the essence of the original spirit and aims stipulated in the *Charter*.

As a founding member of the organization and a proactive member of the global community, Turkey is fully on board to seize the opportunity and meet the challenges of reform.

A Chance for New Leadership in Changing World

Kishore Mahbubani, *former Permanent Representative of the Republic of Singapore to the United Nations. Mr. Mahbubani is currently dean of the Lee Kuan Yew School of Public Policy at the National University of Singapore.**

Mass demonstrations in China against Japan's bid for a permanent seat on the United Nations Security Council is only the latest indication of the difficulties of UN reform. UN Secretary-General Kofi Annan is right—the present UN structures reflect the geopolitical realities of 1945, not 2005. Virtually no one disagrees that Security Council reform is both necessary and inevitable. Yet, there is little agreement on what form the reform should take.

Asia has the biggest stake in this issue. The 21st century, in all likelihood, will be the Asian century. According to many studies, the four largest economies in 2025, in purchasing power parity terms, will be China, America, India and Japan. The Asian share of the global GNP will also rise.

Given Asia's growing influence and power, it is inevitable that all major global institutions, including the UN and its International Monetary Fund, World Bank and World Trade Organization, will have to adjust and adapt to these new realities. The challenge of deciding Asia's representation in a reformed Security Council illustrates this well. Both India and Japan have strong claims to permanent membership. Last year, Japanese Prime Minister Junichiro Koizumi said in his address to the 59th Session of the UN General Assembly that Japan's role has become increasingly vital to the maintenance of international peace and security, providing a solid basis for permanent membership in the Security Council.

Arguing in a similar vein, Indian Prime Minister Manmohan Singh said that making countries like India a permanent member would be the first step toward making the UN a truly representative body. India, for example, is endowed with outstanding human resources and is putting into place policies that will respond to emerging and critical tasks, said Mr. Singh.

Unfortunately, India's claim to permanent membership has caused discomfort in Pakistan, while Japan's claim has led to concern in China and South Korea. This lack of Asian consensus is troubling. But there is an even bigger challenge regarding Security Council reform. Out of the 6 billion people of the world, 1.2 billion are Muslims (most of them live in Asia) and it is no secret that many are disillusioned with global institutions, which they perceive to be dominated by the West. Many are politically quiescent now, but their eroding lack of trust in global institutions could eventually undermine their perceived legitimacy.

It is vital that these 1.2 billion Muslims become stakeholders in a stable and peaceful global order. Many believe that any list of new permanent members should include a Muslim majority state, but there is no agreement on which country should fill the seat.

*The views expressed in this essay are those of Mr. Mahbubani and not of the National University of Singapore.

Meanwhile, India has made it clear that it will accept nothing less than permanent membership with veto powers. Hence, the impression in Asia is that the High-level Panel was trying to tinker with UN reform without addressing the fundamental changes to our global geopolitical landscape. Mere tinkering may not bring about UN reform.

As a member of the group of 18 intergovernmental experts to reform the UN (formerly known as the Group of High-level Intergovernmental Experts to Review the Efficiency of the Administrative and Financial Functioning of the United Nations), I have been involved with these questions for almost 20 years. It has become increasingly clear to me that UN reform will not move forward unless when we reach a consensus on the role and purpose of the Security Council in the 21st century—not just its membership.

Today, we know that a conflict in a distant failed state can impact all corners of the world. Hence, a major new consensus needs to be developed between the major powers and the other UN member states similar to the 1945 San Francisco conference, which gave birth to the UN. A consensus is possible if candidates for permanent membership in a new Security Council simultaneously agree to assume significant new responsibilities as permanent members, such as taking care of any failed state that emerges.

UN observers based in New York are likely to dismiss the prospects of comprehensive UN reform, while UN observers in distant capitals dismiss the possibility of UN reform succeeding if it only attempts to tinker around the edges. This perspective gap needs to be bridged at the SG's heads of state summit and within the General Assembly's 60th session. If it does not happen, however, member states should not give up. The UN's role will become even more indispensable in the 21st century.

And herein lies the rub. Since it is primarily Asian states that will emerge as new major powers, the time has come for Asian states to provide leadership on this issue of UN reform. Asian nations have been among the most vociferous in demanding that the Security Council be reformed, but not one has outlined a vision of the sort of comprehensive reform the UN needs. If serious reform is to come (and serious reform is needed), the Asian states need to step up to the plate and provide the same kind of intellectual leadership that the West provided when the UN was created in 1945. As we go forward, time will tell whether this occurs.

Civil Society: Mobilizing for Change

Gaia Larsen and Stephanie Rossi,
World Federation of United Nations Associations

With Secretary-General Kofi Annan's package of proposals (*In Larger Freedom: Towards Development, Security and Human Rights for All*) in mind, governments have been and will continue to formulate and negotiate their positions on United Nations reform. Civil society groups have been doing this as well—focusing primarily on the *Millennium Declaration* and the Millennium Development Goals (MDGs), agreed to by all 191 member states in 2000.

The World Federation of United Nations Associations (WFUNA), along with the North-South Institute of Canada, has completed its fourth annual online survey of civil society's engagement with the implementation of the MDGs. In 2005, the Federation received 439 responses from nongovernmental organizations (NGOs) and other actors in more than 100 countries. While the complete results of the survey are detailed in the *We the Peoples 2005* report, the overall messages to world leaders are clear:

- Keep the promises made to the world in the *Millennium Declaration*.
- Implement the MDGs, but go beyond them. Get at the roots of poverty and growing inequality; remove obstacles to universal human rights, health and education; eliminate the dangers to the planet's climate and environment; and undertake urgent collective action to build and sustain peace everywhere.
- Strengthen the UN to assure development, social justice, peace and security in our world.
- Commit the necessary resources, both human and financial, to these ends.

Promises made in the *Millennium Declaration* include a life "free from hunger and from the fear of violence, oppression or injustice" for all citizens of the world. To obtain this goal, leaders proclaimed a "collective responsibility to uphold the principles of human dignity, equality and equity at the global level." This implies that "security" means being liberated not only from the violence of war and conflict, but also from the brutality of poverty, disease, discrimination and environmental degradation.

This is a key factor among civil society groups. In order for poor countries to achieve the MDGs, they largely believe that it is essential that the "global partnership for development" envisioned in Goal 8 be implemented and that rich countries deliver their side of the bargain. To this end, civil society groups are rallying behind the Global Call for Action Against Poverty (GCAP), a worldwide alliance of organizations "committed to forcing world leaders to live up to their promises, and to make a breakthrough on poverty in 2005." For example, the alliance is pushing for rich countries to live up to the 0.7 percent commitment they made at the International Conference on Financing for Development held in Monterrey, Mexico, in 2002—that is, to give 0.7 percent of their GDP to official development assistance (ODA).

Today, the alliance includes an expanding number of groups, most of them working nationally for MDG implementation.

There is also strong action being taken to improve, or go beyond, the MDGs. According to the WFUNA survey, many groups feel that the goals do not go far enough to reach the vision of the *Millennium Declaration*. They identify six areas of particular importance: the injustice of inequality; the failures of globalization to diminish this inequality; war, peace and security; AIDS and health systems; climate change; and human rights. Survey respondents would like to see more ambitious targets regarding these topics and deadlines that come before the year 2015.

On a goal-by-goal level, women's organizations and networks were found to be frustrated with gender equality being limited to one MDG in particular, Goal 3. They stressed that for successful development to occur, a gender consciousness must be mainstreamed into all areas of work. To bring about this adjustment, women's groups have worked to incorporate the use of gender indicators into MDG monitoring processes, and to define how the *Convention on the Elimination of All Forms of Discrimination Against Women* (CEDAW) and the Beijing Platform for Action can be used to understand and address gender equality dimensions of the MDGs.

In addition, many NGOs around the world want to see explicit links between peace and development. One Irish survey respondent observed that the "the over-emphasis on security issues" means that existing aid resources are more likely to be used to combat terrorism "rather than more systemic and less visible threats to human security, such as hunger, poverty, disease and human rights violations."

With regard to peace-building, the Global Partnership for the Prevention of Armed Conflict has proposed the implementation of Millennium Peace and Security Goals (MPSGs). These goals would commit UN member states to a more specific set of timetabled, rights-based and gender-sensitive goals, by encouraging the redeployment of military spending to development, thus complementing and enhancing the MDGs.

There are many issues, ideas and demands at stake and clearly, the results of the General Assembly's 60th session will be an important milestone on the way to 2015. WFUNA hopes that world leaders will put in place stronger mechanisms for accountability, make necessary policy changes, strengthen the UN's institutional capacities and ensure the release of more funds for the purposes of achieving the goals of the *Millennium Declaration*. Striving toward these goals with the support of civil society groups via creative and dynamic partnerships will certainly enable the UN to become ever more relevant to the lives of people everywhere.

Appendices

Appendix A: Sixty Important Dates in United Nations History

June 12, 1941 The *Inter-Allied Declaration* was signed in London encouraging free peoples to work together in both times of war and peace.

January 1, 1942 Representatives of 26 allied nations met in Washington, DC to sign the *Declaration by the United Nations*, in which US President Franklin Delano Roosevelt coined the term "United Nations."

September 21–October 7, 1944 The US, Soviet Union, United Kingdom and China agreed on the basic blueprint for a world organization at the Dumbarton Oaks mansion.

February 11, 1945 Roosevelt, Winston Churchill and Joseph Stalin met in Ukraine where they resolved to establish "a general international organization to maintain peace and security."

June 25, 1945 The *United Nations Charter* was unanimously adopted by delegations from 50 nations in the San Francisco Opera House.

October 24, 1945 The five permanent members of the Security Council and a majority of other signatories ratified the *Charter*, creating the UN as we know it today.

January 10, 1946 The first General Assembly meeting was held with 51 nations represented in London.

January 17, 1946 The Security Council met for the first time, establishing its procedural rules.

January 24, 1946 The General Assembly passed its first resolution, which focused on peaceful uses of atomic energy and the abolition of weapons of mass destruction.

February 1, 1946 Norway's Trygve Lie became the UN's first Secretary-General.

June 1948 Established in Palestine, the UN Truce Supervision Organization (UNTSO) launched the first UN Observer Mission.

December 10, 1948 The General Assembly adopted the *Universal Declaration of Human Rights*.

January 7, 1949 A cease-fire was secured between Israel and Arab states by UN envoy Ralph Bunche.

October 24, 1949 Builders laid the cornerstone for the current UN headquarters in New York City.

June 27, 1950 The Security Council, minus the Soviet Union, called on member states to help the southern part of Korea repel an invasion from the north.

November 7, 1956 The General Assembly held its first Emergency Special Session to respond to the Suez Canal Crisis. Two days prior, they established the first UN Peacekeeping force called the UN Emergency Force (UNEF).

November 20, 1959 The General Assembly adopted the *Declaration of the Rights of the Child*.

September 1960 Seventeen newly independent states, 16 from Africa, joined the UN. It was the biggest increase in membership in any single year.

September 18, 1961 Secretary-General Dag Hammarskjöld died in a plane crash while on a mission to Congo.

November 22, 1967 After the Six-Day War, the Security Council adopted Resolution 242, which stipulated the requirements for the end of hostilities.

June 12, 1968 The General Assembly approved *Treaty on the Non-proliferation of Nuclear Weapons*.

January 4, 1969 The *International Convention on the Elimination of All Forms of Racial Discrimination* went into effect.

October 25, 1971 With a General Assembly resolution, the People's Republic of China replaced Taiwan in all UN bodies.

June 1972 In Stockholm, Sweden, the first UN Environment Conference was held resulting in the establishment of the UN Environment Programme (UNEP).

November 13, 1974 The Palestine Liberation Organization was recognized as the "sole legitimate representative of the Palestinian people" by the General Assembly.

June–July 1975 The UN held its first conference on women in Mexico City, coinciding with International Women's Year.

November 10, 1975 The UN passed Resolution 3379 declaring that "Zionism is a form of racism." The resolution passed by 72 votes to 35, with 32 abstentions.

May–June 1978 The General Assembly's first special session on disarmament took place.

December 18, 1979 The General Assembly adopted the *Convention on the Elimination of All Forms of Discrimination against Women*.

May 8, 1980 The World Health Organization (WHO) declared smallpox eliminated.

December 10, 1982 Two entities and 117 states signed the *UN Convention on the Law of the Sea*. It was the largest number ever of signatures affixed to a treaty in one day.

December 10, 1984 The *Convention against Torture and Other Cruel, Inhuman or Degrading Treatment or Punishment* was adopted by the General Assembly.

July 1985 The third UN conference on women is held in Nairobi, marking an end to the UN Decade for Women.

September 1987 The *Treaty on the Protection of the Ozone Layer*, also known as the *Montreal Protocol*, was signed.

1988 UN Peacekeeping was awarded the Nobel Peace Prize. Other UN agencies have received the prize over the years as well.

September 2, 1990 The *Convention on the Rights of the Child* went into effect.

September 29–30, 1990 Seventy-one heads of state attended the World Summit for Children, convened by the UN Children's Fund.

May 31, 1991 The UN Angola Verification Mission (UNAVEM II) negotiated, and then administered, a cease-fire in the 16-year civil war in Angola.

December 16, 1991 The UN passed Resolution 4686 repealing the 1975 Resolution that declared Zionism as a form of racism.

January 31, 1992 Leaders from all 15 member states of the Security Council attended the first Council summit in New York.

June 1992 Rio de Janeiro played host to more than 100 countries at the well-known "Earth Summit." The importance of sustainable development was a major outcome.

June 17, 1992 Secretary-General Boutros Boutros-Ghali released his *An Agenda for Peace* report on diplomacy and peace.

June 1993 The International Year for the World's Indigenous People was observed in Vienna at the World Conference on Human Rights.

October 17, 1993 The General Assembly observed the first International Day for the Eradication of Poverty, inviting all states to devote the day to presenting and promoting activities on the eradication of poverty and destitution.

September 5–15, 1994 Cairo hosted the International Conference on Population and Development where representatives from 179 countries were addressed by 249 speakers.

October 1994 The World Summit on Trade Efficiency, held in Columbus, Ohio, focused on the use of modern information technology to expand international trade.

1995 The UN celebrated its 50th anniversary utilizing the theme "We the peoples of the United Nations - United for a Better World."

March 1995 Copenhagen played host to the World Summit for Social Development in hopes to renew the commitment to combating poverty, unemployment and social exclusion.

September 1995 In Beijing, the Fourth World Conference on Women adopted a "Platform for Action," which analyzed obstacles to women's advancement.

June 1996 The second UN Conference on Human Settlements (Habitat II) convened in Turkey to consider the challenges of human settlements in the 21st century.

September 10, 1996 The General Assembly adopted the *Comprehensive Test-Ban Treaty*.

March 1, 1999 The *Ottawa Convention* on anti-personnel mines entered into force.

September 2000 The General Assembly adopted the *Millennium Declaration* setting on track eight Millennium Development Goals to markedly reduce poverty world-wide by 2015.

November 12, 2001 One of the UN's first steps to address the September 11th terrorist attacks was Security Council Resolution 1377, which called on all states to "eliminate the scourge of international terrorism."

July 1, 2002 The *Rome Statute* established the International Criminal Court.

March 18-22, 2002 At the International Conference on Financing for Development in Monterrey, Mexico, 50 heads of states committed to the *Monterrey Consensus* to attack poverty worldwide, particularly in developing countries.

November 8, 2002 Security Council Resolution 1441 was passed, giving Iraq a final opportunity to disarm. Controversy ensued as to whether another resolution was required to authorize war but was never voted on.

February 16, 2005 In an effort to control the emission of greenhouse gases, the *Kyoto Protocol* came into effect without the US as a signatory.

2005 The UN celebrated its 60th anniversary utilizing the theme "A Time for Renewal."

September 2005 After a special head of state summit, the General Assembly meets to discuss possibly the most significant UN reform in its history.

Sources: Dates compiled from UN website, among others.

Appendix B: The United Nations System Today

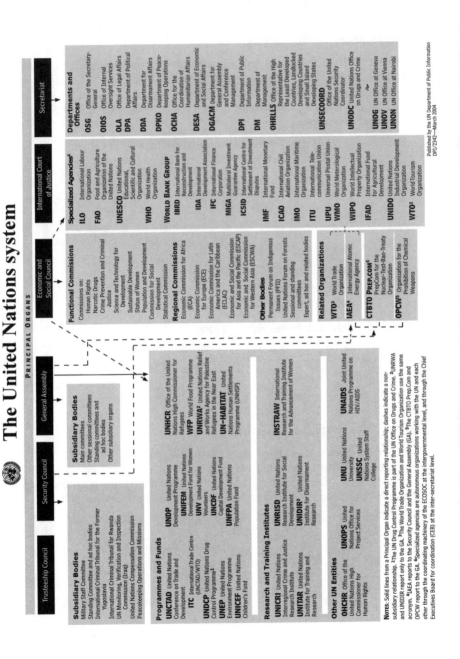

Source: UN Department of Public Information, 2005

Appendix C: Composition of the UN Secretariat

Compiled by Anthony Mango

Table 1: Secretariat Staffing

As of June 30, 2004, the breakdown by grade of the Secretariat was as listed in the table below. In fall 2005, the 59th General Assembly created a new Under-Secretary-General to head the newly established Department of Safety and Security as well as two D-2 posts, 383 new security and safety officers, one P-4, two P-3 and one General Service posts.

POST LEVEL	QUANTITY IN POST
P-1/2	473
P-3	1,350
P-4	1,422
P-5	779
D-1	288
D-2	99
Under-Secretaries-General/ Assistant Secretaries-General	48
Deputy-Secretary-General	1
Sub-total: Professional and above	**4,460**
General Service & related categories	7,120
Total	**11,580**

Source: A/59/299.

Table 2: Geographical Distribution

The number of posts subject to geographical distribution at the UN, as of June 30, 2004, was 2,515. This category of posts comprises non-linguist, professional and senior posts funded by the regular budget. They are divided among member states using a formula that reflects a country's membership, assessment rate and population.

CATEGORY OF MEMBER STATES	2000	2004
Unrepresented	21	15
Under-represented	8	10
Within range	145	145
Over-represented	14	21
Total	**188**	**191**

Source: A/59/299.

Appendix D: United Nations Operations and Budgets

Compiled by Anthony Mango

Table 1: Regular Budget Appropriations 2004-2005 (in $US millions)

PART/SECTION	INITIAL APPROP. IN 2004	INCREASE/ (DECREASE)	REVISED APPROP. IN 2004
PART I: Overall Policy-Making, Direction & Coordination	**592.1**	**9.7**	**621.8**
1. Overall policy-making, direction & coordination	58.5	3.0	61.5
2. General Assembly affairs and conference services	533.6	26.7	560.3
PART II: Political Affairs	**356.0**	**189.2**	**545.2**
3. Political affairs	242.5	185.2	427.6
4. Disarmament	18.1	0.6	18.7
5. Peacekeeping operations	89.9	3.0	92.9
6. Peaceful uses of outer space	5.5	0.4	5.9
PART III: International Justice & Law	**70.9**	**4.6**	**75.5**
7. International Court of Justice	31.6	3.3	34.9
8. Legal affairs	39.3	1.3	40.6
PART IV: International Cooperation for Development	**336.5**	**19.8**	**356.3**
9. Economic and social affairs	137.7	5.3	143.0
10. Least-developed countries, land-locked developing countries and small island developing states	4.2	0.1	4.4
11. UN support for the New Partnership for Africa's Development	9.3	0.2	9.6
12. Trade and development	106.2	8.6	114.8
13. International Trade Centre, UNCTAD/WTO	23.5	2.7	26.1
14. Environment	10.5	0.4	10.9
15. Human settlements	15.5	0.5	16.0
16. Crime prevention & criminal justice	9.4	0.6	10.0
17. International drug control	20.0	1.5	21.5
Part V: Regional Cooperation for Development	**389.6**	**5.7**	**395.3**
18. Economic and social development in Africa	95.7	0.6	96.2

PART/SECTION	INITIAL APPROP. IN 2004	INCREASE/ (DECREASE)	REVISED APPROP. IN 2004
19. Economic and social development in Asia and the Pacific	67.2	(2.2)	65.1
20. Economic development in Europe	50.2	4.6	54.8
21. Economic and social development in Latin America & the Caribbean	80.9	4.5	85.4
22. Economic and social development in Western Asia	52.7	(1.7)	51.0
23. Regular program of technical cooperation	42.9	-	42.9
PART VI: Human Rights and Humanitarian Affairs	**170.7**	**19.1**	**189.8**
24. Human rights	56.8	7.8	64.6
25. Protection of & assistance to refugees	56.7	9.5	66.2
26. Palestine refugees	33.9	0.8	34.6
27. Humanitarian assistance	23.3	1.0	24.3
PART VII: Public Information	**156.1**	**6.3**	**162.3**
28. Public information	156.1	6.3	162.3
PART VIII : Common Support Services	**525.1**	**(48.0)**	**477.1**
29. Management and central support services	525.1	(48.0)	477.1
PART IX: Internal Oversight	**23.2**	**1.0**	**24.2**
30. Internal oversight	23.2	1.0	24.2
PART X: Jointly Financed Administrative Activities and Special Expenses	**105.0**	**(13.3)**	**91.7**
31. Jointly financed administrative activities	25.6	(15.1)	10.4
32. Special expenses	79.5	1.8	81.3
PART XI: Capital Expenditures	**58.7**	**45.9**	**104.6**
33. Construction, alteration, improvement and major maintenance	58.7	45.9	104.6
PART XII: Staff Assessment	**382.3**	**28.9**	**411.2**
34. Staff assessment	382.3	28.9	411.2
PART XIII: Development Account	**13.1**	**-**	**13.1**
35. Development account	13.1	-	13.1

Part/Section	Initial Approp. in 2004	Increase/ (Decrease)	Revised Approp. in 2004
PART XIV: Safety and Security	-	**140.1**	**140.1**
36. Safety and security	-	140.1	140.1
Total, Expenditures	**3,179.2**	**429.0**	**3,608.2**
Income Sections			
1. Income from staff assessment	386.5	29.1	415.6
2. General income	24.0	-	24.0
3. Services to the public	4.8	(0.5)	4.2
Total Income Estimates	**415.3**	**28.5**	**443.9**
Total, Net	**2,763.9**	**400.5**	**3,164.4**

Source: A/Res/59/276 and 277A-B, A/59/448/Add.2 and 578 and 591.

Notes:
1. The total increase of $429 million in expenditures includes $79.4 million attributable to the weakness of the US dollar, $32.8 million for inflation and $99.4 million for security measures approved by the General Assembly.
2. By A/Res/59/278 on the proposed program budget outline for 2006-2007, the General Assembly approved a preliminary estimate of $3,621.9 million at revised 2004-2005 rates, and a contingency fund equal to 0.75 percent of the preliminary estimate (i.e., 27.2 million).
3. The General Assembly will finalize the 2004-2005 appropriations and set the 2006-2007 initial appropriations in December 2005.

Table 2: Peacekeeping Operations Appropriations 2004-2005/ Estimates 2005-2006 (in $US millions)

MISSION	2004-2005	2005-2006
UN Mission for the Referendum in Western Sahara (MINURSO)	41.9	45.6
UN Stabilization Mission in Haiti (MINUSTAH)	379.0	470.1
UN Organization Mission in the Democratic Republic of Congo (MONUC)[1]	954.8	383.2
UN Operation in Burundi (ONUB)	329.7	292.3
UN Mission in Sierra Leone (UNAMSIL)	291.6	107.2
UN Disengagement Observer Force (UNDOF)	40.9	41.6
UN Peacekeeping Force in Cyprus (UNFICYP)	49.4	44.2
UN Interim Force in Lebanon (UNIFIL)	93.0	94.3
UN Mission in Ethiopia and Eritrea (UNMEE)	205.3	176.7
UN Interim Administration Mission in Kosovo (UNMIK)	294.6[2]	240.3
UN Mission in Liberia (UNMIL)	822.0	722.4
UN Mission in the Sudan (UNMIS)[3]	279.5	316.0
UN Mission of Support in East Timor (UNMISET)	85.2	3.9[4]
UN Operation in Cote d'Ivoire (UNOCI)	378.5	367.6
UN Observer Mission in Georgia (UNOMIG)	31.9	34.6
Subtotal for missions alone	**4,277.3**	**3,340.0**
UN Logistics Base at Brindisi (UNLB)[5]	28.4	37.7
Support account [5]	121.6	143.7
Total	**4,427.3**	**3,515.2**

Sources: A/59/728, A/59/734–735, A/59/736/Adds.1-7, 9-13, 15, 16, A/59/784
A/C.5/59/18/Rev.1, A/C.5/59/29.

Notes: The financial year for peacekeeping operations is July 1 to June 30.
1. The figure for 2004-2005 is the revised appropriation approved by A/Res.59/285. The amount for 2005-2006 is the commitment authority request for the period July 1 to October 31, 2005.
2. ACABQ recommendation.
3. A/Res/59/292. The 2005-2006 amount is for the period July 1 to October 31, 2005.
4. Secretary-General's estimate.
5. These costs are apportioned pro rata to the missions.

Table 3: International War Crimes Tribunals Appropriations 2004-2005 (in $US millions, gross)

TRIBUNAL	INITIAL	INCREASE	REVISED
International Tribunal for Former Yugoslavia	298.2	31.1	329.3
International Criminal Tribunal for Rwanda	235.3	20.6	255.9
Total	**533.5**	**51.7**	**585.2**

Source: A/Res/59 /273 and 274.

Note: The Special Court for Sierra Leone is financed by voluntary contributions. However, in A/Res/59/276, section VII, the General Assembly authorized the Secretary-General to enter into commitments under the regular budget for 2004-2005 to supplement, if need be, the Special Court's financial resources, in an amount not to exceed US$20 million for the period January 1 to June 30.

Table 4: Assessments of the Top Ten Financial Contributors to the UN and of the Permanent Members* of the Security Council (in percentages)

Member State	Regular Budget	Peacekeeping Operations 01/01/05	Peacekeeping Operations 01/01/06
Canada	2.81	2.81	2.81
China*	2.05	2.47	2.49
France*	6.03	7.26	7.32
Germany	8.66	8.66	8.66
Italy	4.89	4.89	4.89
Japan	19.47	19.47	19.47
Mexico	1.88	0.38	0.38
Russian Federation*	1.10	1.32	1.33
Spain	2.52	2.52	2.52
United States*	22.00	26.50	26.69
United Kingdom*	6.13	7.38	7.43

Source: A/58/157/Add.1

Table 5: Top Member State Arrears to the UN
(in $US millions as of December 31, 2004)

Member State	Regular Budget	International Tribunals	Peacekeeping Operations	Total
United States	240.5	12.0	722.5	975.1
Japan	-	-	758.6	758.6
Ukraine	0.5	-	152.9	153.4
France	-	-	109.0	109.0
China	-	-	108.5	108.5
Germany	-	-	103.3	103.3
Italy	-	-	99.4	99.4
Brazil	47.4	5.4	26.6	79.4
Republic of Korea	-	-	70.3	70.3
Argentina	15.9	3.0	39.2	58.4

Source: SG/ADM/SER.B/642.

Note: Argentina also owed $0.3 million in Capital Master Plan assessments.

Appendix E: Acronyms

ABM Anti-Ballistic Missile Treaty

ACABQ Advisory Committee on Administrative and Budgetary Questions

AMIB African Union's Mission in Burundi

AMIS African Union's Mission in Sudan

ASEAN Association of Southeast Asian Nations

ASP Assembly of States Parties, referring to the International Criminal Court

ATA Afghan Transitional Authority

AU African Union

BONUCA United Nations Peace-building Office in the Central African Republic

BPOA Barbados Programme of Action

CAFTA Central American Free Trade Agreement

CAP Consolidated Appeals Process, for Humanitarian Assistance

CAR Central African Republic

CD Conference on Disarmament

CEDAW Convention on the Elimination of All Forms of Discrimination Against Women

CENI Independent National Electoral Commission, Burundi

CIS Commonwealth of Independent States

CND Commission on Narcotic Drugs

CPA Coalition Provisional Authority

CSD Commission on Sustainable Development

CSW Commission on the Status of Women

CTBT Comprehensive Test-Ban Treaty

CTC Counter-Terrorism Committee

CTR Cooperative Threat Reduction

DDA Doha Development Agenda

DG Director-General

DMZ Demilitarized Zone

DOTS Directly Observed Therapy Short-Course Strategy

DPA United Nations Department of Political Affairs

DPI United Nations Department of Public Information

DPKO United Nations Department of Peacekeeping Operations

DPRK Democratic People's Republic of Korea/North Korea

DRC Democratic Republic of Congo

DSB Dispute Settlement Body of the World Trade Organization

ECOSOC United Nations Economic and Social Council

ECOWAS Economic Community of West African States

EEZ Exclusive Economic Zone

EU European Union

FAB Burundi Armed Forces

FAO Food and Agriculture Organization

FDLR Democratic Forces for the Liberation of Rwanda

FNI Integrationist Nationalist Front, Democratic Republic of the Congo

FRY Federal Republic of Yugoslavia

FTAs Free Trade Agreements

GA General Assembly

G7 Group of Seven

G8 Group of Eight

GATT General Agreement on Tariffs and Trade

GDP Gross Domestic Product

GNP Gross National Product

GNI Gross National Income

GOARN Global Outbreak Alert and Response Network of the World Health Organization

GPHIN Global Public Health Intelligence Network of the World Health Organization

HIPC Heavily Indebted Poor Countries

HRW Human Rights Watch

IAEA International Atomic Energy Agency

ICC International Criminal Court

ICJ International Court of Justice

ICMP Illicit Crop Monitoring Programme

ICRC International Committee of the Red Cross

ICTR International Criminal Tribunal for Rwanda

ICTs Information and Communications Technologies

ICTY International Criminal Tribunal for the Former Yugoslavia

IDF Israel Defense Forces

IDPs Internally Displaced Persons

IEC Independent Electoral Commission

IECI Independent Electoral Commission of Iraq

IEWP International Early Warning Programme

ILC International Law Commission

ILO International Labour Organization

IMF International Monetary Fund

IMO International Maritime Organization

INCB International Narcotics Control Board

INTERPOL International Criminal Police Organization

IOM International Organization for Migration

ISAF International Security Assistance Force, Afghanistan

ITLOS International Tribunal for the Law of the Sea

ITU International Telecommunications Union

JEMB Joint Electoral Management Body

JIU Joint Inspection Unit

JVC Joint Verification Commission

KRT Khmer Rouge Tribunal

LDC Least-Developed Country

LLDC Landlocked Developing Country

MDGs Millennium Development Goals

MINUGUA United Nations Verification Mission in Guatemala

MINURSO United Nations Mission for the Referendum in Western Sahara

MINUSTAH United Nations Stabilization Mission in Haiti

MONUC United Nations Organization Mission in the Democratic Republic of Congo

NAFTA North American Free Trade Agreement

NAM Non-Aligned Movement

NATO North Atlantic Treaty Organization

NEPAD The New Partnership for Africa's Development

NGO Nongovernmental Organization

NPT Nuclear Nonproliferation Treaty

NSS National Security Strategy

OAU Organization of African Unity

OCHA Office for the Coordination of Humanitarian Affairs

ODA Official Development Assistance

OECD Organization for Economic Cooperation and Development

OHCHR Office of the United Nations High Commissioner for Human Rights

ONUB United Nations Operation in Burundi

OSCE Organization for Security and Cooperation in Europe

P-5 Permanent Five Members of the Security Council: the United States, United Kingdom, Russian Federation, France and China

PISG Provisional Institutions of Self-Government

PSI Proliferation Security Initiative

PTBT Partial Test-Ban Treaty

RBM Roll Back Malaria initiative

RTAs Regional Trade Agreements

RUF Revolutionary United Front, Sierra Leone

SARS Severe Acute Respiratory Syndrome

SC Security Council

SCSL Special Court for Sierra Leone

SG Secretary-General

SIDS Small Island Developing States

SFRY Socialist Federal Republic of Yugoslavia

SLM/A Sudan Liberation Movement/Army

SRSG Special Representative of the Secretary-General

TB Tuberculosis

TRC Truth and Reconciliation Commission

TSZ Temporary Security Zone, Ethiopia/Eritrea

UK United Kingdom

UN United Nations

UNAIDS United Nations Joint Programme on HIV/AIDS

UNAMA United Nations Assistance Mission in Afghanistan

UNAMI United Nations Assistance Mission for Iraq

UNAMIS United Nations Advance Mission in Sudan

UNAMSIL United Nations Mission in Sierra Leone

UNCITRAL United Nations Commission on International Trade Law

UNCLOS United Nations Convention of the Law of the Sea

UNCND United Nations Commission on Narcotic Drugs

UNCTAD United Nations Conference on Trade and Development

UNDAF United Nations Development Assistance Framework

UNDC United Nations Disarmament Commission

UNDCP United Nations International Drug Control Programme

UNDG United Nations Development Group

UNDOF United Nations Disengagement Observer Force

UNDP United Nations Development Programme

UNEP United Nations Environment Programme

UNESCO United Nations Educational, Scientific and Cultural Organization

UNFDAC United Nations Fund for Drug Abuse Control

UNFF United Nations Forum on Forests

UNFICYP United Nations Peacekeeping Force in Cyprus

UNFIP United Nations Fund for International Partnerships

UNFPA United Nations Population Fund

UNHCHR United Nations High Commissioner for Human Rights

UNHCR United Nations High Commissioner for Refugees

UNICEF United Nations Children's Fund

UNIFEM United Nations Development Fund for Women

UNIFIL United Nations Interim Force in Lebanon

UNMEE United Nations Mission in Ethiopia and Eritrea

UNMIBH United Nations Mission in Bosnia and Herzegovina

UNMIK United Nations Mission in Kosovo

UNMIL United Nations Mission in Liberia

UNMISET United Nations Mission of Support in East Timor

UNMOGIP United Nations Military Observer Group in India and Pakistan

UNMOVIC United Nations Monitoring, Verification and Inspection Commission, Iraq

UNOB United Nations Office in Burundi

UNOCHA United Nations Office for the Coordination of Humanitarian Affairs

UNOCI United Nations Operation in Côte d'Ivoire

UNODC United Nations Office on Drugs and Crime

UNOGBIS United Nations Peace-building Support Office in Guinea-Bissau

UNOMIG United Nations Observer Mission in Georgia

UNOMB United Nations Observer Mission in Bougainville

UNOMIL United Nations Observer Mission in Liberia

UNOMSIL United Nations Observer Mission in Sierra Leone

UNOPS United Nations Office for Project Services

UNOTIL United Nations Office in Timor-Leste

UNPOS United Nations Political Office for Somalia

UNPROFOR United Nations Protection Force

UNSCOM United Nations Special Commission for Iraq

UNTAET United Nations Transitional Authority in East Timor

UNTOP United Nations Tajikistan Office of Peace-building

UNTSO United Nations Truce Supervision Organization

US United States

WEHAB Water, Energy, Health, Agriculture and Biodiversity

WFP World Food Programme

WFUNA World Federation of United Nations Associations

WHO World Health Organization

WIPO World Intellectual Property Organization

WMD Weapons of Mass Destruction

WMO World Meteorological Organization

WSSD World Summit on Sustainable Development

WTO World Trade Organization

Appendix F: Glossary

ad hoc For a specific or temporary purpose.

ambassador The highest rank of a diplomatic representative sent by one government to another or to an international organization.

amicus, amici curiae Latin for "third party."

arrears The unpaid portion of a member state's assessment for a given financial period.

appropriations Funds set aside for a specific use.

assessment The amount that a member state must pay as its contribution toward the expenses of the UN in the financial period as set out in the relevant budget adopted by the General Assembly.

atrocities Acts of unusual cruelty or brutality, usually perpetrated on large groups of defenseless persons.

autonomy Self-governance.

bilateral An agreement or exchange involving two parties.

Bonn Agreement This December 5, 2001, agreement created an interim administration to lead Afghanistan until a fully representative government was elected. Elections were held in October 2004.

Bretton Woods Institutions Including the World Bank and International Monetary Fund, the Institutions were set up at a meeting of 43 countries in Bretton Woods, New Hampshire, in July 1944 to help rebuild the shattered postwar economy and to promote international economic cooperation.

Bush Doctrine Also known as the new National Security Strategy (NSS) of the United States, as of September 2002, providing for the preemptive use of force.

Central American Free Trade Agreement (CAFTA) This US proposed agreement, modeled after NAFTA, would initially promote trade liberalization between the US and five Central American countries: Costa Rica, El Salvador, Guatemala, Honduras and Nicaragua.

coalition Temporary alliance between two or more political units, not necessarily including the United Nations, for the purposes of joint action. In the case of the Spring 2003 Iraq war, the "coalition of the willing" involved primarily the United States, the United Kingdom, Australia and Poland.

Coalition Provisional Authority A temporary administration set up by the United States and other coalition members in May 2003 to administer Iraq. The CPA was responsible for restoring security, stability and institutional structures in Iraq until power was turned over to the Interim Government in June 2004.

collective security A concept that seeks to ensure peace through enforcement by the community of nations.

commission A body created to perform a particular function, whether administrative, legislative or judicial.

Commonwealth of Independent States (CIS) A union of 12 of the 15 former Soviet Republics, created in December 1991 to promote a common economic space and humanitarian policy.

Comprehensive Test-Ban Treaty (CTBT) Opened for signature on September 10, 1996, it established a global verification regime regarding nuclear weapons.

consolidated appeals process (CAP) A mechanism used by aid organizations to plan, implement and monitor their activities; they use this data to produce a Common Humanitarian Action Plan and appeal and then present it to the international community every year.

convention A practice or custom followed by states parties. Some international laws are called conventions such as the *Convention on the Rights of the Child*.

coup d'état A sudden, forceful stroke in politics, especially the violent overthrow or alteration of an existing government.

Dayton Peace Accords An agreement among Bosnia, Herzegovina, Croatia, and the Federal Republic of Yugoslavia in 1995 to respect the sovereignty of each nation and to settle future disputes.

delegate A representative.

delegation A group of delegates.

demilitarized zone (DMZ) The area between the forward line of the parties, into which they have agreed not to deploy military forces and which may be placed under the control of a peacekeeping operation.

democracy A form of government in which the right to make political decisions is exercised directly by the whole body of citizens. In direct democracy, citizens rule directly through procedures of majority rule. In representative democracy, citizens exercise the same right not in person but through representatives chosen by them.

developed countries Those with more fully industrialized economies, more productive agriculture and a high standard of living.

developing countries Those not yet fully industrialized and that have limited specialization, not enough financial savings, a population that is outgrowing its resources and a low standard of living.

diplomacy The conduct of relations between nations—often through diplomats, as in making agreements.

diplomatic immunity Special rights given to diplomats, including immunity from the laws that operate in the country to which they are assigned.

disarmament The reduction or removal of armed forces and armaments.

displaced person Someone rendered homeless as a result of war or disaster. An individual fleeing such conditions who crosses a border is considered a "refugee." Anyone who takes flight but never leaves his/her country is an "internally displaced person."

draft resolution A document that has been approved by the chairperson for discussion in formal debate; it is written in the form of a UN resolution but has not been passed by the committee.

dumping In relation to trade, the selling of goods in a foreign market at below the cost of production or at lower than they are sold in the home market.

epidemic Referring to an infectious disease that affects an unusually large proportion of the population within a specific population, community or region.

ethnic cleansing The expulsion, imprisonment or killing of ethnic minorities by a dominant majority group.

European Union (EU) Headquartered in Brussels, Belgium, this group of European countries aims to promote economic and social progress for a strong European presence in the world, as well as to ensure a free, secure and just European citizenship.

free trade Trade carried on without governmental regulations.

G7 Group of Seven First made up of the seven most industrialized nations—Canada, France, Germany, Italy, Japan, the United Kingdom and United States—the group now includes the Russian Federation and is more often referred to as the Group of Eight.

G8 Group of Eight *See above.*

G-22 An informal group of developing nations, now known as the G-20.

G-77 Group of 77 Established on June 15, 1964, by 77 developing countries; now has more than 130 members. As the largest developing coalition in the United Nations, the Group of 77 provides the means for the developing world to promote its collective economic interests and enhance its joint negotiating capacity.

General Agreement on Tariffs and Trade (GATT) This 1947 agreement was incorporated into and superseded by the World Trade Organization in January 1995. The 100-plus members of GATT established the norms and rules of international trade, with the aim of reducing trade barriers. WTO offers a dispute-settlement system for enforcing those rules.

General Assembly (GA) The central deliberative organ of the United Nations. Each of the 191 member states is represented equally and has a vote.

genocide The systematic killing or extermination of a whole people or nation.

Global Fund The Global Fund for HIV/AIDS, Tuberculosis and Malaria is a non-UN body but was initiated by Secretary-General Kofi Annan.

grassroots Originating among or carried on by the common people.

gross domestic product (GDP) An economic measure defining the total value of all products manufactured and goods provided within that territory during a specified period (most often, per year). GDP, like GNP (*see below*) is used as a means of assessing the conditionof a nation's economy.

gross national product (GNP) The value of all the goods and services produced by acountry's nationals in a one-year period.

guerrilla A member of a small force of irregular or "rebel" soldiers, usually volunteers, who make surprise raids, etc.

habeas corpus Latin for "you should have the body," requiringthe government to produce a prisoner before a court and justify his or her imprisonment.

The Hague Home to numerous international courts and tribunals, located in the Netherlands.

High-level Panel on Threats, Challenges and Change A panel established by UN Secretary-General Kofi Annan in September 2003 to recommend clear and practical measures for ensuring collective action among member states to meet today's security problems and challenges.

human rights law The set of obligations that regulate state behavior toward groups and individuals in the spheres of political, civil, economic, social and cultural rights.

immunity Exemption from the application of a rule or jurisdiction.

impunity Exemption from punishment, penalty or harm.

indictment A formal written statement by a court or other authority authorizing a prosecutor to initiate trial on the basis of specified charges.

indigenous Native.

inter alia Latin term for "among other things."

interstate Actions between two or more states or countries.

International Atomic Energy Agency (IAEA) Established in 1957 and headquartered in Vienna, the Agency serves as the world's foremost center for nuclear information and cooperation. IAEA is also the chief inspector of the world's nuclear facilities.

International Court of Justice (ICJ) Also known as the World Court, it is the main judicial organ of the UN for settling civil disputes between member states and giving advisory opinions to the UN and its agencies; it does not hear cases brought by or against individuals or private organizations nor does it hear criminal cases.

International Criminal Court (ICC) A permanent court with jurisdiction over individuals accused of committing serious war crimes, crimes against humanity or genocide after July 1, 2002.

international criminal law Pertaining to those violations of international law that give rise to individual criminal accountability (e.g., very serious war crimes, crimes against humanity and the crime of aggression).

International Criminal Tribunal for the Former Yugoslavia (ICTY) Established by the Security Council on May 25, 1993, the ICTY is mandated to prosecute persons responsible for serious violations of international humanitarian law committed in the territory of the former Yugoslavia since 1991.

International Criminal Tribunal for Rwanda (ICTR) Established by the Security Council on November 8, 1994, the ICTR is mandated to prosecute persons responsible for genocide and other serious violations of international humanitarian law committed in the territory of Rwanda, or by Rwandan citizens in the territory of neighbor states, between January 1 and December 31, 1994.

international humanitarian law Also called the law of war or armed conflict law, aims to protect persons who are not taking part in hostilities, and restricts the means and methods of fighting.

304 · Global Agenda | The 60th General Assembly

international law Traditionally defined as the body of agreements and principles governing relations between states, it increasingly regulates state behavior toward non-state actors.

International Law Commission (ILC) Established in 1947 with a membership of 15 persons of recognized competence in international law, it encourages the progressive development of international law and its codification.

internally displaced person (IDP) *See* displaced person.

intifada The word has come to symbolize the Palestinian uprising against the Israeli occupation.

intrastate Actions within a state or country.

Kyoto Protocol 1997 treaty resulting from the UN *Framework Convention on Climate Change*, this agreement outlines goals to limit greenhouse gas emissions and honor gas reduction commitments among the signatory nations. It went into effect in February 2005.

League of Nations An international organization created after World War I to promote international cooperation and achieve international peace and security. However, when the League became passive in the face of member states' aggressions, it ceased to exist.

least-developed country (LDC) A country characterized by a low standard of living, limited industrial capabilities and long-term impediments to economic growth.

Loya Jirga A Pashtun phrase meaning "grand council." For centuries, leaders in Afghanistan have convened *Loya Jirgas* to choose new kings, adopt constitutions and decide important political matters. The most recent *Loya Jirga* process was set in motion by the **Bonn Agreement** of December 5, 2001.

mandate An authoritative command given by the Security Council or General Assembly to a UN mission or representative.

member state One of the current 191 countries belonging to the United Nations.

microcredit The lending of small amounts of money to the poor and others unable to provide traditional security, especially as part of a social program intended to stimulate improvement in living standards and to provide capital for self-employment.

Millennium Summit Conference that took place from September 6-8, 2000, at UN headquarters in New York City, assembling 150 heads of state and government to tackle global challenges. At this Summit, the *Millennium Declaration* was created, which outlines the eight **Millennium Development Goals.**

Montreal Protocol Originally signed in 1987 and amended in 1990 and 1992, this international pact aims to protect the stratospheric ozone layer.

multilateral Involving or participated in by more than two nations or parties (as in multilateral agreements).

nation Individuals in a specific geographical area who share common customs, history, language, etc., under the rule of one government.

nation-state A state with a single predominant national identity.

national interest Interests specific to a nation-state, especially including survival and maintenance of power.

Non-aligned Countries An alliance of Third World states, it aims to promote the political and economic interests of developing countries. At the United Nations, it is referred to as the Non-aligned Movement.

nongovernmental organization (NGO) A not-for-profit organization that contributes to development through cooperative projects, financial and material aid, the dispatch of personnel and education. Some NGOs are accredited by the United Nations system and can represent their interests before ECOSOC.

North American Free Trade Agreement (NAFTA) An agreement that entered into force in January 1994 among Canada, the United States and Mexico.

North Atlantic Treaty Organization (NATO) Formed on April 4, 1949, when 12 independent nations signed the North Atlantic Treaty and committed to each other's defense, it grew by four more nations between 1952 and 1982 and now has 26 members.

Nuclear Nonproliferation Treaty (NPT) Taking effect in 1970, it was intended to limit the number of states with nuclear weapons to five: the United States, the Soviet Union, the United Kingdom, France and China. More than 140 states have pledged not to acquire nuclear weapons and to accept the safeguards of the International Atomic Energy Agency.

observer mission Unarmed officers to staff observation posts for monitoring cease-fires and armistices.

Official Development Assistance (ODA) Loans, grants, technical assistance and other forms of cooperation extended by governments toward developing countries at concessional financial terms for the purpose of promoting economic development and welfare.

pandemic Referring to an infectious disease that affects an exceptionally high proportion of the population in a very wide geographical area, most often the entire globe.

peace enforcement Also known as third-generation peacekeeping, peace-enforcing does not require consent from the conflicting parties and is undertaken to protect the populace from an aggressor or a civil war.

peacekeeper Person assigned the task of helping to maintain peace where conflict has just ended. Peacekeepers can include civilian staff whereas "peacekeeping soldiers" cannot.

peacekeeping operation An operation involving military personnel, but under the precepts of impartiality and neutrality, undertaken by the UN to help maintain or restore international peace and security in areas of conflict. Peacekeeping has evolved into second-generation peacekeeping (**preventive diplomacy** and **post-conflict peace-building**), which is often multidimensional, based on the consent of the parties involved and has a greater and riskier UN role. Third-generation peacekeeping refers to peace enforcement.

peace-building mission Aimed at development activities in post-conflict regions to ensure that the conflict does not reignite.

peacemaking Diplomatic process of brokering an end to conflict, principally through mediation and negotiation. Military activities contributing to peacemaking include military-to-military contacts, security assistance, shows of force and preventive deployments.

permanent five (P5) Refers to the five permanent members of the UN Security Council: the United States, Russian Federation, United Kingdom, China and France.

political office UN political offices work to support the peacekeeping and peace-building missions through reconciliation and negotiation between parties.

preventive deployment Interposition of a military force to deter violence in a zone of potential conflict where tension is rising among parties.

preventive diplomacy Also known as conflict prevention, this action prevents disputes from arising between parties and limits.

Proliferation Security Initiative (PSI) An effort to enhance and expand efforts to prevent the flow of weapons of mass destruction and their delivery system, announced by US President George W. Bush announced in May 2003.

protocol A document that records the basic agreements reached in negotiations before the final form in which the agreement appears.

recosting This UN budgetary practice provides for adjustments of foreign exchange rates and inflation assumptions during a budgetary cycle.

referendum The principle or practice of submitting to popular vote a measure passed on or proposed by a legislative body or by popular initiative.

regular budget Includes expenditures of the UN Secretariat in New York, the UN offices in Geneva, Vienna and Nairobi, the regional commissions as well as the International Court of Justice and the Center for Human

Rights in Geneva. More than 70 percent of the UN regular budget is earmarked for staff costs. The **scale of assessment** (how much each country owes) is based on the principle of capacity to pay.

repatriate To restore or return to the country of origin, allegiance or citizenship.

resolution A document passed by a committee that expresses the opinions and decisions of the UN.

rule of law A term recently used to describe the activities during peacebuilding that reestablish the rule of law, in opposition to the rule of power. Activities include such things as rebuilding courts and rewriting constitutions.

sanction A coercive economic or military measure, usually adopted by several nations in concert, for forcing a nation violating international law to desist or yield to adjudication.

Security Council (SC) The organ of the United Nations with responsibility for maintaining peace and security is composed of five permanent members (France, China, the Russian Federation, United Kingdom and United States) and 10 rotating members elected to two-year terms by the General Assembly so that they represent a geographical distribution.

Secretariat The UN organ responsible for running the daily affairs of the organization. The Secretariat is made up of international civil servants and led by the Secretary-General.

Secretary-General The chief administrative officer of the UN and head of the Secretariat.

self-determination Freedom of the people of a given area to determine their own political status or independence.

sovereign The highest or supreme political authority.

state-building (nation-building) The concept of rebuilding a post-conflict country, most often so that the sovereignty of the nation is recognized by the international community.

sustainable development A newer, widely used international term for development that meets the needs of the present without compromising the ability of future generations to meet their own needs.

terrorism According to the High-level Panel on Threats, Challenges and Change, any action that is intended to cause death or serious bodily harm to civilians or non-combatants, when the purpose of such act is to intimidate a population, or to compel a government or an international organization to do or to abstain from doing any act.

treaty A formal, binding international agreement. In the United States, treaties proposed by the executive branch and negotiated with a foreign country must be approved by a two-thirds majority in the senate and ratified by the president.

tribunal A committee or board appointed to judge a particular matter.

Trusteeship Council The UN body originally given jurisdiction over 11 former colonies. The Council agenda shrank as one trust territory after another achieved independence or merged with a neighbor.

tsunami A great sea wave produced by a submarine earthquake, volcanic eruption or large landslide.

United Nations Charter The fundamental set of rules according to which the United Nations exists and operates. It was drawn up and signed by the representatives of 50 countries in 1945.

Universal Declaration of Human Rights (UDHR) A historic proclamation of the basic rights and freedoms to which all men and women are entitled adopted by the General Assembly on December 10, 1948, commemorated every year as Human Rights Day.

war crime A crime, such as genocide or maltreatment of prisoners, committed during or in connection with war.

World Bank A multilateral lending agency that aims to reduce poverty by promoting sustainable economic growth.

Index

MEMBERSHIP APPLICATION

Join UNA-USA today and become part of a nationwide movement for a more effective United Nations!

The United Nations Association of the United States of America (UNA-USA) is the nation's largest grassroots foreign policy organization and the leading center of policy research on the UN and global issues. UNA-USA offers Americans the opportunity to connect with issues confronted by the UN and encourages public support for strong US leadership in the United Nations. UNA-USA is a member of the World Federation of United Nations Associations.

For more information, visit our website at **www.unausa.org**.

To join UNA-USA, please return this form, along with your payment to UNA-USA, to:

UNA-USA MEMBERSHIP SERVICES
801 Second Avenue, New York, NY 10017

___ $1,000 Lifetime (one-time dues payment)
___ $500 Patron
___ $100 Sponsor
___ $40 Member
___ $25 Introductory (first year only)
___ $25 Limited Income
___ $10 Student
___ Please send me information on UNA-Student Alliances.
___ Please send me information on making a Planned Gift through the Eleanor Roosevelt Society.

_____
NAME

_____
ADDRESS

_____
CITY, STATE AND ZIP

_____
HOME PHONE

_____
BUSINESS PHONE

_____
EMAIL

In addition to my membership dues, I would like to make a contribution to:

___ UNA-USA National Programs in the amount of $_____

___ My Local UNA-USA Chapter in the amount of $_____

(Contributions are tax deductible to the extent provided by law.)

_____
NAME ON CREDIT CARD

_____
BILLING ADDRESS

Check one:

___ AMEX ___ MasterCard ___ Visa

_____
CREDIT CARD NUMBER

_____
EXPIRATION DATE

_____
SIGNATURE

Membership in UNA-USA is open to any citizen or resident of the United States of America who is committed to the purposes of UNA-USA, a 501(c)3 not-for-profit educational organization.